SAINTS, ANGELS & DEMONS

SAINTS, ANGELS & DEMONS

AN A-TO-Z GUIDE TO THE HOLY AND THE DAMNED

GARY JANSEN

ILLUSTRATIONS BY KATIE PONDER

BLACK DOG
& LEVENTHAL
PUBLISHERS
NEW YORK

Black Dog & Leventhal Publishers
Hachette Book Group
1290 Avenue of the Americas, New York, NY 10104
www.blackdogandleventhal.com
 BlackDogandLeventhal   @BDLev

First Edition: October 2024

Published by Black Dog & Leventhal Publishers, an imprint of Hachette Book Group, Inc.
The Black Dog & Leventhal Publishers name and logo are trademarks of Hachette Book Group, Inc.

The Hachette Speakers Bureau provides a wide range of authors for speaking events.
To find out more, go to hachettespeakersbureau.com or email HachetteSpeakers@hbgusa.com.

Black Dog & Leventhal books may be purchased in bulk for business, educational, or promotional use. For more information, please contact your local bookseller or the Hachette Book Group Special Markets Department at Special.Markets@hbgusa.com.

The publisher is not responsible for websites (or their content) that are not owned by the publisher.

Print book cover and interior design by Katie Benezra

Library of Congress Cataloging-in-Publication Data has been applied for.

ISBNs: 978-0-7624-8485-0 (hardcover); 978-0-7624-8486-7 (ebook)

Printed in China

TLF

10 9 8 7 6 5 4 3 2 1

For Stephen J. Rossetti

CONTENTS

PLATES

INTRODUCTION

W hen I was around thirteen years old, my mother, who worked as a housekeeper for an elderly woman who had survived the Holocaust, gifted me with a book on the saints. It was wrapped in elegant red foil paper. I remember the paper distinctly because money was always tight when we were growing up, and I knew that my mom kept what she thought was a secret collection of used wrapping paper saved from gifts that had been given to and opened by her employer.

As I held the dog-eared, yellowed book, it was apparent that it, too, was used, likely something my mom found at one of the weekend flea markets she loved to scour. Surprisingly, although I had been attending Catholic school since first grade, and perhaps due to my short attention span and difficulty focusing in class, I knew very little about the saints. Regardless, I loved books, I loved reading, and since I was preparing for my Confirmation, the book would definitely come in handy. I thanked my mom, gave her a hug, and told her I would cherish it.

I put the book on my desk in my bedroom and forgot about it for a few weeks.

Then one night, I went to my room, closed the door, and began reading about the holy men and women who dedicated their lives to honoring God, usually by helping others. The book didn't have any pictures (at thirteen, I loved books with pictures, and now, forty years later, I'm not ashamed to say I still do), but what it did have was marginalia: little notes scribbled in the margins of the book that provided a glimpse of the previous owner's spiritual life. "Inspiring," "I can do this," "Amazing," "I want to believe like this," appeared in script next to the stories of the iconic fables of St. Patrick or the bravery of St. Agnes or the miracles of St. Anthony of Padua. And while I enjoyed the stories of the saints and the colorful lives they lived, I was even more fascinated by the reactions of the anonymous person whose life seemed to have been so affected by the examples of heroes and heroines who desired to do good in the world.

Saints, Angels & Demons is inspired by that anonymous reader. This is a book of profiles in courage, tenacity, devotion, reverence, love, and sacrifice. There are more than 10,000 saints within in the Catholic Church; this book introduces you to some of the most popular and influential holy men and women throughout history, a group of diverse people from around the world whose commonality was deep faith, the desire to serve a higher power, and a calling to help others.

As the name attests, this is also a book that profiles the spirits who often assisted and/or sometimes tormented the saints. Angels, or good spirits, and demons, the evil ones, embody the vast spectrum of light and dark, obedience and division, truth and lies, that is part of the Christian tradition.

Saints, Angels & Demons is an encyclopedia for the curious and the faithful. This book, meant to inform and inspire, is divided into three parts. The first, focusing on saints and martyrs who died because of their religious convictions, introduces you to exemplary yet imperfect individuals who epitomized faith in God and provides information about their feast days, patronages, and the signs and symbols associated with them. The second part, which focuses on angels, shines light on the celestial beings of the divine messengers who guide and protect us. The final section of the book explores the sinister nature of demons, also known as fallen angels, and stands as compelling caution against our gravest temptations.

This book spans thousands of years of history and tradition, and, given the vast panorama of topics covered, naming conventions can be intricate. For saints, I've primarily used names from the Roman Martyrology (*Martyrologium Romanum*), a record cataloging the saints and blessed individuals venerated by the Church. At times, I've used the more popular modern spellings. However, the naming of angels and demons, mainly when appearing in Abrahamic folklore traditions, or the Midrash, or the Talmud, is even more complex, so I've selected the most recognized names from contemporary histories.

Having written and edited books on religion and spirituality for more than fifteen years, I always try to find a common vernacular so that the books I have authored and published can spark dialogue among people from all walks of life. This book serves to do just that. Thus, while focused on a panoply of Catholic saints, this book is offered as a showcase of figures who have withstood the test of time, exemplifying the best and the worst of our human condition and beyond.

All this being said, Christianity, especially Catholicism, has intricate terminologies that can be challenging even to the most knowledgeable layperson. Hence, in addition to the three parts noted above, I've included a glossary, timeline, and numerous appendices that put the lives of the saints and the role of angels and demons in historical and theological context. It is also important to note that the time designation BC is used consistently for dates before the Common Era. AD is applied explicitly to first-century dates or when timing is ambiguous. Beyond the first century, AD is omitted.

I owe an immense debt to the brilliant writers, historians, theologians, mystics, and saints who contributed their thoughts to the topic. While the pages ahead may not break new ground, it offers you, the reader, a contemporary introduction to the spiritual realms of the seen and unseen. My hope is that *Saints, Angels & Demons* serves you as more than a reference book; I hope that it rouses you to your own reflections on good, evil, empathy, apathy, kindness, compassion, existence, purpose, and faith.

And while I'm still on the fence about suggesting you add your own marginalia to such a gorgeous book—Is it okay to write on such lovely pages?—beautifully illustrated by Katie Ponder and designed by Katie Benezra, I do hope the lives of the saints and the power of the angels, coupled with the cautionary tales of their fallen brethren, move you to exclaim, as did my anonymous reader, *"Inspiring!"*

GARY JANSEN

NOVEMBER 1, 2023
ALL SAINTS' DAY

SAINTS

Saints appear in various religious traditions and are often regarded as those who exemplify extraordinary holiness, superior virtue, and moral excellence. In Christianity, saints are honored for their righteous lives, miraculous deeds, and for serving as intercessors to God. Islam's Sufism recognizes *awlíya* (spiritual protectors), while Hinduism reveres *sants* or *sadhus* for their spiritual devotion. Buddhism also acknowledges enlightened beings like *arhats* and *bodhisattvas*. Although Judaism does not have formal saints, Jewish mysticism celebrates the thirty-six righteous individuals (like Abraham and Moses) known as *tzadikim*.

In the Catholic Church, saints are people who, after leading lives of holiness and virtue, are formally canonized, meaning that it is officially acknowledged that their souls are in Heaven and they can act as intercessors for the living. The canonization process, which can take decades, meticulously examines a person's life, deeds, and writings, and any posthumous miracles credited to them.

While "saint" denotes this official acknowledgment of sanctity, it is vital to recognize that, in a broader sense, the term *saint* includes all of us. Derived from the Latin *sanctus*, meaning "holy" or "sacred," every human, by his or her very nature, is a sacred being that should be honored (though not worshipped) for having been created in God's image. Receiving this divine imprint means that we are sanctified. And indeed, according to the Church, we are all called to sainthood—a life devoted to love, service, and unity with God.

To be named a saint, an individual must no longer be among the living. Death is an intricate part of sainthood, and the history of the saints is frequently the history of martyrs who died for their religious beliefs. To be a martyr is to follow in the footsteps of Jesus Christ, who was killed for his beliefs and teachings. The term *martyr* originates from the Greek *mártys* (μάρτυς), which means "witness." Martyrs undergo suffering and ultimately pay for their convictions with their lives; most often, they did not seek martyrdom, but neither did they flee from it when confronted with the choice of renouncing their faith or being killed.

Many martyrs are recognized as saints by the Catholic Church, and they, too, go through a process of canonization, though it is often less rigorous than for those who died a natural death.

Once canonized, martyrs, like other saints, are given a specific feast day in the liturgical calendar of the Church. On this day, their lives and sacrifices are remembered and celebrated. Like saints, martyrs usually have patronages. They are sometimes depicted in art with a martyr's palm branch, which alludes to the palms that were thrown at the feet of Jesus in the days before his arrest, torture, and crucifixion.

ACHILLEUS

BORN: 1st century AD, place unknown

DIED: 1st century AD, place unknown

FEAST DAY: May 12 (with St. Nereus)

PATRONAGE: Martyrs

SYMBOLS AND ATTRIBUTES: Palm branch, Roman soldier attire

Known for his strength and bravery, the soldier Achilleus, along with his brother Nereus, served as a personal bodyguard to Emperor Domitian's niece, Domitilla, in Rome.

The two men-at-arms, possibly eunuchs, converted to Christianity around the same time as Domitilla and her fiancé (some accounts suggest that St. Peter himself baptized them). Thereafter, when asked to participate in a pagan sacrifice, they refused, honoring Christian faith. This act of defiance led to their arrest, but despite threats of torture and death, they did not renounce their beliefs. As a result, both were tortured and eventually martyred for their faith.

By the fourth century, Achilleus and Nereus were held in high regard, as evidenced by statues of them found in the Catacombs of Domitilla, which were excavated in the mid-nineteenth century. The two martyrs' legacy has endured through the centuries, and they are honored among the 140 statues of saints that grace St. Peter's Square in Rome. Their shared feast day is celebrated on May 12. (See Nereus.)

ADALBERT OF PRAGUE

BORN: c. 956, Libice nad Cidlinou, Bohemia

DIED: 997, near Gdańsk, Poland

FEAST DAY: April 23

PATRONAGE: Poland, Hungary, Czechia

SYMBOLS AND ATTRIBUTES: Bishop's attire, spear, palm branch

St. Adalbert of Prague, also known as Vojtěch or Wojciech, was a prominent bishop and martyr of the early Middle Ages. Born around 956, he came from the noble Slavic family of the Libice nad Cidlinou region in Bohemia, which is present-day Czechia.

Adalbert was educated at Magdeburg, a prestigious center of learning at the time, and was ordained as a priest. He soon became disillusioned, however, with the secular and corrupt practices of the clergy. This motivated him to seek a life dedicated solely to spiritual pursuits.

Around 982, Adalbert was appointed the bishop of Prague, a position he reluctantly accepted. During his time as bishop, he actively promoted Christian reforms, emphasizing the importance of morality, discipline, and the proper observance of religious practices.

Adalbert faced strong opposition from the local nobility and other influential figures who resisted his reforms, notably, Duke Boleslaus II, also known as Boleslav the Brave, who ruled over Bohemia. While initially supportive of Adalbert's reformist efforts, Boleslaus's commitment to Christian ideals wavered over time, and he grew resentful of the bishop's influence and attempts to impose moral and disciplinary standards on the ruling elite.

The turning point in their relationship came in 989, when Adalbert, frustrated by the resistance and politics, decided to resign from his position as bishop. He then embarked on a pilgrimage to Rome, seeking solace and spiritual guidance from the pope.

During Adalbert's absence, Duke Boleslaus faced a series of political challenges and external threats to his rule. To secure his position and consolidate power, Boleslaus sought the support of the pagan nobility and resorted to violent means to suppress Christian opposition. Adalbert would eventually return as bishop, and his presence and leadership abilities helped to ease political tensions.

This period of calm was soon torn apart, however, when a noblewoman accused of adultery was murdered after taking refuge in a local church. Political leaders, ignoring an ecclesiastical custom that granted temporary asylum to those accused of crimes or immoral behavior, pulled the woman out into the street and murdered her in cold blood. This killing outraged Adalbert, who condemned the barbaric act not only as an unjustified attack on an individual but also an unpardonable assault against the Church. Adalbert excommunicated those responsible, drawing the ire of many powerful people.

These events contributed to growing tension between Boleslaus and Adalbert, which culminated in Adalbert's decision to leave Prague behind for good and embark on missionary journeys to pagan territories, seeking to spread the Christian faith and convert non-believers. This newfound purpose took him to Prussia, Hungary, and other parts of Central Europe.

Adalbert's missionary work was met with considerable challenges and, at times, outright hostility, and in 997, while attempting to convert some pagan inhabitants of Prussia, he was martyred in a violent encounter. The exact circumstances of his death vary, but it is believed that he was murdered by a group of pagans who opposed his efforts.

Following his death, Adalbert was venerated as a martyr, and his remains were initially interred in Gniezno, Poland. His relics were later transferred to Prague, where he became the patron saint of the city and the Czech nation. His martyrdom and dedication to spreading the Christian faith have made him a revered figure in Eastern European history and an important symbol of Czech national identity. Years later, his life would be immortalized by Bruno of Querfort (they had met in Rome) in the work *Life of Adalbert of Prague*. (See Bruno of Querfort.)

AGATHA

BORN: c. 231, Catania or Palermo, Sicily
DIED: c. 251, Catania, Sicily
FEAST DAY: February 5

PATRONAGE: Breast cancer patients, rape survivors, bellfounders
SYMBOLS AND ATTRIBUTES: Pincers, shears, breasts on a plate

A Christian martyr who lived in Sicily during the third century, St. Agatha is widely venerated as the patron saint of those with breast cancer and other breast diseases.

Agatha was born into an affluent and influential family. She grew up as a devout Christian and as a young woman she refused to marry any of the suitors who pursued her. During a time of religious persecution, a Roman prefect named Quintianus made advances toward her as well. Agnes spurned him, and he in turn reported her to the authorities for her Christian beliefs. She was imprisoned and suffered horrific torture and mutilation, including having her breasts cut off. Throughout it all she remained committed to Christ. She ultimately died from her injuries.

Agatha's story has inspired many works of art over the centuries, including paintings by Spanish artists Raphael Vergos and Francisco de Zurbarán. Her image is often depicted holding a palm branch and a platter with two severed human breasts. Many churches and shrines worldwide are dedicated to her, including the Cathedral of St. Agatha in Catania, which houses her relics.

AGNES

BORN: c. 291, Rome, Italy
DIED: c. 304, Rome, Italy
FEAST DAY: January 21

PATRONAGE: Engaged couples, chastity, children of Mary, gardeners, rape survivors
SYMBOLS AND ATTRIBUTES: Lamb, palm branch, sword

St. Agnes, a Christian martyr and saint who lived in Rome in the third century, was known for her unwavering faith and refusal to renounce her beliefs, even when faced with persecution and death. Born into a wealthy and noble Christian family, she took a vow of chastity at an early age and dedicated her life to Christ. Agnes is celebrated as a symbol of purity and faithfulness in the face of adversity.

Agnes's beauty and virtue attracted numerous suitors. However, her vow to remain celibate and her commitment to God angered many of these men. In retaliation, some accused her of being a Christian, a crime punishable by death in ancient Rome. She was arrested. The governor at the time ordered her to be stripped and thrown into a brothel, but a supernatural veil appeared and covered her body, protecting her chastity.

The governor ordered the girl to be burned alive. Miraculously, the flames had no effect on her. Agnes continued to proclaim her faith until, at the age of twelve or thirteen, she was beheaded.

Agnes's tomb resides in the Church of Sant'Agnese in Rome and is an important pilgrimage site for the faithful. Her skull is kept in a reliquary in the church of Sant'Agnese fuori le mura, also in Rome. St. Agnes Cathedral in Rockville Centre, a suburb of New York City, houses one of her relics beneath its altar.

Throughout history, St. Agnes has inspired numerous works of literature and art. English poet John Keats's famous love poem, "The Eve of St. Agnes," set on the night before the saint's feast day, is revered for its vivid imagery and romantic themes.

St. Agnes has also been the subject of many paintings and sculptures. Many of which depict her surrounded by angels or other heavenly beings. One of the most famous depictions is a statue by Gian Lorenzo Bernini, housed in Rome's Borghese Gallery.

AGNES OF ASSISI

BORN: c. 1197, Assisi, Italy
DIED: November 16, 1253, Assisi, Italy
FEAST DAY: November 16

PATRONAGE: Religious communities
SYMBOLS AND ATTRIBUTES: Lamb, Franciscan habit

Agnes of Assisi, also known as St. Agnes or St. Agnes of Assisi, was the younger sister of Clare of Assisi, who would also become a saint. Agnes belonged to a noble family and grew up in a wealthy household.

In her early life, Agnes was radically influenced by the religious fervor of her older sister, Clare, and their mutual acquaintance, Francis of Assisi. Inspired by their example, at fourteen, Agnes left her family's home against her father's wishes and entered the Monastery of San Damiano, which housed the Order of the Poor Ladies (renamed the Poor Clares after the founder, Clare).

Agnes dedicated herself to a life of prayer, poverty, and service to others. Alongside her sister and the other nuns, she lived according to the Rule of St. Clare, which emphasized simplicity, humility, and contemplation. Agnes served for many years as the abbess of a new community near Florence and was known for her spiritual wisdom and holiness.

While Agnes's life was marked by a commitment to solitude and prayer, she also engaged in acts of charity and cared for the sick and poor. She was known for her compassion and selflessness, and her example inspired many others to embrace a similar path of devotion to God.

Agnes of Assisi died on November 16, 1253, and was canonized as a saint by Pope Benedict XIV in 1753. She is venerated as a patron saint of young girls and is often invoked for help with issues related to purity and chastity. (See Clare of Assisi.)

AGNES OF MONTEPULCIANO

BORN: 1268, Gracciano, Italy

DIED: April 20, 1317, Montepulciano, Italy

FEAST DAY: April 20

PATRONAGE: Sienna, those suffering from bodily ills

SYMBOLS AND ATTRIBUTES: Dominican habit, lily, cross, book

Agnes of Montepulciano was a Dominican nun and a mystic born into a wealthy family in the small town of Gracciano-Vecchio, near Montepulciano in Tuscany.

At the age of nine, Agnes had a mystical experience in which she saw a vision of St. Dominic, the founder of the Dominican order, who told her that she would one day join his flock. This experience had a profound impact on Agnes, and later that year, she entered a monastery near her home called the Sisters of the Sack.

Agnes's life in the convent was marked by deep devotion to prayer and fasting. She was known for her humility and her willingness to serve her fellow nuns. Her reputation for kindness and holiness soon spread throughout Tuscany.

Agnes had many mystical experiences throughout her life, including visions of the Virgin Mary, the infant Jesus, and various saints. One of her most famous spiritual encounters occurred in 1288 when, during a time of scarcity, she prayed for God's intervention. In response to her prayers, a large quantity of bread miraculously appeared in the convent's pantry, which fed the nuns and the poor. This miracle became known as the Miracle of the Loaves. She was also known to have experienced levitations.

Another notable mystical experience occurred in 1306, when Agnes was praying in the chapel of the convent. She saw a vision of Jesus, who appeared to her and gave her a ring as a symbol of their spiritual marriage. After this vision, Agnes's devotion to Christ increased even further.

Agnes died on April 20, 1317, at the age of forty-nine. She was buried in the convent of Montepulciano, which became a site of pilgrimage and veneration for many Catholics. In 1796, her bones were transferred to the church of Sant'Agostino in Montepulciano, where they remain to this day.

St. Agnes of Montepulciano was canonized by Pope Benedict XIII in 1726. She is considered the patron saint of Sienna.

AILBE OF EMLY

BORN: 6th century, Ireland

DIED: c. 528-534, Emly, Ireland

FEAST DAY: September 12

PATRONAGE: Archdiocese of Cashel and Emly

SYMBOLS AND ATTRIBUTES: Bishop's attire, Celtic cross

According to legend, St. Ailbe of Emly was left as a baby on a mountain by his cruel parents, only to be adopted by a mother wolf who raised him alongside her own cubs. A hunter eventually discovered him and took him into his home, where he was raised by the man's wife.

Tradition holds that Ailbe was a disciple of St. Patrick and ministered in County Tipperary, Ireland, where his love of animals, especially dogs and wolves, became well known. One tale tells of how Ailbe, forced into exile for his beliefs, blessed a faithful hound who never left his side. In another story, Ailbe saved an old wolf from hunters. The animal placed its head on the preacher's chest and Ailbe realized it was the same wolf that had nursed him as a baby.

Ailbe was said to have performed many miracles, including healing the sick, restoring sight to the blind, and calming storms at sea. He was known for his power of persuasion and is often credited for convincing King Aengus of Munster to donate land for the creation of a monastery. Remembered as the first bishop of Emly, he is often depicted in art standing beside either a dog or a wolf.

ALBERT THE GREAT

BORN: c. 1200, Lauingen, Swabia, Germany
DIED: November 15, 1280, Cologne, Holy Roman Empire
FEAST DAY: November 15

PATRONAGE: Scientists, philosophers, medical technicians, natural sciences
SYMBOLS AND ATTRIBUTES: Bishop's attire, book, globe, quill

,Albert the Great, also commonly referred to as Albertus Magnus, is a towering figure in medieval scholarship who combined a deep religious commitment with a wide-ranging intellectual curiosity. According to varioius sources, he was born in either 1193 or 1206 in Lauingen, Swabia, to the Count of Bollstädt. Little is known of his early life, but as a teen, he attended the prestigious University of Padua.

Excelling at his studies, he was drawn to a religious life and joined the Order of St. Dominic in 1223. Subsequently, he embarked on a distinguished career in academia, teaching in prominent cities such as Cologne and Paris. It was in Paris that he met and began to teach a quiet student named Thomas Aquinas, who displayed a genius intellect. Albert became Thomas's mentor and predicted the future greatness of this occasionally insecure young man. Albert's roles were not just confined to the classroom: he also took on administrative and religious responsibilities, serving as the provincial of his order in Germany, defending Mendicant orders in Rome, and becoming the bishop of Ratisbon.

Always a scholar, Albert wrote extensively, covering diverse subjects ranging from logic, physical sciences, biology, and psychology to morals, metaphysics, and theology. His *De animalibus* delved deep into the study of animals, a subject that garnered significant attention during the medieval period, as scholars sought to understand the natural world and humanity's place within it. And his *Summa theologiae*, which should not be confused with St. Thomas Aquinas's work of the same name, was a magisterial work that provided a comprehensive examination of theological issues at the time. His prowess in assimilating and commenting on a wide array of knowledge led to his title "Doctor Universalis," or Universal Doctor.

St. Albert the Great died on November 15, 1280, and was beatified by Pope Gregory XV in 1622. Pope Pius XI canonized him in 1931, and he is recognized as the patron saint of scientists. His contributions to the fields of philosophy, theology, and natural science continue to be studied and celebrated to this day.

ALEXIS OF ROME

BORN: c. 4th century, Rome, Italy
DIED: c. 5th century, Rome, Italy
FEAST DAY: July 17

PATRONAGE: Beggars, pilgrims, travelers
SYMBOLS AND ATTRIBUTES: Cross, alms, stairs

Alexis of Rome, also known as St. Alexius, is traditionally believed to have lived in the fifth century, although the dates and specific details of his life are not definitively known. According to some sources, Alexis was the only son of a wealthy Roman senator, Euphemianus, and his wife, Aglais. Alexis was deeply religious from a young age. When his parents arranged a marriage for him, Alexis complied but fled on his wedding night to live a life of asceticism and poverty. He gave away his wealth and set sail to Edessa (in modern-day Turkey), where he lived in anonymity, helping the poor and the sick.

After living in Edessa for many years, Alexis had a divine revelation that instructed him to return to his parents' house in Rome. He did so but chose to remain disguised. His father, not recognizing his son, allowed him to live under the stairs of his family home. During the day, Alexis begged for alms, which he would distribute among the poor.

He lived in this manner for seventeen years, his true identity revealed only after his death. Alexis's body was discovered at Euphemianus's house with a document, possibly written by Alexis himself, telling his story. His parents and his wife mourned him, realizing that the beggar they had housed was their son and husband. During the eighth century, Alexis became titular saint of a church on the Aventine in Rome, originally dedicated to St. Boniface and associated with a local home for the poor. The church houses his relics and includes the stairs under which Alexis is said to have lived (*Catholic Encyclopedia*).

ALOYSIUS GONZAGA

BORN: March 9, 1568, Castiglione delle Stiviere, Duchy of Mantua
DIED: June 21, 1591, Rome, Italy
FEAST DAY: June 21

PATRONAGE: Young students, persons with AIDS, caregivers
SYMBOLS AND ATTRIBUTES: Lily, cross, skull, rosary

Also known as Luigi Gonzaga, St. Aloysius Gonzaga was an Italian Jesuit who lived during the sixteenth century. He was born into a noble family in Castiglione delle Stiviere, Italy. A sickly child, Aloysius spent many hours in prayer and reading the Bible. As he grew older, he eventually gave up his status as a member of nobility to focus his attention on God. When Aloysius was twelve, St. Charles Borromeo became his spiritual mentor and administered his First Communion. In 1581, Aloysius went to Spain, serving as a page for Philip II's son, James. At eighteen, Aloysius joined the Jesuit order after finishing his studies and took vows of chastity, poverty, and obedience. He dedicated himself to serving the poor and the sick and even gave up his bed to a leper in need.

Aloysius's compassion and kindness earned him a reputation as a healer and a seer. In 1591 he was living in Rome when plague ravaged the city and he spent countless hours caring for the sick and dying. During this time Aloysius had a vision of St. Gabriel and St. Anthony of Padua, who relayed the message that he would pass away on the eighth day following the feast of Corpus Christi (known as an octave). He continued ministering to those in need. St. Aloysius Gonzaga fell ill and, true to the vision, died on June 21, 1591, the exact date foretold.

In art, Aloysius is often depicted wearing the clothes of a Jesuit, and he is frequently shown holding a crucifix or a rosary. In some depictions, he is also shown with a skull, which serves as a reminder of the brevity of time on earth and the importance of preparing for the afterlife. Another common symbol associated with Aloysius is a lily, which represents his purity and devotion to God. *The Miracle of St. Aloysius Gonzaga and the Novice Nicolás Celestini*, a famous eighteenth-century painting by Miguel Cabrera, housed at the Metropolitan Museum of Art in New York City, depicts the miraculous healing of a novice priest after prayers to Aloysius.

In 1621, Aloysius was canonized by Pope Gregory XV and was declared the patron saint of youth and students.

St. Aloysius Gonzaga's impact on the world can be seen in various ways, including education; Gonzaga University in Spokane, Washington, is named after him. His intercession is often invoked for those affected by AIDS. (See Charles Borromeo, Gabriel, and Anthony of Padua.)

ALPHONSA OF THE IMMACULATE CONCEPTION

BORN: August 19, 1910, Kudamaloor, Kerala, India

DIED: July 28, 1946, Bharananganam, Kerala, India

FEAST DAY: July 28

PATRONAGE: Foot diseases

SYMBOLS AND ATTRIBUTES: Clarist habit, rosary, Bible

Alphonsa of the Immaculate Conception, also known as St. Alphonsa, was an Indian Catholic nun and a member of the Franciscan Clarist Congregation. Born Anna Muttathupadathu in Kudamaloor, a village in the state of Kerala, India, she was the eldest child of Joseph Muttathupadathu and Mary Muttathupadathu.

Anna's early years were defined by adversity and illness. She lost her mother at a young age, after which her upbringing was entrusted to her maternal aunt, Annamma Muricken. In spite of health problems, she demonstrated remarkable academic prowess, attending a local school in Arpookara.

Anna joined the college of the Congregation of the Franciscan Clarists in 1927 as an intern student after initially being rejected due to her physical frailty. She began her postulancy on August 2, 1928, and received her religious habit on May 19, 1930. She took the name Sister Alphonsa of the Immaculate Conception after St. Alphonsus Liguori. Throughout her time in the convent, she faced various health issues, including stomach ailments and severe arthritis in her feet. Sister Alphonsa saw her physical afflictions as a way of participating in Christ's passion and centered her life through prayer, penance, and the cultivation of virtues.

Sister Alphonsa's reputation for sanctity grew, and many people sought her intercession and spiritual guidance. Her life became a testimony to the power of faith in the midst of suffering. In death, she became a powerful intercessor, and miraculous cures were attributed to her, especially for those who had foot problems.

On October 12, 2008, Alphonsa became the first woman of Indian origin to be canonized. She is the patroness of the sick, the suffering, and those who face physical ailments. (See Alphonsus Liguori.)

ALPHONSUS LIGUORI

BORN: September 27, 1696, Naples, Kingdom of Naples

DIED: August 1, 1787, Pagani, Kingdom of Naples

FEAST DAY: August 1

PATRONAGE: Lawyers, arthritis

SYMBOLS AND ATTRIBUTES: Bishop's attire, book, cross

St. Alphonsus Liguori, an Italian bishop, writer, theologian, and founder of the Redemptorists (also known as the Congregation of the Most Holy Redeemer), was born into a noble family in Naples. His parents, devout Catholics, instilled in him a strong devotion to the faith. As a child, Alphonsus dedicated many of his waking hours to prayer.

A gifted student, Alphonsus earned a law degree at sixteen. He became a successful lawyer around the age of nineteen. Later, he felt called to the priesthood and was ordained at around the age of thirty. As a priest, he gained a reputation for having an exceptional ability to connect with his congregation. Alphonsus's simple, direct, and thoughtful preaching style resonated with parishioners, and his sermons often provided practical advice for living a holy life. A great lover of the poor, he devoted much of his time to ministering to those in need.

In 1732, Alphonsus founded the Congregation of the Most Holy Redeemer, a religious order dedicated to preaching the Gospel and serving the poor. The order was a disaster at first and many of its members left, but years later it found success, and Alphonsus became known as a spiritual leader and advocate for the impoverished.

Throughout his lifetime, Alphonsus wrote numerous works, one of the most famous being *The Glories of Mary*, a collection of meditations on the Virgin Mary that has been translated into multiple languages. He also composed many hymns, including the famous Christmas carol "Tu Scendi Dalle Stelle."

In 1762, Alphonsus was appointed bishop of the diocese of Sant'Agata dei Goti but retired four years later due to poor health. Though he struggled with illness for much of his life, and was often bedridden, he remained a dedicated servant of God, stressing the importance of regular participation in the sacrament of Penance and nurturing a devotion to the Eucharist and the Sacred Heart of Jesus.

Alphonsus died on August 1, 1787. He was declared a Doctor of the Church in 1871 by Pope Pius IX. He was canonized by Pope Gregory XVI in 1839.

St. Alphonsus Liguori experienced many supernatural phenomena, including visions, miracles, and levitation. His commitment to the poor and emphasis on the sacrament of Penance still influence the Catholic Church today. His writings on moral theology have had a lasting impact on Catholic theology, and his deep devotions to the Eucharist and the Sacred Heart of Jesus continue to inspire the faithful around the world.

ALPHONSUS RODRIGUEZ

BORN: July 25, 1532, Segovia, Spain

DIED: October 31, 1617, Palma, Majorca, Spain

FEAST DAY: October 31

PATRONAGE: Jesuit lay brothers

SYMBOLS AND ATTRIBUTES: Jesuit habit, rosary, door (as he was a doorkeeper)

A Spanish Jesuit lay brother, Alphonsus Rodriquez was born into a humble family in Segovia, Spain. Before joining the Jesuit order, he worked as a cloth merchant; when he was twenty-six years old, he married Maria Suarez. The couple had three children, but Maria and two of their children passed away in quick succession.

Following this tragic loss, Alphonsus sought solace in Jesus and joined the Jesuit order as a lay brother in 1571. Although he lacked formal education, he dedicated himself to his work and gained a reputation for his gentle demeanor, humility, and compassionate nature.

St. Alphonsus is best known as a humble porter at the Jesuit college in Majorca, Spain, where he served others and assisted those in need. Though he tended to be overlooked by some of the Jesuits, students and visitors to the college often sought his spiritual guidance and comforting words of encouragement. Alphonsus's unpretentious manner endeared him to both the Jesuit community and the people of Majorca.

Some accounts say his life was marked by several miracles attributed to his intercession. One of the most notable stories involved a young, ailing student named Peter Claver. St. Alphonsus took Peter under his wing, praying for his recovery. During one of these prayers, he experienced a vision of the Virgin Mary, who assured him that Peter would heal and become a missionary in the New World. As foretold, Peter recovered and went on to serve the enslaved population in South America as a dedicated Jesuit priest. Today, Peter Claver is recognized as the patron saint of Colombia and of enslaved people.

Another remarkable event linked to St. Alphonsus took place after his death. In 1633, a fire threatened to engulf the Jesuit college in Majorca. The desperate Jesuits implored St. Alphonsus's intercession, and the fire abruptly extinguished itself, saving the building.

St. Alphonsus Rodriguez died on October 31, 1617, at eighty-five years old. His beatification by Pope Clement X in 1671 and canonization in 1716 attest to his enduring impact on the spiritual lives of countless individuals. His life embodied humility, simplicity, and devotion to God and has inspired people from all walks of life to nurture their faith, pursue a deeper connection with the divine, and selflessly serve others. (See Peter Claver.)

AMBROSE OF MILAN

BORN: c. 340, Trier, Gallic Empire
DIED: April 4, 397, modern-day Milan, Western Roman Empire
FEAST DAY: December 7

PATRONAGE: Beekeepers, learning, students, Milan
SYMBOLS AND ATTRIBUTES: Bishop's attire, bees, beehive, whip, book

St. Ambrose of Milan, also known as Ambrosius or Ambrogio, was a prominent figure in the early Church during the late fourth century. He was a prolific writer, a renowned orator, and a skilled theologian and was critical in shaping and defending Christian doctrine and practice.

Ambrose was born in Trier, in what is now modern-day Germany, around 340. His father, also named Ambrose, was a high-ranking official in the Roman Empire, while his mother was believed to have been a Christian. After his father's death, Ambrose and his brother Satyrus moved to Rome with their mother, where they received a classical education. Ambrose studied law and rhetoric in Milan, becoming a successful lawyer and eventually rising in 374 to the position of governor of the city.

It was during this time that Ambrose's life took a dramatic turn. In the same year that he became governor, the bishop of Milan died. The Christian community was divided over his successor. When Ambrose attended the election process to nominate a candidate, he was called upon by the people to mediate and address the crowd. His speech was so powerful and persuasive, those in attendance demanded that he be made the bishop. Ambrose accepted the position. He was quickly baptized and within a week was ordained and consecrated as bishop.

Ambrose learned all he could about Christianity. He worked diligently as bishop to build up the Church in Milan and defend orthodoxy against various heresies, most famously Arianism, that threatened to undermine the Church. Ambrose's writings also significantly impacted Christian thought, particularly in the areas of liturgy, music, and the difficult and complex relationship between church and state.

Ambrose produced a large body of writing that included sermons, letters, and hymns on various theological and pastoral issues. His most famous work is his treatise on the sacraments, which he wrote in response to the heretical teachings of the Arians, who denied the divinity of Christ. Ambrose emphasized the importance of these sacred rites, particularly Baptism and the Eucharist, in the life of the Christian community. He argued that the sacraments were not merely symbolic gestures but were actual channels of divine grace through which believers could receive forgiveness of sins and be united with Christ.

Ambrose was also an accomplished hymnologist whose musical compositions were widely used in the early Church. He believed that music played an essential role in the worship of God and could be used to convey theological truths to the faithful. His hymns are still used today and his influence on Christian music continues to be recognized.

In addition to his theological and musical contributions, Ambrose's influence shaped the relationship between church and state in the Roman Empire. At the time of his appointment as bishop, Christianity was still a minority religion. Nevertheless, Ambrose believed the Church should be independent of the state and not be subject to its authority. He argued that the Church's mission was to proclaim the gospel and care for people's spiritual needs, while the state's role was to maintain order and justice in society. This did not mean that the Church should turn a blind eye to injustice. In retribution for the lynching of a commanding soldier, Emperor Theodosius massacred Thessalonican citizens in 390. Ambrose famously rebuked the emperor and demanded he do penance. Though tensions continued, Ambrose won favor among many Roman officials who agreed with his ideas.

Several signs and symbols are associated with Ambrose, including the bee. According to tradition, when Ambrose was an infant, a swarm of bees settled on his face without harming him. This was interpreted as a sign of his future eloquence and wisdom. In art, he is often depicted with a crosier, representing his role as a shepherd of the Church and symbolizing his authority and pastoral care; a book and pen, illustrating his importance as a prolific writer and theologian; and a baptismal font. Of note, Ambrose was integral in the conversion of St. Augustine, who authored *Confessions* and *The City of God*, two seminal works of Christian thought. Legends tell of Ambrose's exploits as an exorcist who drove out many demons.

As a bishop and leader, Ambrose demonstrated an unwavering dedication to the spiritual well-being of his flock and a deep commitment to preserving and promoting Christian orthodoxy. He is believed to have died on Good Friday, April 4, 397. Today, his writings continue to be studied and admired, and his hymns remain a cherished part of many Christian worship services. (See Augustine of Hippo.)

ANANIAS OF DAMASCUS

BORN: 1st century, place unknown

DIED: 1st century, Damascus

FEAST DAY: January 25

PATRONAGE: Eye problems

SYMBOLS AND ATTRIBUTES: Older man, presenting a hand to Saul (Paul)

Ananias of Damascus was a disciple of Jesus who appears in the Acts of the Apostles, where he is described as a dutiful follower of the law and an esteemed member of the Jewish community living in Damascus. He played a vital role in Saul's journey of conversion to Christianity.

In Acts 9:10–18, Ananias is told in a vision by God to go to a man from Tarsus named Saul, who at the time was known for persecuting Christians. Saul had been struck blind after experiencing a heavenly vision on the road to Damascus.

Ananias obeys the command to seek out Saul, whom he finds. After finding the man, Ananias lays his hands on him, and something like scales fall from Saul's eyes. The persecutor of Christians regains his sight. Following this, Ananias baptizes Saul, who takes the name Paul. The healed man begins his ministry, spreading the teachings of Jesus Christ, and radically changed the course of human history. (See Paul.)

ANASTASIA OF SIRMIUM

BORN: c. 280, Rome, Italy

DIED: c. 304, Sirmium (modern-day Serbia)

FEAST DAY: December 25

PATRONAGE: Martyrs, weavers, widows, exorcists

SYMBOLS AND ATTRIBUTES: Palm branch, chalice

Often identified as Anastasia of Sirmium or Anastasia the Pharmakolytria, St. Anastasia is celebrated as a martyr. Her title "Pharmakolytria" translates to "deliverer from potions" or "she who breaks the spell," emphasizing her alleged power to heal those afflicted by curses, poison, or disease. She is venerated as a patron saint of exorcists.

Most of what we know about Anastasia stems from legends. Born in the late third century, she hailed from a Roman province in present-day Balkans. She married a pagan named Publius, who, according to some accounts, died while Anastasia was still young. In the wake of his passing, she directed her efforts toward charity, particularly aiding imprisoned Christians, and her devout actions led to her capture during the Diocletian persecutions. After enduring various tortures, she was martyred. While one narrative claims her final moments were in Sirmium, another recounts her being beheaded or burned alive on the island of Palmaria.

The mention of Anastasia in the Roman Canon of the Mass underscores her significant role from the Middle Ages to the twentieth century. Throughout the years, the Christian community's respect for her has inspired the establishment of many churches in her name, most notably the Basilica di Sant'Anastasia al Palatino in Rome.

The title "Pharmakolytria" stands as a testament to her distinct protective role. The belief in her ability to counteract poisons and shield against malevolent spells and witchcraft makes her as a potent symbol against harmful spiritual forces. The tenth-century hagiography *The Life of St. Andrew the Fool* indicates that those afflicted with demonic possession were frequently brought to a church dedicated to her in Constantinople.

ANASTASIUS

BORN: 3rd century, possibly Aquileia

DIED: c. 304, maybe Salona

FEAST DAY: September 7

PATRONAGE: Fullers

SYMBOLS AND ATTRIBUTES: Palm branch

St. Anastasius the Fuller was a Christian martyr who lived during the late third century and early fourth century. He was known as "the fuller" because of his profession, which included cleaning and thickening woolen cloth by beating and washing it.

According to tradition, Anastasius was a resident of Aquileia in modern-day Italy. He was known for having a cloth with an image of Christ, which he displayed outside his workshop. This act of devotion angered the pagan authorities, and during the Diocletian persecutions, Anastasius was arrested and ultimately martyred for his faith. He died by drowning, around the year 304.

ANDREW

BORN: c. 5 AD, Bethsaida, Galilee

DIED: Mid-to-late 1st century AD, Achaea, Greece

FEAST DAY: November 30

PATRONAGE: Scotland, Greece, Russia, fishermen

SYMBOLS AND ATTRIBUTES: X-shaped cross (St. Andrew's Cross), fish, fishing net

St. Andrew, also known as Andrew the Apostle, was one of Christ's twelve apostles and a key figure in early Christianity. Born in Bethsaida, Galilee, in the first century AD, he was the brother of Simon Peter (also known as Peter), both of whom were fishermen. According to the Gospel of John, Andrew was initially a disciple of John the Baptist, but left him to follow Jesus after the Baptizer identified Jesus as the "Lamb of God." Soon thereafter, Andrew became convinced that Jesus was the long-awaited Messiah and immediately shared this revelation with his brother Peter. The Gospels of Matthew and Mark tell a different story, in which Andrew and Peter are called while they were fishing and Jesus famously says that he will make them fishers of men. Without hesitation, they left behind their nets to follow the Christ.

Throughout the Gospels, Andrew is depicted as an eyewitness to significant events in Jesus's life. He was present during moments such as the feeding of the 5,000 and the Last Supper. Notably, his devotion to Jesus was unwavering.

Tradition holds that after the crucifixion and resurrection of Jesus, St. Andrew embraced his role as a missionary. He embarked on journeys to spread Christ's teachings, and is believed to have traveled through various regions, including Greece, Romania, and Russia. His efforts to preach the Gospel contributed to the early growth of Christianity and the dissemination of Jesus's message of love and salvation.

Andrew's Christ-centered life ultimately led to his martyrdom. It is said that he met his fate in the city of Patras in Achaea, Greece, where he was crucified on an X-shaped cross, which became known as St. Andrew's Cross or a saltire.

Andrew's significance extends beyond his apostolic role and martyrdom. He is highly revered in the Eastern Orthodox Church, where he is considered the founder and patron saint of the Church of Constantinople, present-day Istanbul. His legacy as a martyr and missionary has made him the patron saint of several countries, including Russia and Greece, and various cities and regions worldwide.

Scotland, in particular, holds a deep connection to St. Andrew. Legend suggests he visited the country and performed miracles, establishing him as its patron saint. The Saltire, Scotland's national flag, featuring a white saltire cross on a blue background, represents this patronage. St. Andrew's Day, celebrated on November 30, is a national holiday in Scotland and an important feast day in the Eastern Orthodox Church.

St. Andrew's influence also extends to Romania, where he is recognized as the country's patron saint. The Romanian Orthodox Church commemorates him with special liturgies and vibrant festivities, including traditional dances and musical performances.

St. Andrew is often depicted in Christian art holding a fishing net, representing his former life as a fisherman and his transformation into a disciple of Jesus and a fisher of men. (See Peter, John the Baptist.)

ANDREW DUNG-LAC

BORN: 1795, Vietnam

DIED: December 21, 1839, Vietnam

FEAST DAY: November 24 (with Vietnamese martyrs)

PATRONAGE: Vietnam

SYMBOLS AND ATTRIBUTES: Priest's attire, palm branch, cross

St. Andrew Dung-Lac was a Vietnamese Catholic priest martyred in the nineteenth century. Little is certain about his early years, but it is believed he was born sometime around 1795 in a small town in what is now Vietnam. He was the son of a poor family and was orphaned at a young age. He proved to be a bright student and was sent to study at the seminary in Hanoi. In 1823, Andrew was ordained a priest and was assigned to the parish of Ke Sai. He was a devoted pastor and spent much of his time ministering to the sick and the poor. In 1839, Emperor Minh Mạng of Vietnam began a campaign of persecution against Christians, which would continue for several decades. Andrew and several other priests and believers were arrested and imprisoned. Tortured and humiliated, Andrew refused to renounce his beliefs. On December 21, 1839, he was beheaded in Hanoi, along with other Vietnamese Christians imprisoned for their faith. He is one of the 117 Vietnamese martyrs canonized by Pope John Paul II on June 19, 1988, in Rome.

St. Andrew Dung-Lac is the patron saint of Vietnam, along with the other martyrs of that country.

ANDREW KIM TAEGON

BORN: August 21, 1821,
Chungcheong-do, Korea
DIED: September 16, 1846, near modern-
day Seoul, Korea

FEAST DAY: September 20
PATRONAGE: Korean clergy
SYMBOLS AND ATTRIBUTES: Priest's attire,
cross, palm branch

St. Andrew Kim Taegon was born in Chungcheong-do, Korea. He was the first native-born Korean Catholic priest and martyr. He came from a noble family that had converted to Catholicism, a relatively new religion in Korea at that time. As a young man, he traveled to China to study Catholicism, and was eventually baptized in Shanghai. He was later ordained as a priest in Macau, a Portuguese colony in China, in 1845.

Upon returning to Korea, Andrew embarked on his mission to evangelize his country. He faced severe opposition from the Korean government, which regarded Catholicism as a foreign threat. Undeterred, he continued to spread the Gospel, which led to his arrest and subsequent execution.

On September 16, 1846, at the age of twenty-five, Andrew, alongside several other martyrs, was beheaded. Their death inspired others to embrace the faith, and Catholicism continued to expand in Korea. Today, he is considered a powerful symbol of the Catholic faith.

Andrew Kim Taegon is recognized as the patron saint of Korea, alongside St. Paul Chŏng Hasang and other martyrs who lost their lives for their Catholic faith in the nineteenth century. Additionally, he is revered as the patron saint of Asian youth and seminarians.

ANGADRISMA OF BEAUVAIS

BORN: 615, Lognes, France
DIED: c. 695, Beauvais, France
FEAST DAY: October 14

PATRONAGE: Diocese of Beauvais
SYMBOLS AND ATTRIBUTES: Nun's habit,
staff, holding a church in her hands

St. Angadrisma of Beauvais was born in 615 in what is now northern France. From the time she was young, Angadrisma dedicated her life to God. Years later, when she was betrothed to a courtier, she fervently prayed to avoid the union. She contracted leprosy, which led to the dissolution of her engagement. After her fiancé wed another woman, she miraculously recovered. She subsequently chose the monastic life, immersing herself in prayer, contemplation, and asceticism.

Angadrisma was known within her community for her kindness, compassion, and generosity toward the poor and needy. She experienced mystical visions, including one where Jesus Christ appeared to her in a dream and instructed her to stay faithful to her calling as a nun and to persevere in prayer and good works.

Throughout her life, St. Angadrisma remained humble and devoted to her faith. She passed away around the year 695, at the age of eighty, and was laid to rest at the church of Saint-Pierre in Beauvais. Her tomb became a pilgrimage site, attracting countless devotees seeking her intercession.

ANGELA MERICI

BORN: March 21, 1474, Desenzano del Garda, Lombardy, Italy

DIED: January 27, 1540, Brescia, Lombardy, Italy

FEAST DAY: January 27

PATRONAGE: Sickness, people with special needs, parental loss

SYMBOLS AND ATTRIBUTES: Cloak with Ursuline "A," ladder, book

St. Angela Merici was the founder of the Ursuline order, a Roman Catholic congregation of women devoted to spiritual development and charitable work. Angela lived during a period of significant religious and social unrest in Europe, coinciding with the Protestant Reformation and the Council of Trent.

Born in Desenzano del Garda near Lake Garda, Italy, Angela was the youngest of three children. In her youth, she experienced a vision of the Virgin Mary that influenced her spiritual journey and ignited a divine sense of purpose. She joined the Third Order of St. Francis, a lay organization enabling individuals to live a religious life without formal vows.

She founded the Company of St. Ursula, a community that eventually became the renowned Ursuline order, dedicated to education and the empowerment of women. Ursuline institutions taught girls practical skills like sewing and embroidery while also enriching their minds with subjects such as Latin and mathematics. These schools have evolved into prestigious institutions of learning consistently equipping their students to emerge as leaders, scholars, and agents of change within their societies. Prominent among the Ursuline schools today are the Ursuline Academy in New Orleans, established in 1727, which was instrumental in educating girls in the southern United States, and the Ursuline Convent School in Cork, Ireland, established in 1771.

In art, Angela is often depicted holding a book, symbolizing her dedication to the study of knowledge. Lilies frequently accompany her image, symbolizing her virtuous life. The Ursuline habit comprises a black gown and veil.

She was canonized by Pope Pius VII in 1807.

ANGELA OF FOLIGNO

BORN: 1248, Foligno, Umbria, Italy

DIED: January 4, 1309, Foligno, Umbria, Italy

FEAST DAY: January 7

PATRONAGE: Widows

SYMBOLS AND ATTRIBUTES: Religious habit, cross

Angela of Foligno was a medieval mystic and saint who lived during the thirteenth century. She is recognized for her spiritual experiences and writings, which have significantly impacted Christian mysticism.

Angela was married and had children. At around age forty she had a vision of St. Francis of Assisi. A few years after this experience, her mother, husband, and children died, after which she underwent a profound spiritual transformation and dedicated her life to God through prayer and penance. Angela continued throughout her life to have mystical experiences characterized by visions, ecstasies, and encounters with divine beings.

She became a member of the Third Order of St. Francis and received guidance from Franciscan friars. Throughout her spiritual journey, she dictated her spiritual experiences and teachings to scribes, resulting in the compilation of her work known by various names but often referred to as *The Book of Divine Consolations of the Blessed Angela of Foligno.* The work contains her autobiographical account, descriptions of her visions, and spiritual insights. Her teachings highlighted the importance of spiritual self-emptying, detachment from worldly desires, and humility to draw closer to God. Angela's book served as an inspiration for Christian mystics who sought guidance and insight into their own faith journeys.

Angela of Foligno died on January 4, 1309, and was beatified on July 11, 1701. Though many miracles were attributed to her intercession, it took more than three hundred years for her to be canonized, even though she had been highly venerated for centuries. Pope Francis declared her a saint on October 9, 2013, by order of equipollent canonization, meaning the Church bypassed the formal process and declared her a saint even without evidence of a miracle attributed to her intercession. (See Francis of Assisi)

ANNA

BORN: 1st century BC, place unknown

DIED: 1st century AD, place unknown

FEAST DAY: September 1

PATRONAGE: Unknown

SYMBOLS AND ATTRIBUTES: Scroll, depicted with the Baby Jesus

FEAST DAY: September 1

Anna was a prophetess who appears briefly in the New Testament after the birth of Jesus. According to the Gospel of Luke, Anna was a devout and elderly woman who had lived as a widow for many years, described as "a prophetess, the daughter of Phanuel, of the tribe of Asher," one of the twelve tribes of Israel. She resided in the temple of Jerusalem, where she worshipped day and night, fasting and praying. When Mary and Joseph presented the baby Jesus at the Temple in accordance with Jewish law, Anna recognized him as the Messiah and gave thanks to God. She subsequently shared the good news about Jesus with everyone who was anticipating the deliverance of Jerusalem.

Anna's brief appearance in the Bible serves as a witness to the fulfillment of Old Testament prophecies and emphasizes both her devotion to God and her recognition of Jesus's significance. She was the subject of the artist Rembrandt, who featured her in the painting *The Prophetess Anna.*

ANNE

BORN: c. 1st century BC, Bethlehem

DIED: 1st century BC, place unknown

FEAST DAY: July 26

PATRONAGE: Grandmothers, mothers, pregnancy, miners, cabinetmakers

SYMBOLS AND ATTRIBUTES: Door, book, Mary as a child

The mother of the Virgin Mary, St. Anne does not appear in the Bible, however; her story comes primarily from the "Protoevangelism of James," an infancy narrative that dates to the second century AD. According to tradition, Anne was Joachim's wife, and the couple longed for a child but could not conceive. They remained faithful to God and, at last, an angel appeared to Anne in her old age and promised that she would bear a child who would become the mother of the Messiah.

Through the will of God, the union of Joachim and Anne resulted in Mary miraculously being born without original sin. This is known as the Immaculate Conception, which, when Pope Pius IX issued the papal bull *Ineffabilis Deus* in 1854, became a core tenet of the Catholic dogma.

Anne is often depicted in art and literature either holding the infant Mary in her arms or holding a lily, symbolizing her purity and the purity of her daughter. She is also sometimes depicted with a book, as she is believed to have taught Mary how to read and write. Anne's feast day is celebrated on July 26, and she is widely venerated as the patron saint of mothers, grandmothers, and childless couples as well as women in labor, miners, and cabinetmakers. Many churches and shrines worldwide are dedicated to her, including the Basilica of St. Anne de Beaupré in Quebec, Canada, a popular destination for pilgrims. Today, St. Anne inspires many who seek to follow God's will in their lives. Her unwavering faith and devotion, and her essential role in raising the mother of Jesus, make her an important figure in Catholicism, someone who highlights the importance of family in the Christian faith.

For the faithful, the story of St. Anne and Joachim is a reminder to trust in God even in the face of disappointment and hardship.

ANNE-MARIE RIVIER

BORN: December 19, 1768,
Montpezat-sous-Bauzon, France
DIED: February 3, 1838,
Bourg-Saint-Andéol, France
FEAST DAY: February 3

PATRONAGE: Sisters of the Presentation of
Mary, catechists, those persecuted for
religious beliefs
SYMBOLS AND ATTRIBUTES: Image of Mary,
cross, nun's habit, children, book

Anne-Marie Rivier was a French Roman Catholic nun and the founder of the Sisters of the Presentation of Mary, also known as the Rivier Sisters.

In 1792, during the French Revolution, she and a group of women formed a small religious community in Thueyts, France, seeking to educate young girls and provide them with a strong religious and academic foundation.

In 1796, Anne-Marie Rivier made a private vow to God, committing herself to establish a larger, religious congregation dedicated to expanding her earlier mission. On July 24, 1802, with the local bishop's approval, she founded the Sisters of the Presentation of Mary with the objective to educate young girls, particularly those from poor and marginalized communities. Under Anne-Marie Rivier's guidance, the congregation grew and established schools across France. The sisters extended their work to other countries, including Switzerland, England, Canada, and the United States.

Anne-Marie Rivier served as the superior general of the Sisters of the Presentation of Mary until her death in 1838, in Bourg-Saint-Andéol, France. She was beatified by Pope John Paul II on May 23, 1982. Pope Francis declared her a saint on May 15, 2022.

ANSELM

BORN: 1033, Aosta, Burgundy
DIED: April 21, 1109, Canterbury, England
FEAST DAY: April 21

PATRONAGE: Philosophers, theologians
SYMBOLS AND ATTRIBUTES: Archbishop's
attire, miter, ship, book

St. Anselm, also known as Anselm of Canterbury, was a Benedictine monk, theologian, and philosopher. He is widely regarded as one of the greatest Christian thinkers of the Middle Ages and is celebrated for his contributions to theology and philosophy, as well as for the miracles attributed to him.

Born in 1033, Anselm exhibited a deep spiritual nature from a young age, mainly due to his mother's influence. As a child, he experienced a defining vision where he saw himself dining with God, which shaped his religious path. Anselm felt drawn to monastic life in his teen years and eventually left home after disagreements with his father. He traveled across Burgundy, France, and Normandy before finding solace at the Abbey of

Bec. Under the mentorship of a monk named Lanfranc, Anselm quickly ascended the abbey's hierarchy, succeeding Lanfranc (who was promoted to archbishop of Canterbury) as prior, and subsequently wrote many foundational philosophical and theological works.

With evident leadership skills, Anselm was named abbot of Bec after its founder, Herluin, passed away. He accepted the appointment, and his growing prestige marked him as the likely successor to Lanfranc, who died in 1089, as archbishop of Canterbury. It would be nearly four years before King William Rufus, the son of William the Conqueror, appointed Anselm as archbishop. Throughout his term, Anselm and King William often disagreed, especially on matters of Church lands and the authority of Pope Urban II.

Beyond these political and religious skirmishes, which lasted until his death, Anselm left an indelible mark as a theologian and philosopher. He is best known for his contributions to the field of theology, especially with the *Proslogion*, which introduces his famous ontological argument for the existence of God. In this meditation, Anselm proposes that God is the greatest conceivable being, and since existing in reality is greater than in thought alone, such a being therefore must exist in reality.

Anselm's contributions to Christian thought have had a lasting impact on the Church and philosophy. His emphasis on reason and logic as tools for understanding the nature of God helped to lay the groundwork for the development of scholasticism, the medieval, philosophical, and theological tradition that sought to reconcile faith and reason. His writings on the existence of God continue to be studied, considered, and debated by philosophers today.

ANSGAR

BORN: September 8, 801, Amiens, West Francia
DIED: February 3, 865, Bremen, East Francia

FEAST DAY: February 3
PATRONAGE: Scandinavia
SYMBOLS AND ATTRIBUTES: Archbishop's attire, cross, crosier

St. Ansgar, also known as the Apostle of the North, was a pivotal figure in spreading Christianity in Scandinavia during the ninth century. He lived in a time when much of Europe remained pagan, and the Church was actively evangelizing the lands beyond the Roman Empire's borders.

Ansgar was educated in the monastic tradition and joined the Benedictine order at a young age. A promising scholar and an accomplished linguist, fluent in several languages, including what would today be called Old Norse, he was chosen to lead a mission to Scandinavia in 826 at the behest of the Danish king, Harald Klak. Ansgar faced challenges in his mission, as the Scandinavians were wary of foreigners and fiercely protective of their traditional beliefs.

However, he persisted, working to spread the Gospel throughout Scandinavia, and eventually established several churches and monasteries in Denmark and Sweden. His tenacity and devotion laid the foundation for the region's eventual Christianization.

One miracle attributed to St. Ansgar occurred during his mission to Denmark, where he sought to free Christian slaves captured by pagan Danes. Legend has it that as Ansgar prayed for their release, the prisoners' chains miraculously fell away, allowing them to escape. This story, possibly inspired by similar stories of the apostles in the years after Jesus's death and resurrection, helped convert many pagan Scandinavians to Christianity.

The *Vita Ansgarii*, a ninth-century hagiography penned by Archbishop Rimbert of Hamburg-Bremen, serves as both a historical document and testament to Ansgar's sanctity. The narrative prominently features Ansgar's guiding visions, which played a pivotal role in his missionary undertakings. One vision featuring his mother alongside Mary inspired his monastic commitment. Another significant vision directed Ansgar toward his missionary work in Scandinavia.

St. Ansgar is often depicted wearing traditional ecclesiastical vestments and symbols, such as a miter and a crosier. In many parts of Sweden and Denmark, the feast day is observed with special church services, processions, traditional foods, and decorations.

ANTERUS

BORN: c. late 2nd century, place unknown

DIED: January 3, 236, Rome, Italy,
Roman Empire

FEAST DAY: January 3

PATRONAGE: Martyrs

SYMBOLS AND ATTRIBUTES: Papal tiara

Anterus became the nineteenth or twentieth bishop in 235. During his brief papacy, Emperor Maximinus Thrax intensified his persecution of Christians. Anterus remained resolute in his duty to guide the Church and protect its members, but his papacy was cut short when he was martyred in 236. According to the accounts documented in the *Liber pontificalis*, a book of biographies of the popes, his death can possibly be traced back to his visionary decision to commission a compilation of the acts of the martyrs, aiming to preserve and enshrine the heroic tales of those who had bravely sacrificed their lives for their faith. Ironically, he would die like those followers of Christ he wished to memorialize.

ANTHONY MARY CLARET

BORN: December 23, 1807, Sallent,
 Catalonia, Spain

DIED: October 24, 1870, Fontfroide,
 Narbonne, France

FEAST DAY: October 24

PATRONAGE: Weavers, savings (financial),
 technical and vocational students

SYMBOLS AND ATTRIBUTES: Bishop's
 attire, book

Anthony Mary Claret, also known as Antonio Maria Claret y Clará, was a Spanish Roman Catholic archbishop and missionary who lived during the nineteenth century. He was born in Sallent, Spain, to a devout Catholic family in 1807, during a time when Spain was experiencing significant political and religious turmoil (Napoleon Bonaparte would invade Spain during this time, leading to the Peninsular War for control of the Iberian Peninsula).

At the age of twelve, Anthony entered the diocesan seminary in Vic, and he was ordained a priest in 1835. In 1849, after serving as a parish priest for several years, Anthony founded the Congregation of the Missionary Sons of the Immaculate Heart of Mary, also known as the Claretians. As a missionary, Anthony traveled throughout Spain and the Canary Islands, preaching the Gospel and advocating for social justice amid the challenges of nineteenth-century Spanish society, which included the struggle for religious freedom. He was a prolific writer and published numerous books and pamphlets on a wide range of topics: prayer, the sacraments, and the importance of family life. His most famous work, which has come to be known as *The Autobiography of St. Anthony Mary Claret*, has been translated into many languages and remains a beloved spiritual classic. He wrote, "A son of the Immaculate Heart of Mary is a man on fire with love, who spreads its flames wherever he goes."

Nurturing a devotion to the Eucharist, Anthony prayed before the Blessed Sacrament many hours every day. He also had many mystical experiences throughout his life, including visions of Jesus and Mary, and experienced locutions, or inner voices, through which he received spiritual guidance and insights. He was known to levitate during prayer and exuded the odor of sanctity while he was alive. He was believed to be able to control earthquakes, and he healed many petitioners through prayer during his lifetime.

Anthony Mary Claret was beatified by Pope Pius XI in 1934 and canonized by Pope Pius XII in 1950.

ANTHONY MARY ZACCARIA

BORN: 1502, Cremona, Duchy of Milan

DIED: July 5, 1539, Cremona, Duchy of Milan

FEAST DAY: July 5

PATRONAGE: Physicians, bodily ills, the Barnabite order

SYMBOLS AND ATTRIBUTES: Crucifix, book, lily

St. Anthony Mary Zaccaria was an Italian priest and founder of the Barnabites, a religious order dedicated to the care of souls. His family was wealthy, and Anthony received an excellent education in the humanities and theology. Ordained a priest at the age of twenty-six, he soon became known for his eloquent speech and his zeal for Jesus. In 1530, he, along with two other priests, Bartholomew Ferrari and James Morigia, founded the Congregation of Clerics Regular of St. Paul, also known as the Barnabites. The Barnabites took their name from the Church of St. Barnabas in Milan, where their first community was established.

The Barnabites focused on preaching the Word of God, caring for the sick and the poor, and promoting the importance of the Holy Eucharist. They also dedicated themselves to the reform of the clergy, both in their own order and in the wider Church.

Anthony was known for his penances and his devotion to the Holy Eucharist. He often spent long hours in prayer before the Blessed Sacrament and encouraged others to do the same. He also had a special devotion to the Holy Spirit, which he often invoked in his preaching and personal life. He is depicted in art holding a chalice and a ciborium, symbolizing his love for the Holy Eucharist, or with a dove, representing his devotion to the Holy Spirit.

Though he was only thirty-six at the time of his death, Anthony's order continued to spread throughout Italy and beyond and is still active today. The Barnabites help in the formation of priests for ministry, and their schools provide academic and spiritual guidance. Additionally, they engage in parish ministry, offering pastoral care and guidance, and have extended their reach through foreign missions, providing spiritual and practical support to communities worldwide.

St. Anthony Mary Zaccaria was beatified by Pope Urban VIII in 1627 and canonized by Pope Leo XIII in 1897.

ANTHONY OF PADUA

BORN: August 15, 1195, Lisbon, Portugal

DIED: June 13, 1231, Padua, Italy

FEAST DAY: June 13

PATRONAGE: Lost items, travelers, shipwrecks, harvests, the poor

SYMBOLS AND ATTRIBUTES: Baby Jesus, lily, book, bread

St. Anthony of Padua, also known as St. Anthony of Lisbon, was born Fernando Martins de Bulhões. His parents seem to have been influential Catholics, devoted to the Church, and lived near the cathedral of Lisbon.

At the age of fifteen, he joined the Augustinian Canons Regular and was ordained a priest. He first resided at the St. Vincent convent just outside Lisbon's city walls. Two years later, he relocated to the Convent of Santa Croce in Coimbra to pursue a more contemplative environment. Over the following eight years, he dedicated himself to study and prayer, honing his theological knowledge by delving into Sacred Scriptures and the writings of revered Church Fathers.

In 1220, Anthony was inspired to join the Order of Friars Minor after encountering the bodies of the first Franciscan martyrs. He set sail for Morocco, intending to preach the faith and potentially suffer martyrdom for Christ. However, a severe illness forced him to redirect toward Portugal, and a violent storm eventually cast him ashore on the Sicilian coast. After recovering, he traveled to Italy and met Francis of Assisi, who was impressed by Anthony's humility and intelligence, and soon thereafter began teaching other Franciscans theology.

As a Franciscan friar, Anthony gained a reputation as a powerful preacher, theologian, and miracle worker throughout Italy, France, and Portugal. He was known as the Hammer of Heretics for his defense of Catholic doctrine.

He was devoted to the Eucharist and the Virgin Mary, which was often reflected in the many stories of miracles linked to him over the years. One time, a novice left the monastery after stealing Anthony's book of Psalms. After Anthony prayed, the novice felt compelled to return to the monastery with the book and give it back to its rightful owner. In another instance, a heretic questioned the true presence of Christ in the Eucharist. To prove it, the heretic thought it a good idea to starve his mule for three days. When given the choice between hay and the Eucharist offered by Anthony, the mule knelt before the Eucharist, acknowledging Christ's presence, and the heretic was inspired to convert. In a separate event, a young man, remorseful after severing his foot, was healed when Anthony prayed, and his foot was supernaturally restored. Lastly, when other heretics ignored Anthony's preaching, he turned to the sea and began addressing the fish. The fish breached the waters so that they could hear his preaching. The heretics, witnessing the miracle, converted to Christianity.

Anthony died on June 13, 1231, in Padua, Italy. He was canonized by Pope Gregory IX in 1232. In 1946, Pope Pius XII declared him a Doctor of the Church.

St. Anthony is the patron saint of various groups and causes, including the poor, travelers, pregnant people, those suffering from infertility, and people searching for lost items or animals. He is also the patron saint of several cities and regions, such as Padua, Italy, and Lisbon, Portugal.

ANTOINE DANIEL

BORN: May 27, 1601, Dieppe, France

DIED: July 4, 1648, Teanaostaye, New France

FEAST DAY: October 19

PATRONAGE: Missionaries and martyrs of North America

SYMBOLS AND ATTRIBUTES: Palm branch, cross

Antoine Daniel was a Jesuit missionary and martyr who lived during the seventeenth century. He went to New France (now Canada) as a missionary in 1632 and spent much of his time working among the Huron people. He learned their language, customs, and traditions, and established North America's first boys' school.

During an Iroquois attack on the village of Teanaostaye, Antoine was shot and killed while reportedly trying to assist the besieged Huron people.

Antoine Daniel and seven other Jesuit missionaries are collectively known as the North American Martyrs or the Canadian Martyrs. They were canonized as saints in 1930.

ANTONY THE ABBOT

BORN: 251, Herakleopolis Magna, Egypt

DIED: 356, Mount Colzim, Egypt

FEAST DAY: January 17

PATRONAGE: Gravediggers, skin diseases, farmers, basket makers

SYMBOLS AND ATTRIBUTES: Bell, pig, book, T-shaped cross

St. Antony the Abbot, also known as St. Antony of Egypt, is considered the father of Christian monasticism. He was born in 251 in Upper Egypt to wealthy parents. At the age of twenty, after hearing the words of the Gospel, he sold all his possessions and gave the money to the poor. He then began a life of asceticism, living in solitude in the desert. He is known for his spiritual teachings, miraculous healings, and mystical experiences.

His biography by Athanasius of Alexandria helped popularize a monastic way of life, especially in Western Europe. Tales of Antony facing supernatural temptations in Egypt's Eastern Desert have left a profound impact on art and literature. He is famously known for defending himself against demons who attacked him regularly. In one story often attributed to him, Antony was tempted by Satan, who appeared to him in the form of a boy. The child tried to frighten Antony with visions of monsters and beasts, but Antony remained bold in his faith, and the demon eventually fled. In another mystical experience, Antony was praying in his cave when he saw a light shining above him. He looked up and saw Christ, surrounded by angels, descending. Jesus spoke to Antony, encouraging him to have the strength he needed to continue his asceticism. This vision is often depicted in art with Antony kneeling before his Lord.

APOLLONIA

BORN: 2nd century, Alexandria, Roman Egypt
DIED: 249, Alexandria, Roman Egypt
FEAST DAY: February 9

PATRONAGE: Dentists, tooth problems
SYMBOLS AND ATTRIBUTES: Pincers holding a tooth, palm branch

Known also as Apollonia of Alexandria, St. Apollonia was a deaconess in Egypt, possibly during the reign of the Roman Emperor Philip the Arab. Because this was a time of persecution against Christians, she was arrested and subjected to severe torture, including having all of her teeth forcibly removed or shattered. Apollonia's response to her tormentors embodied Jesus's example by courageously enduring her pain and suffering and even praying for her persecutors.

Apollonia eventually succumbed to her injuries and died as a martyr. Her story and martyrdom have been recorded in various accounts of the lives of saints, including the widely known *Acts of St. Apollonia*.

APOLLOS

BORN: 1st century, place unknown
DIED: 1st century, place unknown
FEAST DAY: February 13

PATRONAGE: Unknown
SYMBOLS AND ATTRIBUTES: Cross

Apollos appears in Acts 18:24–28, where he is described as a Jew living in Ephesus and an eloquent speaker.

Aquila and Priscilla, a married Christian couple, heard him speak in the synagogue and recognized that he had an incomplete understanding of the Gospel. They took Apollos aside and privately discussed Jesus's teachings more thoroughly with him. Apollos was receptive to their instruction and went on to contribute significantly to the Christian community.

After his time in Ephesus, Apollos traveled to Corinth, where he engaged in debates over Jesus and the Church's future there. He is mentioned in 1 Corinthians 1:12 and 3:4–6, where the apostle Paul refers to divisions among the Corinthians, some of whom aligned themselves with Apollos.

While Apollos's later life is not explicitly mentioned in the Bible, he is regarded as a prominent early Christian teacher and evangelist. Many believe his example underscores the importance of ongoing learning and correction within the Christian community, as well as the cooperative effort of various individuals in spreading the Gospel.

ATHANASIUS

BORN: c. 296, Alexandria, Roman Egypt
DIED: May 2, 373, Alexandria,
Roman Egypt
FEAST DAY: May 2

PATRONAGE: Theologians
SYMBOLS AND ATTRIBUTES: Bishop's
attire, book

A doctor of the Church and an influential bishop and theologian in Alexandria during the fourth century, St. Athanasius is remembered for defending the orthodox Christian faith against the heresy of Arianism.

Born in Egypt around 296 and raised in a Christian family when being a follower of Jesus was still considered dangerous, Athanasius was educated in Greek philosophy and Christian theology. He was ordained as a deacon at age twenty-one. In 328, he was appointed as the bishop of Alexandria, a position he held until his death in 373.

During his time as bishop, Athanasius was involved in a bitter conflict with the Arians, who rejected the full divinity of Jesus Christ and asserted that Jesus, though exalted and unique, was a created being and not equal to God the Father in essence or nature. The Arian heresy had gained a foothold in the Eastern Roman Empire, and many bishops and theologians had succumbed to its teachings. Athanasius, however, was a staunch defender of orthodox Christianity, and he saw the Arians as a threat to the very foundations of the faith.

Athanasius wrote extensively in opposition to to this heresy, and his writings, most notably "Against the Arians," were instrumental in defeating the heresy in the Eastern Roman Empire. Athanasius attended the Council of Nicaea, convened by Emperor Constantine in 325. The council aimed to resolve the Arian controversy and reaffirm orthodox belief. The Nicene Creed was formulated. After the council, Athanasius became a staunch supporter of the creed and is also credited with being one of the first to compile the list of books that would eventually become the New Testament canon. Though it took time for parties to come to agreement, his Festal Letter of 367 listed the twenty-seven books now recognized as the authoritative writings of the New Testament.

In addition to his theological writings, St. Athanasius, known in the Eastern Orthodox Church as the "Father of Orthodoxy," was also a prolific writer of letters. His missives provide valuable insight into the challenges and controversies of the early Christian Church and reveal his deep pastoral concern for the well-being of his flock. For his beliefs, Athanasius spent many years in exile but eventually returned to Alexandria, where he died in 327.

AUGUSTINE OF CANTERBURY

BORN: 6th century, Italy

DIED: May 26, 604, Canterbury, Kingdom of Kent

FEAST DAY: May 26

PATRONAGE: England

SYMBOLS AND ATTRIBUTES: Monk's attire, holding a model of the church

St. Augustine of Canterbury, the Apostle to the English, is considered one of the most important figures in the history of Christianity in England. Born in the last half of the sixth century, he was a Benedictine monk sent to England in 597 by Pope Gregory the Great to lead a mission to convert the Anglo-Saxon people to Christianity. This mission was highly successful, and Augustine is credited with being the first archbishop of Canterbury, laying the foundation for the Christian Church in England. Augustine was not the first missionary to arrive in England; there were some Christian communities in the country at the time, but they were few and far between. Augustine's mission was significant as it was the first major attempt to establish Christianity as the dominant religion in the country.

Augustine's mission not only converted a kingdom but also influenced the relationship between the Church and the state. The Christianization of the Anglo-Saxon tribes led to the integration of Christianity into the political and legal systems, shaping the future of England to this day.

AUGUSTINE OF HIPPO

BORN: November 13, 354, Thagaste, Numidia (now Souk Ahras, Algeria)

DIED: August 28, 430, Hippo Regius, Numidia (now Annaba, Algeria)

FEAST DAY: August 28

PATRONAGE: Printers, theologians, brewers, those who suffer eye problems

SYMBOLS AND ATTRIBUTES: Bishop's attire, heart on fire, pen

St. Augustine, also known as Augustine of Hippo, is one of the most influential figures in the history of Western thought and theology. Born in North Africa in the fourth century, he lived during a time of great political and religious upheaval, as the Roman Empire was in decline and Christianity was emerging as the dominant religion of the region. Augustine's life and writings provide a critical window into this period, as well as into the development of Christian thought and doctrine.

Augustine was born into a family of modest means, to a pagan father named Patricius and a Christian mother named Monica. He was educated in the Roman tradition of rhetoric and philosophy. He was a promiscuous young man and fathered a child out of wedlock. Although he was a prodigious learner, Augustine found himself constantly searching for

PLATE I

Augustine of Hippo

something more. He pursued a variety of religious and philosophical traditions, eventually rejecting his mother's Christianity for Manichaeism, a form of Gnosticism that emphasized a dualistic struggle between spiritual forces of light and darkness.

It was not until Augustine's encounter with the Christian bishop Ambrose of Milan that he began to consider the claims of Christianity seriously. Ambrose's eloquence and intelligence impressed Augustine, and he soon became convinced of the truth of Christian doctrine. In his autobiography, known as *Confessions,* Augustine describes his conversion experience in vivid detail. He recounts how he heard a voice in a garden in Milan urging him to "take up and read" the Bible and how he was immediately struck by a passage from the book of Romans. "Let us live honorably as in the day," he read, "not in reveling and drunkenness, not in debauchery and licentiousness, not in quarreling and jealousy. Instead, put on the Lord Jesus Christ, and make no provision for the flesh, to gratify its desires" (Romans 13: 13–14).

Arguably, Augustine's mother, Monica, played as significant a role in his life, particularly concerning his spiritual journey and eventual conversion to Christianity. As a devout Christian, Monica raised Augustine with Christian values and enrolled him among the catechumens, exposing him to the teachings of Christianity from an early age. She fervently prayed for Augustine's conversion throughout his life. In defiance of Augustine's wayward behavior and involvement with heretical beliefs, Monica provided unwavering support during his periods of doubt and philosophical exploration, accompanying him to Milan, where her presence allowed her to be close to him during his interactions with Bishop Ambrose and his ultimate acceptance of Christianity.

His conversion experience had a powerful impact on Augustine's life and work. He became a priest, then a bishop, and devoted himself to studying and explicating Christian doctrine. He wrote *The City of God,* a monumental work that explores the relationship between Christianity and the secular world, hundreds of sermons and treatises, and his most famous work, *Confessions*. This intensely personal reflection on his life, struggles, and faith, widely read and admired for its honesty and insight, has influenced Western literature, psychology, epistemology, and philosophy for more than 1,500 years. It is in this book that he famously wrote of his early life, "Give me chastity and continence, Lord, but not yet."

One of Augustine's most significant contributions to Christian thought was his doctrine of original sin. Augustine believed that all human beings are born with a sinful nature, a legacy passed down from Adam and Eve's act of disobedience in the Garden of Eden. This belief stands in contrast to earlier Christian teachings, which held that sin resulted from individual choice and action. Augustine's doctrine of original sin had important implications for Christian theology, shaping how Christians thought about the nature of God, the role of Jesus Christ, and the purpose of salvation.

Another key element of Augustine's thought was his emphasis on the importance of grace in the Christian life. Augustine believed that human beings could not achieve salvation through their own efforts but must instead rely on the grace of God. This emphasis on grace has been a central feature of Christian theology ever since, shaping how Christians understand the relationship between faith and works.

Augustine's teachings on original sin and grace were controversial. Several Christian thinkers, including the monk and theologian Pelagius (sometimes known as Pelagius the Heretic), challenged his ideas, arguing that human beings could indeed achieve salvation through their own efforts. The controversy over Pelagianism eventually led to a series of Church councils and declarations, culminating in the Council of Ephesus in 431, which officially condemned Pelagianism as a heresy.

Augustine died on August 28, 430, and his feast day is celebrated every year on that day. In art, he is often depicted dressed as a bishop with a burning heart, which symbolizes Augustine's passionate pursuit of truth, his fervent love for God, and his intense devotion to the Christian faith.

B

BALBINA OF ROME

BORN: c. early 2nd century, place unknown
DIED: 130, Rome, Italy, Roman Empire
FEAST DAY: March 31

PATRONAGE: Throat diseases, thyroid disorders
SYMBOLS AND ATTRIBUTES: Chains, fetters

St. Balbina was an early Christian saint and martyr. According to tradition, she was the daughter of Quirinus, a Roman official, who converted to Christianity and was subsequently martyred. Balbina is said to have been healed from a throat ailment, possibly a goiter, after touching the chains that bound St. Peter during his imprisonment in Rome. As a result, she venerated these chains, and they are now kept as a relic in the church of San Pietro in Vincoli (St. Peter in Chains) in Rome.

BARBARA

BORN: Mid-3rd century, Heliopolis,
Phoenicia (present-day Lebanon)
DIED: Late 3rd century,
Heliopolis, Phoenicia
FEAST DAY: December 4

PATRONAGE: Artillerymen, architects,
miners, protection from lightning
and thunderstorms
SYMBOLS AND ATTRIBUTES: Tower, palm
branch, chalice, lightning

Barbara, an early Christian martyr, is one of the Fourteen Holy Helpers, a group of saints believed to be powerful intercessors in times of illness and adversity.

According to tradition, Barbara lived in Nicomedia during the third century. She was the daughter of Dioscorus, a rich pagan, and was well known for her striking beauty and sharp intellect. Tradition holds that Barbara's pagan father imprisoned her in a tower to protect her not only from suitors but also from the influence of Christianity. Nevertheless, during her confinement, Barbara devoted herself to prayer and study and converted to Christianity. When her father discovered her conversion, he became so enraged that he decided to kill her. Dioscorus took Barbara to the top of a mountain, tortured, and beheaded her. Shortly thereafter, he was struck by the fire of God, probably lightning, and was burned alive.

Barbara is often regarded as the patron saint of, among others, artillerymen and lightning, and is often invoked for protection against sudden and violent death.

BARNABAS

BORN: Early 1st century, Cyprus
DIED: 61 AD, Salamis, Cyprus
FEAST DAY: June 11

PATRONAGE: Cyprus, Antioch, protection
from hailstorms, peacemakers
SYMBOLS AND ATTRIBUTES: Scroll,
book, cross

St. Barnabas, also known as Joses Justus, or Joseph, was one of the earliest proponents of Jesus Christ's teachings and played a significant role in the spread of Christianity. His life and ministry are recorded in the New Testament, particularly in the Acts of the Apostles.

According to Acts 4:36–37, Barnabas was born in Cyprus and was a Levite, a member of the tribe of Levi, which was responsible for the leadership of worship and religious rituals in ancient Israel. He was a wealthy man who owned land, which he sold, giving the money to the apostles to support the Christian community in Jerusalem.

Barnabas is best known for his association with the apostle Paul. In Acts 9:26–30, Paul attempts to join the disciples in Jerusalem after his conversion. These followers of Jesus feared Paul because of his past as a persecutor of Christians. Barnabas, however, vouched for Paul and introduced him to the apostles. Later, in Acts 11:25–26, Barnabas traveled to Antioch and worked with Paul to establish the first Christian community there. Together, they undertook missionary journeys to spread the Gospel throughout the Mediterranean world.

Though the Bible does not provide detailed information about Barnabas's later years, tradition holds that he continued his missionary endeavors, particularly in Cyprus, and eventually met his martyrdom. The exact circumstances surrounding his death remain uncertain, but he is believed to have been stoned to death in Salamis, Cyprus, around 61 AD. (See Paul.)

BASIL THE GREAT

BORN: c. 330, Caesarea, Cappadocia (present-day Turkey)
DIED: January 1, 379, Caesarea
FEAST DAY: January 2

PATRONAGE: Russia, Greek Orthodox Church, education, exorcism, monastics
SYMBOLS AND ATTRIBUTES: Bishop's attire, Gospel book

St. Basil the Great was a bishop of Caesarea in modern-day Turkey and a Doctor of the Church. The son of Basil the Elder, he was educated in Caesarea, Constantinople, and Athens, and excelled in rhetoric, grammar, and medicine. He grew enamored with the Christian teachings, which ignited a spiritual awakening that propelled him toward monastic life. Influenced by monks in Egypt and Mesopotamia, he established a monastery in Pontus, thus pioneering community monastic life in Asia Minor.

Theologically, Basil was a stalwart. He actively participated in debates, championing orthodox beliefs against heretical views, and he was instrumental when the Church combatted the Arian threat from Emperor Valens in the fourth century.

In 370, Basil became the bishop of Caesarea in Asia Minor, an important region for Christianity at the time. In this role, he became a staunch defender of orthodoxy and committed himself to helping those in need, especially during times of famine. Basil's leadership remained resilient despite challenges, including opposition from bishops and confrontations with Emperor Valens. His correspondence underscores the interplay between the Eastern Church and the Roman See, highlighting their significance despite disagreements.

Basil's extensive theological writings, especially his emphasis on the divinity of the Holy Spirit, helped to bolster the Nicene Creed against attacks from pagans and heretics. His legacy also includes liturgical contributions, with the Divine Liturgy of St. Basil being a testament to his enduring influence on Christian worship. Basil the Great passed away on January 1, 379, but his teachings and works continue to be celebrated in the Eastern Orthodox and Roman Catholic traditions.

BARTHOLOMEW

BORN: 1st century, Cana, Galilee

DIED: 1st century, Armenia

FEAST DAY: August 24

PATRONAGE: Tanners, vintners, butchers, cobblers, bookbinders, and butchers

SYMBOLS AND ATTRIBUTES: Knife, flayed skin

St. Bartholomew, also known as Nathanael, was one of the twelve apostles Jesus Christ chose to be his closest followers. His life and ministry are celebrated in the Christian Church as a testament to the power of faith and the importance of spreading the Gospel to all corners of the world.

Little is known about the life of Bartholomew. According to the Gospel of John, he was a close friend of Philip, another disciple of Jesus. Philip introduced Bartholomew (identified as Nathanael in the Gospel of John) to Jesus, who recognized him as a man of true faith. After the death and resurrection of Jesus, Bartholomew and the other apostles traveled throughout the world, preaching the Gospel and converting people to Christianity. According to tradition, Bartholomew preached in India, Armenia, and Ethiopia before being martyred in Albanopolis, Armenia, purportedly by being flayed alive.

According to tradition, Bartholomew was involved in numerous miracles. In one account, he healed a paralyzed man by praying for him and then instructing him to walk. In another, a woman struggled to pour oil into Bartholomew's lamp. Someone proposed the oil might not be worthy of such a holy vessel. When she tried a different lamp, the oil poured effortlessly. Another tale describes a vision of Bartholomew protecting a preacher from the devil's influence.

St. Bartholomew is often depicted in Christian art holding a knife or flaying instrument, symbolizing his martyrdom. He is also sometimes shown holding a book or a scroll, illustrating his role as a teacher of the Gospel. (See Philip.)

BATHILDES

BORN: c. 626, probably England

DIED: January 30, 680, Chelles, Francia

FEAST DAY: January 30

PATRONAGE: Unknown

SYMBOLS AND ATTRIBUTES: Crown, coins, alms

A powerful queen and an inspiring example of faith and charity, St. Bathildes was likely born in Anglo-Saxon England in the seventh century. She was taken as a slave by traders and brought to France, where she was sold to a local mayor. She caught the eye of King Clovis II, who fell in love with her and married her in 649. As queen, Bathildes used her influence to protect the poor and vulnerable. She founded hospitals and monasteries and worked diligently to abolish the slave trade. Bathildes helped enact legal reforms that protected the rights of serfs and peasants, improving their conditions and preventing their exploitation. She also established the Abbey of Chelles near Paris, which became a center for learning and spirituality. Her compassion and generosity were widely recognized, and she became known as a patron of the sick, the imprisoned, and the enslaved.

After the death of her husband, Bathildes served as regent for her young sons, and she continued to rule with wisdom and kindness. Today she is revered as a model of Christian virtue and compassion. Bathildes was canonized as a saint by the Catholic Church in the ninth century.

BEDE THE VENERABLE

BORN: c. 673, Monkwearmouth, Kingdom of Northumbria (present-day England)
DIED: May 26, 735, Jarrow, Kingdom of Northumbria

FEAST DAY: May 25
PATRONAGE: Writers and historians
SYMBOLS AND ATTRIBUTES: Elderly monk with quill and book

Often referred to as the "Father of English History," Bede the Venerable was a scholar, theologian, and monk who lived in seventh- and eighth-century Northumbria, now part of modern-day England. Born to noble parents, Bede was sent, at the age of seven, to the nearby monastery of St. Peter, where he received a comprehensive education under the guidance of the local monks. He moved to the St. Paul's monastery in Jarrow, where he would spend the remainder of his life as a devoted monk.

Bede's intellectual prowess and teaching abilities were remarkable. He displayed fluency in Latin, Greek, and even Hebrew, which he employed in his Biblical studies. Bede authored numerous books and treatises covering diverse topics such as history, theology, and science. His magnum opus, the *Ecclesiastical History of the English People*, stands as a testament to his scholarship and remains an invaluable source for understanding the early English Church and the conversion of the Anglo-Saxon populace to Christianity. Within these pages, he frequently discussed miracles as divinely ordained events that underscored the sanctity of saints and the veracity of Christianity. For Bede, these miracles were tangible evidence of God's active presence in the world, especially in guiding the English people toward Christian conversion.

Other notable works include his *Commentary on the Gospel of Mark*, *Homilies on the Gospels*, and *De natura rerum*, a treatise on natural science. Bede's hymns and poems also continue to resonate within the liturgy of modern times. His works *Musica theoretica* and *De arte metrica* are invaluable for scholars studying the early forms of sacred chant.

Bede's devotion to God was punctuated by miracles and mystical experiences, some of which he chronicled in his writings. Notably, as he approached death, Bede recounted and dictated to his fellow monks a vision of angels gathering to escort his soul to Heaven.

Depictions of St. Bede often portray him holding a book, symbolizing his academic brilliance. In some representations, he is shown with a quill pen and inkwell, signifying his prolific writing. In recognition of the immensity of his contributions, Pope Leo XIII bestowed upon him the title of Doctor of the Church in 1899.

BENEDICT OF NURSIA

BORN: c. 480, Nursia, Kingdom of the Ostrogoths (present-day Italy)

DIED: c. 547, Monte Cassino, Eastern Roman Empire

FEAST DAY: July 11

PATRONAGE: Europe, agricultural workers, schoolchildren, cavers, civil engineers, dying people, antidote to poison, breaker of curses

SYMBOLS AND ATTRIBUTES: Rule of St. Benedict, raven, chalice, broken tray, Benedict Medal, broken cup with a serpent, poison

St. Benedict of Nursia is venerated as the pioneer of Western monasticism. He was born in 480 to a noble family in Nursia, Italy. Tradition holds he had a twin sister named Scholastica, who would grow up to become a famous saint in her own right.

Benedict spent his boyhood in Rome, immersed in his studies until he left his privileged life in his late teens or early twenties to serve God. Initially, he left the Eternal City not to become a hermit but to escape the sinfulness of life in the city. He settled in Enfide, near a church dedicated to St. Peter, with his old nurse and a group of virtuous men. His first reported miracle, where he restored a broken wheat-sifter (sometimes depicted in art as a cup), happened here, and he became popular among the locals who sought his consult. Uncomfortable with the attention he was receiving, he moved to the more secluded area of Subiaco, committing to labor and live in poverty.

In this tranquil setting, Benedict faced and overcame an encounter with the devil, who tempted him with worldly desires. This seminal experience solidified his commitment to a life of devotion and self-denial. His mystical journey and unshakeable faith in God soon began to draw followers.

As his reputation as a holy man grew, Benedict established a monastery at Monte Cassino around the year 529. It was here he penned *The Rule of St. Benedict*, a groundbreaking guide for monastic life that emphasized prayer, labor, and communal living. This spiritual manual, composed of seventy-three brief chapters, tackled various aspects of the religious life, stressing obedience, humility, balance, and moderation, including temperance in food and drink. Monastic communities that chose to strictly adhere to Benedict's *Rule* expanded throughout Italy. The *Rule's* impact on Western monasticism is undisputed, serving as a prototype for religious communities worldwide as well as informing the lives of modern-day leaders and writers including prominent social justice advocate Sr. Joan Chittister and author Rod Dreher, whose book *The Benedict Option*, on embracing the teachings of Benedict in the present day, became a *New York Times* bestseller in 2017.

Centuries later, the Benedict Medal, frequently worn by Catholics, became a powerful symbol of the monk's life and miracles. The front of this sacramental shows St. Benedict with a cross and a book, encircled by the inscription "Ejus in obitu nostro praesentia muniamur," translating to "May we be strengthened by his presence in the hour of our death." The reverse displays symbols including a cross, a cup, and a raven, along with the letters "C S S M L" and "N D S M D," representing "Crux Sacra Sit Mihi Lux" ("May the Holy Cross be my light") and "Non-Draco Sit Mihi Dux" ("Let not the Dragon be my guide"). This medal, kept close for protection, carries an aura of spiritual safeguarding. The medal is often presented to individuals seeking spiritual guidance or safety and is commonly used as a sacramental in exorcisms.

Benedict died in 547 in the Abbey at Monte Cassino. (See Scholastica of Nursia.)

BENEDICT THE MOOR

BORN: 1526, San Fratello, Sicily, Kingdom of Naples

DIED: April 4, 1589, Palermo, Sicily, Kingdom of Spain

FEAST DAY: April 4

PATRONAGE: African Catholic Youth Action, Black missions, Palermo

SYMBOLS AND ATTRIBUTES: Franciscan habit, crucifix, bread, holding a baby

St. Benedict the Moor, also known as St. Benedict the Black or St. Benedict of Palermo, was an Italian Franciscan friar.

Benedict, who was of African descent, was born into slavery in 1526. He was either granted his freedom days after his birth or when he was a young man. Pious in his thoughts and words, he joined the Friars Minor, a religious order founded by St. Francis of Assisi, when he was around thirty-eight. Benedict was initially assigned to the Franciscan friary in Palermo, Sicily. There, he served as a cook and devoted himself to a life of prayer, penance, and caring for others.

Benedict's reputation for sanctity and dedication to the poor and the sick became widely known. He was also known for humility, his ability to work miracles, and the wisdom of his counsel and spiritual guidance.

Benedict died on April 4, 1589, in Palermo. He was beatified in 1743 by Pope Benedict XIV and canonized as a saint on May 24, 1807, by Pope Pius VII.

BERNADETTE SOUBIROUS

BORN: January 7, 1844, Lourdes, France
DIED: April 16, 1879, Nevers, France
FEAST DAY: April 16

PATRONAGE: Sick, poor, shepherds and shepherdesses, Lourdes
SYMBOLS AND ATTRIBUTES: Rosary, candle, vision of Our Lady of Lourdes

St. Bernadette Soubirous was a young French peasant who became famous for her extraordinary visions of the Virgin Mary in the mid-nineteenth century.

She was the eldest of six surviving children. Her family was poor, and they lived in a small room in the basement of a former prison. Bernadette's mother suffered from asthma and often could not care for her children, so Bernadette and her siblings were sent to live with various relatives. Even though life for the Soubirous family was difficult, Bernadette was known for her sweet and gentle nature and deep faith in God.

In February 1858, at the age of fourteen, Bernadette experienced a life-altering encounter while gathering firewood near a grotto by a local river. It was there that she witnessed the appearance of a beautiful lady. This ethereal figure, clothed in a white robe with a blue sash and adorned with a rosary, smiled at Bernadette and made the sign of the cross, dispelling the young woman's initial fear. Bernadette fell to her knees in prayer. For several weeks, the lady revealed herself to Bernadette on multiple occasions. She urged Bernadette to visit the grotto daily for fifteen days, and faithfully Bernadette obeyed. On the ninth day, the lady instructed Bernadette to dig in the dirt and drink from the spring that emerged. Bernadette followed her instructions, and an astonishing spring of water burst forth. This water was believed to possess miraculous healing properties, attracting pilgrims from all corners of France who sought solace in its powers.

The lady appeared to Bernadette Soubirous eighteen times, with the final encounter taking place on July 16, 1858. However, the local government had barricaded the grotto by this time due to the overwhelming number of people seeking to witness the apparitions. As a result, Bernadette could not access her usual spot and instead knelt by the riverbank. Nevertheless, Bernadette still experienced the presence of Our Lady and described her as even more beautiful than before.

Initially met with skepticism, Bernadette faced rigorous interrogation from Church and government officials who doubted the veracity of her accounts. She never wavered in her narrative of what she had experienced.

Eventually, Bernadette reported, the lady identified herself as the Immaculate Conception, which is a title bestowed by the Catholic Church upon Mary, the mother of Jesus, signifying her sinless nature. Embracing her newfound calling, Bernadette entered a convent and dedicated the remainder of her life to prayer and contemplation.

In 1862, the Catholic Church officially declared the apparitions authentic, leading to the construction of a shrine at the grotto. Nearby, a magnificent basilica named the Basilica of Our Lady of the Rosary was erected and was completed in 1899.

Bernadette's health deteriorated over the years, and she passed away on April 16, 1879, at the age of thirty-five. In 1933, recognizing her holiness, Pope Pius XI canonized Bernadette as a saint.

The significance of Bernadette's visions at Lourdes endured through subsequent generations. Pope John Paul II visited Lourdes three times, reaffirming the site's enduring importance and expressing his personal devotion to the Virgin Mary. Pope Benedict XVI commemorated the 150th anniversary of the apparitions at Lourdes on September 15, 2008.

St. Bernadette's story captivated twentieth-century author Franz Werfel, who wrote the novel *The Song of Bernadette*, published in 1941. Werfel, a German-speaking Jewish playwright born in Prague in 1890, had become famous for his satirical plays targeting the Nazi regime. Fleeing from the Nazis amid the chaos of war, Werfel and his wife ended up in Lourdes, France, where they were sheltered by brave families. Inspired by the story of Bernadette, Werfel vowed to write about her if he and his wife survived their ordeal. The couple did survive. Werfel's fictionalized account of Bernadette's life and visions gained tremendous popularity and, in 1943, was adapted into a critically acclaimed film. Starring Jennifer Jones as Bernadette, the film earned four Academy Awards.

Through the ages, St. Bernadette has been a source of inspiration for countless artists. Paintings and sculptures depict her in moments of prayer, receiving the apparitions, or standing in the presence of the Virgin Mary. These artistic creations attempt to capture the essence of her simplicity, piety, and the awe-inspiring nature of her visions, and serve as visual reminders for the faithful of one child's extraordinary spiritual journey.

St. Bernadette's story and her visions have become a beloved part of Catholic history, resonating with believers around the world. Every year, people seeking solace and healing at the grotto, known as the Grotto of Massabielle or the Grotto of Apparitions, make pilgrimages to Lourdes. Many drink from the spring, which is believed to hold miraculous powers. The shrine at Lourdes receives millions of visitors annually, serving as a focal point for pilgrimage and a center of hope and spiritual renewal.

The reputation of Lourdes as a place of miracles and healing has been firmly established. Over the years, more than 7,000 healings have been reported, with the Catholic Church officially recognizing seventy as miracles. The Lourdes Medical Bureau, established in 1884, diligently examines claims of miraculous healings and has meticulously documented thousands of cases. These testimonies and the ongoing stream of pilgrims further reinforce the significance of St. Bernadette's visions and their lasting impact.

BERNARDINO OF SIENA

BORN: September 8, 1380, Massa
Marittima, Italy

DIED: May 20, 1444, L'Aquila, Italy

FEAST DAY: May 20

PATRONAGE: Advertisers, communications,
gambling addicts

SYMBOLS AND ATTRIBUTES: Monogram of
the Holy Name (IHS), book

St. Bernardino of Siena, also known as St. Bernardine, was an Italian Franciscan friar and preacher known for his devotion to Christ and his powerful, sometimes incendiary sermons.

Bernardino was born into the noble Albizzeschi family. He was raised by a devout aunt after being orphaned at a young age. He was educated in literature and the arts and studied law at the University of Siena. In 1397, he became a member of the Confraternity of Our Lady and worked in the Santa Maria della Scala hospital.

With great zeal, Bernardino attended to those afflicted by the Black Death plague that had been ravaging Italy since the mid-1300s. Although he managed to evade the disease, his exhaustive efforts weakened him, and he fell ill with a fever that kept him confined for several months.

In 1403, inspired by the example of St. Francis of Assisi, he joined the Franciscan order, and was ordained a priest a year later. Bernardino became known for his exceptional, fiery preaching skills as well as his ability to inspire conversions. He traveled throughout Italy, preaching to large crowds in the cities and towns he visited.

Bernardino was known for his devotion to the Holy Name of Jesus. He promoted the use of the monogram "IHS" (a Greek abbreviation for "Jesus") as a symbol of devotion and as a way to spread the message of Christ's love. He would often inscribe the monogram on banners and flags, and it became a widely recognized symbol of the Franciscan order.

Not everyone, however, held this symbol in such high regard. In 1426, Bernardino's zeal for the Holy Name led to charges of heresy. After theologians, including Paul of Venice, provided their opinions on the matter, he was found innocent. Bernadino impressed Pope Martin V during these events, who asked him to preach in Rome. Bernardino delivered passionate sermons for eighty consecutive days, and the pope offered to make him a bishop. Bernardino declined, preferring his monastic ways and his freedom to preach. In subsequent years, Bernardino traveled extensively, counseled rulers, and was defended against condemnation by cardinals and popes. He even accompanied the Holy Roman Emperor Sigismund to Rome for his coronation in 1433.

Bernardino had several mystical experiences throughout his life. He claimed to have received a vision of Christ crucified, while praying before an image of the crucifix. He also reported seeing the Blessed Virgin Mary and St. John the Evangelist in another vision.

Bernardino was credited with performing several miracles during his lifetime. One such miracle involved a man who had been declared dead and was being carried to the cemetery. Bernardino intervened and prayed over the man, who stood up and walked home. In another instance, Bernardino was said to have healed a man who was suffering from a severe illness simply by touching him and invoking the name of Jesus.

Bernardino's passionate devotion to God made him a beloved figure among the people of Italy. He was known for his selfless service to the poor and for his willingness to help those in need. He died on May 20, 1444, in L'Aquila, Italy, and was canonized as a saint by Pope Nicholas V in 1450.

One notable event that occurred more than fifty years after Bernadino's death was the Bonfires of the Vanities in Florence in 1497. Possibly inspired by the fiery preaching of Bernardino as well as others at the time, the faithful set great bonfires ablaze with frivolous possessions like expensive clothes, mirrors, cosmetics, books, and artwork associated with vanity and materialism that were considered irreligious. The bonfires were organized by followers of Girolamo Savonarola, a Dominican friar who shared Bernardino's ideals of moral reform. Even though Bernardino had passed away five decades earlier, his powerful sermons against vanity and materialism continued to reverberate after his death. The Bonfires of the Vanities remain a notable chapter in Florence's history, illustrating the influence of religious fervor and the impact of charismatic preachers on societal values and practices.

Ironically, Bernardino is not only the patron saint of communications and public relations professionals but also advertisers, who are often characterized as exploiting society's vanities.

BERNARD OF CLAIRVAUX

BORN: 1090, Fontaine-lès-Dijon, Kingdom of Burgundy

DIED: August 20, 1153, Clairvaux, Kingdom of France

FEAST DAY: August 20

PATRONAGE: Cistercians, candlemakers, Gibraltar, beekeepers

SYMBOLS AND ATTRIBUTES: White dog, beehive, devils on a chain

Known as St. Bernard, Bernard of Clairvaux was a key figure in medieval Christianity. Born into Burgundy nobility, he was well educated and displayed remarkable writing skills at a young age. The death of his mother sparked a religious awakening, shifting his focus from worldly pursuits to prayer and devotion to God. In 1112, he joined the nascent Cîteaux monastery, which, with its strict adherence to the Rule of St. Benedict, became known as the Order of Cistercians. He founded the Clairvaux monastery, became its abbot, and, in his leadership style, retained his admiration for the Cistercian order. He influenced the founding of new communities like the Clairvaux monastery.

Bernard, a prolific writer and preacher, penned theological works on humility, God's love, and the Virgin Mary. His writings also defended the Cistercians and criticized other monastic orders while expressing respect for the Benedictines of Cluny.

Over the years he became a well-respected spiritual advisor and mediator. Active in ecclesiastical and political matters, he continued to work toward reform, emphasizing spiritual renewal and moral integrity. He drafted synodal statutes at the Council of Troyes in 1128 and helped form the Rule of the Knights Templar. His influence extended to the Crusades, preaching the Second Crusade and rallying European support to seek to recapture the city of Edessa from the Muslims. Due to political and strategic failures, the crusade was disastrous for the Church, but Bernard continued to shape the religious and political landscape. In 1140, he denounced the errors of philosopher and theologian Peter Abelard, leading to Abelard's condemnation for heresy. Bernard continued to contribute to the religious discourse of his time until his death in 1153.

Bernard's life and teachings helped steer the direction of medieval theology and spirituality, emphasizing humility and intimacy with God. Just over two decades after his death, in 1174, he was canonized a saint. In 1839, in recognition of his theological prowess, Pope Pius XII named him a Doctor of the Church.

Bernard's work continues to be studied in theological and philosophical circles, providing great insight into a medieval thinking that influenced such writers as fourteenth-century poet Dante Alighieri, who celebrated him by placing Bernard in a prominent part of Heaven in the last book of his *Divine Comedy*, the "Paradiso." In art, he is often depicted wearing a white monastic habit symbolizing his leadership within the Cistercian order and the broader Church. (See Benedict of Nursia.)

BIBIANA

BORN: 4th century, Rome, Italy
DIED: c. 361-363, Rome, Italy
FEAST DAY: December 2

PATRONAGE: People with epilepsy, single women, torture victims, those with headaches
SYMBOLS AND ATTRIBUTES: Palm leaf, pillar, whip

The story of St. Bibiana, also known as Viviana or Vibiana, is steeped in legend. A virgin martyr of the early Christian era, the primary source of her life comes from a fifth-century account, and historical facts about her are scarce.

According to tradition, Bibiana was born into nobility in Rome during the fourth century to a devout Christian family. During the persecutions under the Roman Emperor Julian the Apostate, Bibiana's father, Flavian, was tortured, exiled, and died from his ordeals. Her mother, Dafrosa, was beheaded.

After the death of their parents, Bibiana and her sister, Demetria, were left destitute. They were summoned by the city's governor, Apronianus, who demanded they abandon their beliefs. Demetria died on the spot. Bibiana refused and was handed over to a malicious woman who tried to coerce her into prostitution. Undeterred, Bibiana preserved both her chastity and unwavering faith, consistently refusing to renounce Christ.

As a result, Bibiana was tied to a pillar and cruelly scourged until she died. According to tradition, her body was left for the wild beasts, but none dared touch it. After two days, a priest named John buried her body under cover of nightfall.

The church of Santa Bibiana in Rome is entrusted with her relics. She is often depicted in art holding a palm branch, a symbol of martyrdom, and sometimes with a pillar or whip, signifying her manner of death.

BLAISE

BORN: 3rd century, Sebastea, Armenia (present-day Sivas, Turkey)
DIED: c. 316, Sebastea, Armenia
FEAST DAY: February 3

PATRONAGE: Throat illnesses, animals, wool combers, veterinarians
SYMBOLS AND ATTRIBUTES: Two crossed candles, wool comb, palm branch

St. Blaise, also known as St. Blaise of Sebaste or St. Vlas, is primarily remembered for his miraculous healing powers and his role as a protector against diseases of the throat.

Blaise was born in the late third century in the city of Sebastea, now in modern-day Turkey. He was a physician and bishop who was known for his kindness, compassion, and dedication to caring for the sick and the poor.

Blaise's most famous miracle is said to have occurred when he was living in a cave in the mountains near Sebastea. One day, a woman brought her young son to Blaise, seeking his help because the boy was choking on a fishbone. Blaise prayed over the boy and miraculously removed the bone from his throat. This story became the basis for Blaise's role as a protector against throat diseases. He is now celebrated on February 3 each year with a blessing of the throats in many Catholic churches worldwide.

Blaise was martyred during the reign of Emperor Licinius, who ordered the persecution of Christians. He was arrested and brought before the governor of Sebastea, who ordered him to renounce his faith. When Blaise refused, he was brutally tortured and beheaded.

BONAVENTURE

BORN: 1221, Bagnoregio, Papal States

DIED: July 15, 1274, Lyon, Kingdom
of Arles

FEAST DAY: July 15

PATRONAGE: Bowel disorders

SYMBOLS AND ATTRIBUTES: Cardinal's
attire, ciborium, Holy Communion, book
and quill

A Doctor of the Church also known as the Seraphic Doctor, St. Bonaventure was a prominent medieval Franciscan theologian and philosopher. He is widely recognized as one of the greatest intellects of his time and made significant contributions to the development of Franciscan theology and spirituality. His life and work have left a lasting impact on the fields of theology, philosophy, and mysticism.

Bonaventure joined the Franciscan order at age twenty-two. He studied theology and philosophy at the prestigious University of Paris under the tutelage of Alexander of Hales, a famous Franciscan scholar. Bonaventure's brilliance and ability to synthesize diverse theological and philosophical insights became quickly evident, leading to a position as a university professor. He would gain his doctorate in October 1257 on the same day that Thomas Aquinas received his. That year, when the Franciscan order was divided between the Spirituales and the Relaxati factions, Bonaventure was elected Minister General of the Friars Minor. The Spirituales wished for a literal interpretation of the original Rule of St. Francis, particularly regarding poverty, while the Relaxati wanted to introduce changes to the Rule. As the new general, Bonaventure took swift action against both extremes within the order, and worked hard to ensure unity between them. In 1263, he wrote what became at that time the definitive biography on St. Francis. In 1265, Bonaventure declined an offer from Pope Clement IV to become archbishop of York. He continued to lead the Order of Friars Minor until 1274, when Jerome of Ascoli was elected his successor.

St. Bonaventure is known as the Seraphic Doctor for his spiritual insights and deep understanding of divine love. The title "Seraphic" refers to the seraphim, the highest choir of angels described in the Bible. In the book of Isaiah, the seraphim are depicted as surrounding the throne of God, praising Him and proclaiming His holiness. St. Bonaventure's writings and teachings commend the Almighty and reflect a profound contemplation of God's love and a desire to experience union with the divine.

One of Bonaventure's most influential works is *Itinerarium mentis in Deum* (The journey of the mind to God), in which he lays out a path to contemplative prayer and spiritual union with God. This seminal work has impacted the development of Christian mysticism, guiding many on their spiritual journeys and encouraging them to seek communion with the divine. (See Seraphim.)

BONIFACE

BORN: c. 675, Crediton, Kingdom
of Wessex

DIED: June 5, 754, near Dokkum, Frisia
(present-day Netherlands)

FEAST DAY: June 5

PATRONAGE: Germany, brewers, tailors

SYMBOLS AND ATTRIBUTES: Book, sword,
oak tree, fountain, raven

St. Boniface, also known as the Apostle to Germany, is revered for his missionary work and evangelization efforts in Germany during the eighth century. Boniface was born circa 675, in Crediton, a town in Devon, England, and became a part of the Benedictine monastic community at Nursling in Hampshire. Around 716, he left England and traveled south, where he conducted a series of missionary journeys across Germany to evangelize the people living there. His work was supported by both secular and ecclesiastical authorities, including Pope Gregory II, who commissioned Boniface as a missionary bishop to Germany in 722.

Boniface's missionary work involved confronting and challenging paganism. According to numerous sources, he cut down an oak tree sacred to the thunder god Thor at Geismar, near Fritzlar, demonstrating the perceived impotence of pagan gods. This act became a prophetic symbol of the fall of heathenism, leading to many conversions to Christianity. Other variations tell of how Boniface consecrated the tree to Christ and hence began the tradition of the Christmas tree.

In addition to his evangelism, Boniface faced significant challenges in correcting heretical beliefs and pagan customs that had become intertwined with Christian practices. Many of these were perpetuated by Celtic missionaries who taught doctrines and practices at odds with the Roman Church. Regardless of these obstacles, Boniface received support from the pope and clergy who provided him with ecclesiastical articles, books, and words of encouragement. His efforts led to a further increase in the number of faithful, including many nobles and educated individuals, who assisted in the building of churches and chapels.

After Pope Gregory II died in 731, Boniface began working with Gregory III, who ordered Boniface to set up the Church in Bavaria and create several dioceses, or centers of worship. This action helped Bavaria join the Carolingian empire. Boniface became the archbishop of Mainz and aimed to improve the Church's practices in Frankish regions. With the help of leaders in the Frankish kingdom, the reforms took hold.

Boniface significantly shaped the future of Christianity in Western Europe. One of his most lasting legacies was the establishment of a clear Church hierarchy in Germany, mirroring that of the Roman Catholic Church at the time. He founded and reformed numerous bishoprics, including those in Eichstatt, Salzburg, Freising, Regensburg, and Passau.

His efforts set the stage for the formation of the Holy Roman Empire. Unfortunately, Boniface's success in converting souls eventually led to him being murdered by a group of pagans in 754.

Boniface also left a significant body of written work, including sermons, letters, and Latin grammar, which provides invaluable insights into his life, mission, and the historical and cultural context of the eighth century. His correspondence with the papacy highlights his unwavering commitment to maintaining the unity of the Church.

His influence transcended his lifetime by shaping Germany's Christian identity and influencing Europe's religious and cultural development. Boniface is celebrated as a martyr by Roman Catholic and Eastern Orthodox Churches.

BRENDAN

BORN: c. 484, Fenit, County Kerry, Ireland
DIED: c. 577, Clonfert, County
   Galway, Ireland
FEAST DAY: May 16

PATRONAGE: Sailors, mariners,
   elderly adventurers
SYMBOLS AND ATTRIBUTES: Boat, map,
   whale, harp

Also known as Brendan the Navigator, St. Brendan is an emblematic figure in Irish history and Christian lore. Brendan was born in Ireland to a Christian family. St. Íta of Killeedy oversaw his early education for five years before he continued his studies at Jarlath's monastery school at Tuam. He is recognized as one of the "Twelve Apostles of Ireland" tutored by Finnian of Clonard.

Brendan eventually committed himself to monastic life, helping to found the community at Clonfert, where he was ordained a priest. Brendan's legendary voyages form the core of his enduring fame. His maritime adventures are chronicled in the ninth-century text *The Voyage of St. Brendan*. The narrative describes a seven-year journey from Ireland, in which he and his fellow monks explored far-off lands filled with marvels and curiosities.

Their expedition was marked by several fascinating occurrences, including encounters with pig people, sea monsters, and a colossal fish that threatened to capsize Brendan's vessel. The monks also encountered a large rock in the sea that began to shake violently, emitting a voice claiming to be a demon imprisoned within. The voice offered to guide them to the "Land of Promise" in exchange for freedom. Brendan refused, and the rock sank back into the ocean.

Although Brendan's voyages are the stuff of legend, some scholars argue that there could be elements of truth within the tales, even suggesting that Brendan may have reached North American shores long before the Vikings; stories of early Irish settlements in regions such as Newfoundland and Nova Scotia endure.

Miracles attributed to St. Brendan during his lifetime extend beyond his voyages. He was legendary for his mystical experiences. He was reputed to possess healing abilities and the power to calm stormy seas, communicate with animals and inanimate objects, and resurrect the dead. Throughout his life, he reportedly had several visions of angels and saints.

In art, Brendan is often depicted with a boat or a map, symbolizing his journeys and missionary endeavors. A whale or fish is another common symbol, as is a harp representing his love for music and poetry.

St. Brendan's feast day is celebrated on May 16, the day of his death circa 577. Irish Catholics worldwide honor his memory and contributions to Christian spirituality and the culture of their homeland. (See Íta.)

BRIDGET OF SWEDEN

BORN: c. 1303, Upland, Sweden

DIED: July 23, 1373, Rome, Italy, Papal States

FEAST DAY: July 23

PATRONAGE: Europe, Sweden, widows

SYMBOLS AND ATTRIBUTES: Book, staff, quill

St. Bridget of Sweden, also known as Birgitta Birgersdotter, was a fourteenth-century Swedish saint and mystic. She was the daughter of Birger Persson, a governor and wealthy landowner, and Ingeborg Bengtsdotter, a pious and virtuous woman. Educated by her family, she was married at thirteen to Ulf Gudmarsson, a nobleman who served in the royal court. They had eight children together, including Catherine of Vadstena, who would become a saint in her own right.

After her husband died in 1344, Bridget devoted herself to a life of prayer and good works. She founded the Bridgettine order in 1346, with the approval of Pope Innocent VI. Also known as the Order of the Most Holy Savior, Bridget's group was dedicated to the care of the sick and poor and educating young girls. Bridget wrote extensively on spiritual topics, including visions she had received from God. Her most famous work is the *Revelations of St. Bridget*, a collection of visions she experienced over many years.

Bridget was a tireless advocate for the reform of the Church and the papacy. She believed that the Church had become too worldly and corrupt, and that the pope needed to return to a more humble and spiritual way of life. She traveled extensively throughout Europe, meeting with kings, nobles, and other important figures and urging them to support her causes. Her writings have been translated into many languages and are still widely read across the globe.

Bridget died in Rome on July 23, 1373. She was canonized by Pope Boniface IX in 1391. St. Pope John Paul II declared her Co-Patroness of Europe, calling her a feminine model of holiness who "stands as an important witness to the place reserved in the Church for a charism lived in complete docility to the Spirit of God and in full accord with the demands of ecclesial communion."

Her relics are enshrined in the Church of Santa Brigida in Rome. (See Catherine of Vadstena.)

BRIGID OF IRELAND

BORN: c. 451, Faughart, Dundalk, Ireland

DIED: c. 525, Kildare, Ireland

FEAST DAY: February 1

PATRONAGE: Ireland, dairy workers, cattle, healers, poets, blacksmiths

SYMBOLS AND ATTRIBUTES: Cloak, crosier, cow, flame

St. Brigid of Ireland shines brightly in the rich history of Ireland as one of the country's most important saints. Her story, passed down through generations, has been immortalized in hymns, prose, and legends, offering valuable insights into Ireland's religious and cultural heritage. While the details of her life remain a topic of debate, she is widely revered as one of Ireland's most beloved figures.

Though accounts vary, it is generally believed Brigid was born circa 451 in Faughart, a region north of Dundalk in the Kingdom of Ulaid. Her mother, Broicsech, was a slave who had been baptized by St. Patrick; her father, Dubhthach, was a chieftain from the province of Leinster. Legends from her early life depict a young Brigid embodying holiness and spiritual devotion. One tale recounts how her prayers miraculously replaced her mother's entire supply of butter, which she had given away to the needy.

Brigid led pioneering efforts to establish communal religious life for women in Ireland. It is believed that around 480, she founded a monastery at Kildare in a location originally dedicated to the Celtic goddess Brigid. This former pagan shrine, situated beneath a grand oak tree, would evolve into a center of worship and learning, eventually becoming a cathedral city.

Beyond establishing a place of worship, Brigid's monastery served as a hub of creative endeavors. She is credited with founding a school of art that was particularly celebrated for its metalwork and illumination. The scriptorium at Kildare supposedly produced the now lost *Book of Kildare*, a legendary Christian manuscript whose contents remain a mystery to this day.

Brigid's accomplishments extended beyond Kildare. The *Trías Thaumaturga* documents her journeys throughout Ireland, where she founded numerous churches in Connacht and the Diocese of Elphin and visited regions as far-reaching as Longford, Tipperary, Limerick, and South Leinster.

Brigid was thought to have known St. Patrick, another of Ireland's patron saints. Although historical discrepancies exist regarding their actual interaction, their friendship, symbolizing a shared purpose and spirit in the Christianization of Ireland, is recorded in the *Book of Armagh*.

While the details of Brigid's life are debated, her influence is unquestionable. Her name and deeds are interwoven into Ireland's spiritual, cultural, and artistic heritage, establishing her as an enduring symbol of Irish identity. Through her pioneering contributions to the monastic tradition, she provided a template for female leadership in a male-dominated religious world.

Today, St. Brigid symbolizes empowerment, compassion, and Irish womanhood's resilience, inspiring individuals globally. Honored as the Patroness of Ireland, her feast day on February 1 merges the Christian observance with the pagan festival of Imbolc, symbolizing spring's arrival, fertility, and renewal. Her celebration includes cultural festivities across the Emerald Isle, showcasing the nation's rich traditions.

BRUNO OF QUERFURT

BORN: c. 974, Querfurt, Holy
  Roman Empire
DIED: February 14, 1009, near
  Braunsberg, Poland

FEAST DAY: October 19
PATRONAGE: Martyrs
SYMBOLS AND ATTRIBUTES: Sword,
  palm branch

Bruno of Querfurt was a medieval missionary and martyr. He was born into a noble family around 974 in Querfurt, a town in present-day Germany. In the early eleventh century, he became a canon at the cathedral in Magdeburg, and joined the Benedictine monastery of St. Emmeram in Regensburg. He dedicated himself to a life of prayer, study, and asceticism.

Bruno, inspired by the missionary work of Adalbert of Prague, felt called to spread the Christian faith in foreign lands, particularly among the pagan peoples of Eastern Europe. In 1003, he embarked on a missionary journey to the Slavic territories, accompanied by several companions.

While attempting to convert the Prussians, Bruno and his companions encountered opposition and were captured by a band of pagan raiders. Enduring harsh treatment and imprisonment, Bruno remained faithful to God and continued to preach to his captors.

On February 14, 1009, Bruno and his friends were martyred. While the exact details of their death is unclear, it is believed they were beheaded, and their bodies were left unburied. Bruno's remains were eventually collected and interred at the monastery of St. Emmeram.

BRUNO OF COLOGNE

BORN: c. 1030, Cologne, Holy
   Roman Empire
DIED: October 6, 1101, Calabria, Italy
FEAST DAY: October 6

PATRONAGE: Calabria, exorcists,
   possessed people
SYMBOLS AND ATTRIBUTES: Carthusian
   habit, book, cross, skull

St. Bruno of Cologne was a revered Catholic monk and the founder of the Carthusian order. His austere, contemplative way of life left an indelible mark on the history of monasticism. He hailed from a prominent family, studied theology and canon law in France, and, in 1055, in Cologne, became a priest.

While serving as a canon of the cathedral of Reims, Bruno felt a desire to pursue a more contemplative existence. After he and others were instrumental in deposing a corrupt prelate, who retaliated by destroying and confiscating their property, he chose to act on that desire. In 1080, he left his ecclesiastical position and retreated to a hermitage nestled in the French Alps. There, he embraced a life of solitude, prayer, and minimalist living. Eventually, a small group of like-minded individuals joined him, and this group became known as the Carthusian order, monks who mostly remained in isolation from one another.

Bruno dedicated the remainder of his life to seclusion, rarely venturing beyond his hermitage. Years after Bruno's death, his customs for leading a holy life became the foundation for *The Carthusian Statutes*, which meticulously outlines the rules and practices of the Carthusian order.

Bruno passed away in 1101 and was buried in the monastery he had founded. Recognizing his sanctity, Pope Gregory XV canonized him as a saint in 1623.

C

CAJETAN

BORN: October 1, 1480, Vicenza, Republic of Venice

DIED: August 7, 1547, Naples, Spanish Naples

FEAST DAY: August 7

PATRONAGE: Job seekers, workers, the unemployed

SYMBOLS AND ATTRIBUTES: Lily, book

A prominent Italian Catholic priest and co-founder of the Theatine order, St. Cajetan, also known as St. Gaetano, was born into a noble Italian family. According to numerous sources, he pursued law at the University of Padua, earning his doctorate at the age of twenty-four. While he achieved success as a diplomat for Pope Julius II and then as a courtier for the king of Naples, Cajetan felt a growing inner calling to become a priest. In 1516, he was ordained. Throughout his life, Cajetan dedicated himself to preaching and providing spiritual and material support to the sick and the marginalized. He was particularly concerned about the suffering caused by wars and political turmoil of his time. Cajetan worked incessantly to assist those who were affected, offering them comfort and aid.

Cajetan's strong devotion to the Church led him to actively participate in various reform movements. One of these movements was the Oratory of Divine Love, a group of priests dedicated to reform and to helping those lacking resources and afflicted by illness. In 1524, Cajetan and a group of like-minded clergy established the Theatine order. The order emphasized the pursuit of virtue and a return to the simplicity and austerity of the early Church. Theatines quickly gained recognition for their holiness and their charitable work.

Numerous stories of good deeds and miracles are associated with Cajetan, including healings, conversions, and the provision of food and shelter to those in need. One well-known story recounts how Cajetan interceded to halt a fire that threatened the city of Vicenza. As the flames approached, Cajetan led a procession of the faithful, carrying a monstrance and singing hymns. Miraculously, the fire stopped just short of the city, and Cajetan was credited with saving it from destruction.

CALLISTUS I

BORN: c. 160, Rome, Italy, Roman Empire

DIED: c. 223, Rome, Italy, Roman Empire

FEAST DAY: October 14

PATRONAGE: Cemetery workers

SYMBOLS AND ATTRIBUTES: Papal tiara, palm branch

St. Callistus I is a revered figure in the early Christian Church, having served as the bishop of Rome from 217 to 222. He was born in the late second century, but little is known about his early life.

As pope, Callistus I faced significant challenges from within the Church. One notable issue was the readmission of lapsed Christians to the Church, to which Callistus I dedicated himself to resolving by promoting unity and orthodoxy. He also helped develop Christian doctrine, in particular by establishing a distinction between mortal and venial sins.

His contributions to the organization of the Church were substantial. He staunchly defended the authority of the bishop of Rome and the primacy of the papacy. His efforts in securing burial grounds for Christians earned him the patronage of cemetery workers.

Still, Callistus I faced opposition and criticism during his lifetime. Some accused him of being too lenient toward those who had lapsed from the faith, and others disapproved of his lenient approach to resolving conflicts within the Church. Notably, Hippolytus of Rome, a theologian and priest, opposed Callistus I and accused him of promoting heresy.

Callistus I may have been martyred; his legacy grew after his death. The early Church venerated him as a saint, and theologians studied and debated his teachings and contributions to Christian doctrine for centuries. His work in organizing the structure of the Church laid some of the foundations for the Catholic Church as we know it today. (See Hippolytus of Rome.)

CAMILLA BATTISTA DA VARANO

BORN: April 9, 1458, Camerino, Italy

DIED: May 31, 1524, Camerino, Italy

FEAST DAY: May 31

PATRONAGE: Martyrs, those that suffer

SYMBOLS AND ATTRIBUTES: Franciscan habit, book, quill

Camilla Battista da Varano was a nun of the Order of Poor Clares and the founding abbess of the monastery of St. Clare in Camerino, Italy. She was the daughter of Giulio Cesare da Varano and noblewoman Cecchina di Maestro Giacomo. Growing up as a princess, she displayed a deep devotion to her faith from a young age. When Battista was twenty-three, she made a life-changing decision to enter the Poor Clares monastery in Urbino, where she dedicated herself entirely to a life of prayer, poverty, and service.

In 1484, Battista's dedication led her to establish a new community of Poor Clares in Camerino. At the age of thirty-five, she was appointed the abbess, and assumed a position of leadership and responsibility within the religious order. However, her path was not devoid of hardships. Cesare Borgia, a notorious figure, murdered her father and brothers during a time of political upheaval. Battista experienced immense grief from their deaths, and her faith was challenged, though she ultimately remained committed to her religious calling.

Amid the turmoil, Battista found herself in constant danger. She feared not only for her life but also for the safety of her fellow nuns. To ensure their well-being, she had to make the difficult decision to flee her beloved community and seek refuge in the Kingdom of Naples, far from the enemies who threatened her life.

In 1505, Pope Julius II recognized Battista's exceptional qualities and entrusted her with reforming and reestablishing the Poor Clares in Fermo, Italy.

Battista's life was cut short by a devastating plague that ravaged the area. Centuries later, Pope Benedict XVI canonized her as a saint on October 17, 2010, in recognition of Battista's devout life and her impact on religious communities. This canonization reaffirmed the significance of her spiritual journey and her unwavering commitment to God and the Poor Clares. Her feast day, celebrated on May 31, serves as a dedicated occasion to honor and commemorate her inspiring life, sincere faith, and enduring dedication to the principles of the Order of Poor Clares.

CAMILLUS DE LELLIS

BORN: May 25, 1550, Bucchianico, Kingdom of Naples

DIED: July 14, 1614, Rome, Italy, Papal States

FEAST DAY: July 18

PATRONAGE: Hospitals, nurses, sick people

SYMBOLS AND ATTRIBUTES: Red cross, attending to the sick

St. Camillus de Lellis was a sixteenth-century Italian Roman Catholic priest. At sixteen, after the passing of his mother, he joined the Venetian army and fought against the Turks. A brave solider, he had a boisterous nature and a love of gambling that got him into trouble and would eventually leave him destitute.

With little to his name, Camillus began working as an assistant at a Capuchin friary, had a spiritual awakening, and made the decision to become a friar. Unfortunately, a chronic leg ailment prevented his acceptance into the order. Moving to Rome, he became a caregiver at the hospital of San Giacomo degli Incurabili (St. James of the Incurables), soon ascending to superintendent. Discontented with subpar patient care, he gathered a group of men to aid him, thereby laying the foundation for a religious community focused on health care. With support from his confessor, Philip Neri, and a benefactor, Camillus pursued seminary studies.

Ordained in 1584 by Bishop Thomas Goldwell, he founded the Order of Clerks Regular, Ministers of the Infirm, also known as the Camillians. Recognizable by their red cross, symbolizing charity, they specialized in battlefield medical care. Pope Sixtus V acknowledged the Camillians in 1586 and gave them Rome's Church of St. Mary Magdalene as their headquarters.

Camillus emphasized compassionate end-of-life care and, in an effort to prevent premature burials, instated a fifteen-minute waiting period after death to declare someone dead. In 1591, Pope Gregory XIV granted the Camillians order status, emphasizing their vow to serve the sick even at personal peril.

Under Camillus's leadership, the order grew and expanded, notably during a plague outbreak in Naples in 1594 during which Camillus personally aided the afflicted.

Health issues plagued Camillus throughout his life, but he displayed perseverance, even if it meant crawling when he was unable to walk. He passed away in Rome in 1614. Acknowledging his immense holiness, Pope Benedict XIV beatified him in 1742 and canonized him in 1746. Pope Leo XIII named him the patron saint of hospitals and the sick. Several congregations, including the Congregation of the Servants of the Sick of St. Camillus and the Daughters of St. Camillus, owe their origins to Camillus's visionary ministry. (See Philip Neri.)

CASTULUS

BORN: 3rd century, place unknown
DIED: c. 286, Rome, Italy, Roman Empire
FEAST DAY: March 26

PATRONAGE: Shepherds, skin disorders, protection against lightning and wildfires
SYMBOLS AND ATTRIBUTES: Palm branch

According to tradition, Castulus served as a chamberlain in the court of the Roman emperor Diocletian. He was a devout Christian and, along with his friend Tiburtius, secretly assisted and supported persecuted Christians. When the two friends were discovered, they were arrested and brought before a local official. They were sentenced to death for their belief in Christ. Castulus was reportedly beaten and thrown into a pit filled with quicklime, where he died as a martyr.

Many churches in Germany and Austria are dedicated to Castulus. He is also known as the husband of St. Irene of Rome, who aided St. Sebastian after his attempted execution. (See Tiburtius, Irene of Rome, Sebastian.)

CATHERINE DEI RICCI

BORN: April 23, 1522, Florence, Republic
of Florence
DIED: February 2, 1590, Prato, Grand
Duchy of Tuscany

FEAST DAY: February 13
PATRONAGE: Sick people, loss of parents
SYMBOLS AND ATTRIBUTES: Lily, crucifix,
nun's habit

An Italian nun, Catherine dei Ricci was baptized with the name Alessandra. She was the daughter of a wealthy merchant named Piero dei Ricci, a member of the famous Ricci family, and his wife, Fiammetta degli Strozzi. The family, highly respected in Florence, was known for their generosity to the poor. Her mother died after giving birth to Alessandra. At the age of twelve, Alessandra entered the Dominican convent of San Vincenzo in Prato, a city near Florence. She took the name Catherine in honor of St. Catherine of Siena, who had lived more than a century earlier. Catherine dei Ricci quickly became known for her prayerfulness and dedication to the religious life, and her superiors chose her to be the novice mistress, then prioress, of the convent.

Catherine reported that Jesus appeared to her many times, often bringing her comfort during challenging moments. Catherine also had a vision of the Holy Spirit, in which she saw a dove descending upon her and filling her with spiritual gifts. She also experienced the stigmata, or the wounds of Christ, on her hands, feet, and side, although she reportedly asked Jesus to take away these physical signs of her devotion.

One of the most famous mystical experiences of Catherine dei Ricci was her vision of the infant Jesus. In 1542, while she was praying before the crucifix in the convent chapel, she saw the infant Jesus in the arms of the Virgin Mary. Jesus smiled at Catherine and then the apparition disappeared. It was in this same year that Catherine received a mystical ring from Jesus, which symbolized her sacred, spiritual marriage with Christ.

Catherine dei Ricci died on February 2, 1590, at the age of sixty-seven. She was beatified by Pope Clement XII in 1732 and canonized by Pope Benedict XIV in 1746. (See Catherine of Siena.)

CATHERINE LABOURÉ

BORN: May 2, 1806,
Fain-lès-Moutiers, France
DIED: December 31, 1876, Paris, France
FEAST DAY: November 28

PATRONAGE: The Miraculous Medal, the
elderly, the infirm
SYMBOLS AND ATTRIBUTES: The Miraculous
Medal, Daughters of Charity habit

St. Catherine Labouré, also known as Catherine Labouré of the Miraculous Medal, was a French Roman Catholic nun who lived during the nineteenth century. She was the daughter of Pierre Labouré, a farmer, and Louise Madeleine Gontard, and grew up in a devout Catholic family.

Catherine's mother died when she was just nine years old, leaving her and her siblings under the care of their older sister, Marie-Louise. Catherine took on household duties and worked on the family farm to help support her siblings. The young girl found solace in prayer.

Later that year, Catherine received her First Holy Communion, which further deepened her spiritual life. She often visited the local church, dedicating time to prayer and attending Mass regularly. Catherine had a strong devotion to the Blessed Virgin Mary, frequently seeking her intercession and guidance.

When Catherine turned twenty-two, she expressed her desire to pursue a religious vocation. Her father initially opposed her decision, but after much persuasion, he eventually relented and allowed her to follow her calling.

In 1830, Catherine entered the Daughters of Charity, a religious order founded by St. Vincent de Paul and St. Louise de Marillac. She moved to Paris and began her novitiate, dedicating herself to a life of prayer, service, and charitable works.

On July 18, 1830, Catherine had a series of three visions that would come to be known as the apparitions of the Miraculous Medal. According to her account, the Virgin Mary appeared to her in a chapel. Mary spoke to Catherine, revealing her desire to create a medal that would bear her image.

In these visions, Mary described the design of the medal: an oval frame with the words "O Mary, conceived without sin, pray for us who have recourse to thee" encircling an image of Mary standing on a globe, her hands outstretched, with rays of light surrounding her. Mary instructed Catherine to have the medal made and spread its devotion, promising abundant blessings to those who wore it and who trusted in her intercession.

Catherine shared these visions with her confessor, Father Jean-Marie Aladel, who initially had reservations about the authenticity of her experiences. However, through a series of events and the intervention of a bishop, the medal was eventually produced and distributed. It quickly became known as the Miraculous Medal due to the numerous reported miracles and conversions associated with its use.

After the apparitions, Catherine lived a life of humility and anonymity. She continued her work as a caretaker of the elderly at the motherhouse of the Daughters of Charity in Paris. She remained devoted to the Virgin Mary throughout her life. After her passing, Catherine's body was relocated to the Chapel of Our Lady of Graces of the Miraculous Medal in Paris. Today visitors can see her body preserved in a glass enclosure beneath the side altar.

Pope Pius XII canonized Catherine Labouré on July 27, 1947. Her visions and the subsequent devotion to the Miraculous Medal continue to inspire and comfort countless individuals worldwide.

CATHERINE OF BOLOGNA

BORN: September 8, 1413, Bologna, Papal States

DIED: March 9, 1463, Bologna, Papal States

FEAST DAY: March 9

PATRONAGE: Artists, liberal arts, against temptations

SYMBOLS AND ATTRIBUTES: Cross, crown of thorns, easel

Born on September 8, 1413, in Bologna, Italy, Catherine of Bologna, also known as St. Catherine de' Vigri, was an Italian nun, mystic, and saint. She came from a well-to-do family, but at the age of seventeen, she chose to enter the Poor Clare monastery in Ferrara, where she embraced a life of poverty and prayer. Catherine was known for her deep spirituality and experiences of mystical visions and revelations.

Catherine was a skilled painter, illuminator, and calligrapher, and her works were highly praised. She produced beautiful manuscripts, including her own prayer books and copies of the Gospels. Her artwork includes a painting of St. Ursula, now in Venice's Galleria dell'Accademia, and an illuminated manuscript once used by Pope Pius IX, now in Oxford, England.

Her spiritual writings, including her letters and prayers, have been collected and preserved. They provide insights into her great love for God and her devotion to the Passion of Christ. Her writings also express her desire for the salvation of souls and her dedication to spreading the Gospel. Her seminal work, *The Seven Spiritual Weapons,* is a guide that explores essential virtues—humility, obedience, poverty, chastity, patience, charity, and devotion—required to lead a robust spiritual life. Further, these virtues encourage the cultivation of an unblemished purity, enable endurance through life's myriad challenges, promote the practice of altruistic selflessness, and facilitate a loving and loyal bond with the Divine. The book also provides insights into the spiritual challenges faced by believers, addressing in particular encounters with divine revelations as well as temptations from Satan. The text serves as a guide for those seeking to navigate the complexities of their spiritual journey, and provides strategies for resisting and overcoming various temptations.

Catherine of Bologna was known for her humility, obedience, and care for the poor. During her lifetime, she was esteemed for her holiness. After she died, her body was discovered to be incorrupt, meaning it did not undergo the typical decomposition post-mortem. It was placed in the Church of Corpus Domini, and became a place of pilgrimage. In 1712, she was canonized as a saint by Pope Clement XI.

CATHERINE OF SIENA

BORN: March 25, 1347, Siena, Republic of Siena

DIED: April 29, 1380, Rome, Italy, Papal States

FEAST DAY: April 29

PATRONAGE: Europe, Italy, Philippines, firefighters, nurses, the sick, women who have suffered miscarriages, those ridiculed for their faith

SYMBOLS AND ATTRIBUTES: Stigmata, crown of thorns, heart, crucifix, skull, model of a church

A Dominican nun, mystic, theologian, reformer, and Doctor of the Church, St. Catherine of Siena is regarded as one of the most important saints of the Catholic Church and is a patron saint of Europe, Italy, and the Philippines.

Born in 1347 in Siena, Italy, she was the second youngest of twenty-five children, who grew up in a devoutly religious family. According to the *Catholic Encyclopedia*, her father was a tradesman, a dyer of textiles and fabrics, and her mother was the daughter of a local poet. Catherine belonged to the lower-middle-class faction known as the Party of the Twelve, which held significant political power in Siena from 1355 to 1368.

Catherine's spiritual journey began when she was a child. She had a mystical experience at the age of six, when Jesus appeared to her in a vision and put a ring on her finger, which symbolized her spiritual marriage to Christ. From that day forward, her years were marked by intense prayer and fasting as she sought to strengthen her relationship with God. She joined the Dominican order at the age of sixteen and began a life of service to God and the Church.

Her spirituality was characterized by devotion to the Eucharist, a deep prayer life, and the experience of mystical visions and ecstasies. She believed that the Eucharist was the apex of the Christian life and that through it, one could be united with Christ. She experienced many mystical visions and ecstasies, including one in which she received the stigmata, otherwise known as the wounds of Christ. Her mystical journey included what she called "spiritual espousals"—a sacred union with Christ, an extension of the experience she had as a child—and she had visions of Hell, Purgatory, and Heaven. Enduring physical pain and subsisting on meager food, Catherine nevertheless committed herself to serving the sick, poor, and sinners.

PLATE II
Catherine of Siena

Her life as a religious person was a challenging one. She faced many obstacles, both within the Church and without. As a spiritually ambitious woman in a male-dominated society, she had to fight to be heard and taken seriously. And yet, many people did listen to Catherine. She was also often at odds with Church authorities, whom she believed were not doing enough to reform the Church and bring it back to its original mission of putting Jesus before everything else. Still, she continued to work relentlessly for the Church. She was a gifted speaker and traveled extensively, meeting with popes, bishops, and other religious leaders to advocate for the reform of the Church.

Catherine's most significant contribution to the Church was her role in helping to end the Western Schism, a tumultuous period in Church history from 1378 to 1417, during which there were two and sometimes three competing popes. She helped convince Pope Gregory XI to return to Rome from Avignon, where the papacy had been situated for many years, and later lent support to Pope Urban VI, the first pope to be elected in Rome in more than seventy years.

Catherine's writings are an essential part of her legacy and are considered classics of spiritual literature. *The Letters of Catherine of Siena*, which comprise multiple volumes, are a collection of missives written by Catherine to various individuals, including popes, bishops, and political leaders, in which she offers spiritual guidance and advice. The *Dialogue of Divine Providence*, written in the form of a conversation between Catherine and God, is a mystical work that explores the nature of God and the relationship between God and humanity.

Catherine's commanding nature and devotion to God still inspire many to this day. In recent years, Illinois native Nancy Murray, a Dominican nun, and sister to famed actor Bill Murray, has brought Catherine's life into the contemporary spotlight with a one-woman play she wrote and performed titled *Catherine of Siena: A Woman for Our Times*. Catherine is often depicted in art with the stigmata and wearing a crown of thorns.

Catherine died in Rome, Italy, on April 29, 1380. She was only thirty-three years old; her death was reportedly due to a series of strokes. She was canonized in 1461. Her relics, including her severed, mummified head and finger, are housed in the Basilica San Domenico in Siena, a popular pilgrimage site for many faithful and curious.

CATHERINE OF VADSTENA

BORN: c. 1332, Vadstena, Sweden

DIED: March 24, 1381, Vadstena, Sweden

FEAST DAY: March 24

PATRONAGE: Women who suffer miscarriages

SYMBOLS AND ATTRIBUTES: Book, chalice, a red deer (female)

Catherine of Vadstena, also known as Catherine of Sweden, was a distinguished Swedish noblewoman revered as a saint in the Roman Catholic Church. She was born in 1332 to Ulf Gudmarsson, Lord of Ulvåsa, and St. Bridget of Sweden.

Catherine's life was marked by remarkable piety and devotion. She married Lord Eggert van Kyren at a young age and, through her influence, persuaded him to commit to a life of chastity, the two remaining virgins together.

Notably, Catherine played a pivotal role as the co-founder of the Bridgettines, a religious order dedicated to the teachings and spiritual principles established by her mother, St. Bridget. Catherine continued her mother's legacy, fostering the growth of the Bridgettine community and their adherence to a strict religious rule. She was canonized in 1484. (See Bridget of Sweden.)

CECILIA

BORN: Early 3rd century, Rome, Italy
DIED: 235, Rome, Italy,
FEAST DAY: November 22

PATRONAGE: Musicians, poets, singers, luthiers
SYMBOLS AND ATTRIBUTES: Organ, roses, lute, violin, songbird

Though her biography is shrouded in legend and myth, St. Cecilia's legacy endures to this day. Born into a wealthy Roman family in the early third century, Cecilia was raised in the Christian faith, devoting herself to God from a young age. Despite her beliefs, her parents arranged for her to marry a pagan man named Valerian.

On their wedding night, Cecilia revealed to her husband that she had dedicated her virginity to God and that an angel was present to guard her purity. Moved by her words, Valerian converted to Christianity. Cecilia's brother-in-law, Tiburtius, and an officer named Maximus also converted to Christianity. When news of their conversion became public, the prefect Turcius Almachius condemned Valerian, Tiburtius, and Maximus to death. Cecilia sought to bury their remains and, for doing so, was arrested and sentenced to death. Some versions say she was suffocated and then beheaded when the suffocation failed, while others say she was ordered to be beheaded directly. However, it's widely accepted that she suffered three blows of an axe and still did not die immediately but lived for three more days. She was buried in the catacombs of Callistus.

During the ninth century, Pope Paschal I undertook a search for her remains in order to have them transferred to the Church of Cecilia in the Trastevere quarter of Rome. At the time, the relics were believed to have been stolen by the Lombards. However, Pope Paschal saw Cecilia in a vision, who encouraged him to persist in his search. Motivated by this revelation, he resumed his quest and eventually discovered her body in the Catacomb of Prætextatus. The remains were adorned in elaborate gold brocade and accompanied by cloths soaked in her blood. It is speculated that the relics were moved from the Catacomb of Callistus to protect them from previous Lombard raids near Rome. Pope Paschal also collected the remains of Valerian, Tiburtius, Maximus, and Popes Urbanus and Lucius. These sacred relics were later reinterred beneath the high altar of Cecilia's church.

Her association with music varies among sources. The most common tale is that during her wedding to Valerian, while musical instruments played, Cecilia sang to God in her heart to keep her pure. It is also believed that she had a voice of an angel, could play multiple instruments, and composed hymns of praise to God and encouraged others to sing and make music. This aspect of her life has inspired artists and musicians throughout history; many churches and schools have been named in her honor.

Cecilia's story has been the subject of numerous works of art and musical compositions. One of the most famous depictions of Cecilia is the painting by Raphael, which shows her holding a small organ and surrounded by saints with musical instruments at their feet. This painting has become an iconic representation of Cecilia's role as the patron saint of music.

Cecilia's legacy has also been celebrated through musical compositions. Many composers, including Henry Purcell, George Frideric Handel, and Benjamin Britten, have written works in her honor. One of the most famous pieces of music associated with Cecilia is the "Ode to St. Cecilia" by Handel, written in 1739 and still performed today.

The historical reality of Cecilia's life story has been the subject of much debate among scholars. Some argue that she was a real person, while others believe that she is a purely legendary figure. There is little historical evidence to support the traditional account of her life, and some scholars have suggested that earlier pagan myths influenced her story.

Regardless, the enduring popularity of St. Cecilia can be attributed to her role as a symbol of creativity and faith. Her story also serves as a reminder of the importance of loyalty and devotion in a world that often values materialism and power over spiritual values.

CELESTINE V

BORN: 1215, Molise, Kingdom of Sicily

DIED: May 19, 1296, Ferentino, Papal States

FEAST DAY: May 19

PATRONAGE: Bookbinders

SYMBOLS AND ATTRIBUTES: Papal tiara, dove

St. Celestine V, also known as Pope Celestine V, was born Pietro Angelerio in Italy in 1215. He was a hermit and a monk before becoming pope and is often remembered for his brief and troubled papacy, which lasted only a few short months from July 5 to December 13, 1294.

Pietro was elected pope at the age of seventy-nine after a lengthy papal conclave. He was chosen for his reputation for holiness and simplicity. However, his lack of experience and administrative skills proved to be a challenge during his pontificate.

One of the most significant acts of Pope Celestine V was his decision to issue a decree allowing the pope to resign (until then, the papal office was for life). In December 1294, feeling overwhelmed by the responsibilities of his office, Celestine V abdicated the papacy, becoming the first pope in history to do so willingly (Pope Benedict XVI would become the second pope to step down from his office in 2013). He returned to his previous life as a hermit.

Celestine V's abdication led to a power vacuum and subsequent political and ecclesiastical turmoil. His successor, Pope Boniface VIII, viewed Celestine V as a potential threat and imprisoned him to prevent any potential challenges to his authority. Celestine V died in captivity on May 19, 1296, and was canonized as a saint in 1313 by Pope Clement V. He is revered as a symbol of humility, simplicity, and the willingness to renounce power for the sake of the greater good.

CHARLES BORROMEO

BORN: October 2, 1538, Arona, Duchy of Milan

DIED: November 3, 1584, Milan, Duchy of Milan

FEAST DAY: November 4

PATRONAGE: Bishops, cardinals, seminarians, spiritual directors, apple orchards, and stomach diseases

SYMBOLS AND ATTRIBUTES: Cardinal's attire, Bible

St. Charles Borromeo was an Italian Catholic cardinal who lived during the Counter-Reformation. He was the third of six children, and his family was one of the most prominent in Milan at that time.

From the time he was a boy, Charles showed a deep desire to serve God. He was well educated, studying at the University of Pavia and the University of Padua, where he earned a doctorate in canon and civil law. After completing his studies, Charles returned to Milan and was appointed to several important positions in the Church hierarchy. He was made a deacon at the age of twenty-two and a bishop at the age of twenty-five. At twenty-seven, Charles took charge of the Archdiocese of Milan, instituting various reforms, founding seminaries, building ecclesiastical structures, and donating to the poor. In 1560, he was appointed cardinal by Pope Pius IV and quickly became one of the most influential figures in the Catholic Church. A man of deep devotion who stressed the importance of relics in the Church, he played a vital role in the relocation of the Holy Shroud (now known as the Shroud of Turin) from France to Milan.

When Charles became cardinal, the Catholic Church was facing a severe crisis. The Protestant Reformation had led many Catholics to question their faith, and the Church was plagued by corruption and abuses. Charles recognized that the Church needed to rectify itself from within, and he set about implementing a series of reforms that would restore its credibility and authority.

One of the most significant of these reforms was the establishment of seminaries to train priests. At the time, many priests were poorly educated and ill-prepared for their ministry. Charles established the first seminary in Milan in 1563, and it quickly became a model for others throughout Europe. For Charles, the path to sanctity for the clergy wasn't merely in their titles or daily duties but in their deep commitment to prayer and the act of penance. This unyielding faith not only steered his personal actions but also inspired those around him, establishing an ethos of genuine devotion.

However, his efforts toward reformation were not without challenges. The Humiliati, a religious order, viewed him as a threat, and one of its members made an assassination attempt on his life. In a turn of events that has been deemed miraculous, Charles emerged unscathed, with the bullet fired from an arquebus causing him no harm.

In addition to his efforts to reform the clergy, Charles also worked to improve the lives of the poor and sick. He established hospitals and charitable organizations and personally ministered to the ill and dying, especially during the plague that gripped Milan during the 1570s.

He died on November 3, 1584, in Milan, Italy, and was canonized as a saint by Pope Paul V on November 1, 1610.

CHARLES GARNIER

BORN: May 25, 1606, Paris, France
DIED: December 7, 1649, Petun,
   New France
FEAST DAY: October 19

PATRONAGE: Missionaries to the Petun and
   Huron peoples
SYMBOLS AND ATTRIBUTES: Palm
   branch, cross

Charles Garnier was one of the North American Martyrs, a group of Jesuit missionaries murdered during their work among the Huron and Iroquois peoples in the seventeenth century in what is now Canada.

Born on May 25, 1606, in Paris, France, Charles came from a privileged family. He joined the Society of Jesus, known as the Jesuits, in 1624. After his ordination, he expressed a deep desire to work among the missions in New France.

Charles arrived in Quebec in 1636 and spent much of his missionary work among the Petun Nation (also known as the Tobacco Nation) near the Hurons. He made significant efforts to learn the language and customs of the Indigenous people so that he might better serve them. He was known for his gentle nature and dedication to his work.

On December 7, 1649, an Iroquois raiding party attacked the Petun village, and Charles was shot and martyred in the battle.

CHARLES LWANGA

BORN: 1860–1862, Buganda Kingdom (now Uganda)
DIED: June 3, 1886, Namugongo, Buganda Kingdom (now Uganda)
FEAST DAY: June 3

PATRONAGE: African Catholic Youth Action, converts, torture victims
SYMBOLS AND ATTRIBUTES: Palm branch, fire

St. Charles Lwanga is a martyr and well-loved Ugandan saint. He was a member of the Buganda tribe, known for its loyalty to their king and adherence to traditional customs. However, Lwanga was drawn to Christianity and eventually converted to Catholicism under the guidance of the White Fathers, a group of French missionaries who had come to Uganda in the late 1800s.

Charles's conversion was not without challenges. Many members of the Buganda tribe saw Christianity as a threat to their way of life, and those who converted to the faith were often subject to persecution and even death.

In 1886, King Mwanga II of Buganda ordered the execution of a group of Catholic converts who had refused to renounce their faith. Charles was among this group. They became known as the Ugandan Martyrs. Before his execution, Charles was said to have instructed his executioners to kill him quickly, adding, "My friend, you are going to kill me. But know that I forgive you with all my heart."

Beyond the violent circumstances of their deaths, the Ugandan Martyrs are remembered not for their suffering but for their commitment to their faith. Charles Lwanga shares his feast day with his companions, which is celebrated on June 3.

CHRISTOPHER

BORN: c. early 3rd century, place unknown

DIED: c. 251, Asia Minor

FEAST DAY: July 25

PATRONAGE: Travelers, drivers, sailors, storms, bachelors, fruit dealers, athletes, surfers, and those suffering from toothaches

SYMBOLS AND ATTRIBUTES: Carrying the Christ Child, staff, depicted as having a dog's head, sometimes illustrated as a giant

What is known about St. Christopher, also known as Christopher of Lycia, comes mainly through tradition. He was a third-century martyr who lived during a time of Christian persecution and was said to have been a tall, strong man who served as a soldier in the Roman army. One of the best-known legends associated with Christopher is the story of him carrying the Christ Child across a river.

According to the legend, Christopher encountered a child who wanted to cross a river but could not do so due to his small size and the strength of the currents. Christopher carried the child on his shoulders, and as he crossed the river, the child became increasingly heavy. When they reached the other side, the child revealed himself to be Christ and explained that the weight the soldier felt was the weight of the sins of the world that Christ carried.

This story became the basis for Christopher's association with travelers and motorists, as he was believed to offer protection and safe passage. His image, often depicted as a tall, bearded man (and shown as a giant) carrying a child on his shoulders, became a popular symbol for protection during journeys. Other tales of Christopher, particularly in Eastern Orthodox traditions, portray him as a monstrous, dog-headed man, representing his possible brutish nature before becoming a venerated Christian figure.

While St. Christopher is revered by many Christians, historical evidence and details of his life are not well documented. Because of this, the Catholic Church removed Christopher's feast day from the liturgical calendar in 1969. However, he is still recognized as a saint and many still celebrate his feast day. He is most widely known as the patron of travelers.

CLARE OF ASSISI

BORN: July 16, 1194, Assisi, Kingdom of Italy

DIED: August 11, 1253, Assisi, Papal States

FEAST DAY: August 11

PATRONAGE: Television, goldsmiths, eye disease

SYMBOLS AND ATTRIBUTES: Monstrance, lily, pyx, lamp, book

St. Clare of Assisi was an Italian mystic, writer, and the founder of the Poor Clares, a contemplative order for women. Clare was born the eldest daughter of a wealthy family in Assisi, Italy. She was influenced by the preaching of Francis of Assisi and his call to a life of poverty and simplicity. At the age of eighteen, she left her family's home and joined Francis's movement, taking a vow of poverty and dedicating herself to caring for those in need. In 1212, Clare founded the Poor Clares and served as the abbess for forty years, leading the sisters in their devotion to God and service to the poor.

Francis and Clare became close friends. They shared a deep love for the Gospel and a commitment to living it authentically. Francis provided Clare with guidance and spiritual direction, helping her establish her own religious community of women. Clare, in turn, admired Francis and looked to him as her spiritual father and mentor. Throughout their lives, Francis and Clare maintained a correspondence, exchanging letters expressing their spiritual insights, encouragement, and support. Their friendship continued until Francis's death in 1226. Before he passed away, the monk reportedly visited Clare at the San Damiano convent to visit, blessing his friend and her dedicated community.

Clare was known for her numerous miracles, one of the most famous being the Miracle of the Eucharist, which took place in 1240. At the time, the town of Assisi was in danger of attack by an approaching army of Saracens. Clare, who was bedridden at the time, had a vision of the Eucharist. She instructed her sisters to bring her the Blessed Sacrament; she held the monstrance up to the window, and the Saracens outside the town were suddenly struck with terror and fled in fear.

Clare was a prolific writer, and her writings have been admired for centuries. Her most famous work is the *Rule of St. Clare*. Written just before her death, it outlined a set of guidelines for the Poor Clares, emphasizing the importance of poverty, chastity, and obedience, and is still followed by the Poor Clares today. She also wrote many letters and prayers, collected in various volumes over the years. Her missives are often deeply personal, revealing her profound spirituality and love for God. Her prayers are also notable for their beauty and simplicity, and they continue to be used by people worldwide as a source of inspiration and comfort.

In artistic representations, St. Clare is frequently shown with a monstrance, representing her devotion to the Eucharist (and possibly as a reminder of her miracles against the Saracens). She is also often depicted holding a book, symbolizing her writings and her commitment to study and contemplation.

She died in 1253 at the age of fifty-nine and was canonized by Pope Alexander IV in 1255.

In 1958, Pope Pius XII formally proclaimed Clare as the patron saint of television. According to one account from 1255, Clare was too sick to go to Christmas Mass. She stayed in bed and said she saw a vision of the service on her wall. As television rose in popularity during the mid-twentieth century, an increasing number of the faithful came to believe that Clare's vision was a foreshadowing of the miracle of TV. (See Francis of Assisi.)

CLAUDE DE LA COLOMBIÈRE

BORN: February 2, 1641, Saint-Symphorien-d'Ozon, Kingdom of France

DIED: February 15, 1682, Paray-le-Monial, Kingdom of France

FEAST DAY: February 15

PATRONAGE: Devotees of the Sacred Heart of Jesus

SYMBOLS AND ATTRIBUTES: Sacred Heart, cross, quill

Claude de la Colombière was a French Jesuit priest and the confessor of St. Margaret Mary Alacoque. He was born in 1641 and entered the Society of Jesus in 1659. He was known for his deep spirituality, humility, and dedication to the Jesuit mission.

In 1675, he was sent to the town of Paray-le-Monial, where he became the spiritual director of Margaret Mary Alacoque, a Visitation nun who claimed to have received revelations from Jesus about His Sacred Heart. Claude played a vital role in confirming the authenticity of Margaret Mary's visions and helped spread the devotion to the Sacred Heart throughout France.

In 1676, he was sent to London to serve as a preacher to the duchess of York amid anti-Catholic conditions in England. He resided at St. James's Palace, delivering sermons, providing spiritual guidance, and instructing those seeking reconciliation with the Catholic Church.

In late 1678, however, he was falsely accused in connection with the Titus Oates "papist plot," a fabricated conspiracy alleging Catholics were trying to overthrow King Charles II and the Protestant government. Claude spent time in King's Bench Prison amid poor conditions before being expelled from England by royal decree. He returned to France in poor health in 1681 and died in 1682, perhaps from tuberculosis, at the age of forty-one. In recognition of his contributions, Claude de la Colombière was beatified in 1929 and canonized in 1992. (See Margaret Mary Alacoque.)

CLEMENT I

BORN: c. 35 AD, Rome, Italy, Roman Empire

DIED: c. 99 AD, Chersonesus, Crimea

FEAST DAY: November 23

PATRONAGE: Mariners, stonecutters

SYMBOLS AND ATTRIBUTES: Anchor, fish, palm branch

St. Clement I, also known as Pope Clement I, was an early Christian leader and the fourth bishop of Rome. He is considered to be one of the Apostolic Fathers, a group of early Christian writers who lived in the first and second centuries AD and were believed to have a direct connection to the apostles.

Little is known about Clement's early life. According to tradition, it is believed he was born in Rome and may have been a contemporary of St. Peter and St. Paul. He was likely of Jewish heritage and was a Roman citizen. Some sources indicate that he may have been a slave before his conversion to Christianity.

Clement served as the bishop of Rome from around 88 to 99, during the reigns of the Roman emperors Domitian and Nerva. During his tenure, he is said to have emphasized the importance of unity among Christians and established a system of Church governance that stresses the authority of bishops. He intervened in a dispute between two factions of the Church in the city of Corinth, Greece. In a letter to the Corinthians, he urged them to set aside their differences and respect the authority of the Church's leaders. The letter, known as The First Epistle of Clement, is regarded as one of the earliest writings in Christianity, apart from the New Testament..

In addition to this letter, several other writings have been attributed to him, including the Second Epistle of Clement and a homily on repentance. However, there is some debate among scholars as to whether these works were written by him or by others in the early Christian community.

Beyond the uncertainties surrounding his life and writings, St. Clement I remains an important figure in early Christian history. His emphasis on unity and his establishment of a system of Church governance helped lay the foundation for the development of the Catholic Church, and his writings continue to be studied and revered by Christians worldwide.

CLOTILDE

BORN: c. 474, Lyon, Burgundian Kingdom
DIED: June 3, 545, Tours, Kingdom of
the Franks
FEAST DAY: June 3

PATRONAGE: Disappointing children,
brides, adopted children
SYMBOLS AND ATTRIBUTES: Crown, model
of a church

A queen consort of the Franks and a prominent figure in early medieval history, St. Clotilde, also known as St. Clotilda, was born a Burgundian princess around 474–475. She married Clovis I, the king of the Salian Franks, in 493.

Clotilde played a significant role in converting the Frankish kingdom to Christianity. As a devout Christian, she greatly influenced her husband's religious beliefs, eventually succeeding in converting Clovis to Catholicism. As tradition holds, Clovis was facing defeat during the Battle of Tolbiac in 496. Clotilde prayed for his victory, and Clovis vowed that if he won, he would convert. Clovis did indeed win and subsequently was baptized, marking the conversion of the first king of the Franks to Christianity. Soon after, the couple ordered the construction of a church that would become the Abbey of St. Genevieve.

Clovis's conversion had far-reaching consequences, as it laid the foundation for the alliance between the Catholic Church and the Frankish monarchy, which would shape Europe's religious and political landscape for centuries to come.

After Clovis died in 511, Clotilde's sons divided the Frankish kingdom among themselves, which led to conflict between the brothers. Looking to escape the mayhem that followed her husband's passing, she spent her later years in Tours, where she dedicated herself to religious activities and charitable works. She died in 545. Clotilde is venerated on her feast day, June 3. She is the patron saint of parents, especially those who face challenges with their children.

COLETTE

BORN: January 13, 1381, Corbie, Kingdom of France

DIED: March 6, 1447, Ghent, Burgundian Netherlands

FEAST DAY: March 6

PATRONAGE: Women seeking to conceive, sick children

SYMBOLS AND ATTRIBUTES: Book, cross

St. Colette, also known as St. Colette of Corbie, was a fifteenth-century French religious reformer. Her birth name was Nicolette Boëllet, but she is commonly referred to as Colette.

Colette entered religious life as a young woman and became a member of the Poor Clares. In 1406, Colette received a vision in which she believed God commanded her to reform the order. She founded several of her own convents throughout France, Belgium, and the Netherlands, adhering to the principles of strict poverty and a return to the original ideals of St. Clare. This reformed order would come to be known as the Colettines.

Colette and the Colettines were known for asceticism, prayer, and deep devotion to the Passion of Christ. Members of this order took vows of poverty and went barefoot throughout the day. Colette was reputed to have performed many miracles, including the restoration of life to a stillborn child. And though not a midwife, she was known for the care she provided women during childbirth.

She died on March 6, 1447, in Ghent, Burgundian Netherlands, and was canonized as a saint by Pope Pius VII in 1807. (See Clare of Assisi.)

COLOMBAN

BORN: c. 540, Nobber, Kingdom of Meath (now Ireland)

DIED: November 23, 615, Bobbio, Lombard Kingdom (now Italy)

FEAST DAY: November 23

PATRONAGE: Motorcyclists

SYMBOLS AND ATTRIBUTES: Monastic robe, Celtic cross, dove

St. Colomban, also known as St. Columbanus or Columban of Luxeuil, was an Irish missionary and monastic founder. He was born in Ireland around 540 and is regarded as one of the great saints of the early medieval period.

Educated in Irish monastic schools, Colomban eventually joined the monastery of Bangor in Northern Ireland. Inspired by the examples of St. Patrick and St. Brendan, he felt a calling to spread Christianity on the European continent. Around 590, he embarked on a missionary journey with twelve companions.

They traveled first to England and then crossed the channel to Gaul (modern-day France). Colomban and his companions established several monastic communities, including the famous Abbey of Luxeuil in Burgundy. The monasteries founded by Colomban became known for their asceticism, scholarship, and, ultimately, their strict adherence to the Rule of St. Columbanus, a set of guidelines emphasizing a life focused on humility, poverty, obedience, devotion to God, and the cultivation of silence.

In his later years, Colomban traveled to Italy, where he established the Monastery of Bobbio, which became a center of learning and culture. Colomban died in 615 and his relics remain enshrined in the Abbey of Bobbio. (See Patrick, Brendan.)

COLUMBA

BORN: December 7, 521, Gartan, Kingdom of Tir Chonaill (now Ireland)

DIED: June 9, 597, Iona, Kingdom of Dál Riata (now Scotland)

FEAST DAY: June 9

PATRONAGE: Derry, floods, bookbinders, poets, Ireland, Scotland

SYMBOLS AND ATTRIBUTES: Monk's robes, dove, book, crosier

An important figure in early Christianity, St. Columba, also known as St. Colum Cille or Columba of Iona, is considered a warrior saint and one of Ireland's patron saints. He was born on December 7, 521, in Gartan, County Donegal, Ireland, and was a member of the ruling family of the northern Irish kingdom of Tír Chonaill (now known as County Donegal). He was baptized by a priest named Cruithnechán at Tulach-Dubhglaise (Temple-Douglas) and studied at the monastic school of Movilla under St. Finnian. Here, he received the diaconate. At the monastery of Clonard, he became one of the Twelve Apostles of Ireland, and was ordained a priest by Bishop Etchen of Clonfad.

Columba was a strong, boisterous man who came from a family with warrior blood. He was instrumental in converting the Picts, a people who inhabited what is now Scotland, to Christianity. He traveled extensively throughout the region, preaching and establishing several monasteries in Ireland, including, around 546, the influential monastery at Derry (also known as Londonderry). His most significant establishment was a monastery on the island of Iona, located off the west coast of Scotland. The monastery at Iona became a center of learning, religious teaching, and manuscript production, playing a crucial role in the spread of Christianity in Scotland and northern England. Of note, some traditions hold that St. Columba and St. Finnian had a disagreement over a psalter (an ancient religious text). Columba had copied it from Finnian's original, and the dispute over the ownership of the copy led to a significant rift between the two. Supposedly, a battle between followers of the two men led to the deaths of thousands. This event might have inspired Columba's penitential journey to Scotland and his establishment of the monastery on Iona.

Many legends surround Columba; some suggest he had an encounter with what would become known as the Loch Ness Monster around the year 565. Columba challenged the creature after it has supposedly killed a local, and using the sign of the cross banished it beneath the murky water of Scotland's most famous lake.

An author and a poet, Columba transcribed and wrote numerous manuscripts. The monastic communities he established were known for their scriptoria, where manuscripts were produced, copied, and illuminated, making him a significant figure in the history of bookbinding and manuscript production, and the patron saint of bookbinders and poets.

Columba died on the island of Iona, where he spent the latter part of his life. Along with the monk's robes, Celtic tonsure, and crosier, he is often depicted in art with a dove (which is what his name means in Latin) and sometimes with a book or a psalter. (See Finnian.)

CONSTANTINE THE GREAT

BORN: February 27, c. 272, Naissus, Moesia (now Niš, Serbia)

DIED: May 22, 337, Nicomedia, Bithynia (now İzmit, Turkey)

FEAST DAY: May 21

PATRONAGE: Kings, Byzantine Empire

SYMBOLS AND ATTRIBUTES: Chi Rho, labarum, crown

Constantine the Great, also known as Constantine I, was a Roman emperor from 306 to 337. He played an indispensable role in the rise of Christianity in the Roman Empire and left a lasting impact on its history. Additionally, he established Constantinople (modern-day Istanbul) as the empire's new capital.

Born on February 27 around 272 in Naissus (present-day Niš, Serbia), Constantine hailed from a military background. His father, Constantius Chlorus, served as a Roman general, and Constantine followed in his father's footsteps, gaining military experience and steadily climbing the ranks of the Roman army.

In 306, following his father's death during a military campaign in Britain, Constantine's troops declared him junior emperor. This marked the beginning of his journey to sole rulership, which he achieved after a series of civil wars known as the Tetrarchy. In 324, Constantine emerged as the solitary ruler of the Roman Empire.

A pivotal moment in Constantine's path to absolute power occurred on October 28, 312, at the battle of Milvian Bridge near Rome. This conflict pitted Constantine against his rival, Maxentius, the emperor of the Western Roman Empire. Constantine experienced a vision during the fighting, as recounted in Christian tradition and the writings of Eusebius of Caesarea, a fourth-century bishop and historian. The vision involved a cross of light in the sky, accompanied by the inscription "In hoc signo vinces" (In this sign, you will conquer), often referred to as the "Chi-Rho Vision" due to the cross's resemblance to the Chi-Rho symbol. Believing himself divinely favored by the Christian God, Constantine attributed his subsequent victory over Maxentius's forces to this divine encounter. While accounts of this pivotal moment in history differ (for instance, Lactantius, an early Christian author, suggests Constantine had a dream in which he was commanded to mark his soldiers' shields with the "heavenly sign"), the triumph at the Battle of Milvian Bridge represented a significant turning point in Constantine's life and reign, prompting him to take steps to support and protect the Christian faith within the empire.

The Battle of Milvian Bridge set the stage for Constantine's subsequent actions, greatly influencing Christianity in the Roman Empire and laying the groundwork for his pro-Christian policies, most notably the Edict of Milan in 313. This edict granted religious tolerance to Christians, effectively ending the persecution they faced under previous emperors. The Edict of Milan stands as a turning point for Christianity, enabling its flourishing and granting it official recognition throughout the Roman Empire.

Constantine's significance to Christianity extends beyond the Edict of Milan. He actively promoted Christianity and oversaw the construction of notable churches, including the Church of the Holy Sepulchre in Jerusalem. In 325, he called the Council of Nicaea, where he contributed to the resolution of theological disputes and the establishment of a unified Christian doctrine. Around this time, Constantine's mother, Helena, converted to Christianity and became instrumental in the building of churches in Rome and Jerusalem.

In 330, Constantine embarked on a monumental endeavor, establishing a new capital for the Roman Empire in Byzantium, which he renamed Constantinople. This move had far-reaching implications for the empire's future, as Constantinople flourished as a vibrant center of culture, trade, and political power. It functioned as the capital of the Eastern Roman Empire, subsequently referred to as the Byzantine Empire, for more than a thousand years.

While Constantine was crucial in advancing Christianity within the Roman Empire, he wasn't baptized until shortly before his death, which occurred on May 22, 337, in Nicomedia (modern-day İzmit, Turkey). His death marked the end of an era and left a lasting legacy that shaped the course of history. His contributions to the rise of Christianity, his establishment of Constantinople, and his shaping of politics and religion continue to be studied and admired to this day. As one of the most influential figures of late antiquity, Constantine the Great remains an enduring symbol of religious transformation and imperial power.

CORNELIUS

BORN: c. late 2nd century

DIED: June 253, Centumcellae (now Civitavecchia), Roman Empire

FEAST DAY: September 16

PATRONAGE: Lovers, against earache, cattle, twitching

SYMBOLS AND ATTRIBUTES: Horn, papal tiara, crosier

St. Cornelius, also known as Pope Cornelius, was the twenty-first bishop of Rome and a saint of the Catholic Church. He lived in the third century and is revered for his contributions to the development of the Church during a time of great persecution.

Cornelius was born in Rome and served as a priest in the Church before being elected as bishop of Rome in 251. His term was marred by controversy, including a schism within the Church over the question of whether Christians who had renounced their faith during persecution could be readmitted to the Church. Cornelius maintained that these Christians could be absolved and readmitted to the Church after performing acts of penance, but a rival bishop, Novatian, often considered the first anti-pope, argued that they could not be readmitted.

The dispute between Cornelius and Novatian led to a split in the Church, with Novatian establishing his own sect, the Novatianists. Facing this division, Cornelius continued to work to strengthen the Church, and he is remembered for his commitment to unity and reconciliation.

Cornelius was exiled to Civitavecchia, Italy, during the persecution of Emperor Decius, and he died there in 253. He was buried in the Catacomb of St. Callistus in Rome.

Cornelius, whose name is derived from the Latin word for horn, is the patron saint of cows, cattle, and domestic animals, as well as of earaches and people with epilepsy. He is often depicted in art wearing the papal tiara and holding a book, symbolizing his role as bishop and teacher. He is also sometimes shown with a horn, which represents his patronage of cattle.

COSMAS

BORN: 8th century, Damascus, Syria
DIED: 8th century, Maiuma, Gaza
FEAST DAY: October 14

PATRONAGE: Hymnographers
SYMBOLS AND ATTRIBUTES: Pharmacist's vials, surgical instruments, twins

A renowned writer of hymns, St. Cosmas of Maiuma, also known as Cosmas the Hymnographer, was believed to have been born in the early eighth century in the city of Maiuma, near Gaza, located in modern-day Israel. He was either the foster brother or close friend of St. John of Damascus. As a young man, Cosmas became a monk and spent many years studying and writing music. He was known for his beautiful, poetic hymns, often sung during church services and reflecting his intense love for God and his faith in Jesus Christ.

Cosmas lived during the Eastern Roman Empire's great religious and political turmoil. Invasions from outside forces beset the empire, and the Church had many disputes over theological and political issues. He continued to write hymns that uplifted the hearts and minds of his fellow believers. Cosmas is highly regarded for his numerous compositions, including canons for significant occasions such as Lazarus Saturday, Palm Sunday, and the Nativity. His best-known work is the "Canon for Christmas Day." (See John of Damascus.)

CRISPIN AND CRISPINIAN

BORN: 3rd century, Rome, Italy,
DIED: c. 286–305, Soissons, Roman Gaul
FEAST DAY: October 25

PATRONAGE: Cobblers, tanners, leather workers
SYMBOLS AND ATTRIBUTES: Shoemaker's tools, shoes

Sts. Crispin and Crispinian, also known as the Martyrs of Gaul, were brothers born to a noble Roman family in the third century. They traveled to Gaul (modern-day France) as missionaries to spread the teachings of Christianity, working as shoemakers during the day and preaching the Gospel at night. They were known for their generosity and humility, often providing shoes to the poor and needy without charge. They converted many people to Christianity through their preaching and acts of kindness.

During the persecutions by Roman Emperor Maximian, Crispin and Crispinian were arrested for their faith. They were brought before the governor of Gaul, who tried to convince them to renounce their Christian beliefs. The brothers refused to abandon Christianity, and as a result, were beaten, whipped, and thrown into a river with giant stones around their necks. They survived and continued to profess their faith. The brothers were eventually decapitated somewhere between 286 and 305.

Sts. Crispin and Crispinian are revered as the patron saints of cobblers, tanners, and leatherworkers, and are depicted holding a shoemaker's awl or a shoemaker's knife. St. Crispin's Day is observed on October 25, the traditional feast day of Sts. Crispin and Crispinian. The day gained significant cultural and historical importance due to its association with the famous St. Crispin's Day speech delivered by King Henry V of England in William Shakespeare's play *Henry V*.

In the play, Henry V leads his outnumbered English troops against the French army at the Battle of Agincourt during the Hundred Years' War in 1415. On the eve of the battle, he delivers the rousing speech to motivate his soldiers, boosting their morale and inspiring them to fight with valor and determination.

The St. Crispin's Day speech highlighted the camaraderie among soldiers and the honor of facing adversity. The speech begins with Henry acknowledging the small size of his army and the overwhelming odds they face. However, he emphasizes that victory will bring them great glory and eternal honor. Henry's words encourage his troops to put their faith in God and trust in their unity as they face their enemies.

The St. Crispin's Day speech has become celebrated for its powerful rhetoric and portrayal of heroism in the face of adversity. It celebrates the spirit of unity and bravery during times of great danger, just as Crispin and Crispinian stood united in their faith with death looming before them.

CRISTÓBAL MAGALLANES JARA

BORN: July 30, 1869, Totatiche,
Jalisco, Mexico

DIED: May 25, 1927, Colotlán,
Jalisco, Mexico

FEAST DAY: May 21 (collectively with other
Cristero martyrs)

PATRONAGE: Cancer

SYMBOLS AND ATTRIBUTES: Priestly attire,
palm branch

Cristóbal Magallanes Jara, also known as St. Cristóbal Magallanes, born in Jalisco, Mexico, was a Roman Catholic priest and martyr.

Magallanes was ordained as a priest in 1899 and served in various parishes throughout Mexico. He became a parish priest in Totatiche and helped establish vocational schools and sought outreach to the Indigenous Huichol, which led to the founding of a mission in Azqueltán.

During the Cristero War, a violent conflict between the Mexican government and Catholic rebels in the 1920s, Magallanes openly opposed the anti-Catholic measures implemented by the powers that be and refused to stop celebrating Mass and administering the sacraments.

In May 1927, Father Magallanes, along with several other priests, was arrested while traveling to celebrate Mass in a nearby town. They were imprisoned and subjected to harsh conditions. Undeterred, Magallanes continued to minister to his fellow prisoners and provide them with spiritual guidance.

On May 25, 1927, without a fair trial or due process, Father Cristóbal Magallanes Jara was executed by a firing squad in Colotlán, Jalisco. He died as a martyr for his faith and unwavering commitment to Jesus and the Church.

Pope John Paul II canonized Cristóbal Magallanes Jara on May 21, 2000, as one of the twenty-five saints and martyrs of the Cristero War. He is considered a significant figure in Mexican Catholicism and is venerated as a patron saint of priests in Mexico.

CUNEGUND

BORN: c. 975, Luxembourg

DIED: March 3, 1033, Kaufungen, Holy
Roman Empire

FEAST DAY: March 3

PATRONAGE: Poland, Lithuania

SYMBOLS AND ATTRIBUTES: With Emperor
Henry II, model of a church, salt

St. Cunegund, also known as St. Kunigunde or St. Cunigunde, was a medieval nun and empress. She was born around 975 in the Duchy of Luxembourg, a member of a noble family, and became known for her virtue and charitable works. She married Henry II, who became the Holy Roman Emperor.

According to some accounts, Cunegund and Henry II took a vow of conjugal virginity (abstaining from sexual relations within the marriage). This decision was likely motivated by their desire to dedicate themselves fully to their religious commitments and to focus on their spiritual lives. They ruled the Holy Roman Empire together, and were illustrious for their devotion to the Christian faith and their efforts in promoting religious reforms.

Throughout her life, Cunegund was committed to helping the poor and the sick. She founded several monasteries and supported various charitable institutions. Cunegund was also known for her personal humility and modesty; even though she was an empress with power and riches, she lived a simple and humble life.

After the death of Henry II in 1024, Cunegund dedicated herself to religious pursuits. She entered the monastery of Kaufungen near Kassel, Germany, where she lived a life of prayer and penance. She became abbess of the monastery and was highly respected for her wisdom and holiness.

Cunegund was canonized as a saint by Pope Alexander III in 1200, in recognition of her exceptional virtue. (See Henry II.)

CYPRIAN

BORN: c. 200, Carthage, Roman Empire (now Tunisia)

DIED: September 14, 258, Carthage, Roman Empire

FEAST DAY: September 16

PATRONAGE: North Africa

SYMBOLS AND ATTRIBUTES: Bishop attire, crosier, book

St. Cyprian was an early theologian and bishop of Carthage. Born around 210 in North Africa to wealthy pagan parents, Cyprian was a strong student and pursued a career in law. Around 246, he experienced a profound conversion to Christianity. He renounced his sinful ways and was baptized. Within a short period, Cyprian was elected as the bishop of Carthage. His episcopacy coincided with the Decian persecution, initiated by the Roman Emperor Decius in 250. The Decian persecution was a period of widespread and intense persecution against Christians throughout the Roman Empire. Emperor Decius issued an edict requiring all citizens to participate in a religious ceremony acknowledging the Roman gods and the divine command of the emperor. This decree presented a significant challenge to Christians, who refused to engage in pagan rituals due to their monotheistic beliefs and loyalty to Christ.

Faced with the threat of persecution, Cyprian went into hiding. However, the Decian persecution took a toll on the Christian community, with many believers renouncing their faith or obtaining *libelli pacis* certificates falsely claiming allegiance to pagan gods to avoid persecution.

After the persecution subsided, Cyprian returned to Carthage in 251 and convened a council of bishops to address the issue of the lapsi, or lapsed Christians, who had lied to save their lives. The council resolved that although no individual should be completely barred from penance, those who had truly renounced their faith (known as the sacrificati) would only be allowed reentry at the time of their death. Meanwhile, those who had acquired certificates (the libellatici) would be permitted reentry after completing different durations of penance. This ruling set significant precedents for Church disciplinary practices, emphasizing the authority of the bishops in matters of penance and the acceptance of unworthy members into the Christian community.

Cyprian's theological views were not confined to matters of discipline alone. He emphasized the unity and uniqueness of the Church, considering it the central pillar of salvation. For Cyprian, schism and rebellion against the priesthood were grave sins, and he viewed the consensus of bishops as vital for preserving the integrity of the Church.

Cyprian also faced tensions with the papacy, particularly concerning the restoration of lapsed bishops and the validity of baptism. Moreover, disagreements arose between Cyprian and Pope Stephen I primarily over the agency of the priesthood. These conflicts highlighted the diverse theological perspectives within early Christianity and the complexities of ecclesiastical authority.

Cyprian's unwavering commitment to his beliefs and his bravery in the face of persecution earned him admiration and respect among his followers. However, his leadership and influence attracted the attention of the Roman authorities. Under a new wave of persecution initiated by Emperor Valerian in 257, Cyprian was summoned before the authorities and asked to profess his devotion to pagan gods. He refused and was sentenced to death.

CYRIACUS

BORN: 3rd century, place unknown
DIED: c. 303, Rome, Italy, Roman Empire
FEAST DAY: August 8

PATRONAGE: Against eye disease, viticulture, protection against temptation when dying
SYMBOLS AND ATTRIBUTES: Chains, demon underfoot, palm branch

St. Cyriacus was a fourth-century Christian martyr. Considered one of the Fourteen Holy Helpers, he is believed to have been a deacon in Rome. Known for wise and insightful guidance, his counsel was sought by many in Rome and elsewhere. Cyriacus's sanctity and spiritual wisdom led many to view him as a living saint who was revered for his unwavering faith and devotion to God. It is said he performed many exorcisms and ministered to those possessed by unclean spirits, including a young girl name Artemisia, who was the daughter of Emperor Diocletian. Both daughter and her mother converted to the faith, but Diocletian was unmoved; eventually, Cyriacus was executed under his rule.

CYRIL OF ALEXANDRIA

BORN: c. 376, Alexandria, Roman Empire

DIED: June 27, 444, Alexandria, Roman Empire

FEAST DAY: June 27

PATRONAGE: Teachers

SYMBOLS AND ATTRIBUTES: Bishop's attire, pen, scroll

Known also as Cyril the Great, St. Cyril of Alexandria was a powerful figure in early Christian history and a prominent bishop of Alexandria in the fifth century. He was born around 376 in Egypt and received a comprehensive education in political and theological studies, preparing him for his future role as a Church leader. He may have studied under the scholar and theologian Didymus the Blind, whose teachings greatly influenced Cyril's understanding of the Scriptures.

In 412, Cyril became the patriarch, or bishop, of Alexandria, succeeding his uncle, Theophilus. As patriarch, he faced numerous challenges and controversies, particularly concerning the nature of Christ and the relationship between the divine and human aspects of His person.

One of the most notable conflicts during Cyril's tenure was his involvement in the Nestorian controversy. Nestorius, the patriarch of Constantinople, espoused a belief that suggested Christ's divine and human natures were separate and distinct. Cyril vehemently opposed Nestorius and argued for the unity of Christ's nature, affirming the doctrine of the hypostatic union, meaning that Jesus was fully God and fully man.

Cyril's writings helped to resolve the Nestorian controversy. His best known work, *On the Unity of Christ*, systematically articulated his Christological views asserting that Christ's divinity and humanity were united in one person. This treatise was instrumental in shaping the Council of Ephesus in 431, where Nestorius was condemned and Cyril's theological stance was upheld. Some of his other writings, which are still studied today, include *Commentary on the Gospel of John* and *On the Incarnation of the Only-Begotten*. *Against Julian* is a polemical response to the writings of pagan philosopher Julian the Apostate, who sought to undermine Christianity.

Although Cyril's theological acumen was widely respected, his leadership was not without its problems. His confrontational approach and strong-handed tactics led to strained relationships with other Church leaders and political figures. Nevertheless, Cyril made significant contributions to the early Church, not only in the field of Christology, which explores and defines the nature, person, and work of Jesus Christ, but also in Biblical interpretation, pastoral care, and the defense of orthodox Christianity. He emphasized the Eucharist's importance and the Virgin Mary's role as Theotokos, the Mother of God.

St. Cyril of Alexandria is revered as a saint in various Christian traditions, including the Eastern Orthodox Church, the Roman Catholic Church, and the Oriental Orthodox Churches. His theological insights and writings, which continue to be studied and appreciated by scholars and theologians today, have made a lasting impact on the development of Christian thought and doctrine.

CYRIL OF JERUSALEM

BORN: c. 313–315, Jerusalem,
 Roman Empire
DIED: 386, Jerusalem, Roman Empire
FEAST DAY: March 18

PATRONAGE: Catechists, Catechumens
SYMBOLS AND ATTRIBUTES: Bishop's attire,
 Jerusalem cross

St. Cyril, also known as Cyril of Jerusalem, was a theologian and bishop who lived in the fourth century. He is celebrated in the Orthodox and Catholic Churches and is revered for his contributions to Christian theology and his defense of orthodoxy against heretical beliefs.

In about 349, Bishop Maximus consecrated Cyril as a bishop, hoping to secure a steadfast defender of orthodox Christian doctrine. However, Cyril's refusal to endorse Arianism led to accusations of heresy and the allegation that he had sold Church property to assist the poor, culminating in his summons to a council of bishops. His refusal to attend resulted in charges of disobedience and exile to Tarsus in southern Turkey, where he won the hearts of the people through his preaching. Upon his return to Jerusalem, the region remained troubled by heresy, strife, and criminal activities. Cyril faced exile twice more due to Arian disputes before his passing in 386.

Throughout his life, Cyril was known for his devotion to the faith and his tireless efforts to defend it against heretical teachings. He authored several important works, including the *Catechetical Lectures*, a series of instructions given to new converts to Christianity. These lectures emphasized the importance of the sacraments and the proper interpretation of Scripture.

Pope Leo XIII proclaimed him a Doctor of the Church on July 28, 1882. (See John Chrysostom.)

D

POPE DAMASUS I

BORN: c. 305, Roman Empire
DIED: December 11, 384, Rome, Italy,
Roman Empire

FEAST DAY: December 11
PATRONAGE: Archeologists, fever sufferers
SYMBOLS AND ATTRIBUTES: Papal tiara,
book, cross, model of the church

The tenure of Pope Damasus I was instrumental in shaping the Catholic Church. Born around 305, he ascended the papacy in 366. Amid the religious upheavals of his era, Damasus stood firm as a staunch defender of orthodox Christianity. He grappled primarily with the Arian controversy, which debated the nature of Christ and the Trinity. Throughout the tense times, Damasus remained a fierce advocate for the Nicene Creed, upholding the belief in Jesus Christ's divinity.

Two significant events punctuated his papacy. The first was the First Council of Constantinople in 381. Recognized as the Catholic Church's second ecumenical council, this assembly delved into theological concerns, especially regarding the nature and divinity of the Holy Spirit. While political divides prevented Pope Damasus I from attending, he sent representatives to ensure the Church's orthodox position remained intact. The second was the Council of Rome in 382, which addressed Church discipline and reaffirmed its orthodoxy and unity.

A hallmark of his papacy was his dedication to the saints and martyrs. Damasus relocated the remains of many holy men and women to notable religious sites, amplifying the bond between believers and these divine figures. His backing of St. Jerome, whom he appointed as his secretary and tasked with translating the Scripture into Latin, culminated in the creation of the Vulgate—the foundational Bible in Western Christian thought.

Pope Damasus I also prioritized the Church's physical presence in Rome, embarking on extensive construction and rejuvenation projects, notably enhancing the basilicas of St. Peter, St. Lawrence, and St. Sebastian. Meanwhile, his focus on internal reforms ensured greater unity and discipline within the Church.

Pope Damasus I passed away on December 11, 384, which is celebrated as his feast day. Today, he is the patron saint of archeologists and often depicted in art adorned in papal attire with his patriarchal cross.

DAMIEN

BORN: January 3, 1840, Tremelo, Belgium
DIED: April 15, 1889, Molokai, Hawaii
FEAST DAY: May 10

PATRONAGE: Lepers, Hawaii, outcasts
SYMBOLS AND ATTRIBUTES: Cross, tree, dove

St. Damien, also known as St. Damien of Molokai, is a well-known figure in the Catholic Church. He was born Jozef De Veuster on January 3, 1840, in Tremelo, Belgium. Around the age of eighteen, he entered the Congregation of the Sacred Hearts of Jesus and Mary and took the name Damien.

Damien is primarily known for his missionary work and selfless service to those affected by leprosy (Hansen's disease) on the island of Molokai in Hawaii. In 1873, he volunteered to go to Molokai to minister to the lepers isolated there to prevent the spread of the disease. He worked without rest to provide physical, spiritual, and emotional support to the afflicted individuals, establishing a sense of community and offering them love, compassion, and dignity.

Setting aside the risk of contracting the disease himself, Damien spent sixteen years caring for the lepers until he too contracted leprosy and died on April 15, 1889. He is widely regarded as a martyr of charity and an example of selflessness and devotion.

Damien's dedication to the lepers of Molokai has made him a revered figure, not only within the Catholic Church but also in the broader context of humanitarian and missionary work. In 1937, John Farrow, a famous Australian film director and the father of actress Mia Farrow, wrote a biography of Damien entitled *Damien the Leper.* Farrow provides an account of Damien's journey from his early years in Belgium to his missionary work in Hawaii and the legacy he left behind.

Pope Benedict XVI canonized Damien on October 11, 2009.

DAVID

BORN: c. 500, Wales
DIED: c. 589, Wales
FEAST DAY: March 1

PATRONAGE: Wales, vegetarians, poets
SYMBOLS AND ATTRIBUTES: Dove, daffodil, leek

Also known as Dewi Sant, St. David is the patron saint of Wales. He was a Celtic monk, bishop, and prominent figure in Welsh history.

According to tradition, David was born around the year 500 in the region of Pembrokeshire, Wales, and helped establish monastic communities. He promoted a disciplined way of life among his followers and advocated for a vegetarian diet, with water as the preferred drink instead of wine. He promoted the idea of "*Gwnewch y pethau bychain mewn bywyd*" or "Do the little things in life," a saying that encourages individuals to focus on performing small acts of kindness and carrying out their duties faithfully.

One of the best-known miracles associated with David is the Synod of Brefi to deal with the heresy of Pelagianism. As the legend goes, during the council, St. David caused the ground beneath him to rise, enabling him to be seen and heard by all the attendees. This act is said to have affirmed his status as the chosen leader of the Welsh Church.

St. David's Day, celebrated annually on March 1, commemorates his death, around the year 589, and serves as a day of national celebration of Welsh culture, heritage, and language. It is customary to wear daffodils or leeks, traditional symbols associated with the saint, during the holiday.

DENIS

BORN: c. early 3rd century, Roman Italy
DIED: c. 250, Paris, Roman Gaul
FEAST DAY: October 9

PATRONAGE: France, Paris, headache sufferers
SYMBOLS AND ATTRIBUTES: Decapitated bishop with his head in hands

St. Denis, also known as St. Dionysius or Dionysius the Areopagite, was a Christian martyr in the third century and a prominent figure in the early Church. According to Christian tradition, Pope Fabian sent him to Gaul (modern-day France) to preach the Gospel. He is traditionally believed to have been the first bishop of Paris.

Denis was known for his evangelistic efforts and converted numerous individuals to Christianity. However, this attracted the attention of the Roman authorities. During the reign of the Roman emperor Decius, Denis and his companions were arrested, tortured, and executed for their faith.

The story of St. Denis is closely linked to a legendary account of his martyrdom. According to tradition, Denis was beheaded on the hill of Montmartre in Paris. Death, however, did not deter the holy man from performing his godly duties. After his execution, Denis reportedly stood, picked up his head, and walked several miles while preaching the Gospel.

Christian art and iconography often portray St. Denis as a cephalophore: a saint holding his own decapitated head. These artistic representations serve as a visual reminder of his martyrdom. Paintings, sculptures, stained glass windows, and other artistic works featuring St. Denis can be found in churches, museums, and galleries around the world.

The Basilica of Saint-Denis, constructed above his burial site in the northern suburbs of Paris, houses the relics of the bishop. Pilgrims visit the basilica to pay their respects, seek his intercession, and deepen their spiritual connection to the saint. The basilica remains an architectural landmark and the final resting place for many French nobles. (See Clement I.)

DIDACUS OF ALCALÁ

BORN: c. 1400, San Nicolás del Puerto, Kingdom of Seville, Spain

DIED: November 12, 1463, Alcalá de Henares, Kingdom of Castile, Spain

FEAST DAY: November 13

PATRONAGE: Franciscan lay brothers

SYMBOLS AND ATTRIBUTES: Cross, lily

Born around the year 1400 in the town of San Nicolás del Puerto, near Seville, Spain, St. Didacus of Alcalá, also known as San Diego de Alcalá or St. James of Alcalá, was a Franciscan lay brother.

Didacus may have worked as a shepherd in his youth. He entered the Third Order of St. Francis where, as a lay brother, he performed manual labor and served in various capacities, including cook, gardener, and porter.

Didacus was known for his devotion to God and commitment to living a holy life. He was sent to evangelize and convert the people of the Canary Islands. He moved back to Spain some years later and in 1450 attended the canonization of Bernardino of Siena. A plague broke out in the city, and Didacus attended to the ill and dying. It is believed that many were healed by his prayers.

He spent his last years at the Franciscan friary of Santa María de Jesús in Alcalá de Henares, near Madrid, Spain and was admired for his compassion and care for the poor and the sick. He would often give away his food and clothing to those in need, even if it meant going without.

Didacus was also known to spend long hours in prayer; he experienced ecstasies, many of which happened during contemplation before the crucifix. He had a deep devotion to the Eucharist and the Passion of Christ. Known as a wonder worker, Didacus was canonized as a saint by Pope Sixtus V in 1588.

DISMAS

BORN: c. early 1st century AD,
place unknown
DIED: c. 33 AD, Golgotha
FEAST DAY: March 25

PATRONAGE: Prisoners, condemned
people, repentant thieves,
funeral directors
SYMBOLS AND ATTRIBUTES: Broken fetters,
cross, crucifixion, loincloth

Though not named in the Gospel accounts, St. Dismas, known as the Good Thief or the Penitent Thief, was one of the two thieves crucified alongside Jesus Christ.

The Gospel of Luke (Luke 23:32–43) makes mention of two criminals crucified with Jesus, one on his right and the other on his left. As Jesus was suffering on the cross, one of the thieves mocked him, while the other, traditionally identified as Dismas, acknowledged his own guilt and recognized Jesus's innocence. Dismas expressed his faith in Jesus and asked him to remember him when he entered his kingdom. In response, Jesus told Dismas, "Truly I tell you, today you will be with me in paradise."

The story of St. Dismas serves as a reminder of the importance of humility, repentance, forgiveness, and salvation. Over the centuries, St. Dismas has been venerated as the patron saint of thieves, prisoners, and those condemned to death as well as those who have turned their lives around or seek redemption. He is often depicted as an older man, contrite of heart, and wearing the loincloth of a crucified criminal. Occasionally, he is portrayed with a halo to indicate his sainthood.

DOMINIC

BORN: August 8, 1170, Caleruega,
Kingdom of Castile, Spain
DIED: August 6, 1221, Bologna,
Papal States
FEAST DAY: August 8

PATRONAGE: Astronomers, the
Dominican order
SYMBOLS AND ATTRIBUTES: Rosary, dog,
star, lily

St. Dominic was a Catholic priest and the founder of the Dominican order. His birth name was Domingo de Guzmán, and his parents were Felix de Guzmán and Joan of Aza.

Strong religious influences shaped Dominic's upbringing. His mother was a devout woman known for her commitment to prayer and acts of charity. According to tradition, she experienced a vision of a dog holding a torch in its mouth during her pregnancy, interpreted as a sign that her child would dedicate his life to God. Joan of Aza would eventually be beatified by the Catholic Church.

In his early years, Dominic received his education at the Cathedral School of Palencia in Spain, where he studied the liberal arts, philosophy, and theology, displaying exceptional intellectual abilities and an intense thirst for knowledge. After completing his studies, Dominic entered the priesthood and became a canon regular at the cathedral at Osma. He devoted his life to prayer, asceticism, and acts of charity and dedicated his life to serving God by serving others.

In 1203, Dominic accompanied his bishop, Diego de Acebo, on a diplomatic mission to Denmark. During their journey, they traveled through southern France, where they witnessed the spread of the Albigensian heresy. The Albigensians held Gnostic beliefs including the thought that the universe was ruled by both a benevolent spiritual god and an evil material god, a philosophy that went against the basic Christian tenet of monotheism. This attack against his cherished faith deeply impacted Dominic and fueled his determination to combat heresy and restore people to the true faith.

In response to the spread of heresy, Dominic established the Order of Preachers, commonly known as the Dominicans, in 1214. Individuals who shared his passions for preaching and for promoting the teachings of Jesus joined him in his mission. The rule Dominic created as a framework for the governance and organization of the order underscored the significance of preaching, study, common prayer, and communal living. Members of the order embraced a life of poverty, relying on begging for sustenance while pursuing rigorous study and engaging in intellectual debates. This emphasis on intellectual pursuits distinguished the Dominican order from other religious orders of the time.

In 1216, Pope Honorius III officially recognized the Order of Preachers as a religious order within the Catholic Church. This formal recognition gave the Dominicans a stable foundation and enabled its rapid expansion throughout Europe. Dominic and subsequent leaders established priories, convents, and schools that produced numerous influential theologians, scholars, and saints, including St. Thomas Aquinas.

Dominic's legacy is also intertwined with the practice of the rosary. According to tradition, the Virgin Mary appeared to Dominic and bestowed upon him the rosary as a spiritual tool to combat heresy and promote devotion to Jesus and Mary. The Dominicans popularized this sacramental as a form of prayer, and it has since become a cherished devotion in the Catholic Church.

St. Dominic is often depicted in religious art with a dog holding a torch, symbolizing his role as the "hound of the Lord" who brought the light of truth to the world. He is portrayed in numerous paintings and literature, including *Saint Dominic in Prayer* by El Greco, a famous depiction of Dominic immersed in deep contemplation and prayer. Bartolomé Murillo's painting *St. Dominic* showcases him with a book and a rosary, symbolizing his devotion to preaching and the rosary. Other artists who have depicted St. Dominic include Fra Angelico, Francisco de Zurbarán, and Giovanni Bellini.

Dante Alighieri, the distinguished Italian poet and author of the *Divine Comedy*, highlights St. Dominic in the "Paradiso," the third part of the *Divine Comedy*. Dante encounters St. Dominic in the sphere of the Sun, which represents the realm of the wise and the theologians. Dante portrays St. Dominic as a radiant figure and praises him for his zeal in combating heresy and defending the Catholic faith, depicting him as an exemplar of religious fervor and an instrument of divine truth. Dante also highlights St. Dominic's role as a preacher and attributes to him the power of eloquence. He describes how St. Dominic's persuasive words had a transformative impact on the world, proclaiming that from Dominic, "there sprang then various streams by which the Catholic garden is watered so that its sapling have new life."

Pope Gregory IX canonized Dominic as a saint in 1234, recognizing his exemplary life, the founding of the Dominican order, and his contributions to the Church. (See Thomas Aquinas.)

DOMINIC SAVIO

BORN: April 2, 1842, Riva di Chieri, Kingdom of Sardinia

DIED: March 9, 1857, Mondonio, Kingdom of Sardinia

FEAST DAY: May 6

PATRONAGE: Choirboys, juveniles, falsely accused people

SYMBOLS AND ATTRIBUTES: Lily, cross, book, prayer card, school papers (notes)

St. Dominic Savio was an Italian student who died at the age of fourteen due to complications related to tuberculosis, possibly from pleurisy, which is an inflammation of the outer layer of the lungs. He became widely recognized for his deep faith and unwavering commitment to serving God.

Born on April 2, 1842, Dominic Savio was a student at the Oratory of St. John Bosco in Turin, Italy, where he lived and studied under the guidance of John Bosco, who would be canonized. Dominic Savio had a deep devotion to the Eucharist and dedicated many of his waking hours to prayer, meditation, and the study of Scripture. Impressed by Dominic's virtuous qualities, Bosco developed a special bond with him and took on the role of Dominic's mentor and spiritual director, affectionately referring to him as "the saint" and treating him as a spiritual son.

Dominic had various mystical encounters that deepened his faith and intensified his devotion to God. And after he died, it is believed that young Dominic appeared as an apparition to say goodbye to his dear friend and teacher Don Bosco, and to inform him of a request from Jesus to love the Blessed Virgin and tell the children of the world to pray to her.

Dominic is widely believed to have served as an intercessor in cases of illness and affliction, with numerous accounts reporting his presence in moments of dire need. One remarkable instance involves a young boy named Albano Sabatino, who was stricken with a life-threatening illness. Placing a relic of Dominic beneath Albano's pillow resulted in his swift recovery. In yet another account, Dominic's intercession is credited with the miraculous healing of a mother of six who was suffering from a heart ailment, enabling her to continue her loving care for her family.

On June 12, 1954, Pope Pius XII canonized Dominic Savio as a saint. He is venerated as the patron saint of teenagers, choirboys, the falsely accused, and juvenile delinquents. (See John Bosco.)

DOROTHY

BORN: 3rd century, place unknown
DIED: c. 311, Caesarea, Cappadocia
FEAST DAY: February 6

PATRONAGE: Gardeners, brides, florists, victims of torture
SYMBOLS AND ATTRIBUTES: Flowers, especially roses

Dorothy was a young Christian woman of the fourth century who lived in Caesarea, a city in the Roman province of Palestine. She was known for her beauty, virtue, and devotion to her faith.

During the Diocletian persecution of Christians, Dorothy was arrested and brought before the governor, Sapricius. Refusing to abandon her beliefs, she was tortured and jailed. According to tradition, while imprisoned, Dorothy was visited by an angel who comforted her and told her that she would soon be in paradise. On the way to her execution, a soldier named Theophilus mocked Dorothy, requesting apples and roses from heaven. The young woman prayed, and an angel appeared with three apples and roses on a linen cloth. She asked for them to be given to Theophilus before her execution. Theophilus, amazed at the miracle, especially because apples and roses were out of season at the time, professed Christ as the true God, but not before Dorothy was beheaded. Theophilus would soon meet the same fate for his conversion.

Dorothy is often depicted in Christian art holding a basket of flowers or roses and is the patron saint of gardeners, florists, brides, and victims of torture.

DROGO

BORN: c. 1105, Epinoy, County of Artois
DIED: April 16, 1186, Sebourg, County
of Hainaut
FEAST DAY: April 16

PATRONAGE: Shepherds, baristas, those
with physical deformities
SYMBOLS AND ATTRIBUTES: Sheep,
shepherd, cattle, bag of coffee beans

St. Drogo, also known as St. Druon, was a twelfth-century Belgian saint who is often associated with miraculous abilities and extraordinary gifts. He was born in Epinoy, near Valenciennes, France, around the year 1105. Orphaned shortly after his birth and raised by an uncle, Drogo was said to have contracted an illness when he was a young man that led to various physical deformities. Ostracized by some in his community, Drogo developed a deep devotion to God and sought solace in prayer and meditation. He lived as a hermit for many years, residing in a small cell attached to a church in Sebourg, France, where he spent hours in deep contemplation.

One of the most notable aspects of Drogo's life is the phenomenon of bilocation, the ability to be present in two places simultaneously. It is said that while attending Mass in one location, Drogo could also be seen by others working in the fields or performing manual labor in a different place. These extraordinary experiences gained him a reputation as a wonder worker.

Many people sought his intercession for various ailments, and numerous miracles were attributed to his prayers. Reports claimed he could cure the sick, heal the blind, and even restore life to the dead.

St. Drogo is venerated as the patron saint of shepherds, coffeehouse keepers, and those who suffer from bodily ailments and deformities.

DUNSTAN

BORN: 909, Baltonsborough, Kingdom
of England
DIED: May 19, 988, Canterbury, Kingdom
of England

FEAST DAY: May 19
PATRONAGE: Blacksmiths, goldsmiths
SYMBOLS AND ATTRIBUTES: Harp, anvil,
bellows, an army of angels

St. Dunstan, also known as Dunstan of Canterbury, was a tenth-century abbot and bishop. His early life was spent in the area surrounding Glastonbury, England, where he became known for his skills as a scholar, blacksmith, musician, and artist. He entered the service of King Edmund and played an integral role in the political events of the time. However, he found little favor in the king's court, and was often falsely accused of black magic and bewitching the royal family.

When Edmund died, Dunstan faced persecution under the succeeding king, but he escaped and spent a period of exile in Europe. While abroad, Dunstan further developed his skills and knowledge in various fields, including metalworking and monasticism. In time, he returned to England and became the abbot of Glastonbury Abbey, where he revitalized the monastic community and implemented reforms.

Dunstan's reputation as a wise and capable leader grew, and he was appointed as the bishop of Worcester and, subsequently, the archbishop of Canterbury. As archbishop, he continued his reforms, focusing on the clergy's moral conduct, the restoration of monasticism, and the promotion of education and art within the Church.

St. Dunstan is often depicted in folklore and hagiography as having various supernatural encounters, including legends of him outwitting the devil and performing miracles. St. Dunstan's legacy endured long after his death, and he became one of the most celebrated saints in England.

DYMPHNA

BORN: 7th century, Ireland
DIED: 7th century, Geel, Brabant, Belgium
FEAST DAY: May 15

PATRONAGE: Mental and nervous disorders, runaways, people with epilepsy
SYMBOLS AND ATTRIBUTES: Lily, sword, lamp

The story of Dymphna revolves around her tragic life and martyrdom. According to tradition, Dymphna, also known as Dympna or Dimpna, lived for much of her life in the village of Geel in present-day Belgium. She was the daughter of a pagan Irish king named Damon. Her mother died when she was very young, and her grief-stricken father sought to marry someone who resembled his late wife. However, because Dymphna resembled her mother so closely, her father's desires took a disturbing turn, and he developed an incestuous attraction toward her.

Dymphna, guided by her Christian faith, resisted her father's advances and fled Ireland to preserve her chastity. Accompanied by a small group of friends, including a priest named Gerebernus, she sought refuge in Geel, Belgium. Unfortunately, her father discovered their whereabouts and traveled to Geel in pursuit of his daughter.

Upon their reunion, Dymphna once again refused her father's immoral requests. Enraged, the king ordered the execution of Gerebernus and then beheaded Dymphna.

After their deaths, Dymphna's body was buried in Geel, and her tomb became a pilgrimage site. Many miracles and healings were attributed to her intercession, particularly in cases of mental illness and epilepsy. The town of Geel eventually became known as a place of care for those with psychological illnesses, and Dymphna is its patron saint.

The details of St. Dymphna's life and martyrdom come from a medieval account known as the *Acta Sanctorum*, a compendium of the lives of the saints written by Jesuit scholars in the seventeenth century. While the historical accuracy of the account is debated, devotion to Dymphna has remained strong, and she is widely venerated as a compassionate intercessor for those facing mental and emotional challenges. (See Gerebernus.)

E

EDITH STEIN

BORN: October 12, 1891, Breslau, German Empire (now Wrocław, Poland)
DIED: August 9, 1942, Auschwitz-Birkenau, German-occupied Poland
FEAST DAY: August 9

PATRONAGE: Europe, loss of parents, converted Jews
SYMBOLS AND ATTRIBUTES: Cross, Star of David

St. Edith Stein, also known as St. Teresa Benedicta of the Cross, was a Jewish philosopher and Catholic convert who was martyred at the concentration camp at Auschwitz, Poland. Born on October 12, 1891, in Breslau, Germany (now Wrocław, Poland), she was the youngest of eleven siblings in a devout religious Jewish family. Edith's exceptional aptitude for learning emerged early on, and by the age of fifteen, she had already completed her secondary education with honors.

In 1911, Edith enrolled at the University of Breslau, where she pursued philosophy and developed an interest in women's studies. In 1913, she studied philosophy under Edmund Husserl at the University of Göttingen. Husserl was impressed with Edith's intelligence and encouraged her to pursue a career in academia. In 1916, Edith received her PhD in philosophy, becoming one of the first women to earn a doctorate in the field.

During her doctoral studies, Edith attended the lectures of influential Catholic philosopher Max Scheler. Scheler's work greatly influenced Edith's philosophical development and sparked her exploration of Catholic thought.

In 1921, Edith came across the autobiography of St. Teresa of Ávila. The saint's unwavering faith and commitment to Christ immediately struck her.

Edith delved deeper into the study of Catholicism, and later that year, she decided to convert. She was baptized on January 1, 1922. Her conversion caused significant consternation among her family and friends, who saw it as a betrayal of her Jewish heritage.

Following her conversion, Edith Stein continued her academic pursuits and became a prominent lecturer and writer on philosophical and theological topics. She taught at various institutions and gained recognition for her insightful analyses of phenomenology and her ability to harmonize philosophy and faith.

In the early 1930s, as Germany's political climate grew increasingly hostile toward Jews, Edith faced escalating discrimination and persecution as a Jewish Catholic intellectual. Recognizing the dangers of remaining in Germany, she sought refuge in the Carmelite monastery in Cologne in 1933. There, she embraced the contemplative life, assuming the name Sister Teresa Benedicta of the Cross.

Unfortunately, religious institutions were not safe from the Nazi regime's aggressive persecution of Jews. In 1938, Sister Teresa Benedicta, fearing for her safety, was sent by her superiors to the Carmelite monastery in Echt, the Netherlands. Amid the turbulent times, she continued to devote herself to prayer, reflection, and contemplation, seeking solace and strength in her faith.

Her sanctuary in the Netherlands proved temporary, however. In 1940, the Nazis invaded and occupied the country. On August 2, 1942, Sister Teresa Benedicta and her sister Rosa, who was also a convert to Catholicism, were arrested by the Gestapo as part of their retaliatory response to a pastoral letter written by the bishops of the Netherlands on July 26, 1942 that denounced antisemitism. They were taken to the Westerbork concentration camp and deported to Auschwitz.

On August 9, 1942, Sister Teresa Benedicta, along with her sister and others, was killed in the gas chambers.

Her life, characterized by sacrifice and unwavering devotion, inspired many in the years after World War II, and calls for her sainthood stirred.

During this time, Edith Stein's contributions to philosophy and theology, particularly in the realm of phenomenology, became better known. Her dissertation on empathy and explorations of consciousness and human experience has left a lasting impact. Scholars worldwide continue to study and appreciate her writings. Some of her notable works include *Finite and Eternal Being*, in which she engages with Thomas Aquinas's philosophy, discussing the structure of reality, the nature of God, and the relationship between faith and reason. Another important work, *The Science of the Cross*, delves into the spirituality of St. John of the Cross, emphasizing the transformative power of embracing suffering and spiritual self-emptying. Additionally, her book *Essays on Woman* examines the nature, dignity, and role of women in society, advocating for equal opportunities and presenting a holistic vision of womanhood.

On May 1, 1987, Edith Stein was beatified by Pope John Paul II in Cologne, Germany, her home during her time as a Carmelite nun. The beatification ceremony recognized her martyrdom and death in Auschwitz during World War II, underscoring her sanctity and unwavering faith amid persecution. It highlighted her exemplary life as a model of holiness and her witness to the Catholic faith.

In that same year, two-and-a-half-year-old Benedicta McCarthy from Brockton, Massachusetts, who had accidentally ingested sixteen times the lethal dose of Tylenol, recovered from a severe overdose-induced coma and organ failure following nationwide prayers to Edith Stein. Benedicta's complete recovery was considered "miraculous" by her treating physician, Dr. Ronald Kleinman, and was investigated by the Roman Catholic Church for its potential status as a miracle attributable to Edith Stein.

Her path to sainthood culminated on October 11, 1998, when Pope John Paul II canonized Edith Stein as a saint in Rome. Benedicta, her family, Dr. Kleinman, and the nurses who treated her attended the canonization Mass at St. Peter's. The ceremony at St. Peter's Square acknowledged Stein's heroic virtues and elevated her to the esteemed status of a saint. It affirmed her enduring legacy as a model of faith, courage, and dedication to God. Moreover, she was recognized as an embodiment of Christian-Jewish dialogue, promoting understanding and unity among different cultures and religions. Her canonization designated her as an intercessor and a source of inspiration for Catholics worldwide.

Through the beatification and canonization process, Edith Stein's profound example of the power of faith and the intellect became recognized and celebrated. As a saint and martyr, she continues to shine as a light of hope for those in pursuit of truth in the face of adversity.

The feast day of St. Edith Stein is celebrated on August 9, commemorating the day of her martyrdom at Auschwitz.

EDMUND CAMPION

BORN: January 24, 1540, London, Kingdom of England

DIED: December 1, 1581, Tyburn, London, Kingdom of England

FEAST DAY: December 1

PATRONAGE: British Jesuits, United Kingdom

SYMBOLS AND ATTRIBUTES: Palm branch, book

St. Edmund Campion was a scholar, Jesuit priest, and martyr. He was born into a Catholic family during the reign of Henry VIII, a turbulent time for religion in England. It is believed that to protect him from persecution, Campion was raised in the newly formed Church of England. He displayed an exceptional aptitude for learning and attracted the attention of prominent figures, including Sir Thomas White, the founder of St. John's College, Oxford. White became his patron, and under his guidance, Campion went to Oxford. In 1557, he became a junior fellow at St. John's College.

In 1566, Queen Elizabeth I visited Oxford, and Campion was selected to deliver a speech to the assembly who gathered in her honor. The queen was so impressed with Campion, she offered him the deanship of St. John's College. However, Campion, who had started to reconnect to his Catholic faith, declined the offer. This decision marked the beginning of a significant spiritual transformation.

In 1571, feeling increasingly uncomfortable with the religious ambivalence in England, Campion decided to leave his homeland and travel to Dublin, where he hoped to establish a university. The venture failed due to political reasons, leading him to depart for Douai, France. There, he officially joined the Catholic Church and commenced his studies to become a priest.

In 1573, he traveled to Rome and entered the Society of Jesus (the Jesuits). As a novice, he was sent to Prague, where he spent much of the next six years.

His time in Prague was transformative. He was ordained as a Jesuit priest in 1578 and, together with fellow Jesuit Robert Persons, penned a significant work on the life of St. Alexis, demonstrating his continuing prowess in scholarship even as he pursued his spiritual path.

Following his ordination, Campion was convinced that his mission was to return to England to minister to Catholics who were increasingly oppressed by the Protestant regime. In 1580, he returned to England undercover, facing religious tension and the threat of persecution.

Back in his homeland, Campion celebrated clandestine Masses, administering the sacraments and giving spiritual guidance to the beleaguered Catholics. His exceptional oratory skills and persuasive arguments in defense of the Catholic faith made him both a source of inspiration for Catholics and a prime target for the Protestant authorities.

At this time, he composed a manifesto called "Challenge to the Privy Council," which has become known as "Campion's Brag." The statement outlined his mission and challenged the religious authorities of the time. It is believed to be the earliest defense of the Catholic faith to emerge in English during the Reformation. It also further inflamed the authorities against him, intensifying their efforts to capture him. Campion remained undeterred in his beliefs.

His bravery would not go unnoticed, but neither would it go unpunished. He was arrested during Mass at Lyford Grange in Berkshire in 1581. After his capture, he was confined in the Tower of London, where he underwent torture and interrogation regarding his religious beliefs and loyalty.

His trial took place later that year, where he defended himself eloquently despite the physical and psychological toll of his imprisonment. This did little to deter his final punishment. On December 1, 1581, he was executed by hanging, drawing, and quartering at Tyburn, London. His martyrdom significantly impacted the Catholic community in England and inspired others to remain faithful to their beliefs during a time of persecution.

After his death, Campion's fame grew, and he became an emblem of Catholic martyrdom. He was beatified by Pope Leo XIII in 1886 and canonized as one of the Forty Martyrs of England and Wales by Pope Paul VI in 1970. He often appears in artistic displays holding a Bible.

ELIGIUS

BORN: c. 588, Chaptelat, Kingdom of
the Franks

DIED: December 1, 660, Noyon, Neustria

FEAST DAY: December 1

PATRONAGE: Goldsmiths,
blacksmiths, mechanics

SYMBOLS AND ATTRIBUTES: Hammer, anvil

St. Eligius, also known as St. Eloi or St. Elois, was a seventh-century saint and bishop. He was trained as a goldsmith and became highly skilled in his craft. His reputation reached the court of Frankish king Clotaire II, and he was eventually appointed as the chief mint master for the kingdom. He produced many beautiful, intricate pieces in gold and silver, including jewelry, liturgical vessels, and reliquaries.

As time went on, Eligius felt called to a religious vocation and became a priest. He was ordained as a bishop of Noyon-Tournai in present-day Belgium in 642. As bishop, he worked diligently to promote Christian teachings, provide care for the poor, and reform the Church. He used his skills to serve the needy and advocate for fair treatment of the poor, converting precious metals into practical objects for the less fortunate.

St. Eligius was renowned throughout his life for his holiness and miraculous acts. He passed away on December 1, 660, and was laid to rest in Noyon after his passing. Though many of his writings have been lost to time, there still exists a sermon denouncing the pagan customs prevalent during his era, a homily focusing on the last judgment, and a letter penned in 645. He is often depicted wearing bishop's vestments, holding a crosier in his right hand and a small gold church in his left.

ELIZABETH

BORN: 1st century BC, Judea,
Roman Empire
DIED: 1st century AD
FEAST DAY: November 5

PATRONAGE: Expectant mothers
SYMBOLS AND ATTRIBUTES: Pregnancy,
embracing Mary

As the cousin of the Virgin Mary and the mother of John the Baptist, St. Elizabeth holds significant importance in the Christian tradition. According to the Gospel of Luke in the New Testament, Elizabeth was married to Zechariah, a priest among the Jewish people. She was beyond child-bearing years, but she and her husband were told by the angel Gabriel that Elizabeth would bear a child, who would be filled with the Holy Spirit.

After an angel told the Virgin Mary she would conceive the Son of God, Mary went to see her elderly cousin, Elizabeth. To Mary's surprise, Elizabeth was six months pregnant with a child who would become John the Baptist. Moved by the Holy Spirit, Elizabeth proclaimed the importance of Mary's unborn child and proclaimed, "Blessed are you among women, and blessed is the child you will bear!" This makes Elizabeth the first to recognize the significance of Jesus's special conception.

St. Elizabeth is revered for her faith, for preparing the way for Jesus via the birth of her son John the Baptist, and her exemplary hospitality and humility. The scene of the Visitation, featuring Elizabeth and Mary, has been depicted in art by luminaries such as Raphael, Andrea Mantegna, and Correggio. (See John the Baptist.)

ELIZABETH ANN SETON

BORN: August 28, 1774, New York City,
New York, USA
DIED: January 4, 1821, Emmitsburg,
Maryland, USA

FEAST DAY: January 4
PATRONAGE: Catholic schools, seafarers,
widows, converts
SYMBOLS AND ATTRIBUTES: Book, rosary

Elizabeth Ann Seton was the first native-born American saint canonized by the Catholic Church. She was born Elizabeth Ann Bayley in New York City to a prominent Episcopalian family. When she was three years old, her mother died; her father, wanting to ensure that Elizabeth and her younger sister Catherine had a mother figure, married Charlotte Amelia Barclay, an Anglican whose mother was related to the well-to-do Roosevelt family. Charlotte often took her stepdaughters on trips around New York to help serve the poor.

Well educated and devout, Elizabeth's faith played a central role in her life from an early age. In 1793, at the age of nineteen, she married William Magee Seton, with the inaugural Episcopal bishop of New York, Samuel Provoost, officiating the wedding ceremony. The couple went on to have five children, but their marriage was cut short in 1803, when William passed away from tuberculosis.

After William's death, Elizabeth turned to her faith for solace and guidance, and she soon became drawn to the Catholic Church. The Church's commitment to charity, community, and service resonated with her, and she felt a strong connection to its teachings and traditions. In 1805, Elizabeth was accepted into the Catholic Church and dedicated herself to her new faith. In 1809, she relocated to Emmitsburg, Maryland, where she founded the Sisters of Charity of St. Joseph's, the first American religious community for Catholic women. Their mission focused on aiding the poor and providing education to children. Elizabeth and her community established St. Joseph's Academy and Free School, the country's first Catholic school for girls. Over time, the institution expanded, underwent name changes, and evolved into a high school and a four-year college. In 1973, St. Joseph College merged with Mount Saint Mary's University.

Elizabeth Ann Seton passed away on January 4, 1821, and was beatified on March 17, 1963, by Pope John XXIII. Prayers for her intercession are credited with the healing of a four-year-old girl with leukemia, which ultimately provided the necessary miracles that led to her canonization as a saint on September 14, 1975, by Pope Paul VI.

ELIZABETH OF HUNGARY

BORN: July 7, 1207, Kingdom of Hungary
DIED: November 17, 1231, Marburg, Holy Roman Empire
FEAST DAY: November 17

PATRONAGE: Bakers, beggars, brides, hospitals, lacemakers, dying children, widows
SYMBOLS AND ATTRIBUTES: Roses, bread, crown, alms

St. Elizabeth of Hungary, also known as St. Elizabeth of Thuringia, lived in the thirteenth century in what is now Germany. She was a princess, wife, and mother who dedicated her life to serving the poor and marginalized.

Elizabeth was born in 1207 in Hungary to King Andrew II and Queen Gertrude. At the age of four, she was promised in marriage to Louis, the son of the landgrave of Thuringia, and at six years old, she went to live with his family, Christians who instilled in her the importance of compassion and service.

When Elizabeth married Louis at fourteen, she committed herself to helping the poor and sick in the surrounding area. While raising three children and fulfilling her duties as a wife and mother, she began giving away her belongings and worked to care for those in need. Influenced by the teachings of St. Francis of Assisi, Elizabeth embraced a life of prayer and selflessness. She personally attended to the needy and marginalized, providing them with food, clothing, and shelter.

Although Elizabeth's generosity and compassion earned her widespread admiration, some members of the royal court criticized and opposed her actions. After her husband's death, she faced a complex set of challenges, including securing her children's inheritance. She eventually distanced herself from the court and her brother-in-law, Henry Raspe, who refused to support her charitable acts. Elizabeth then dedicated the rest of her life to religious devotion, joining the Third Order of St. Francis and embracing a life of poverty.

In 1231, Elizabeth passed away at twenty-four. She was canonized by Pope Gregory IX in 1235. She is often depicted in art holding roses.

ELIZABETH OF PORTUGAL

BORN: 1271, Zaragoza, Kingdom of Aragon

DIED: July 4, 1336, Estremoz, Kingdom of Portugal

FEAST DAY: July 4

PATRONAGE: Peace, brides, queens, charitable societies, the falsely accused, difficult marriages, invoked during times of war

SYMBOLS AND ATTRIBUTES: Crown, dove, rose, coins

A medieval queen who became a revered Catholic saint, St. Elizabeth of Portugal, also known as St. Elizabeth of Aragon, was born in Zaragoza, Aragon (now modern-day Spain), the daughter of King Peter III of Aragon and Queen Constance of Sicily. She was named in honor of her great-aunt, St. Elizabeth of Hungary.

In 1282, Elizabeth married King Denis of Portugal, which made her the queen consort of Portugal. Despite political challenges and her husband's infidelity, she remained steadfast in her faith and dedicated to the well-being of her subjects.

Fabled for her compassion and charitable endeavors, Elizabeth founded hospitals and orphanages and personally cared for the sick and needy. On several occasions, she acted as a peacemaker, notably intervening between her husband and their son, Alfonso IV, to prevent violent conflict.

Following King Denis's death in 1325, Elizabeth embraced a life of deep religious devotion. She joined the Poor Clares, dedicating her days to prayer and acts of penance. Elizabeth passed away in 1336 and was canonized by Pope Urban VIII in 1625.

EPAPHRAS

BORN: 1st century, Colossae

DIED: 1st century

FEAST DAY: July 19

PATRONAGE: Friendship

SYMBOLS AND ATTRIBUTES: Letter, scroll, book

St. Epaphras was an early Christian mentioned in the letters of Paul, specifically in the Epistle to the Colossians and the Epistle to Philemon. In the letter to Philemon, Epaphras is mentioned as Paul's fellow prisoner.

Epaphras was a laborer and a faithful minister of Christ. He was originally from Colossae, a city in ancient Phrygia, which is now part of modern-day Turkey. Epaphras is described as a beloved fellow servant and a faithful representative of the Church who helped spread the Gospel in his hometown and the surrounding regions. It is believed that Epaphras was instrumental in establishing the Christian community in Colossae and in helping to address certain issues and false teachings that had arisen among the believers there. He exemplifies the qualities of a faithful servant and collaborator in the early Christian community. (See Paul.)

ERASMUS

BORN: 3rd century

DIED: 303, Formia, Roman Empire

FEAST DAY: June 2

PATRONAGE: Sailors, abdominal pain sufferers

SYMBOLS AND ATTRIBUTES: Windlass, boat, halo

St. Erasmus, also known as St. Elmo, was a third-century bishop who lived during the reign of the Roman emperor Diocletian, a time of great Christian persecution. Erasmus refused to renounce his faith and was subjected to various tortures including being boiled alive, and was finally disemboweled, his intestines wound around a wheel until he died. Throughout his ordeals he remained faithful to Christ and Church until his last breath. An angelic light was believed to have surrounded him during this torture, a sign of divine presence and protection. Nevertheless, Erasmus succumbed to the brutality and died a martyr.

Over time, the light that protected Erasmus became associated with a weather phenomenon known as Saint Elmo's fire, a glowing plasma discharge around a ship's masthead during thunderstorms at sea. Sailors often invoked Erasmus's intercession for protection during storms and lightning.

EULALIA

BORN: c. 290, Mérida, Roman Empire
DIED: December 10, 304, Mérida, Roman Empire
FEAST DAY: December 10

PATRONAGE: Seville, Barcelona, sailors
SYMBOLS AND ATTRIBUTES: Palm branch, cross

St. Eulalia, also known as Eulalia of Mérida, is a revered Christian martyr who lived during the late third and early fourth century. According to the popular narrative, Eulalia was a young girl, around thirteen or fourteen years old, at the time of her martyrdom. She lived during the reign of Emperor Diocletian, a persecutor of Christians. Her rejection of the Roman gods and refusal to participate in pagan rituals and sacrifices made her a target for abuse.

The account of Eulalia's martyrdom describes a series of tortures inflicted upon her. She was subjected to scourging, beatings, and various cruel punishments, including being stripped naked and paraded through the streets of Mérida as a form of public humiliation. However, as one account relates, a sudden snowfall covered her body as she walked, shielding her from the view of onlookers. One account of her martyrdom states that she was crucified, while another suggests that she burned at the stake.

Eulalia is revered as a courageous and pious young girl with an unwavering devotion to Christ, and she is honored through various religious festivities and celebrations in Spain, particularly in Barcelona, where her relics are believed to be enshrined. She is often depicted in art on an X-shaped cross, the possible instrument of her death.

EXPEDITUS

BORN: 3rd century, Armenia, Roman Empire
DIED: 303, Melitene (modern-day Turkey), Roman Empire

FEAST DAY: April 19
PATRONAGE: Urgent causes, students, merchants, navigators
SYMBOLS AND ATTRIBUTES: Cross, crow

The origins and details surrounding St. Expeditus are shrouded in legend and myth. According to tradition, he is believed to have been a Roman soldier who embraced Christianity and suffered martyrdom because of his faith.

Expeditus is often depicted as a man-at-arms holding a cross with the word *HODIE* (Latin for "today") written on it, symbolizing the urgency and importance of embracing Christianity immediately. According to one legend, Expeditus witnessed a vision of an angel holding a cross. Inspired by this vision, he decided to convert to Christianity but subsequently was tempted by Satan, who took the form of a crow at his feet and urged him to delay his conversion until the next day. In response, Expeditus stomped on the bird, exclaiming, "I will be a Christian today!" He was later beheaded for his decision.

He is revered in Chile, Brazil, Argentina, and other countries as the patron saint of those seeking fast solutions, prompt actions, and overcoming procrastination. Many people believe that invoking his intercession can bring about quick resolutions to their problems or urgent needs.

F

FABIAN

BORN: Late 2nd century, place unknown
DIED: January 20, 250, Rome, Italy
FEAST DAY: January 20

PATRONAGE: Potters, farmers
SYMBOLS AND ATTRIBUTES: Dove, papal attire

Born in Rome, St. Fabian initially worked as a farmer before being unexpectedly elected to the papacy in 236. Fabian's tenure as pope witnessed notable growth in the Christian faith and the completion of significant architectural projects.

The manner of Fabian's elevation to pope astonished many. According to tradition, during the election, a dove descended from the sky and hovered over his head, symbolizing his divine selection by God. His papacy brought about several significant developments within the Church. He is credited with dividing the Roman diocese into seven regions, known as deaconries, each led by a deacon. This organizational structure decentralized the early Church and facilitated improved communication among its local leaders.

Alongside his ecclesiastical contributions, Pope Fabian supervised the restoration of the catacombs of St. Callistus. Additionally, some accounts list Fabian as establishing the traditional practice of consecrating chrism—a mixture of oil and balsam used in sacraments—on Holy Thursday.

The feast day of St. Fabian is celebrated on January 20, which commemorates his martyrdom in 250 during the reign of Emperor Decius. Decius had issued a decree mandating that all Roman citizens offer sacrifices to the pagan gods, a command to which St. Fabian refused to do. Consequently, he was arrested and tortured, and although accounts vary on the exact manner of his death, it is widely believed that he was beheaded.

St. Fabian's final resting place is the celebrated catacomb of Callixtus in Rome, an underground crypt initially established by Pope Callixtus. Within this historic site, his tomb bears a Greek inscription that can still be read today: "Fabian, Bishop, Martyr." He is often depicted in art in his papal vestments and sometimes with a dove.

FAUSTINA KOWALSKA

BORN: August 25, 1905, Głogowiec, Poland

DIED: October 5, 1938, Kraków, Poland

FEAST DAY: October 5

PATRONAGE: Divine Mercy

SYMBOLS AND ATTRIBUTES: Image of Divine Mercy

St. Faustina Kowalska was a Polish nun well known for her unwavering devotion to the Divine Mercy and for receiving numerous visions and revelations from Jesus Christ. Born Helena Kowalska, she was the third of ten children. Her parents, Stanisław and Marianna Kowalska, were poor but devout Catholics who instilled in their children a deep love for God and the Church. From a young age, Helena felt a strong calling to religious life, but her family's financial difficulties initially prevented her from pursuing this vocation. Instead, she worked as a housekeeper and as a factory worker to help provide for her family.

In 1925, at the age of twenty, Helena entered the Congregation of the Sisters of Our Lady of Mercy in Warsaw and took the name Sister Maria Faustina of the Blessed Sacrament. Her spiritual life was marked by a deep love for Jesus Christ and an intense desire to imitate His self-giving love.

A remarkable aspect of Faustina's life was her mystical experiences, which began in 1928 and continued until her death. She reported receiving numerous visions of Jesus Christ, who spoke to her and revealed to her the depths of His mercy and love. These revelations were recorded in her diary, which has since become a classic of Catholic spirituality that is widely read and studied by believers around the world.

One of the most famous of these visions occurred on February 22, 1931, when Faustina saw an image of Jesus Christ as Divine Mercy. In this image, Jesus is shown with two rays of light emanating from His heart—one red and one white. According to her diary, "The pale ray stands for the Water which makes souls righteous. The red ray stands for the Blood which is the life of souls. These two rays issued forth from the very depths of My tender mercy when My agonized Heart was opened by a lance on the Cross." Jesus instructed Faustina to have this image painted, promising that those who venerated it would receive great graces and mercy.

Another significant revelation occurred on September 13, 1935, when Jesus appeared to Faustina and requested that a feast day be established in honor of the Divine Mercy. He said, "I want the Feast of Mercy to be a refuge and sanctuary for all souls, and especially for poor sinners. On that day the depths of My mercy are open; I pour out a whole sea of graces on souls that approach the fount of My mercy." This feast day was established by Pope John Paul II and is celebrated on the first Sunday after Easter.

Faustina's spirituality was rooted in the message of the Divine Mercy, which emphasizes God's infinite love and compassion for all humanity, especially for sinners. The message is encapsulated in the phrase "Jesus, I trust in You," which Faustina heard repeatedly in her visions and which appears at the bottom of the famous painting of the image of Divine Mercy by Eugene Kazimierowski. These words reflect a sincere faith in God's goodness and an unwavering trust in His love and care for each person. The revelations also highlight the importance of kindness and compassion toward others.

Faustina Kowalska was canonized by Pope John Paul II on April 30, 2000, when the pope recognized her as the "Apostle of Divine Mercy." Pope John Paul II had a particular devotion to the Divine Mercy, and it was under his papacy that the Divine Mercy Sunday (the first Sunday after Easter) was officially instituted in the Roman Catholic Church.

FELICITY OF ROME

BORN: c. 101 Rome, Italy
DIED: c. 165, Rome, Italy
FEAST DAY: November 23

PATRONAGE: Mothers, expectant mothers, parents who have lost children
SYMBOLS AND ATTRIBUTES: Palm branch, martyr's crown

St. Felicity of Rome was a second-century martyr.

Little historical evidence exists concerning Felicity, but according to tradition, she was a wealthy Roman noblewoman who lived in the second century and who suffered for her faith in Christ. She and her seven sons had converted to Christianity. All eight were arrested and ordered to renounce their faith before the emperor Marcus Aurelius. Even with the emperor's threats and promises of rewards for abandoning their faith, Felicity and her sons refused to denounce Christ. They were tortured and thrown into a pit of wild animals.

Felicity is celebrated for her unwavering faith and her remarkable courage in the face of persecution.

FINNIAN OF CLONARD

BORN: c. 470, Ireland
DIED: 549, Clonard, Ireland
FEAST DAY: December 12

PATRONAGE: Teaching, Clonard Abbey
SYMBOLS AND ATTRIBUTES: Book, monastery, cross, staff, torch

St. Finnian of Clonard, also known as Finnian the Leper, was an Irish Christian monk and one of the early saints of the Christian church in Ireland.

Finnian established a monastic school of Clonard, attracting many students, including some who would become influential saints and scholars. Finnian's monastic rule was known for its emphasis on scholarship, asceticism, and missionary work. One of his most famous students was St. Columba, who went on to found an important monastery at Iona, which was instrumental in spreading Christianity in Scotland and Northern England. (See Columba.)

FRANCES OF ROME

BORN: July 1384, Rome, Italy, Papal States
DIED: March 9, 1440, Rome, Italy, Papal States

FEAST DAY: March 9
PATRONAGE: Rome, Italy; motorists
SYMBOLS AND ATTRIBUTES: Angel, book

Francesca Bussa de' Leoni, St. Frances of Rome, is one of that city's patron saints. Born into a noble family, she wanted to be a nun from a very early age but was forced to marry Lorenzo Ponziani when she was twelve. Even though this was an arranged marriage, Frances embraced her life as a wife, loved her husband, and together they had three children (though two died from plague). Frances and Lorenzo were married for forty years.

Rome faced political upheaval during her life, causing hardships for her family. Yet Frances's faith increased as her commitment to prayer, charity to the poor, and merciful care of the sick grew.

Though she had wished to become a nun, her family responsibilities took precedence. According to Vatican sources, after nearly three decades of marriage, she and her husband chose to live a chaste life. Frances went on to establish the Oblates of Santa Francesca in 1433, a lay congregation focusing on piety and service. However, after her husband's death two years later, she founded the Oblates of Mary. This group of married and single women lived secular lives while adhering to religious vows, which was a progressive idea at the time.

Fr. Giovanni Mattiotti, her confessor and spiritual director, chronicled Frances's mystical encounters. Among these was a revelation about the end of the Western Schism, visions of Heaven and Hell, and intimate exchanges with an angel who served as her trusted guide and companion.

She passed away in 1440 and was canonized in 1608. Due to a legend about an angel lighting her path, she is also recognized as the patron saint of motorists.

FRANCES XAVIER CABRINI

BORN: July 15, 1850, Sant'Angelo
Lodigiano, Lombardy, Italy
DIED: December 22, 1917, Chicago,
Illinois, USA
FEAST DAY: November 13

PATRONAGE: Immigrants,
hospital administrators
SYMBOLS AND ATTRIBUTES: Cross,
nun's habit

St. Frances Xavier Cabrini, also known as Mother Cabrini, was the first American citizen canonized by the Catholic Church. Born on July 15, 1850, in a small town near Milan, Italy, she was the youngest of thirteen children born to Agostino Cabrini and Stella Oldini. Francesca was academically gifted and aspired to become a missionary in China, but she suffered from poor health. As a young woman she applied to two religious congregations but was turned away because of her frail constitution.

With the help of benefactors, Frances founded the Missionary Sisters of the Sacred Heart of Jesus in 1880. She assumed the name Sister Frances Xavier in honor of St. Francis Xavier, the patron saint of missionaries, but would be best known as Mother Cabrini. She was an exceptional teacher and served in various schools affiliated with her order.

One of the first roles of the order was to assume control of a local orphanage, which would become known as House of Providence, a school for girls in Codogno, Italy. Recognizing that young people required more than just an education, she endeavored to provide them with a loving, caring home.

Under Mother Cabrini's leadership, the congregation rapidly expanded, and she opened schools, orphanages, and hospitals across Italy, focusing on instructing girls and caring for the sick, particularly those afflicted by tuberculosis, prevalent during that era.

A move to the United States opened a new chapter in Mother Cabrini's journey. In 1889, at the request of Pope Leo XIII, she embarked on a mission to establish a house in New York City to aid the influx of Italian immigrants. Encountering numerous challenges, including limited resources and opposition from some local clergy members, she persisted and gained the respect and support of many individuals, which allowed her and the sisters to establish schools, orphanages, and hospitals throughout the United States.

They offered spiritual guidance to immigrants, many of whom were impoverished and grappling with the adjustments demanded by their new surroundings. She believed the Catholic faith could give these immigrants a sense of community and belonging.

Mother Cabrini had a great love for the United States and became a U.S. citizen in 1909. After an illness, she passed away on December 22, 1917, in Chicago, Illinois, leaving behind a legacy that endures to this day.

Numerous miracles were attributed to her, including the restoration of sight to a young boy named Peter Smith who had received an incorrect dosage of silver nitrate after birth. The sisters at Mother Cabrini Memorial Hospital affixed a fragment of Cabrini's habit to Peter's clothing and fervently prayed for two days, resulting in the remarkable recovery of his sight.

On July 7, 1946, the Catholic Church canonized Mother Cabrini, bestowing upon her the distinction of becoming the first American citizen to be declared a saint. She was honored for her exceptional acts of charity and unwavering devotion to God. Her canonization also symbolized recognition of the contributions of Italian immigrants to the United States and paid tribute to all those who dedicate their lives to serving others.

The Missionary Sisters of the Sacred Heart of Jesus continue to serve the poor, sick, and marginalized in numerous countries. In the United States, many schools, hospitals, and institutions bear her name as a testament to her influence. She is venerated as the patron saint of immigrants, particularly Italian immigrants. (See Francis Xavier.)

FRANCIS DE SALES

BORN: August 21, 1567, Château de
Thorens, Savoy
DIED: December 28, 1622, Lyon, Kingdom
of France

FEAST DAY: January 24
PATRONAGE: Journalists, writers, the deaf
SYMBOLS AND ATTRIBUTES: Cross,
pen, book

St. Francis de Sales was a Roman Catholic bishop and theologian known for his work as a spiritual writer and his efforts to promote the Catholic faith during the Counter-Reformation.

Born in 1567 in the Duchy of Savoy (present-day France), Francis was raised in a devout Catholic family. He studied law in Paris and became a lawyer when he was twenty-four. However, he felt a strong calling to the priesthood and eventually pursued a religious vocation.

Francis was ordained a priest in 1593; he quickly gained a reputation for his preaching and for providing spiritual guidance. He was known for his gentle and compassionate approach, emphasizing the importance of God's love and mercy. He believed in reaching out with kindness and understanding rather than through the use of harsh or confrontational methods.

In 1602, Francis was consecrated as the bishop of Geneva, a mainly Protestant area. He faced numerous challenges in his efforts to reestablish Catholicism in the region and to reconcile with the Protestant community. His approach was marked by constructive dialogue and gentle persuasion, and he sought to find common ground with his detractors by emphasizing the importance of personal holiness and inner conversion.

To spread his teachings and guidance to a broader audience, Francis wrote several influential books, including the still-popular *Introduction to the Devout Life*. This beloved guide is structured as a series of letters and conversations between Francis de Sales, who assumes the role of a spiritual director, and a fictional character named Philothea, who represents an earnest seeker of God's will (the name Philothea is derived from Greek and means "lover of God"). The book emphasizes that holiness is attainable for all people, regardless of their state in life. It addresses various aspects of spiritual life, including prayer, pursuing virtue, overcoming temptations, and embracing a spirit of humility, love, and detachment. Francis's message is one of universality, as he famously wrote, "My purpose is to instruct those who live in town, within families, or at court, and are obliged to live an ordinary life as to outward appearances."

Francis's approach to spirituality, characterized by a balance between the active life and the contemplative life, greatly influenced Catholic spirituality and the development of the Order of the Visitation of Holy Mary, commonly known as the Visitandine order or the Salesian Sisters, a Roman Catholic religious order for women. It was founded by Francis de Sales and Jane Frances de Chantal in 1610. The order, named after the Visitation of the Virgin Mary to her cousin Elizabeth as described in the Gospel of Luke, was established to provide a religious vocation for women who desired a contemplative life but were unable to meet the strict requirements of other existing religious orders. Francis and Jane Frances envisioned a community where women could dedicate themselves to a life of prayer and spiritual reflection while engaging in active works of charity and service to their local communities.

Francis de Sales died in Lyon, France, on December 28, 1622, at the age of fifty-five. In 1623, his remains were transferred to the church of the Visitandine monastery in Annecy, France. He was beatified by Pope Alexander VII in 1665 and canonized as a saint the following year. In 1877, Pope Pius IX elevated him to Doctor of the Church, acknowledging his exceptional influence on Catholic theology and spirituality. (See Jane Frances de Chantal.)

FRANCIS OF ASSISI

BORN: 1181 or 1182, Assisi, Papal States
DIED: October 3, 1226, Assisi, Papal States
FEAST DAY: October 4

PATRONAGE: Animals, the environment, Italy, the poor, the Franciscan order
SYMBOLS AND ATTRIBUTES: Animals, stigmata, tau cross, birds, Franciscan habit, skull

St. Francis of Assisi, an Italian Catholic friar, mystic, and preacher, founded the Order of Friars Minor, the Third Order of Saint Francis, and the Custody of the Holy Land. Born in the late twelfth century to a prosperous family, Francis renounced his wealth to dedicate himself to a life of poverty and service to the underserved. His teachings of humility and love have touched people worldwide for centuries, establishing him as a cherished figure in the Catholic Church.

Born Giovanni Francesco di Bernardone in 1181 or 1182 in Assisi, Italy, he was the eldest son of Pietro di Bernardone, a cloth merchant, and Pica de Bourlemont, a noblewoman from Provence. As a young man, Francis's vibrant and charismatic nature made him a natural leader. In his early twenties, Francis joined the military, participating in a war between Assisi and Perugia. He was eventually captured, imprisoned for a year, and fell seriously ill. During this tumultuous period, Francis began his spiritual awakening, seeking solace in prayer and Scripture and experiencing divine visions. He was eventually released from captivity and though he attempted to join the military again, something had radically changed inside of him.

A notable transformative moment in his life occurred when he encountered a leper in the countryside. Overcoming his initial aversion, Francis kissed the leper's hand. When he turned around, the leper had vanished. This meeting, coupled with other dreams and visions, marked a pivotal shift in his life. In one revelation at the dilapidated San Damiano chapel, Christ instructed him to restore his house. Francis took the message literally—personally mending the chapel—and figuratively by setting his heart on getting back to the basics of Jesus's teachings.

This change in focus and beliefs caused friction with his father, who saw his son's actions as reckless. The tension culminated in a public confrontation where Francis renounced his familial ties, symbolically disrobing in front of the local bishop. Embracing his spiritual calling, he donned a simple worker's cloak, marking his commitment to spiritual richness over material wealth.

Subsequently, Francis's teachings began attracting followers who shared his desire to live by vows of poverty, obedience, and chastity. This community eventually became the Order of Friars Minor, a prominent religious order that is active in the Catholic Church even today.

PLATE III
Francis of Assisi

One of many notable episodes in Francis's life was his encounter with Sultan Malik al-Kamil of Egypt in 1219 during the Fifth Crusade. Venturing into enemy lines, he hoped to broker peace, an initiative that highlighted his dedication to harmony and understanding between faiths. While he couldn't secure a peace agreement or convert the sultan, the meeting remains an emblematic representation of interfaith dialogue and respect.

Among his many contributions, Francis is celebrated for establishing, around 1223, the tradition of the Nativity scene. He organized a live reenactment of Christ's birth that emphasized the poverty and humility of the event. This influential event spurred the global tradition of creating Nativity scenes during Christmas. He is also believed to have created the first crèche.

Francis is said to have experienced the stigmata, which he received in 1224 during the Feast of Exaltation of the Cross. While in prayer, he witnessed a vision of a seraph, a six-winged angel, bearing the image of a crucified man. As the vision faded, Francis experienced intense pain and discovered wounds resembling those of Christ's crucifixion on his hands, feet, and side. The appearance of these stigmata stirred significant controversy both during his life and afterward. Yet, to his followers, they symbolized his deep sanctity and divine affirmation of Francis's belief in the central values of poverty, humility, and love in Christian living. Historically, Francis is recognized as the first documented person to exhibit the stigmata.

Francis of Assisi died on October 3, 1226, and was swiftly canonized by Pope Gregory IX in 1228.

Celebrated on October 4, Francis's feast day honors him as the patron saint of animals, the environment, Italy, and the Franciscan order. In works of art he is often depicted with the stigmata and surrounded by animals, symbolizing his life and teachings.

Several miracles and fantastical stories are revealing of Francis's love of nature and animals. One is the tale of the wolf of Gubbio. In this legend, Francis approached a wolf who was terrorizing a town, made the sign of the cross, and commanded the animal to not hurt anyone else. The wolf listened and the town adopted it as a companion, providing it with food and care. Francis also preached to birds and trees. Another story tells of a winter that was especially harsh. All the plants were barren. But Francis spoke to an almond tree, asking it to demonstrate the might and love of God, and the tree immediately blossomed in response.

Though he was not a prolific writer, St. Francis's few works, such as the *Canticle of the Sun* and his *Admonitions*, hold significant weight in the Catholic Church. Pope Francis, elected in 2013, named himself after the great saint, in honor of Francis's enduring values of peace, love for nature, and commitment to the poor.

FRANCIS OF NAGASAKI

BORN: 1562, Japan

DIED: February 5, 1597, Nagasaki, Japan

FEAST DAY: February 6

PATRONAGE: Nagasaki

SYMBOLS AND ATTRIBUTES: Palm branch, crucifix

St. Francis of Nagasaki, also known as St. Francis Takeya, was a Japanese Christian and Franciscan tertiary who was martyred for his faith in Nagasaki, Japan, in the seventeenth century. Born in 1562, he converted to Christianity and joined the Third Order of St. Francis. During a period of intense persecution of Christians in Japan, Francis was arrested and imprisoned along with other Christians.

On February 5, 1597, Francis and twenty-five other Christians, including several missionaries and laypeople, were crucified on the orders of Toyotomi Hideyoshi, the ruler of Japan at that time. This event is known as the Crucifixion of Twenty-Six Martyrs of Japan. They were subjected to brutal torture and execution to suppress the spread of Christianity in Japan. The martyrs, including Francis, were canonized as saints by the Catholic Church.

St. Francis of Nagasaki is revered as a symbol of the enduring faith of the early Christian community in Japan. His feast day is celebrated on February 6, along with the other Martyrs of Japan.

FRANCIS OF PAOLA

BORN: March 27, 1416, Calabria, Kingdom of Naples

DIED: April 2, 1507, Plessis-lez-Tours, Kingdom of France

FEAST DAY: April 2

PATRONAGE: Sailors, boatmen

SYMBOLS AND ATTRIBUTES: Staff, rosary

St. Francis of Paola was born Francesco Martolilla in 1416 in the Italian town of Paola, Calabria. His parents, who had long struggled to have a child, turned to prayer, and invoked the intercession of St. Francis. Their prayers were heard. In gratitude for the miracle of their son's birth, they named him after the great saint.

From a young age, Francis was seemingly marked by divine favor. An eye ailment in infancy threatened his sight, but his parents' prayer yielded miraculous results once again, and the boy's sight was restored. As thanks, Francis's parents consecrated him to Christ.

Francis's spiritual journey led him to seek solitude, initially on his father's property, and subsequently in a coastal cave. The year 1435 marked a turning point as two companions joined him in his isolation, and together they constructed hermitage cells and a chapel. This marked the birth of the Order of Minims, with "minims" meaning "the smallest," an apt descriptor for their ascetic and humble lifestyle.

The Minims were marked by their strict adherence to a life of poverty, humility, and fasting. They adopted a simple diet, eschewing meat, eggs, and dairy products. They lived by a rule that Francis penned and which was granted papal permission by Pope Sixtus IV in 1474. The order was officially recognized by Pope Alexander VI, who affirmed their rule.

Gifted with healing and prophecy, Francis also could discern the conscience of others. He was sent to the French court of the ailing King Louis XI. Though his prayers did not heal the monarch, he did win the king's respect with his words of comfort and wisdom. Louis XI's heir showered Francis with favor, helping him establish a monastery.

Even in the face of death in old age, Francis's spiritual authority was undiminished. He continued to guide his followers, delivering his final exhortations on Good Friday and passing away as the Passion according to St. John was being read. He was canonized by Pope Leo X in 1519.

Though Huguenots desecrated his tomb, devout Catholics managed to save some of his relics, which are now enshrined in various churches of the order. (See Francis of Assisi.)

FRANCIS XAVIER

BORN: April 7, 1506, Navarre, Kingdom of Spain

DIED: December 3, 1552, Shangchuan Island, China

FEAST DAY: December 3

PATRONAGE: Navarre, Spain, missionaries, travelers, epidemics

SYMBOLS AND ATTRIBUTES: Crucifix, globe, boat, Bible

St. Francis Xavier was the co-founder of the Society of Jesus and is widely regarded as one of the greatest missionaries of all time. Born on April 7, 1506, in the Castle of Xavier near Sanguesa, in Navarre, which is now part of Spain, Xavier was a well-educated man and received a degree in philosophy from the University of Paris.

While studying in Paris around 1525, he met Pierre Favre, a Savoyard, at the esteemed Collège de Sainte-Barbe in Paris. A friendship flourished between the two, and sometime thereafter they encountered Ignatius of Loyola, who would become a pivotal figure in their lives.

Impressed by the charismatic Ignatius and his vision for a new religious order, Xavier and Favre eagerly joined him in forming the Society of Jesus, otherwise known as the Jesuits. Along with James Laínez, Simon Rodrigues, Alfonso Salmerón, and Nicholás Bobadilla, Xavier, Favre, and Ignatius made their religious vows at Montmartre on August 15, 1534. They would come to be known as the First Companions of the Society of Jesus.

Xavier was ordained a priest in 1537 and worked closely with the members of the new society. Two years later he received a request from King John III of Portugal to evangelize the East Indies. Eager to embark on this divine mission, Xavier set foot on Indian soil in 1542, commencing an odyssey that would span many lands and touch countless lives.

Arriving in Goa, India, Xavier dedicated himself to preaching and ministering to the sick in hospitals. He also engaged in various forms of social service to assist the marginalized and those in need. He cared for the sick, looked to provide food and shelter to the poor, and advocated for the fair treatment of all people. Xavier faced numerous obstacles, including persecutions instigated by local rulers and the detrimental influence of Portuguese soldiers. Yet, he persevered, converting many and even reaching the distant shores of Ceylon (modern-day Sri Lanka).

In 1545, Xavier proceeded to Malacca, in what is now Malaysia, continuing to preach the Gospel. From there, he would perform missionary work on the Molucca Islands in Indonesia and at Amboyna, Ternate, and other islands in the Pacific. Though historical records remain inconclusive, some suggest he may have stepped foot on the shores of Mindanao, making him the first Apostle of the Philippines. After his return to Malacca, Xavier's attention turned to Japan.

Xavier's long-cherished dream of introducing Christianity to Japan materialized when he arrived in Kagoshima in August 1549. For a year, he diligently studied the Japanese language and, with the help of a convert named Pablo de Santa Fe, translated important articles of faith. Xavier nevertheless faced resistance from local leaders, which led to his banishment from Kagoshima. Undeterred, he journeyed through various cities in Japan, establishing Christian communities and nurturing their growth.

After spending two and a half years in Japan, Xavier entrusted the mission to his fellow Jesuits and returned to India in early 1552. Xavier's eyes then turned toward China, a land that beckoned with its vast potential for spreading the Gospel. Determined to reach the Celestial Empire, he planned an expedition and secured an appointment as an ambassador. Accompanied by a small group, Xavier set sail, but fate had other ideas. During his journey to China, Xavier fell ill on the island of Sancian and later died on December 3, 1552.

Xavier was considered a miracle worker, and his aboveground casket housed in the Basilica of Bom Jesus in Goa is adorned with sculptures that feature many of the notable and miraculous events associated with him, including healing the sick and curing the deaf and mute.

The canonization of Francis Xavier in 1622, together with Ignatius, underscores his lasting legacy. His relics, including a severed arm, once connected to a hand that supposedly baptized more than 100,000 people, is housed in Rome's Church of the Gesù. He is often depicted in art wearing a cassock, surplice, and crucifix. Francis Xavier is the patron saint of Navarre as well as navigators and missions. (See Ignatius of Loyola.)

G

GABRIEL LALEMANT

BORN: October 3, 1610, Paris, France
DIED: March 17, 1649, St. Ignace,
New France
FEAST DAY: October 19

PATRONAGE: Jesuit missionaries to
North America
SYMBOLS AND ATTRIBUTES: Palm
branch, cross

Gabriel Lalemant was one of the North American Martyrs, a group of Jesuit missionaries who were martyred in the seventeenth century while serving among the Huron and Iroquois nations in what is now Canada.

Born in Paris on October 3, 1610, Gabriel entered the Jesuit novitiate in 1630. He was sent to New France (present-day Canada) in 1646 to assist in the missions there.

After a brief period in Quebec, the Jesuits assigned Gabriel to join John de Brébeuf, another Jesuit missionary, in the Huron missions. His time there was short-lived. In March 1649, the Iroquois attacked the Huron village of St. Ignace. Gabriel and Brébeuf were set on fire and burned alive by the Iroquois.

Gabriel Lalemant was canonized alongside the other North American Martyrs by Pope Pius XI in 1930 (See John de Brébeuf.).

GABRIEL OF OUR LADY OF SORROWS

BORN: March 1, 1838, Assisi, Papal States
DIED: February 27, 1862, Isola del Gran
Sasso, Kingdom of Italy
FEAST DAY: February 27

PATRONAGE: Abruzzo, students, young
religious, seminarians
SYMBOLS AND ATTRIBUTES: Passionist
habit, lily

Gabriel of Our Lady of Sorrows, also known as St. Gabriel Possenti, was an Italian Passionist religious brother. Born in Assisi, Italy, as Francesco Possenti, he was known for his deep devotion to the Virgin Mary and his commitment to the Passion of Christ.

Francesco entered the Passionist order in 1856, taking the name Gabriel of Our Lady of Sorrows. He lived a life of simplicity, obedience, and self-denial, dedicating himself to prayer, penance, and the service of others. Gabriel had a special devotion to the mourning of the Blessed Virgin Mary over the sins of the world and sought to console her through his life of sacrifice.

Numerous legends are associated with Gabriel. One widely known tale recounts an assault on a town by bandits. In various accounts, Gabriel, through his serene and sacred presence, confronted and pacified the intruders, avoiding conflict. Another more dramatic and violent rendition portrays Gabriel like a modern-day mercenary, outgunning the villains in the name of God, and emerging as the town's hero. In modern times, he is sometimes unofficially referred to as the patron saint of handguns and gangs.

Gabriel of Our Lady of Sorrows died on February 27, 1862, after contracting tuberculosis. He was twenty-three. He was canonized as a saint by Pope Benedict XV in 1920.

GAETANO CATANOSO

BORN: February 14, 1879, Chorio di San Lorenzo, Reggio Calabria, Italy

DIED: April 4, 1963, Chorio di San Lorenzo, Reggio Calabria, Italy

FEAST DAY: April 4

PATRONAGE: Priests, chaplains

SYMBOLS AND ATTRIBUTES: Rosary

St. Gaetano Catanoso was an Italian Roman Catholic priest. He was born on February 14, 1879, in Chorio di San Lorenzo, Reggio Calabria, Italy, and died in the same city on April 4, 1963. He was ordained in 1902 and served in various parishes in southern Italy. He was known for his holiness, devotion to the Eucharist, and deep love for the Blessed Virgin Mary.

In 1934, Gaetano Catanoso founded the Congregation of the Veronican Sisters of the Holy Face, a religious order of nuns dedicated to prayer, contemplation, and apostolic works. The congregation focused on promoting devotion to the Holy Face of Jesus, following the example of St. Veronica, who, according to tradition, wiped the face of Jesus during His Passion, leaving behind a relic now known as the Veronica.

Gaetano Catanoso dedicated himself to the spiritual formation of the Veronican Sisters and worked with great determination to spread devotion to the Holy Face of Jesus among the faithful. He was particularly concerned with the conversion of sinners and the sanctification of priests.

After his death, Gaetano Catanoso was recognized for his holiness and was beatified by Pope John Paul II on May 4, 1997. He was canonized as a saint by Pope Benedict XVI on October 23, 2005. (See Veronica.)

GALLA

BORN: 5th century, Rome, Italy, Western Roman Empire

DIED: 550, Rome, Italy, Byzantine Empire

FEAST DAY: October 5

PATRONAGE: Patients, the sick

SYMBOLS AND ATTRIBUTES: Cross

St. Galla, also known as St. Galla of Rome or St. Galla of the Palatine, was a Roman noblewoman who lived in the sixth century. She was born into a wealthy and influential family and was married to a Roman consul. After her husband's death, however, she dedicated her life to serving God.

Galla became known for her ascetic lifestyle and acts of charity. She gave away her wealth and possessions to the poor and lived a life of prayer and fasting. She joined a community of religious women and founded a hospital and monastery on Vatican Hill, one of the seven hills in Rome. (It is believed that the seven mountains on which the Whore of Babylon sits in the book of Revelation is a reference to the geography of this area.)

Pope Gregory the Great praised Galla and mentioned her in his writings, specifically in his famous work *Dialogues*, which contains accounts of the lives of various saints. He honors her virtues and describes her ascetic practices, including her acts of charity and her deep devotion to St. Peter. Galla died around the year 550. (See Gregory the Great.)

GASPAR BERTONI

BORN: October 9, 1777, Verona, Republic of Venice

DIED: June 12, 1853, Verona, Austrian Empire

FEAST DAY: June 12

PATRONAGE: Stigmatines

SYMBOLS AND ATTRIBUTES: Priest attire, crucifix

St. Gaspar Bertoni was an Italian Roman Catholic priest and the founder of the Congregation of the Sacred Stigmata of Our Lord Jesus Christ, also known as the Stigmatines. He was born in 1777 in Verona. A sickly child, Gaspar began having mystical experiences at the age of eleven, after he received his first Holy Communion. He came of age during the French Revolution. He witnessed the challenges faced by the Catholic Church and the suppression of religious orders in neighboring countries. The revolution's anti-Catholic sentiment only intensified the strength of his beliefs and faith.

Gaspar received an excellent education at home and in school after the municipality in Verona suppressed the local Jesuit order. Young Bertoni studied with Fr. Louis Fortis, who would become the first Jesuit General after the reinstatement of the Society of Jesus. Fr. Louis helped groom Gaspar for the holy orders.

Gaspar entered the seminary in 1796 and was ordained a priest in 1800. He began his work as an educator in 1808 at the Diocesan Seminary of Verona. Gaspar served as a spiritual director, retreat master, and confessor, offering religious instruction in parishes and establishing an oratory for young people. Known for his holiness and spiritual insights, he became sought after for advice from bishops, priests, religious, and laypeople.

In 1816, inspired by St. Ignatius of Loyola and the Society of Jesus, Gaspar founded the Stigmatines to support missions, conduct retreats, and provide formation for seminarians and clergy. The Stigmatines derive their name from the stigmata, the wounds of Christ, symbolizing their dedication to spreading Christ's love in the world. The congregation's primary mission is to promote the greater glory of God through the sanctification of its members, the consecration of the clergy, and the blessing of youth. They engage in various pastoral and educational ministries to fulfill this mission.

Gaspar Bertoni passed away on June 12, 1853. He was beatified by Pope Paul VI in 1975 and canonized as a saint by Pope John Paul II in 1989. (See Ignatius of Loyola.)

GEMMA GALGANI

BORN: March 12, 1878, Camigliano, Tuscany, Italy

DIED: April 11, 1903, Lucca, Tuscany, Italy

FEAST DAY: April 11

PATRONAGE: Students, pharmacists, sufferers of headaches and back pain, paratroopers and parachutists

SYMBOLS AND ATTRIBUTES: Cross, stigmata, lily

Also known as Gemma of Lucca or the Flower of Lucca, St. Gemma Galgani was an Italian mystic and stigmatist who lived during the end of the nineteenth century. A deep devotion to God, profound spiritual experiences, and numerous miracles characterized her life.

Born in 1878 in Camigliano, a Tuscan city in Italy, she was the fifth child in a devoutly Catholic family of eight. Tragedy struck with the passing of her mother when Gemma was only seven years old. Gemma took the Blessed Virgin Mary as her spiritual mother and dedicated her life to her faith.

As a child, Gemma had mystical visions and encounters with the supernatural. She claimed to have been visited by the Virgin Mary, Jesus, saints, angels, and even demons. Daily she saw and conversed with her guardian angel, who personally instructed, guided, and, at times, admonished her in the spiritual life. Once, when Gemma was ill, her angel gave her a cup of coffee that, she said, tasted delicious and instantly healed her.

When Gemma turned eighteen, she fell seriously ill with spinal meningitis. Miraculously, she recovered after praying to St. Gabriel of Our Lady of Sorrows, a recently canonized young Italian saint. This experience deepened her faith and prompted her to become a lay member of the Passionist Third order.

Gemma had an intense love of Jesus and the Eucharist. Her spiritual life was particulary marked by an earnest devotion to the Passion, or suffering, of Christ. She prayed incessantly and subjected herself to rigorous penances, often fasting and going without sleep for long periods. One of the best-known aspects of Gemma's mystical life was her stigmata. According to her own account, she first received the wounds of Christ on June 8, 1899, while praying in her room. She described feeling a sudden and intense pain in her hands, feet, and side, as if nails had pierced her. The wounds bled profusely, causing her immense physical suffering, but she accepted them as a sign of her heartfelt love for Christ.

Over the following years, Gemma continued to experience a range of mystical phenomena, including ecstasies, levitation, and bilocation. She also received visions and revelations, notably a series of visions of Hell that she believed were meant to inspire her to pray for sinners.

In early 1903, she contracted tuberculosis and succumbed quickly to the disease. She passed away on April 11, 1903, at the age of twenty-five and was laid to rest in the cemetery of Lucca, Italy. Her grave swiftly became a pilgrimage site for those seeking her intercession. In 1940, she was canonized by Pope Pius XII, and her relics are held in the Passionist's Monastery in Lucca, Italy.

Throughout her life, Gemma was renowned for performing miracles. These miracles included healing the sick, calming storms, and prophesying future events. Even more miracles were attributed to St. Gemma after her death. Benedict Williamson's book, *Blessed Gemma Galgani,* reports numerous miracles attributed to Gemma. For example, Maria Menicucci of Vitorchiano had a severe knee condition called synovitis, which was deemed incurable. After a novena to Gemma and the application of a relic, her knee was found to be perfectly normal. Filomena Bini of Pisa had a malignant stomach disease diagnosed as cancerous, but after falling asleep with a relic of Gemma, she woke up to find all traces of the disease vanished. Isolina Serafini of Vicopelago suffered from acute meningitis for months until she turned to Gemma. After a sound sleep, the disease completely disappeared. Giovanna Bortolozzi had a large tumor in her armpit and was scheduled for surgery, but after a novena and the application of a relic, the tumor disappeared, astonishing her doctor. Gioocchino Nuccio of Palermo was gravely ill with tubercular peritonitis and nephritis, but after a picture of Gemma was placed upon him, he regained consciousness, was completely cured, and even went for a walk the next day. Dom Thommaso, a monk, had suffered from chronic spinal pain for twelve years, but after beginning a novena to Gemma, he was cured in just two days. (See Gabriel of Our Lady of Sorrows.)

GENESIUS OF ROME

BORN: 3rd century, Rome, Italy
DIED: c. 303, Rome, Italy
FEAST DAY: August 25

PATRONAGE: Actors, comedians, dancers, clowns
SYMBOLS AND ATTRIBUTES: Comedy and tragedy masks

Genesius of Rome, also known as St. Genesius or Genesius the Actor, is a legendary Christian martyr from the third century. According to tradition, Genesius was a Roman thespian and comedian who performed in plays that mocked Christianity. It was during one of these performances that something unexpected happened: Genesius experienced a vision of angels and underwent a conversion. Refusing to continue with the performance, Genesius openly confessed his newfound Christian faith. His actions enraged the Roman authorities, and he was subsequently arrested and brought before Emperor Diocletian, who was known for his severe persecution of Christians.

Genesius refused to renounce his new faith. He was eventually martyred, possibly by beheading, around 303. His story became popular among early Christians, and he came to be venerated as a saint as his tale of conversion and courage spread throughout the empire.

GENEVIEVE

BORN: c. 419–422, Nanterre, Western Roman Empire
DIED: c. 500–512, Paris, Kingdom of the Franks

FEAST DAY: January 3
PATRONAGE: Paris, France
SYMBOLS AND ATTRIBUTES: Candle, keys, bread

Considered a significant figure in French history and religious tradition, St. Genevieve, also known as Sainte Geneviève, was a French saint and a patroness of Paris. Genevieve was born in Nanterre, a small town near Paris, to a respectable family. From a young age, she displayed a great devotion to God and a strong desire to serve Him. She often visited the local church and was known for her kindness toward the poor and the sick. At the age of fifteen, Genevieve decided to dedicate her life to God and became a nun. She moved to Paris and joined a community of religious women.

Genevieve gained a reputation for giving sound spiritual guidance and for her prophetic abilities. She is said, through a vision, to have foreseen the invasion of Attila the Hun. She encouraged the citizens of Paris not to abandon their city, but to pray to God for protection against the Huns. Miraculously, Attila turned his attention away from Paris and invaded Orléans instead. This event solidified her status as a revered protector of Paris.

In another vision, Genevieve encountered the soul of St. Denis, the first bishop of Paris. She interpreted the spiritual visitation as a sign that a church in honor of him should be built, and she convinced authorities to begin building.

Genevieve was also a persuasive diplomat. According to the traditional narrative, during the reign of King Childeric I of the Franks in the fifth century, Paris experienced a severe famine. Genevieve took it upon herself to help alleviate the suffering of the people. According to one legend, Genevieve persuaded King Childeric to assist the starving population, convincing him to distribute the remaining grain from the royal stockpiles to those in need. As a result, the king ordered the release of the reserves. Genevieve's actions saved many lives and earned her admiration and gratitude from the people.

Genevieve died somewhere between 500 and 512, and her relics are housed in the Church of Saint-Étienne-du-Mont in Paris. Over the centuries, her influence grew, especially during times of crisis. Many invoked her intercession during the Hundred Years' War, the French Revolution, and both world wars.

Genevieve is the patron saint of Paris (as is Joan of Arc). Her name is often associated with the city's history and culture, and her image can be found in many churches throughout Paris. Her feast day is celebrated on January 3. She is often depicted holding a candle or a torch, representing the light of faith that she brought to the people of Paris. (See Denis, Joan of Arc.)

GENOVEVA

BORN: January 3, 1870, Almenara, Spain
DIED: January 5, 1956, Zaragoza, Spain
FEAST DAY: January 5

PATRONAGE: Daughters of the Sacred Heart of Jesus and of the Holy Angels
SYMBOLS AND ATTRIBUTES: Religious habit, scapular

Genoveva Torres Morales was a Spanish Catholic nun known for her role as the founder of the Daughters of the Sacred Heart of Jesus and of the Holy Angels. She was born on January 3, 1870, in Almenara, Spain. Her life took a challenging turn at the age of twelve, when her leg was amputated due to a knee infection. Subsequently, she relied on crutches for mobility and found comfort in spiritual literature.

Sometime after 1885, Genoveva encountered Carlos Ferrís, a priest who inspired her faith. Although she aspired to join an existing congregation, her health posed an obstacle. However, this setback did not deter her from establishing her own community. In 1895, in Valencia, Spain, she founded the Daughters of the Sacred Heart of Jesus and of the Holy Angels, which focused on providing care and schooling for women, especially the elderly and infirm. The sisters within her community engaged in charitable endeavors, including managing schools, orphanages, hospitals, and elderly care homes. Additionally, they offered support to at-risk young girls, protecting them from exploitation and trafficking.

Genoveva was esteemed for her humility, simplicity, and unwavering love for God and humanity. Her life exemplified a selfless commitment to service, as she worked to alleviate the suffering of those in need. Even today, her compassionate work continues to inspire others.

She was often called Angel of Solitude for her peaceful and quiet demeanor. Pope John Paul II beatified Genoveva Torres Morales in 1995, and she was canonized in 2003, solidifying her status as a revered figure in the Catholic Church.

GEORGE

BORN: c. 280, Lydda, Roman Palestine
DIED: April 23, 303, Nicomedia,
　Roman Empire
FEAST DAY: April 23

PATRONAGE: Soldiers, England, farmers,
　field workers, archers; those suffering
　from skin diseases, leprosy, and syphilis
SYMBOLS AND ATTRIBUTES: Dragon, lance,
　horse, shield

St. George, a third-century saint and martyr, is celebrated for heroic deeds, the legends of which have been passed down through generations. Of Greek origin, he served as a Roman soldier and was a member of the Praetorian Guard during Emperor Diocletian's reign. George was famed for his courage, especially in secretly protecting Christians from persecution and safeguarding the Christian faith. He was martyred for his actions.

George is the central character in the popular legend of St. George and the dragon. This tale of faith and chivalry gained prominence through the medieval hagiography the *Golden Legend*. Authored by Jacobus de Voragine in the thirteenth century, the text chronicles the lives and legends of numerous saints.

One story tells the tale of a horrifying dragon terrorizing a kingdom near a city called Selena in Libya. The dragon's breath caused pestilence; the monster also demanded daily offerings of two sheep from the populace. When the sheep supply dwindled, the dragon required a human sacrifice chosen by lottery.

Eventually, the lot fell on the king's daughter. George, a brave knight and a stalwart soldier, happening to pass by, encountered the distressed princess. Fearing for the knight's safety, she urged him to leave. However, he decided to stay. Upon the dragon's appearance, George fearlessly attacked it with his lance after making the sign of the cross. He successfully subdued the dragon and used the princess's garter to lead the creature back to the city as if it were a tame lamb.

Once in the city, George reassured the citizens and encouraged them to embrace baptism before he beheaded the dragon. Many of the townsfolk complied. The grateful king offered George half of his kingdom, which he declined. Instead, he advised the king to tend to God's churches, respect the clergy, and show compassion to the poor.

George, a symbol of courage and righteousness, is recognized as a defender of good and an enemy of evil, leading to his widespread veneration throughout Europe and beyond. In England, he's honored as the country's patron saint, and his feast day is celebrated on April 23 in the Western Christian tradition. St. George's Day marks the beginning of the

PLATE IV
George

agricultural season in some regions. In Bulgaria, it's known as Gergyovden, and it's associated with the arrival of spring. In other Eastern European cultures, St. George's Day holds significant importance, particularly in regions rooted in folk traditions and supernatural beliefs. For centuries, the eve of St. George's Day was seen as a time of heightened activity for *moroi* (akin to malevolent spirits or vampires), witches, and other dark entities, especially between midnight and dawn. To ward off these creatures of the night, people participated in protective rituals like inscribing crosses on doors and windows, bathing in streams or rivers, and invoking St. George for protection. While some of these practices have faded in modern times, the regional folklore is remembered and celebrated in parts of Romania and in the Caucasus region.

St. George has also been a celebrated figure in art history. Notable depictions include Raphael's *St. George and the Dragon* from the Renaissance period, now in the National Gallery of Art in Washington, DC; Peter Paul Rubens's *St. George Fighting the Dragon* from around 1605–1607, which can be found at the Museo del Prado in Madrid; Gustave Moreau's *St. George and the Dragon* from 1889 to 1890 in the National Gallery in London; and a stained glass window in the Cathédrale Notre-Dame de Paris, to name but a few.

GEREBERNUS

BORN: 7th century, place unknown

DIED: 7th century, Ardennes

FEAST DAY: May 15

PATRONAGE: Fever

SYMBOLS AND ATTRIBUTES: Palm, lance

St. Gerebernus was a central figure in the life of St. Dymphna, a thirteenth-century Christian maiden and the daughter of a pagan Irish king. According to tradition, when Dymphna's father expressed intentions of marrying his own daughter following her mother's death, Dymphna fled with a group of friends and a trusted priest named Gerebernus. They landed at Antwerp and settled near a chapel in Geel. However, they were eventually located by her father's spies. When Dymphna again refused her father's advances, he ordered the killing of Gerebernus and personally beheaded Dymphna. Dymphna's remains were entombed in Geel and Gerebernus's remains were transferred to Xanten. (See Dymphna.)

GERTRUDE THE GREAT

BORN: January 6, 1256, Eisleben, Thuringia

DIED: November 17, 1302, Helfta, Saxony

FEAST DAY: November 16

PATRONAGE: West Indies

SYMBOLS AND ATTRIBUTES: Heart, book, pen, cross

St. Gertrude the Great, also known as Gertrude of Helfta or Gertrude the Great of Helfta, was a German Benedictine nun, mystic, and theologian from the thirteenth century. She is recognized for her profound spiritual experiences and writings.

Gertrude was born in Eisleben, in what is now Germany, and entered the Benedictine monastery of Helfta in Saxony when she was five years old. From that young age, she dedicated her life to prayer, contemplation, and religious studies. Her spiritual journey was characterized by a deep devotion to Christ and a passionate love for God. She possessed an unwavering devotion to the Sacred Heart of Jesus, which encompassed a deep love for Christ and a desire to honor and console His Heart.

Gertrude firmly believed that through devotion to the Sacred Heart, one could draw closer to Jesus and experience His abundant mercy and compassion. She regarded the Sacred Heart as a symbol of divine love, a source of spiritual nourishment, and a means of healing. In her writings, Gertrude described various mystical experiences and conversations with Jesus, often centered on the Sacred Heart.

Gertrude's devotion to the Sacred Heart extended beyond personal prayer and contemplation. She emphasized the importance of sharing this devotion with others, inviting them to partake in the love and mercy of Jesus. To that end, Gertrude promoted the practice of offering one's heart to Christ. This practice involved presenting one's desires to the Sacred Heart of Jesus, seeking alignment with God's will, and striving to love as God loves. Gertrude taught that this offering united the individual's intentions with the infinite love of Christ, enriching their spiritual life and contributing to the salvation of souls.

One of Gertrude's most significant contributions was her mystical writings, which have had a lasting impact on Christian spirituality. *The Herald of Divine Love* is a collection of spiritual exercises, prayers, and revelations that reflect her passionate relationship with God. In this work, Gertrude vividly portrayed her mystical visions of Jesus, the Virgin Mary, and other saints; she also included prayers and meditations that exemplified her spiritual life. Her writings offer guidance on deepening one's relationship with God, emphasizing the value of humility, trust, and surrender. Readers are encouraged to seek union with God and to live a life of holiness and love.

Although *The Herald of Divine Love* initially gained recognition and appreciation within Gertrude's monastery, it was not widely known or published during her lifetime. It was only in later centuries that her works were compiled and published, thereby contributing to her posthumous recognition as a significant figure in Christian mysticism.

GIANNA BERETTA MOLLA

BORN: October 4, 1922, Magenta,
Kingdom of Italy
DIED: April 28, 1962, Monza, Italy
FEAST DAY: April 28

PATRONAGE: Mothers, physicians,
pediatricians, unborn children
SYMBOLS AND ATTRIBUTES: White doctor's
coat, children

St. Gianna Beretta Molla was an Italian pediatrician, wife, and mother who is often called "a saint of ordinary life." Born in Magenta, Italy, she and Pietro Molla were married in 1955 at the Basilica di San Martino in Milan. The couple had three children.

During her fourth pregnancy, in 1961, Gianna developed a tumor in her uterus. Faced with a difficult decision, she had to choose between potentially life-saving treatment that would have terminated her pregnancy or safeguarding her child's life while putting her own at risk. Gianna chose to prioritize her unborn child's life, refusing any treatment that could harm the child.

On April 21, 1962, Gianna gave birth to a healthy baby girl. She named the baby Gianna Emanuela. Unfortunately, Gianna's condition deteriorated, and at the age of thirty-nine, on April 28, 1962, she succumbed to septic peritonitis.

Gianna Beretta Molla's act of sacrificing her own life to save her child made her widely admired for her unwavering dedication to the sanctity of life. Her story is associated with at least two miracles, which add to her revered status.

According to journalist Thomas J. McKenna, in October 1977, Lucia Sylvia Cirilo, a twenty-seven-year-old Protestant woman from Grajau, Brazil, faced a stillborn birth and subsequent complications. After experiencing severe pain, she was rushed to a hospital, where doctors diagnosed her with an inoperable rectal-vaginal fistula. The nearest hospital capable of handling her condition was more than 375 miles away. A nurse named Sister Bernardina, praying to Gianna Beretta Molla for intercession, sought healing for Lucia's illness to avoid the perilous trip. Astonishingly, Lucia's pain vanished immediately and the fistula was healed. Medical experts and theologians thoroughly investigated the incident, and it was recognized as a third-degree miracle on May 22, 1992, by the Special Congress of the Congregation of the Causes of Saints.

In November 1999, Elizabeth Comparini Arcolino, a thirty-five-year-old Brazilian woman, faced a complicated pregnancy that included a serious hemorrhage, blood clot, and deteriorating placenta. Doctors recommended terminating the pregnancy due to the risks involved for both the mother and the baby. However, Elizabeth, a devout Catholic, refused to consider having an abortion. Inspired by Blessed Gianna Beretta Molla, she instead sought the support of a bishop and a priest, who prayed with her. Against all odds, the baby's heart continued to beat, and Elizabeth remained determined to carry the child to term. Through intense prayers and community support, Elizabeth's pregnancy progressed without infection, premature labor, or fetal anomalies. On May 31, 2000, she successfully delivered a healthy baby girl, Gianna Maria. This event, too, was investigated by the Congregation of the Causes of Saints and deemed a miracle. Elizabeth's obstetrician attested that the successful outcome went against all logic and all scientific understanding, attributing it to divine intervention and the intercession of Blessed Gianna.

Pope John Paul II beatified Gianna Beretta Molla on April 24, 1994, with Lucia Sylvia Cirilo present at the ceremony. On May 16, 2004, Gianna was canonized as a saint.

GILES

BORN: 7th century, Athens, Byzantine Empire

DIED: c. 710, Nîmes, Visigothic Kingdom

FEAST DAY: September 1

PATRONAGE: Edinburgh, Scotland, the disabled, beggars, blacksmiths

SYMBOLS AND ATTRIBUTES: Deer, arrow

St. Giles, also known as St. Giles the Hermit or St. Giles of Provence, is believed to have been born in Athens, Greece, around 650. According to legend, Giles was a wealthy nobleman who renounced his wealth and position to live as a hermit in France. He sought solitude and a life of prayer and penance in the forest of Nîmes, in the region of Provence. He lived there for many years, surviving on the milk of a deer that came to him in the forest.

Giles became famous for his holiness and eventually, a community of disciples formed around him. He was also known as a miracle worker, and many people came to him seeking healing and spiritual counsel.

The story of Giles's life became intertwined with various legends and miracles attributed to him. One such story recounts that Charlemagne was hunting in the forest of Nîmes. During the hunt, the king accidentally shot an arrow that wounded Giles, having mistaken him for a deer. Realizing his mistake and learning of the hermit's piety, the king sought forgiveness and begged for Giles's prayers and intercession. According to the legend, Giles miraculously healed from the wound, and the king became a benefactor and protector of the saint and his monastery. Giles would become the king's confessor.

Giles died around the year 710, and his tomb in the forest of Nîmes soon became a popular pilgrimage site. In time, a monastery was established at the site, which became an important center of devotion and veneration.

St. Giles is considered the patron saint of disabled people, beggars, and of the city of Edinburgh, Scotland. His attributes include a hind (a red deer), an arrow, and a crosier. He is considered one of the Fourteen Holy Helpers.

GREGORY THE GREAT

BORN: c. 540, Rome, Italy,
    Byzantine Empire
DIED: March 12, 604, Rome, Italy,
    Byzantine Empire

FEAST DAY: September 3
PATRONAGE: Musicians, teachers, students
SYMBOLS AND ATTRIBUTES: Papal tiara,
    dove, book

Also known as Pope Gregory I, St. Gregory the Great was a prominent figure in the sixth century and one of the most influential popes in the history of the Catholic Church. His contributions as a theologian and statesman left an indelible mark on the development of Christianity and the shaping of Western civilization.

Gregory the Great was born in Rome around the year 540 to a noble family with deep ties to the Church. Well educated as a young man; he became a monk and dedicated himself to a life of prayer and contemplation, spending several years in seclusion.

In 579, Gregory was ordained a deacon by Pope Pelagius II and appointed as the papal ambassador to Constantinople. During his time in Constantinople, Gregory gained recognition for his diplomatic skills and theological knowledge.

After returning to Rome, he served as the abbot of the monastery of St. Andrew, where he was known for his strict discipline and unwavering commitment to the spiritual growth of the monks under his care.

Preferring the monastery to any form of public service, Gregory reluctantly accepted the position of pope after being elected by the clergy and people of Rome in 590. As pope, he devoted himself to reforming the Church and spreading the Gospel across Europe, focusing on the conversion of the Anglo-Saxons in England. In 596, Gregory dispatched a group of missionaries led by St. Augustine of Canterbury to England. Within a few years, the missionaries successfully converted the king of Kent and many of his subjects to Christianity.

Gregory the Great is renowned for his extensive writings on theology, spirituality, and pastoral care. Among his most notable works is *The Book of Pastoral Rule*, a guide for bishops and clergy on how to lead their congregations. In this work, he emphasizes the significance of humility, compassion, and the care of souls. He stresses the need for pastors to act as true shepherds, guiding their flocks with love and wisdom.

The Dialogues, another significant work, is a collection of stories recounting the lives of sixth-century saints. These stories are replete with examples of miracles, healings, courage, compassion, and self-sacrifice, offering continued inspiration to readers. It serves as a powerful testament to the strength of faith and the miracles that can occur when individuals place their trust in God.

Gregory also composed numerous liturgical works, including hymns and prayers. His "Regula Pastoralis," also known as "Pastoral Care," became a standard manual for pastors during the Middle Ages and remains an essential work for clergy to this day.

His writing on angels helped to influence the Church's understanding of these heavenly creatures. In one of his homilies, Gregory explored the topic of guardian angels, emphasizing their role in protecting and guiding individuals. He taught that God assigns a guardian angel to each person from the moment of his or her birth, and that this angel accompanies and guides them throughout their earthly journey. He also discussed the hierarchy of angels, referring to the nine choirs of angels as described by the early Christian theologian Dionysius the Areopagite. They included: Seraphim, Cherubim, Thrones, Dominions, Virtues, Powers, Principalities, Archangels, and Angels. Gregory reflected on their different roles and ranks within the celestial hierarchy, emphasizing their collective worship and service to God.

While Gregory the Great's writings on angels may not constitute an extensive treatise on the topic, they provide valuable insights into the medieval Christian understanding of angelic beings. Furthermore, his work has influenced subsequent theological thought on angels and continues to shape beliefs and devotional practices within the Catholic Church and beyond.

Gregory the Great was officially recognized as a Doctor of the Church in 1298. His theological works, particularly his writings on moral theology and pastoral care, were highly regarded for their depth, clarity, and practical guidance. His influence extended far beyond his own era, shaping theological thought and pastoral practices for many generations to come.

GREGORY VII

BORN: c. 1015, Sovana, Papal States

DIED: May 25, 1085, Salerno, Principality of Salerno

FEAST DAY: May 25

PATRONAGE: Reformers

SYMBOLS AND ATTRIBUTES: Papal tiara, keys

St. Gregory VII, also known as Pope Gregory VII, was a prominent figure in the history of the Catholic Church. He was born Hildebrand of Sovana around the year 1015 and served as pope from 1073 until his death in 1085.

Gregory VII played a crucial role in the Investiture Controversy, a conflict between the papacy and secular rulers, particularly the Holy Roman Emperor, over the appointment of bishops and the control of Church offices.

One of Gregory VII's most significant acts was the issuance of the *Dictatus papae*, a set of decrees that asserted papal supremacy and outlined the powers and privileges of the pope. This document declared that the pope had the authority to depose secular rulers and that the pope himself could not be judged by anyone. Reactions by the nobility to this decree were not kind.

Gregory VII's reforms also aimed to eliminate simony (the buying and selling of Church offices) and clerical marriage, and to establish a rule of celibacy for priests. Before Gregory VII's reforms, clerical celibacy was not universally enforced or strictly adhered to within the Church, but he believed that it was essential for the clergy's spiritual purity and moral authority. He argued that married priests were prone to worldly concerns and divided loyalties, compromising their ability to serve the Church effectively. He saw clerical marriage as a source of corruption and a hindrance to the spiritual mission of the priesthood.

In 1074, Pope Gregory VII issued a decree explicitly forbidding the marriage of priests and demanding that all clergy members uphold the vow of celibacy. To enforce this decree, Gregory VII implemented strict measures against clerics who violated the rule. He insisted that married priests should either divorce their wives or live chastely. He also sought to remove bishops who did not adhere to the celibacy requirement and replace them with individuals who would uphold the reforms.

Gregory VII's stance on celibacy faced significant resistance and opposition, particularly from married clergy members and secular rulers who saw the marriage of priests as a way to secure alliances and control Church appointments.

While Gregory VII's efforts to enforce this edict were not entirely successful during his pontificate, his actions laid the foundation for the implementation of mandatory celibacy rules that still exist in the Catholic Church today.

H

HELENA

BORN: c. 246–250, Drepanum, Bithynia
DIED: c. 330, Nicomedia, Bithynia
FEAST DAY: August 18

PATRONAGE: Archeologists, converts, difficult marriages
SYMBOLS AND ATTRIBUTES: Cross, nails

St. Helena, often referred to as St. Helen, was the mother of Constantine the Great, the first Christian emperor of the Roman Empire.

Believed to have been born in Drepanum, Bithynia (present-day Turkey), around 248, tradition holds that Helena was the daughter of an innkeeper named Ariston. Later in life, she married the Roman soldier Constantius Chlorus and bore a son, Constantine.

As Constantius Chlorus rose to the position of caesar of the Roman Empire, he divorced Helena to marry the stepdaughter of co-emperor Maximian. Nevertheless, Helena and Constantine maintained positions at the imperial court in Trier, Germany.

While it's unclear when Helena converted, it is generally believed that she embraced the faith upon Constantine's proclamation of the Edict of Milan in 313, which legalized Christianity across the Roman Empire. Subsequently, she became an ardent supporter of the Church and a champion of Christian values.

Between 326 and 328, Helena undertook a pilgrimage to the Holy Land. During this journey, she was said to have discovered the True Cross, believed to be the cross on which Jesus was crucified. Assisted by a man named Judas, she reportedly unearthed three crosses at excavation sites in Jerusalem. To determine which was the True Cross, a leper touched each one. The third cross, which miraculously healed the leper, was deemed to be the True Cross. Fragments of it were then sent to various churches throughout the Roman Empire.

Helena's architectural legacy includes the commissioning of two pivotal churches in Palestine: the Church of the Nativity in Bethlehem and the Church of the Holy Sepulchre in Jerusalem. They were erected on the traditional sites of Jesus's birth and resurrection.

Her travels and archeological work marked a significant transition in Christian history, showcasing the evolution of Christianity from a persecuted faith to the empire's official religion under Constantine, setting a precedent for future Christian pilgrimages to the Holy Land.

Helena serves as the patron saint for a variety of groups, including archeologists, empresses, and people experiencing troubled marriages. Notably, she is also considered the patron saint of Colchester, England, believed to have been the location where she founded a church. She is frequently portrayed holding a cross, symbolizing her discovery of the True Cross. (See Constantine the Great.)

HENRY II

BORN: 973, Bavaria
DIED: July 13, 1024, Göttingen, Germany
FEAST DAY: July 13

PATRONAGE: Childless people, the handicapped, those rejected from religious orders
SYMBOLS AND ATTRIBUTES: Crown, scepter

Henry II, also known as Henry II of Bavaria, was the Holy Roman Emperor in the early eleventh century and holds the distinction of being the last emperor from the Ottonian dynasty, a Saxon family of German monarchs and nobility.

The son of Duke Henry the Quarrelsome and Gisela of Burgundy, Henry's early years were marked by the challenges of his father's exile. From these tumultuous beginnings, he emerged as a powerful and influential ruler. In 1002, he was elected and subsequently crowned the king of Germany. A mere two years later, in 1004, he achieved the title of king of Italy. His crowning glory came in 1014 when Pope Benedict VIII officially named him the Holy Roman Emperor.

Even as he navigated the complex world of politics, Henry II was a deeply spiritual man. From a young age, he aspired to join the Benedictine order as a monk. However, his noble birth and subsequent royal duties prevented him from pursuing this monastic dream (though in later years he would become an oblate, a special designation for a life dedicated to God). Instead, he channeled his piety into spearheading various ecclesiastical reforms and fostering religious foundations.

Traditionally, it's believed that Henry II and his wife, Cunigunde of Luxembourg, chose to live their marital life in chastity. This remarkable commitment to faith led both of them to be canonized, marking them as one of the rare married couple saints in the Catholic Church. Henry II was canonized in 1146 by Pope Eugene III, while Cunigunde received this honor in 1200. His legacy is further solidified by being the only German monarch to achieve canonization. The Church commemorates his life and contributions on July 13, marking his feast day.

HILARION

BORN: c. 291, Thabatha, Gaza
DIED: c. 371, Cyprus
FEAST DAY: October 21

PATRONAGE: Mystics
SYMBOLS AND ATTRIBUTES: Monk with cross

St. Hilarion, also known as St. Hilarion the Great, was an early Christian monk and ascetic who lived in the fourth century. He is considered one of the pioneers of monasticism in the Christian tradition.

Born around 291 in Thabatha, a village in the present-day Gaza Strip, Hilarion was of pagan background. However, after encountering a Christian teacher, he embraced the Christian faith and dedicated his life to pursuing spiritual perfection.

He spent much of his life in the wilderness, seeking communion with God through prayer, fasting, and physical mortification. He became known for his wisdom and spiritual insight as well as for his miracles, including healing the sick and driving out demons. As his reputation as a holy man grew, he attracted many followers.

Hilarion's teachings and example significantly impacted the development of monasticism in the Eastern Christian tradition. He emphasized the importance of renouncing worldly possessions and desires, advocating for a life of prayer, contemplation, and detachment from material concerns.

Hilarion died around 371 in Cyprus, where he had established a monastery. His life and teachings inspired many subsequent generations of monks and ascetics, and he is venerated as a saint in the Eastern Orthodox Church, the Oriental Orthodox Churches, and the Roman Catholic Church.

HILARY OF POITIERS

BORN: c. 300, Poitiers, France

DIED: c. 368, Poitiers, France

FEAST DAY: January 13

PATRONAGE: Against snake bites, lawyers

SYMBOLS AND ATTRIBUTES: Bishop holding a book

St. Hilary of Poitiers, also known as the Hammer of the Arians, was a bishop who influenced the further development of the Catholic Church in the fourth century. He was celebrated for his theological writings, defense of the doctrine of the Holy Trinity, and opposition to Arianism, a heretical doctrine that denied the divinity of Christ.

Hilary was born into a wealthy and noble family in France around 300, and was educated in rhetoric and philosophy. A pagan, Hilary was drawn to Christianity later in life. He converted and became a leading figure in the Church. He was ordained as the bishop of Poitiers around 353.

Hilary was a prolific writer, and his works influenced the development of Christian theology. Many of his writings focused on combating Arian heresy and defending the doctrine of the Holy Trinity. The Arians were a group of Christians who followed the teachings of Arius, a presbyter from Alexandria. Arius propagated the belief that Jesus Christ was not co-eternal and consubstantial with God the Father but rather a created being of lesser status. Hilary wrote extensively in response to this controversy to refute the Arians' claims and affirm the orthodox understanding of the Holy Trinity.

During the Synod of Béziers in 356, which was held in what is now France, Hilary staunchly defended the orthodox position. However, the Arian bishops who dominated the council had the support of the imperial authorities, and their Arian-influenced creed was adopted.

Hilary refused to support the creed and continued to advocate for the orthodox faith. His unyielding stance against Arianism and refusal to accept the council's decisions led to his condemnation. He was ordered into exile by Emperor Constantius II, who expelled Hilary from his bishopric in Poitiers and banished him to Phrygia, a region in Asia Minor (modern-day Turkey).

During his exile, Hilary wrote his notable treatise *Ad Constantium Augustum* (To Emperor Constantius), in which he criticized the Arian policies of the emperor. His best-known work is *De Trinitate* (On the Trinity), in which he presents a comprehensive defense of the doctrine of the Trinity, affirming the belief in one God who exists in three persons: Father, Son (Jesus Christ), and Holy Spirit.

In *De Trinitate*, Hilary emphasized the unity, equality, and eternal nature of the three divine persons, employing philosophical arguments, Biblical exegesis, and logical reasoning to counter heretical assertions and highlight the divinity of Jesus Christ. His writings significantly contributed to the development of Trinitarian theology in the Western Church, providing a solid foundation for future theologians.

After Emperor Constantius II's death in 361, Hilary was allowed to return to his diocese in Poitiers. Hilary died around 368 and was named a Doctor of the Church by Pope Pius IX in 1851. He is often depicted in art with a white beard and wearing his bishop's vestments.

HILDEGARD OF BINGEN

BORN: September 16, 1098, Bermersheim vor der Höhe, Holy Roman Empire

DIED: September 17, 1179, Bingen am Rhein, Holy Roman Empire

FEAST DAY: September 17

PATRONAGE: Musicians, writers, receivers of visions

SYMBOLS AND ATTRIBUTES: Quill, book

Hildegard of Bingen, also known as St. Hildegard or Hildegard von Bingen, was a polymath who excelled as a composer, writer, mystic, herbalist, scientist, and abbess. She was born into a noble family in 1098 in Bermersheim, Germany. At the age of eight, she entered the Disibodenberg monastery under the guidance of Jutta von Sponheim, an anchoress. Jutta's spiritual teachings influenced Hildegard, fostering her devotion to God and providing a strong foundation for her future spiritual and intellectual endeavors.

One of the most distinguishing aspects of Hildegard's life was her visionary experiences. She claimed to have received divine revelations from a young age, which she kept secret. It was not until her forties, after experiencing many visions, that she felt compelled to share her insights with others. Hildegard recorded her visions in several volumes, most notably in *Scivias* (Know the Ways of the Lord). This seminal work explored theological concepts regarding the relationship between God, humanity, and the universe. *Scivias* contained text as well as illuminations, which showcased Hildegard's artistic talent. Her visionary experiences were described in two other significant works, *Liber vitae meritorum* (Book of Life's Merits) and *Liber divinorum operum* (Book of Divine Works).

One specific mystical experience that Hildegard of Bingen describes in her work is the vision of the "Living Light." Hildegard describes encountering a luminous, vibrant light that surpasses all earthly brilliance, radiating God's spirit and wisdom. In this mystical experience, the light fills her entire being, and she becomes enveloped in its radiant presence. Hildegard describes receiving divine illumination and understanding through this mystical encounter, including insights into the interconnectedness of all creation, the divine order of the universe, and the mysteries of God's plan. This vision deepened her understanding of theology, cosmology, and the nature of the sacred.

Hildegard's musical talent and compositions hold a special place in her vast creative repertoire. She composed many liturgical songs, known as antiphons, which were performed during religious ceremonies. These compositions revealed her innovative use of melodic lines and harmonies, often accompanied by lyrical texts that reflected her visionary experiences. Her music, marked by its ethereal and haunting beauty, is considered an important contribution to medieval music.

Beyond her spiritual and artistic pursuits, Hildegard exhibited remarkable scientific and medical knowledge, unusual for her time. She wrote extensively on natural history, medicinal plants, and the treatment of various ailments. Her work *Physica* (Natural Science) served as a comprehensive guide to the natural world, describing the healing properties of more than 200 plants. In *Causae et curae* (Causes and Cures), she explored the causes and treatments of diseases, providing a holistic approach to health care.

Hildegard's influence extended beyond her intellectual pursuits. In 1136, she founded and served the Rupertsberg monastery and the Eibingen monastery as abbess. Responsible for her communities' spiritual and administrative affairs, she implemented reforms emphasizing the importance of education, music, and the arts in monastic life. Her leadership elevated women's status and learning during a time when opportunities for women were severely limited.

Hildegard's impact during her lifetime was considerable, and her legacy flourished after her death in 1179. Her teachings and writings attracted a wide following, and her musical compositions remained influential in the centuries that followed. However, it was not until 2012, over eight centuries after her passing, that Hildegard of Bingen was officially canonized as a saint by Pope Benedict XVI. This recognition solidified her position as a spiritual and intellectual luminary, highlighting her enduring significance to the Catholic Church and the world at large. At her canonization she was declared a Doctor of the Church, the fourth woman to hold that honor.

HIPPOLYTUS OF ROME

BORN: c. 170, Rome, Italy

DIED: c. 236, Sardinia

FEAST DAY: August 13

PATRONAGE: Horses

SYMBOLS AND ATTRIBUTES: Horse, book, palm branch

St. Hippolytus of Rome was a prominent Christian theologian, scholar, and martyr who lived primarily in the third century. He was instrumental in the early development of Christian theology and is regarded as one of the most important figures of his time.

Hippolytus was born in Rome, Italy, during the late second century, possibly around 170, becoming a leading figure in the Christian community of Rome. He opposed the teachings of certain heretical groups, most notably the Monarchians, who challenged the relationship between God the Father and God the Son. These conflicts and theological disagreements shaped a significant portion of Hippolytus's life and works.

Hippolytus authored numerous theological treatises and writings, greatly influencing early Christian thought development. His most famous work is *Refutation of All Heresies* (also known as *Philosophumena*), a comprehensive critique of various heterodoxies of his time. This work provided valuable insights into the beliefs and practices of different religious groups during the second and third centuries. Eventually, Pope Callixtus I, whose views Hippolytus opposed, condemned and excommunicated him from the Church. As a result, Hippolytus established his own community and was consecrated as an alternative bishop of Rome, thus becoming an antipope. This schism was resolved when Pontian, the succeeding pope, reconciled with Hippolytus.

In 235, during the reign of Emperor Maximinus Thrax, Hippolytus, along with Pope Pontian and other Christians, was arrested for his beliefs and exiled to the mines of Sardinia. There, he endured harsh conditions until he died a martyr's death. His writings continue to be studied by theologians and historians to this day, providing valuable insights into the early development of Christianity.

I

IGNATIUS OF ANTIOCH

BORN: c. 35 AD, Syria

DIED: c. 108, Rome, Italy

FEAST DAY: October 17

PATRONAGE: Church in the East, throat diseases

SYMBOLS AND ATTRIBUTES: Lions, chains

Ignatius of Antioch was a theologian and martyr who was born around 35 AD. He became the third bishop of Antioch, a prominent Christian center in ancient Syria, now present-day Turkey. He is also considered an Apostolic Father, a group of early Christian leaders who had direct connections to the apostles and were integral to the development of Christian doctrine and the organization of the Church.

Ignatius is revered for his writings, particularly seven letters, which provide valuable insights into early Christian theology, church organization, and spirituality. Written during his journey from Antioch to Rome, where he faced martyrdom, the letters offer a glimpse into the challenges and beliefs of the early Christian community.

Ignatius's life and writings are closely tied to the persecution of Christians under the Roman Empire. Around 107, during the reign of Emperor Trajan, Ignatius was arrested and taken to Rome for trial. While the exact reason for his arrest is unclear, it was likely his refusal to renounce his Christian faith and his influence as a bishop that led to his persecution.

During his journey to Rome, Ignatius wrote letters to seven Christian communities that served as encouragement and exhortation and emphasized the importance of unity and obedience to the bishops. These seven missives are valuable as a historical record that offers insights into early Christian beliefs, practices, and the Church's organizational structure. They also reflect Ignatius's deep commitment to the Christian faith and willingness to sacrifice his life for Christ.

The first letter, addressed to the Ephesians, emphasizes unity among believers, obedience to the bishop, and the central role of Jesus Christ in the life of the Church. In his letter to the Magnesians, Ignatius urges the Christians in Magnesia to remain united and avoid false teachings. He emphasizes the significance of the Eucharist and warns against divisions within the Church. The letter to the Trallians addressed to the Christians in Tralles again stresses the importance of unity and obedience to the bishop. Ignatius warns against heresy and emphasizes the reality of Jesus's Incarnation and suffering. In the letter to the Romans, Ignatius expresses his desire to die for Christ and urges the Roman Christians not to intervene on his behalf. In the letter to the Philadelphians, Ignatius emphasizes the importance of love, unity, and obedience in the Church. He encourages the Philadelphians to support their bishop and warns against false teachers. The letter to the Smyrnaeans commends the Christians in Smyrna for their faith and encourages them to remain steadfast. Ignatius warns against the teachings of certain heretical groups. And finally, in the letter to Polycarp, a fellow bishop and future notable figure in the early Church, Ignatius advises Polycarp on various matters related to the Christian faith, emphasizing unity and obedience.

Some accounts report that upon his arrival in Rome Ignatius was thrown to wild beasts in the Colosseum for Roman entertainment. The exact date of his martyrdom is uncertain, but it is believed to have occurred around 108.(See Polycarp.)

IGNATIUS OF LOYOLA

BORN: 1491, Basque Region of Spain
DIED: July 31, 1556, Rome, Italy
FEAST DAY: July 31

PATRONAGE: Society of Jesus (Jesuits), retreats, soldiers
SYMBOLS AND ATTRIBUTES: Christogram IHS, book with *Ad majorem Dei gloriam*

Born in 1491 to a family of nobles in the Basque region of Northern Spain known as Loyola, Ignatius spent his early years dreaming of becoming a warrior. Enchanted by tales of courtly love and heroic deeds, Ignatius trained as a soldier in the hopes of becoming a knight. He fought valiantly in the Battle of Pamplona in 1521. However, during a siege, he was struck by a cannonball that shattered his leg.

Thirty years old at the time, Ignatius returned to his father's castle in Loyola, broken in body and spirit. While convalescing, bored and depressed, Ignatius requested books on chivalry and romance to be brought to him. None were to be found in the family library. A family member offered him other reading material, including books on the life of Christ and the saints. Reluctant, but with nothing else to do, Ignatius began to read. Ignatius was so captivated by these stories of mystics and miracles, Jesus and his disciples, and humble mendicants like St. Francis, he found himself no longer enchanted by stories of knights in armor and damsels in distress. He experienced a conversion and vowed that once his health improved, he would make a pilgrimage to the Holy Land to honor God.

Ignatius did recover from his injury but would walk with a limp for the rest of his life. In 1523, he kept his promise; against many odds, he made it to Jerusalem, where he spent time with the Franciscans. Because he was uneducated in the basics of theology and Latin, the monks sent Ignatius back to Spain, where he enrolled in a grammar school with students twenty years younger. During this time, he began writing what would come to be known as *Spiritual Exercises*, a guide for finding God in all things. The *Exercises* is a four-week program to strengthen one's faith through daily prayer, reflection, and contemplation; it is a regime designed to help retreatants develop greater spiritual strength, increased courage, deeper love for God, self, and others, and a more acute sense of justice.

In 1539, Ignatius formed the Society of Jesus, otherwise known as the Jesuits, with his friends Francis Xavier and Peter Faber. In 1540, a significant milestone for the Society of Jesus was reached when Pope Paul III formally endorsed and approved the order with the papal bull *Regimini militantis Ecclesiae*. This official recognition from the Vatican set the stage for the Jesuits' expansive outreach in the years to come. As the founder and guide for this fledgling order, Ignatius dedicated himself between 1547 and 1550 to crafting the Constitutions of the Society of Jesus. This pivotal document outlined the governance, mission, and procedures of the Jesuit order, emphasizing its commitments to education, missionary work, and unwavering service to the Church.

Under Ignatius's leadership, the Jesuits wasted no time making their mark across Europe and beyond. They laid the foundations of numerous colleges and universities, including the esteemed Roman College in 1551, which evolved into the Pontifical Gregorian University. As the Society's scholastic footprint grew, so too did its missionary ambitions. Jesuits were dispatched to various corners of the world, from the heart of Asia and the depths of Africa to the newfound lands of the Americas, reflecting the global vision Ignatius held for the order.

While the *Spiritual Exercises* were initially penned by Ignatius as a personal reflection, they soon became a cornerstone of Jesuit formation. Central to the novitiate training of the Society, the *Exercises* sculpted the unique Jesuit approach to spirituality, mission, and ministry, fostering a deep, contemplative relationship with God.

However, the rapid ascent of the Jesuits was not without its challenges. Their growing influence led to tensions both within the Church, particularly as regarded other religious orders, and with local church authorities. Yet, it was precisely this influence and zeal that positioned the Jesuits at the forefront of the Counter-Reformation. As the Catholic Church grappled with the seismic shifts of the Protestant Reformation, the Jesuits became instrumental in re-evangelizing parts of Europe that had veered toward Protestant beliefs.

Ignatius's later years were marked by his continued guidance of the society. Through letters and instructions to Jesuits on distant missions, he provided insight into his vision for the society's direction, leaving behind a trove of historical and spiritual documents that, coupled with the foundational structures he established for the Jesuits, ensured that his impact would continue to resonate long after his passing.

Ignatius died in Rome on July 31, 1556, and was canonized as a saint by Pope Gregory XV in 1622. His motto *Ad majorem Dei gloriam*, "for the greater glory of God," is the guiding principle of the Jesuits, who look to meet people where they are, and honor and serve others regardless of who they are or what they believe. They are known for the numerous educational institutions they established around the world, including Georgetown University, Boston College, and John Carroll University in the United States.

Jesuits and Jesuit education have contributed to significant advancements in social and physical sciences. German Jesuit Athanasius Kircher (1602–1680) has been hailed as the father of Egyptology. Catholic priest Georges Lemaître (1894–1966), a theoretical physicist and a contemporary of Albert Einstein, studied at the College du Sacré-Cœur, a Jesuit secondary school, and would go on to help develop what would come to be called the big bang theory in the 1930s. Paleontologist Pierre Teilhard Chardin, SJ (1881–1955) wrote extensively on evolution in the early twentieth century. Astronomer Brother Guy J. Consolmagno, SJ (1952–), director of the Vatican Observatory, is a recent recipient of the Carl Sagan Award for his work in planetary science.

In 2013, Jorge Bergoglio, the archbishop of Buenos Aires, took the name of Francis, the saint who inspired Ignatius 500 years prior, and became the first Jesuit pope in the history of the Catholic Church.

IRENAEUS

BORN: c. 130, Smyrna, Asia Minor
DIED: c. 202, Lugdunum, Gaul
FEAST DAY: June 28

PATRONAGE: Apologists and catechists
SYMBOLS AND ATTRIBUTES: Bishop holding a book

St. Irenaeus, also known as St. Irenaeus of Lyons, was a second-century Christian bishop and theologian who was instrumental in the development of early Christian thought. Born in Smyrna (present-day Izmir, Turkey) in the early second century, Irenaeus eventually became the bishop of Lyons, a city in present-day France. He is remembered for his defense of orthodox Christian teachings against various heresies and for his contributions to the development of Christian theology and doctrine.

Very little is known about Irenaeus's early life, but he is believed to have been a disciple of St. Polycarp, who was himself a disciple of St. John the Apostle. Irenaeus may have also been familiar with St. Ignatius of Antioch, another prominent Christian bishop of the time. After serving as a presbyter (priest) in Smyrna, Irenaeus was sent to Gaul (present-day France) to serve as a missionary. He eventually settled in Lyons, where he was elected bishop around 177.

During his time there, Irenaeus wrote extensively on Christian doctrine and theology. His most famous work is *Against Heresies*. Written around the year 180, the work consists of five books in which Irenaeus refutes various theological errors threatening to undermine orthodox Christian teachings. The writings are mainly concerned with the heretical movement known as Gnosticism, which claimed to possess secret knowledge of the Divine.

In *Against Heresies*, Irenaeus argues that Christian teachings are public and accessible to all, and that the authority of the Christian Scriptures and the teachings of the apostles are the only reliable sources of knowledge about God. He insists that the Gnostics, with their claims of secret knowledge, lead people astray and endanger their salvation.

In addition to his refutation of heresies, Irenaeus also provides a systematic defense of orthodox Christian doctrine and theology. He emphasizes that all Christians should be united in their beliefs and practices. He also defends the doctrine of the Trinity, which holds that God is one being in three persons, against various heretical interpretations.

Irenaeus was also known for his pastoral work, particularly his care for the poor and the sick. He was respected by his fellow Christians, both in Lyons and beyond, and was widely regarded as a saint even during his lifetime.

St. Irenaeus is often depicted in Christian art holding a book, representing his writings and his defense of orthodox Christian teachings. He may also be shown holding a sword, representing his role as a defender of the faith. (See Polycarp, John the Apostle, Ignatius of Antioch.)

IRENE OF ROME

BORN: 3rd century, Rome, Italy
DIED: 288, Rome, Italy
FEAST DAY: April 3

PATRONAGE: Girls and young women, peace
SYMBOLS AND ATTRIBUTES: Palm branch, caring for St. Sebastian

Irene was a devoted Christian woman known for her compassionate acts during the Diocletian persecution. According to Christian legend, after St. Sebastian was shot with arrows and left for dead because of his faith, Irene discovered him and nursed him back to health. This story has come to symbolize the depth of compassion and support within the early Christian community.

Throughout history, the poignant tale of Irene tending to St. Sebastian's wounds has been a popular subject for artists. One notable example is Benedetto Luti, an Italian painter of the late Baroque period. Luti created several evocative paintings focusing on this theme. His depictions capture the compassion and unwavering devotion of Irene, delving deep into the emotional connection between the two saints. (See Sebastian.)

ISAAC JOGUES

BORN: January 10, 1607, Orléans, France

DIED: October 18, 1646, Ossernenon, New France

FEAST DAY: October 19

PATRONAGE: Americas, Canada

SYMBOLS AND ATTRIBUTES: Tomahawk

St. Isaac Jogues was a French Jesuit missionary who lived during the seventeenth century. He is primarily known for his missionary work among the Indigenous tribes in North America.

He was born on January 10, 1607, in Orléans, France, and entered the Society of Jesus (Jesuits) in 1624. He was ordained as a priest in 1636. Shortly after his ordination, he expressed his desire to go on a mission to New France, encompassing parts of present-day Canada and the northeastern United States. In 1636, Isaac sailed to Quebec, where he was sent to work among the Huron people. He dedicated himself to learning their language and understanding their culture, knowing that he would be more effective in spreading Christianity if he understood their ways. He soon gained their respect and trust.

Isaac faced many challenges and hardships during his missionary work. The Huron people faced frequent attacks and raids from the Iroquois, who were hostile to the French and to their Christian teachings. In 1642, Isaac and his companions were captured by the Iroquois and tortured. During his captivity, Isaac's fingers were mutilated, and he witnessed the martyrdom of his fellow Jesuit and companion, René Goupil.

After spending over a year in captivity, Isaac managed to escape with the help of Dutch traders who ransomed him. He returned to France in 1644, where he was hailed as a hero and a martyr.

Not long after, Isaac expressed a strong desire to return to the mission field. In 1646, he sailed back to New France and continued his missionary work among the Huron people. However, later that year, he was captured by a Mohawk party and tortured yet again. On October 18, 1646, Isaac was martyred near present-day Auriesville, New York.

Isaac Jogues was canonized in 1930. He is revered as one of the North American Martyrs, a group of eight Jesuit missionaries who were killed in the seventeenth century while spreading Christianity among the Indigenous tribes. His feast day is celebrated on October 19 with the other North American Martyrs. (See René Goupil.)

ISIDORE OF SEVILLE

BORN: c. 560, Cartagena, Spain

DIED: April 4, 636, Seville, Spain

FEAST DAY: April 4

PATRONAGE: Internet, computer users, students

SYMBOLS AND ATTRIBUTES: Beehive, book

Also known as Isidore the Great, St. Isidore of Seville was a prominent figure in early Christian history and a scholar. Born around 560 in Cartagena, Spain, he hailed from a prominent family of Visigothic descent. Isidore received an exceptional education from his elder brother, who served as the bishop of Seville. Following his brother's footsteps, he was ordained as a priest and succeeded him as the bishop of Seville in the year 600, a position he held until his death in 636.

Isidore is best known for his magnum opus, the *Etymologiae* (also known as Origines or Origins). This ambitious encyclopedic work, consisting of twenty books, aimed to compile and systematize all knowledge of the time, drawing from a vast range of sources, including the Bible, classical literature, and various theological and secular texts. The *Etymologiae* covered diverse subjects such as grammar, rhetoric, mathematics, theology, philosophy, natural sciences, and even topics like clothing, agriculture, and medicine. Its comprehensive nature and scholarly rigor made it an invaluable resource for centuries to come, shaping the intellectual landscape of medieval Europe.

Etymology is central to the *Etymologiae*, as Isidore believed that the study of word origins could reveal hidden meanings and provide a deeper understanding of concepts. He traces the histories of numerous words, exploring their linguistic roots and often associating them with moral or theological significance. Isidore's etymological explanations, however, can sometimes be fanciful or speculative, reflecting the influence of his sources and the medieval mindset.

The *Etymologiae* quickly gained popularity in the medieval period. Its encyclopedic nature and comprehensive coverage made it a valuable resource for scholars and students across Europe. Moreover, the *Etymologiae* was significant in preserving and sharing ancient texts and ideas during a time when access to classical works was limited, and its wide-ranging influence was acknowledged by luminaries like Dante, Geoffrey Chaucer, Boccaccio, and Petrarch.

Isidore was a vital promoter of education at the time, founding schools in and around Seville in an effort to make learning accessible to clergy and laity alike. He also championed the study of liberal arts, stressing the importance of a worldview that balanced classical learning with spiritual and historical insights.

Recognized for his exceptional visionary thinking, Isidore is venerated as the patron saint of the Internet, computer users, and students. His feast day, celebrated on April 4, commemorates his legacy and his enduring impact on Christian scholarship.

ISIDORE THE FARMER

BORN: c. 1070, Madrid, Kingdom of Castile

DIED: May 15, 1130, Madrid, Kingdom of Castile

FEAST DAY: May 15

PATRONAGE: Farmers, laborers

SYMBOLS AND ATTRIBUTES: Plough, angel, corn, sickle, spade

St. Isidore the Farmer, also known as St. Isidore the Laborer or San Isidro Labrador, is a Spanish Roman Catholic saint who lived during the eleventh century. He is considered the patron saint of farmers, agricultural workers, and rural communities. Isidore was born into a poor but devoutly Christian family around 1070 in Madrid, Spain. He worked as a laborer on the estate of a wealthy landowner and was known to rise early every morning to attend Mass before beginning his day's work in the fields. No matter what he was doing, he maintained a solid commitment to prayer, often praying while working the land.

Numerous miraculous events are associated with Isidore's life. According to legend, angels would assist him with his work so that he could pray while plowing the fields. On one occasion, his fellow workers complained to their employer, claiming that he spent too much time in prayer. However, when the employer investigated, he witnessed angels helping Isidore plow the field, leaving no doubt about his holiness.

Another story tells of Isidore's miraculous multiplication of food to feed the poor. It is said that on numerous occasions, Isidore would give away his own food to the hungry, and miraculously, the supply would replenish itself. These acts of charity and his unwavering devotion to God endeared him to those around him.

Isidore passed away on May 15, 1130, in Madrid. His reputation for holiness multiplied after his death, and numerous miracles were attributed to his intercession.

Isidore is especially revered in Spain and throughout the Spanish-speaking world, where he is seen as a model of hard work, humility, and devotion to God. Farmers often seek his intercession for bountiful harvests, protection from natural disasters, and guidance in their work. His feast day, which is May 15, is celebrated with various agricultural and religious festivities, particularly in Spain.

ITA

BORN: c. 480, County Waterford, Ireland

DIED: c. 570, Killeedy, Ireland

FEAST DAY: January 15

PATRONAGE: Killeedy

SYMBOLS AND ATTRIBUTES: Book, model of a church, roses

St. Ita, also known as Íte of Killeedy, was a sixth-century Irish nun, one of the early female saints of Ireland. She is often called the Foster Mother of the Irish Saints for educating and nurturing many future saints and religious figures.

Born in 480 in County Waterford, she decided at a young age to forgo marriage and live a life of celibacy and spiritual pursuits. Ita opened a school for boys where the young man who would become St. Brendan was educated. She also founded a community of nuns in Limerick, where she became affectionately known as the Brigid of Munster, a reference to the renowned St. Brigid of Ireland.

Legends and stories abound. One of the most famous involved a donkey who was used to transport milk for the nuns in Ita's monastery. One tale recounts how this beloved animal was once attacked in Tournafulla by local hooligans, leading to Ita's curse on the area, which came to be known as the "field of blood." Another tale speaks of Ita removing a thorn from a donkey's hoof. The plucked thorn fell to the ground, and a tree grew in its place. Ita's compassion extended beyond animals to insects. She allowed a large stag beetle to suckle at her side despite the beetle causing her harm. When the nuns at Killeedy killed the beetle, Ita missed her blood-sucking companion and prayed to God to appease her loneliness. In answer to her prayers, God sent the infant Christ to her to care for and foster.

St. Ita is remembered for her teachings, notably the listing of three things loved by God (true faith, a pure heart, and charity) and the three things disliked by the Almighty (a scowling face, stubbornness in wrongdoing, and excessive reliance on wealth). Her influence on early Irish Christianity and her steadfast commitment to a virtuous way of life continue to inspire, emphasizing the enduring power of faith, humility, and compassion.

J

JAMES THE APOSTLE

BORN: c. 5 BC, Galilee

DIED: 44 AD, Jerusalem

FEAST DAY: July 25

PATRONAGE: Spain, pilgrims, veterinarians

SYMBOLS AND ATTRIBUTES: Scallop shell, pilgrim hat or cloak

St. James the Apostle, commonly known as St. James the Greater, was one of Jesus Christ's twelve apostles. He was the son of Zebedee and Salome and was the elder brother of St. John the Evangelist.

Along with Peter and John, James was part of an inner circle that bore witness to significant events in Jesus's life, including the Transfiguration, the agony of Jesus in the Garden of Gethsemane, the raising of Jairus's daughter, and the Mount of Olives discourse.

James's legacy holds immense significance in Christian tradition. According to the Book of Acts, he was the first apostle to be martyred when he was beheaded under the reign of King Herod Agrippa I. His feast day, commemorated on July 25, is believed to mark the day of his martyrdom.

James's legacy is intricately woven into the cultural and religious tapestry of Spain. As the country's patron saint, tradition holds that he preached the Gospel there while journeying through the land. The route he is said to have traversed, now known as the Camino de Santiago or the Way of St. James, has become a renowned pilgrimage path. Each year, it attracts hundreds of thousands of pilgrims. His remains are traditionally believed to be housed in the Cathedral of Santiago de Compostela, constructed in the eleventh century, making it a focal point of pilgrimage. Works such as the *Codex Calixtinus*, a twelfth-century guidebook for pilgrims to Santiago de Compostela, attest to his influential legacy. Various artworks, like paintings, sculptures, and stained glass windows, celebrate his life and martyrdom. One iconic depiction is a statue in the Cathedral of Santiago de Compostela portraying St. James as a pilgrim. St, James's significance endures today, reflected in Brazilian writer Paulo Coelho's 1987 novel *The Pilgrimage* and Emilio Estevez's 2010 motion picture *The Way*, which portrays a father's poignant journey along the Camino after his son's tragic death.

In addition to his historical impact, several miracles are attributed to St. James. One famous tale involves his confrontation with Hermogenes, a magician in Jerusalem. As the story goes, Hermogenes showcased his magical prowess, summoning demons and darkening skies to gain followers. Challenged by the magician, St. James displayed divine power, dispersing the demons and illuminating the skies with a radiant light. Hermogenes eventually sought St. James's healing after being struck blind, leading to his conversion. This story, among others, solidified St. James's stature as a formidable saint in Christian lore.

Symbols associated with St. James include a pilgrim's cloak and a scallop, symbolic of those journeying on the Camino.

JAMES THE LESS

BORN: c. early 1st century AD, Galilee

DIED: c. 62 AD, Ostrakine (Egypt)

FEAST DAY: May 3

PATRONAGE: Pharmacists, hat makers

SYMBOLS AND ATTRIBUTES: Fuller's club

St. James the Less, also known as St. James the Lesser, is recognized as one of Jesus's earliest followers. He is often listed among the twelve apostles in the New Testament, as seen in Matthew 10:3, Mark 3:18, Luke 6:15, and Acts 1:13. While he holds a place of significance among Jesus's disciples, the New Testament doesn't provide as extensive an account of him as it does for some other Apostles, like Peter, John, and James the Greater (the son of Zebedee), though some traditions suggest he served as the first bishop of Jerusalem.

The identification of James the Less has been debated among scholars and theologians. Some posit that he might be the same James mentioned in Mark 15:40, standing near Mary at the crucifixion. Others speculate that he could be the James referred to as the brother of Jesus in Matthew 13:55 and Galatians 1:19. However, it's important to note that the Catholic and Orthodox traditions generally differentiate between James the Less, the Apostle (son of Alphaeus), and James, the brother of Jesus (sometimes known as James the Just). On the other hand, the Protestant tradition often identifies them as one and the same.

Regardless of these complexities, James the Less's legacy is celebrated on his feast day, May 3. In art, he is frequently depicted holding a fuller's club, a nod to the tradition that he was martyred by being beaten with such a tool.

JANE FRANCES DE CHANTAL

BORN: January 28, 1572, Dijon, France
DIED: December 13, 1641, Moulins, France
FEAST DAY: August 12

PATRONAGE: Forgotten people, troublesome in-laws, parents separated from their children, in-law problems
SYMBOLS AND ATTRIBUTES: Nun's habit, cross, heart with a flame

A French Roman Catholic nun, mystic, and founder of the Order of the Visitation of Holy Mary, St. Jane Frances de Chantal was born to a noble family in Dijon, France, in 1572. Her mother died shortly after Jane's birth, and her father raised her, instilling in her a love for God and a deep sense of devotion.

Jane married a nobleman, Baron de Chantal, at the age of twenty. Her marriage was a happy one, and she devoted herself to caring for her family, assisting her husband's estates, and cultivating her faith. However, tragedy struck when her husband was killed in a hunting accident.

After her husband's death, Jane, now a widow with four children, dedicated herself to serving her family and assisting the less fortunate. Through her father, she met St. Francis de Sales, who became her spiritual director. Together they founded the Order of the Visitation of Holy Mary, also known as the Visitandines. This new religious order welcomed women who discerned that they could not live the difficult and austere life of those in traditional convents. It did, however, emphasize virtues like humility, obedience, poverty, charity, and patience. The order took inspiration from Mary's journey of mercy, depicted in the Catholic Rosary as the Visitation (Mary's visit to her cousin Elizabeth, who was pregnant with John the Baptist). The order's charism was one of gentleness, humility, and charity, and it quickly grew in popularity.

During her lifetime, Jane Frances wrote many letters, which have been compiled into various volumes over the centuries. One of her most famous works is the *Letters of Spiritual Direction*, which contains her correspondence with St. Francis de Sales. In these missives, she reveals her deep spirituality and love for God, her struggles with the challenges of religious life, and her acceptance of suffering as a hallmark of the devout life.

Another notable aspect of Jane Frances's spirituality was her devotion to the Sacred Heart of Jesus. She believed that through devotion to the Sacred Heart, one could cultivate a deep and intimate relationship with Christ and be transformed by his love. This devotion is evident in her letters and prayers and in the symbol of the heart with a flame often associated with her.

Jane Frances de Chantal lived the rest of her life as a nun in the order she founded, serving as its superior until her death on December 13, 1641, at the age of sixty-nine. She was canonized by Pope Clement XIII in 1767 and is venerated as a saint in the Roman Catholic Church. (See Francis de Sales.)

JANUARIUS

BORN: c. 272, Benevento, Italy
DIED: 305, Pozzuoli, Italy
FEAST DAY: September 19

PATRONAGE: Naples, blood banks, volcanic eruptions
SYMBOLS AND ATTRIBUTES: Vial of blood, bishop attire

Also known as San Gennaro, St. Januarius was a bishop and martyr who lived in the third century. He is venerated as a saint in the Catholic Church, Eastern Orthodox Church, and several other Christian denominations.

Januarius is believed to have been born around 272 to a wealthy family in Benevento. He became a priest at a young age. He was ordained as a bishop of Naples during a time when the Roman Empire was in a state of turmoil and the persecution of Christians was prevalent. Aware of the dangers of proclaiming his faith, Januarius continued to preach and evangelize to the people of Naples.

Shortly after his ordination, however, he was arrested by authorities. Unwilling to renounce his faith, he was tortured and imprisoned, and eventually beheaded and martyred in 305. His body was buried in what is now called the Catacombs of San Gennaro in Naples. His relics were moved to the Naples Cathedral, where they remain to this day.

Of these relics, the most famous is a vial of Janaurius's blood. According to the Catholic News Agency, the blood, preserved in two glass ampoules in the Naples Cathedral, traditionally liquefies three times a year. Believed to be a response to the prayers and devotion of the faithful, the dried blood turns into liquid, filling the glass when the miracle occurs. The liquefaction process can take hours or days, and sometimes it doesn't happen at all. The faithful view the failure of the blood to liquefy as an omen of misfortune.

Despite scientific investigations, a satisfactory explanation for this phenomenon has yet to be found. Interestingly, the blood has liquefied in the presence of some popes, including Pope Francis, in 2015. However, it did not liquefy during the visits of Pope John Paul II or Pope Benedict XVI.

In the United States, New York City hosts the San Gennaro festival in Little Italy, which spans several days and features a variety of events and activities, including religious processions, parades, live music, traditional Italian food stands, carnival rides, games, and entertainment.

JEAN DE LALANDE

BORN: c. 1620, Dieppe, France
DIED: October 19, 1646, Ossernenon, New France
FEAST DAY: October 19

PATRONAGE: Missionaries to the Huron people
SYMBOLS AND ATTRIBUTES: Palm branch, cross, tomahawk

Jean de Lalande, one of the North American Martyrs, was a French Jesuit lay brother known for his missionary work in present-day Canada. Compelled by his desire to spread Christianity, he immersed himself in efforts to evangelize the Huron people. His endeavors were met with resistance from the Iroquois, who killed him with a tomahawk blow to the head in autumn 1646. Today, he is remembered as a symbol of faith, dedication, and the formidable challenges encountered by early Jesuit missionaries in North America.

JEANNE JUGAN

BORN: October 25, 1792, Cancale, France
DIED: August 29, 1879, Saint-Pern, France
FEAST DAY: August 30

PATRONAGE: Elderly, poor
SYMBOLS AND ATTRIBUTES: Nun's habit, cross, bread

Also known as Sister Mary of the Cross, St. Jeanne Jugan was born on October 25, 1792, in Cancale, France, and died on August 29, 1879, in Saint-Pern, France. At the age of forty-seven, she encountered an old, blind woman who was homeless and destitute. Jeanne

Jugan took the woman into her own home, giving up her bed and sleeping on the floor to care for her. This act of compassion marked the beginning of her mission to provide care and support for elders.

With the help of other like-minded women, Jeanne Jugan established the Little Sisters of the Poor in 1842 in Saint-Servan, France. The congregation's mission was to offer a loving home and provide care for older adults who were poor and alone, ensuring that they were treated with dignity and respect. The sisters relied on divine providence and the generosity of others to support their work.

Jeanne Jugan's selfless dedication and humility attracted other women to join her cause. The Little Sisters of the Poor grew rapidly, and the congregation spread beyond France, establishing homes for the elderly poor in other countries. Today, the Little Sisters of the Poor continue their mission worldwide.

Jeanne Jugan was beatified by Pope John Paul II on October 3, 1982, and canonized as a saint by Pope Benedict XVI on October 11, 2009. Her life and work inspire many in the field of elder care. She stands as a shining example of the Christian virtue of charity.

JEROME

BORN: c. 347, Stridon, Dalmatia

DIED: September 30, 420, Bethlehem, Judaea

FEAST DAY: September 30

PATRONAGE: Librarians, students, translators, archeologists

SYMBOLS AND ATTRIBUTES: Lion, book, skull

Also known as Jerome of Stridon, St. Jerome was a prominent scholar and theologian. His most significant contribution was his translation of the Bible into Latin, which came to be known as the Vulgate, derived from the Latin word *vulgata*, meaning "common" or "popular." While books were relatively scarce during his lifetime, his translation aimed to make the Bible accessible to a broader audience.

Jerome was born Eusebius Sophronius Hieronymus around 347 in Stridon, a town situated in the Roman province of Dalmatia, which is part of modern-day Slovenia. Although it is unclear whether Jerome's family were Christians, he was baptized as a young adult. In his formative years, Jerome received an excellent education, encompassing studies in grammar, rhetoric, classical literature, and philosophy. He enjoyed extensive travels throughout his life, spending time in Rome and Constantinople. Initially living a life of indulgence and pleasure-seeking, Jerome experienced a profound transformation, leading him to pursue a pious and ascetic lifestyle. He embraced monasticism, and journeyed to the East, ultimately settling in Antioch. It was during this period that Jerome began to acquire a deep knowledge of Hebrew, which proved crucial for his future work on the Vulgate.

Jerome's involvement with the Vulgate unfolded during his residence in Bethlehem. There, he founded a monastery and dedicated substantial time to scholarly pursuits. It was in Bethlehem that he undertook the immense job of translating the Bible into Latin.

His translation work aimed to provide a more accurate Latin version of the Scriptures, as existing translations often lacked consistency and fidelity to the original Hebrew and Greek texts. Jerome's translation project spanned several years, commencing in the late 380s and continuing until the early 400s. Throughout this period, he collaborated with fellow scholars, consulted Hebrew and Greek manuscripts, and conducted meticulous research to ensure the accuracy of his translation.

His approach to the translation varied depending on the Biblical books he worked on. For the Old Testament, he primarily relied on traditional Hebrew texts, though it seems he may have also consulted the Septuagint, the Greek translation of the Old Testament. It's worth noting that the Septuagint was generally considered less authoritative than the original Hebrew Scriptures.

When translating the New Testament, Jerome used Greek manuscripts, striving to produce a Latin version that captured the nuances and style of the original Greek text while remaining accessible to Latin-speaking Christians.

While Jerome's Vulgate was not an entirely new translation, his revisions and improvements held significant theological and cultural significance. It rapidly gained popularity and widespread acceptance, becoming the standard Latin translation of the Bible in the Western Church.

Though Jerome's translation was a personal endeavor driven by his scholarly pursuits and the desire to honor Christ, several influential figures within the early Christian Church supported and encouraged his efforts. Pope Damasus I, the bishop of Rome from 366 to 388, endorsed and promoted Jerome's translation work. He recognized the need for a standardized Latin translation of the Bible and encouraged Jerome to undertake the task. Additionally, Jerome received patronage and support from noble and wealthy Christian women such as Paula and Marcella, who admired his scholarly abilities and dedication to Biblical studies. These individuals provided him with resources, including manuscript paper and financial assistance, enabling him to devote himself entirely to his translation project.

Beyond his translation work, Jerome authored numerous theological treatises, commentaries, and letters addressing various theological, moral, and Biblical issues. His writings encompassed a wide array of topics, including Biblical exegesis, asceticism, and controversies within the early Church. Notable contributions to Christian theology include *Commentary on the Book of Isaiah*, which explored theological themes like messianic prophecies, the suffering servant, and the nature of God's covenant with Israel; *Against Jovinian*, a polemical treatise refuting the teachings of Jovinian, an opponent of asceticism, emphasizing the importance of virginity and celibacy as superior states of

Christian virtue; *Lives of the Desert Fathers*, a collection of biographies recounting the lives and spiritual practices of early Christian hermits and ascetics in the Egyptian desert; and *Adversus Helvidium*, a response to the views of Helvidius, who denied the perpetual virginity of Mary. Jerome's defense of this doctrine emphasized Mary's unique role in the Incarnation.

St. Jerome is celebrated as one of the Four Great Western Doctors of the Church, alongside Sts. Augustine, Ambrose, and Gregory the Great. His legacy as a Biblical scholar and translator continues to exert influence, with his translation, the Vulgate, remaining an essential text in Biblical studies. He is often depicted in art with a lion, skull, trumpet, or books, and he is revered as the patron saint of archeologists, librarians, and translators.

JOACHIM

BORN: 1st century BC, Israel
DIED: 1st century AD, Israel
FEAST DAY: July 26 (with St. Anne)

PATRONAGE: Fathers, grandparents
SYMBOLS AND ATTRIBUTES: Lamb, staff, scroll

As the father of the Virgin Mary, St. Joachim, also known as Joachim of Nazareth, occupies an important place in Christian tradition, even though his name is never mentioned in the Bible. The primary source of information about Joachim and his wife, Anne, comes from an apocryphal text called the "Protoevangelium of James," also referred to as the "Gospel of James" or the "Infancy Gospel of James." Scholars believe it was composed around the second century and provides a narrative of Mary's early life. While this text is not considered part of the New Testament and is not recognized as Scripture by most Christian denominations, its stories have inspired writers and artists throughout the centuries.

In the Gospel of James, Joachim is portrayed as a devout and righteous man from the tribe of Judah. However, Joachim and Anne struggled with infertility despite their fervent prayers to be blessed with a child. Their unwavering faith bore fruit when God promised that Anne would conceive; in her old age, Anne became pregnant and gave birth to Mary, the only human being conceived without sin. This event would come to be called the Immaculate Conception.

Joachim's patronage encompasses several areas, primarily associated with fathers, grandfathers, and those experiencing infertility and pregnant women. In addition, he is considered the patron saint of cabinetmakers and linen traders.

In various artistic representations, Joachim is often depicted holding a lamb or his daughter Mary, with Anne by his side. These depictions look to capture the essence of his role as a devoted father and the guardian of Mary. (See Anne.)

JOAN OF ARC

BORN: c. 1412, Domrémy, Kingdom
of France

DIED: May 30, 1431, Rouen,
Normandy, England

FEAST DAY: May 30

PATRONAGE: France, soldiers, prisoners,
those in need of courage and strength

SYMBOLS AND ATTRIBUTES: Armor, sword,
shield, banner, angels

Joan of Arc was a young French peasant who became a national heroine and a symbol of French resistance. Born around 1412 in Domrémy, a small village in northeastern France, Joan was the child of Jacques d'Arc and Isabelle Romée, both farmers. She was the youngest of five children in a devout Catholic family loyal to the French king, Charles VII, amid the turmoil of the Hundred Years' War. Her upbringing was typical of girls of her time: she learned to sew, cook, and manage farm animals.

Around the age of thirteen (some sources say fifteen), Joan began experiencing visions of St. Michael, St. Catherine, and St. Margaret, appearing to her as physical figures, often radiating light or accompanied by angelic auras. Joan described hearing their voices, speaking in sometimes comforting and sometimes assertive tones, quite clearly. These figures implored her to free France from English rule and restore Charles VII to the throne. She initially kept these visions to herself due to fear and uncertainty, but the urgency of her perceived divine mission eventually compelled her to act.

By 1428, with the English army laying siege to Orléans, Joan, age sixteen, convinced the local lord, Robert de Baudricourt, to facilitate a meeting with the Dauphin, the future king of France. She reached Chinon in February 1429. Joan recognized the Dauphin even though he was in disguise to protect himself from attack, a feat many saw as divine intervention.

Impressed by reports of Joan's tenacity and faith, Charles VII granted her permission to join the French army. Adorned in men's armor and wielding a banner depicting Jesus and Mary, she spearheaded the campaign to liberate Orléans in May 1429—a pivotal moment in the war.

However, the tides of fortune shifted in 1430 when the English captured Joan near Compiègne. Accused of heresy and witchcraft by English and pro-English Burgundians, she endured a notoriously biased trial and was subsequently executed by burning in Rouen in 1431.

Controversies around Joan's trial persisted. In 1456, after a thorough review, the Catholic Church declared her innocent. Her fame grew. Celebrated as a divine agent and hero, churches and monuments were erected in her honor, culminating in her beatification in 1909 and canonization in 1920.

Joan's influence on French history and culture is monumental. She played a pivotal role in shaping the national identity, with her image and deeds symbolizing resistance, divine favor, and unity. Many writers, artists, and composers have sought inspiration from her story, with notable examples being Charles Péguy's *Jeanne d'Arc*, George Bernard Shaw's *Saint Joan*, Mark Twain's *Personal Recollections of Joan of Arc*, and Carl Theodor Dreyer's silent film *The Passion of Joan of Arc*.

JOANNA

BORN: 1st century AD, Israel

DIED: 1st century AD, Israel

FEAST DAY: May 24

PATRONAGE: Desperate cases

SYMBOLS AND ATTRIBUTES: Jar of ointment

St. Joanna, also known as Johanna, is mentioned in the Gospel of Luke as a follower of Jesus Christ. According to the Gospel of Luke, Joanna was the wife of Chuza, a steward to Herod Antipas, the ruler of Galilee. Joanna's encounter with Jesus is described in Luke 8:1–3, where it is mentioned that Jesus traveled to several towns and villages, teaching those who would listen about the news of the kingdom of God. He journeyed with twelve apostles and some women who had been cured of evil spirits and diseases, including Joanna. Jesus had healed Joanna, and tradition holds that, in gratitude, she decided to use her own resources to support his ministry and the needs of his disciples.

Joanna's commitment to Christ went beyond financial support. She actively participated in his ministry, traveling with him and the apostles as they journeyed from place to place. She witnessed the miracles performed by Jesus and experienced firsthand the impact of his teachings.

One of the most significant moments in Joanna's story is her involvement in the events surrounding Jesus's crucifixion and resurrection. She was one of the women who discovered the empty tomb of Jesus after his crucifixion. This made her a witness to the resurrection, a pivotal event in Christian faith, and she later played a vital role in spreading the news of Jesus's resurrection, testifying to the truth of his triumph over death.

In Orthodox tradition, Joanna is honored with the title "St. Joanna the Myrrhbearer" and is commemorated alongside the other myrrh-bearing women ("Myrrhbearer" refers to the women who brought spices and myrrh to anoint Jesus's body after his crucifixion). These women symbolize the care, faithfulness, and devotion of the early Christian community.

Joanna's dedication to Jesus continued after his resurrection. Though she is not mentioned again in the Bible, it is believed that she was present during the selection of Matthias as the replacement for Judas Iscariot among the twelve apostles (Acts 1:12–26). She was also present at the Day of Pentecost, where the Holy Spirit descended upon the disciples and inspired them with fire for their mission of proclaiming the Good News (Acts 2:1–4).

JOHN BERCHMANS

BORN: March 13, 1599, Diest, Spanish Netherlands

DIED: August 13, 1621, Rome, Italy, Papal States

FEAST DAY: November 26

PATRONAGE: Altar servers, Jesuit scholastics

SYMBOLS AND ATTRIBUTES: Rule of Jesuits, crucifix

Born on March 13, 1599, in the city of Diest, located in present-day Belgium, John Berchmans was raised in a devout Catholic family that instilled in him a strong religious foundation. His parents, John and Elizabeth Berchmans, recognized their son's spiritual potential and encouraged him to pursue a life dedicated to God. This led John to enter the Jesuit order in 1616, at the age of seventeen.

As a Jesuit novice, Berchmans displayed exceptional intellectual capabilities and sincere devotion to prayer and religious practices. His superiors quickly recognized his spiritual gifts, and he was appointed a tutor to younger students at the Jesuit College of Mechelen, Belgium. Berchmans's exemplary conduct and academic prowess impressed his peers and mentors alike.

On August 13, 1621, at the age of twenty-two, he passed away after a period of intense suffering due to an illness. Following his death, John Berchmans's reputation for holiness grew rapidly. Reports of miracles and intercessions attributed to him began circulating, bolstering his status as a revered figure in Catholicism. Pope Leo XIII beatified John Berchmans in 1865. He was officially canonized by Pope Leo XIII on January 15, 1888. He is the patron saint of altar servers and young people, and his relics are preserved and venerated at various locations, including the Sant'Ignazio Church in Rome and the Church of St. John Berchmans in his hometown of Diest, Belgium.

JOHN BOSCO

BORN: August 16, 1815, Piedmont,
Kingdom of Italy

DIED: January 31, 1888, Turin, Kingdom
of Italy

FEAST DAY: January 31

PATRONAGE: Schoolchildren, young
people, magicians, editors,
publishers, apprentices

SYMBOLS AND ATTRIBUTES: Young people,
two pillars, cassock, biretta

St. John Bosco, also known as Don Bosco, was a nineteenth-century Italian Catholic priest and educator. He is known for working with disadvantaged youth and founding the Society of St. Francis de Sales, the Salesians, an order of Catholic priests dedicated to educating and helping young people. His life and work were also marked by many extraordinary events and experiences, including several supernatural occurrences often cited as evidence of his sanctity.

John Bosco was born in 1815 in Becchi, a small town in the Piedmont region of Italy. His parents were poor farmers, and he was the youngest of three sons. From an early age, John showed a strong inclination toward religious life. When he was nine years old, he had a dream in which he saw himself surrounded by a group of young men engaged in various forms of mischief. In the dream, John spoke to them, urging them to turn away from their sinful ways and to follow the path of righteousness. When he woke up, he felt God was calling him to dedicate his life to following Jesus and helping young people stay on the straight and narrow.

Though money in the Bosco family was always scarce, John was able to attend schools thanks to the generosity of local benefactors. As a teenager, he decided to join the priesthood, and he entered the seminary at the age of twenty.

He excelled at his studies and had powerful dreams and visions. One notable experience involved his friend and fellow classmate Louis Comollo. Bosco and Comollo made a pact to communicate with each other from the afterlife if one was to die. As fate would have it, Comollo, who had always had a sickly constitution, died when he was still a student at the seminary. Bosco, saddened by the death of his friend, nevertheless waited patiently for a sign from the afterlife. One night, Bosco heard a rumbling sound in his dormitory that grew louder and closer. The room vibrated, and a ghostly multicolored light appeared. The sound ceased, and Comollo's voice was heard saying, "Bosco, Bosco, Bosco—I am saved." The dormitory became brighter before the noise erupted again and then stopped abruptly. Bosco interpreted this experience as a sign from his deceased friend that life everlasting awaited them after death.

John was ordained a priest in 1841. He began his ministry in Turin, where he worked with young people who had been abandoned or were at risk of falling into poverty and crime. He was particularly concerned with the plight of street children, who were often subjected to violence and exploitation. John established a series of oratories, or community centers, where young people could come for learning, recreation, and spiritual guidance.

John's work impacted the Catholic Church and society as a whole. He is credited with pioneering a new approach to youth ministry that focused on building positive relationships with young people and helping them develop their full potential. His Salesian Society, which he founded in 1859, continues to this day to provide vocational training and spiritual guidance to young people worldwide. (See Francis de Sales.)

JOHN CHRYSOSTOM

BORN: c. 347, Antioch, Eastern Roman Empire
DIED: September 14, 407, Comana, Pontus
FEAST DAY: September 13

PATRONAGE: Orators, preachers, education, epilepsy, Constantinople
SYMBOLS AND ATTRIBUTES: Bees, dove, pen

St. John Chrysostom is a Doctor of the Church and one of the most revered saints in the Eastern Orthodox Church. He lived in the fourth century, was renowned for his eloquence, and served as a bishop in Constantinople.

John was born in Antioch, Syria, around the year 347 to parents of noble birth, his father being a high-ranking military officer. He excelled in rhetoric, a highly valued discipline in the Roman Empire. Yet his life's path took a turn when John felt a calling to religious life; at the age of twenty-three, he chose to be baptized. He studied under the theologian Diodore of Tarsus, eventually became a monk, and lived for many years in the Syrian mountains.

In 381, John was ordained as a deacon and began preaching in Antioch. His sermons were well received, and he quickly gained a reputation for his eloquence and ability to connect with his audience. His exceptional oratory skills and his ability to connect with others earned him the title "golden-mouthed" (*Chrysostom* in Greek).

In 398, he was appointed archbishop of Constantinople. During his tenure, John made enemies within the imperial court and was exiled twice. Nevertheless, he remained devoted to his followers and continued to write letters and preach the Gospel.

Around 403, John was accused of heresy and exiled—an unopular act among the people. He returned in 404 but was quickly exiled again. He hoped to return home, but his health deteriorated. He died on September 14, 407, marking the end of a turbulent chapter in his life and ministry, but his legacy lived on through his writings and enduring theological influence. His writings, many of which survived, encompass sermons, letters, and theological treatises. Some of his most notable works include *On the Priesthood*, *On the Incomprehensible Nature of God*, and homilies on the Gospel of Matthew and the Epistles of Paul.

John's body was brought back to Constantinople, where it was venerated as a relic.

JOHN DE BRÉBEUF

BORN: March 25, 1593, Condé-sur-Vire, Normandy, France
DIED: March 16, 1649, Wendake, New France

FEAST DAY: October 19
PATRONAGE: Canada
SYMBOLS AND ATTRIBUTES: Hatchet, cross

St. John de Brébeuf, also known as Jean de Brébeuf, was a French Jesuit missionary and one of the North American Martyrs who faced martyrdom in Canada during the seventeenth century. Born in Condé-sur-Vire, Normandy, France, to a family of minor nobility, he studied at the Jesuit College of Caen. In 1617, he entered the Society of Jesus in Rouen, where he advanced his theological and missionary training. By 1622, he was ordained as a priest.

In 1625, John was sent to New France (modern-day Ontario region in Canada) to evangelize the Huron people. Upon reaching Quebec, John spent his initial months living among the Montagnais tribe, gaining insights into their customs and language. His primary focus soon shifted to the Hurons. Dedicated to understanding their unique culture and beliefs, John became proficient in their language, sharing his newfound knowledge of their ways with other missionaries and settlers.

His ambition was to merge Huron beliefs with Christianity, fostering a smooth conversion process. However, John encountered numerous challenges, including harsh weather and smallpox outbreaks. Some of the Hurons accused him of sorcery. As European diseases ravaged the Huron community, John stood beside them, documenting their way of life in hopes of finding harmony between their spiritual practices and Christian teachings. John eventually gained the trust of the Huron people. They fondly named him "Echon," meaning "the man who carries the load."

In 1649, conflict erupted. John and seven other Jesuit missionaries were captured by the Iroquois, who were in a territorial dispute with the Hurons. They were brutally tortured and martyred on March 16, in present-day Midland, Ontario. Nearly 300 years later, Pope Pius XI canonized John de Brébeuf and his companions on June 29, 1930.

John's meticulous journals detailing his time in Canada are invaluable contributions to ethnography. His descriptions of the Huron language and his Huron-French dictionary offer insights into the Huron's sociocultural fabric at the time, illuminating Canada's early history and the nexus between European settlers and North America's Indigenous peoples.

In art, John is depicted in a Jesuit cassock, holding a crucifix—symbols of his dedication to faith. Other depictions include a scroll or book celebrating his life as a scholar or a kettle, signifying his adaptability to the Huron way of life.

Among his notable contributions is the "Huron Carol," penned around 1642. Recognized as Canada's oldest Christmas song, it's sung in the Huron/Wendat language to a traditional French melody.

While St. Joseph is the principal patron saint of Canada, St. John de Brébeuf holds a special place as a secondary patron, revered for his missionary endeavors and sacrifice. He is especially significant for the Huron people and the Martyrs' Shrine in Midland, Ontario.

JOHN EUDES

BORN: November 14, 1601, Ri, Normandy,
Kingdom of France
DIED: August 19, 1680, Caen, Normandy,
Kingdom of France

FEAST DAY: August 19
PATRONAGE: Eudists, missionaries
SYMBOLS AND ATTRIBUTES: Heart with a
cross on top

St. John Eudes, also known as Jean Eudes, was a Catholic priest and missionary who lived in France during the seventeenth century. He was born to a devout Catholic family on November 14, 1601, in the town of Ri, Normandy, France. His parents were farmers. At a young age, he decided to live a chaste life. He was educated by the Jesuits and studied at the University of Caen. He was ordained a priest in 1625. He spent several years preaching and conducting missions throughout France.

In 1641, John Eudes founded the Congregation of Jesus and Mary, renamed the Eudist Fathers, to provide spiritual guidance to the people of France and train priests for spiritual work. In 1644, he also founded the Order of Our Lady of Charity, a religious order dedicated to caring for women who had been abandoned or who had fallen into prostitution.

John Eudes was a prolific writer who left behind a large body of work. He wrote numerous books and treatises, including *The Life and Kingdom of Jesus*, *The Admirable Heart of Mary*, and *The Good Confessor*. He also wrote several sermons and letters, many of which have been preserved and are still read today.

One of John Eudes's most important works is *The Sacred Heart of Jesus*, a book he wrote to promote the Sacred Heart, a devotion that focused on spreading the love, compassion, and mercy of Jesus Christ for all people. In this book, he explains the theology behind this devotion and offers advice for practicing it in daily life. Along with St. Mary Margaret Alacoque, he is considered the co-founder of the devotion to the Sacred Heart. He also wrote extensively about the Immaculate Heart of Mary and was one of the first writers to promote both of these devotions together.

John Eudes died on August 19, 1680, in Caen, Normandy, France. His feast day is celebrated every year on the anniversary of his death. He is often depicted in religious art holding a crucifix and a heart, representing his devotion to the loving hearts of Jesus and Mary.

JOHN HENRY NEWMAN

BORN: February 21, 1801, London, England
DIED: August 11, 1890, Edgbaston, England
FEAST DAY: October 9

PATRONAGE: Seekers, ordinariates, poets
SYMBOLS AND ATTRIBUTES: Cardinal's attire, book

St. John Henry Newman was a theologian, philosopher, and cardinal whose life and work significantly impacted Christian intellectual thought in the nineteenth century, especially in his mission to instruct laypeople about the faith.

Born in London, England, to an Anglican family, John Henry's spiritual and intellectual journey was complex and multifaceted. He became interested at a young age in various ideas from rationalists and religious skeptics like Voltaire and David Hume. These works, which often challenged religious belief, instead may have galvanized his faith. Around the age of fifteen, John Henry had what he called a conversion experience where he began to fully embrace Christianity, becoming more devout in his early Anglican beliefs. He eventually pursued an academic path and attended Trinity College, Oxford, and would become a fellow at Oriel College. Newman would go on to become a leading figure in the Oxford Movement, a group of Anglican theologians who sought to renew the Church of England by emphasizing its Catholic roots.

As Newman delved deeper into theological studies and historical research, he began questioning the legitimacy of the Anglican and Evangelical beliefs and the validity of their claims. His studies led him to convert to Roman Catholicism in October 1845, a decision that caused a significant stir in religious circles and strained his relationships with many of his former colleagues and friends.

After his conversion, Newman dedicated his life to promoting Catholicism and defending its doctrines. He became a Catholic priest in 1847 and established the Birmingham Oratory, a religious community in Birmingham, England, in 1849.

Newman was known for his intellectual prowess and eloquent writings. One of his most significant contributions was his work on the evolution of belief. He argued that the Catholic Church's teachings evolve and deepen over time through a process he termed "the development of doctrine." This concept significantly influenced Catholic theology and continues to do so today.

In 1879, Pope Leo XIII recognized Newman's exceptional intellectual and spiritual contributions by elevating him to the rank of cardinal (without first being appointed a bishop, which was a significant gesture of respect). In this role, Newman continued to write and lecture, addressing various theological and philosophical topics. His works, including the philosophic masterpiece *An Essay in Aid of a Grammar of Assent*, and *Apologia pro vita sua*, remain influential and widely studied to this day. In particular, *Apologia pro vita sua*, which translates to "A Defense of One's Life," serves as Newman's spiritual biography, a personal account and defense of his religious beliefs. In the book, Newman reflects on his early life and challenges at university, providing insights into his intellectual and spiritual development, his struggles with doubt and skepticism, and the events that eventually led him to convert to Roman Catholicism. Newman also meticulously examines his theological and philosophical journey, addressing various topics such as the nature of faith, the authority of the Church, and the relationship between reason and religious belief. He wrote many more books and, in 1877, was named an honorary fellow at Trinity College.

A man of conviction who believed in the importance of cultivating the soul as well as the intellect, John Henry died on August 11, 1890. He was beatified by Pope Benedict XVI during the pope's visit to the United Kingdom on September 19, 2010. On October 13, 2019, John Henry was canonized as a saint by Pope Francis, becoming the first English saint of the modern era.

JOHN I

BORN: c. 470, Populonia, Tuscia
DIED: May 18, 526, Ravenna,
   Ostrogothic Kingdom
FEAST DAY: May 18

PATRONAGE: Prisoners
SYMBOLS AND ATTRIBUTES: Papal
   vestments, two crosses

St. John I, also known as Pope John I, was a prominent figure in the early Christian Church. Before becoming pope, John I had a background in ecclesiastical administration. He served as a deacon in Rome and became the archdeacon of the Roman Church under Pope Hormisdas. His competence and dedication to his duties led to his election as pope on August 13, 523, following the death of Pope Hormisdas.

During his papacy, Pope John I faced several significant challenges. One notable event was his involvement in the dispute between the Eastern Roman emperor, Justin I, and the Arian king of the Ostrogoths, Theodoric the Great.

At the time, Italy was under the control of the Ostrogothic Kingdom, with Theodoric the Great as its king. Theodoric was an Arian Christian, a branch of Christianity that did not believe in the full divinity of Jesus Christ. Theodoric's Arian beliefs put him at odds with the religious practices of the Byzantine Empire. The Byzantines adhered to the teachings of the Council of Chalcedon, which upheld the orthodox view that Jesus is both fully God and fully man, with no division or confusion between His divine and human natures.

In the early 520s, the Byzantine emperor Justin I sought to reassert imperial control over Italy and bring it back under Byzantine authority. Theodoric viewed this as a threat to his kingdom as well as to his Arian faith. Emperor Justin I attempted to exert influence over the appointment of the bishop of Rome, which further heightened tensions between the two rulers.

Pope John I, a man of frail health, found himself caught in the middle of this conflict. Theodoric, suspecting the pope's allegiance to the Byzantine Empire, summoned him to Ravenna, the capital of the Ostrogothic Kingdom. The pope was pressured to secure a favorable reconciliation between Theodoric and Emperor Justin I.

In 525, Pope John I embarked on a diplomatic mission to Constantinople to meet with Emperor Justin I. His primary objective was to advocate for a peaceful resolution and prevent a military confrontation between the Byzantine Empire and the Ostrogoths. Unfortunately, his diplomatic mission did not achieve the desired outcome. Theodoric distrusted the pope's actions and intentions, accused him of conspiring with the Byzantine Empire against his kingdom, and imprisoned him upon his return to Italy in 526.

Pope John I suffered severe mistreatment, which ultimately resulted in his death on May 18, 526. The exact circumstances surrounding his demise and the extent of Theodoric's direct involvement are not entirely clear from historical records.

St. John I is venerated as a martyr in the Catholic Church. His relics were transferred to Rome and interred in the Basilica of St. Peter.

JOHN LEONARDI

BORN: 1541, Diecimo, Italy
DIED: October 9, 1609, Rome, Italy, Papal States
FEAST DAY: October 9

PATRONAGE: Pharmacists
SYMBOLS AND ATTRIBUTES: Mortar and pestle, quill, priest cassock

St. John Leonardi was an Italian priest and founder of the Order of Clerks Regular of the Mother of God, also known as the Leonardini. Born in Diecimo, Italy, he was the youngest of seven children. From a young age, John showed a deep love for God and a desire to serve Him. At the age of seventeen, he went to Rome and studied to be a pharmacist. During that time he became interested in the teachings of St. Philip Neri, who had founded the Congregation of the Oratory. John was impressed by St. Philip's love for God, his devotion to the poor, and his joyful spirit.

After completing his studies, John returned to Tuscany to become a pharmacist. However, he soon realized God was calling him to a different path. In 1572, he was ordained a priest and began his ministry in Lucca, where he worked as a catechist and spiritual director. John soon gained a reputation for his holiness and ability to bring people closer to God.

Inspired by the Counter-Reformation, a series of reforms and actions taken by the Catholic Church in the sixteenth and seventeenth centuries to address criticisms raised by Protestant reformers and to clarify Catholic doctrine, he established a religious group in 1574 with the goal of strengthening Christian faith and devotion. Within this group, he actively encouraged devotion to the Blessed Virgin Mary, participation in the Forty Hours (a period of continuous prayer and adoration of the Blessed Sacrament), and stressed the significance of frequent communion.

Years later, in 1603, John founded a confraternity called the Propagation of the Faith, which focused on the education of the clergy and the promotion of the Gospel message, especially in missionary work. More than ten years after John's death, his order would become known as the Clerics Regular of the Mother of God.

John Leonardi died on October 9, 1609, in Rome, where he had moved in the later years of his life. Pope Clement XIII canonized him as a saint on April 17, 1938. He is remembered for his tireless efforts in promoting religious studies, fostering devotion to the Blessed Virgin Mary, and reforming the clergy. His feast day is celebrated on October 9. (See Philip Neri.)

JOHN OF CAPISTRANO

BORN: June 24, 1386, Capistrano, Kingdom of Naples

DIED: October 23, 1456, Ilok, Kingdom of Hungary

FEAST DAY: October 23

PATRONAGE: Jurists, military chaplains

SYMBOLS AND ATTRIBUTES: Banner, bird, red cross, armor, crucifix

John of Capistrano, also known as John of Capestrano, was a prominent figure in the fifteenth century. He came from a noble family, studied law in Perugia, and became a successful lawyer. However, John's life took a significant turn when he experienced a spiritual awakening and, in 1415, joined the Franciscan order. He embraced a life of poverty, humility, and service to God and quickly rose within the order's ranks, displaying exceptional leadership qualities.

John became known for his fiery preaching, advocating for moral reform and stressing the importance of prayer and devotion. He traveled extensively throughout Europe, organizing religious missions and delivering powerful sermons that emphasized the need for repentance, virtue, and courage, especially during a time when the Church was repeatedly coming under attack.

One of John's most notable achievements was his involvement in the Crusade against the Ottoman Empire. Following the Fall of Constantinople in 1453, Christian Europe was under the ominous threat of the Ottoman forces led by Sultan Mehmed II. In 1454, Pope Callixtus III dispatched John to rally Christian forces against the Turks. Around seventy years old at the time, John embarked on a dangerous journey to the Imperial Diet of Frankfurt, aiming to garner support for a Crusade against the Ottoman Empire. Recognizing the strategic importance of Hungary, he focused his efforts there, where the Ottoman forces were menacingly laying siege to Belgrade.

By July 1456, John had assembled an unconventional yet determined army of more than 40,000 poorly trained peasants and local countryside landowners. This ragtag army, driven by an indomitable spirit, launched a spontaneous assault on the Ottoman positions, defying the orders not to loot their foes. Their unwavering determination swelled the ranks of defenders, and what started as a skirmish swiftly escalated into a full-scale clash between the Christian and Ottoman forces.

After a long and intense battle, the Ottoman forces retreated, ending the siege. And though John managed to live through war, he died shortly thereafter from the bubonic plague on October 23, 1456. He was buried in the Franciscan Church in Ilok in what is now Croatia, and his tomb became a place of pilgrimage.

John of Capistrano was canonized as a saint by Pope Alexander VIII on April 28, 1690. He is revered as a soldier priest, a powerful preacher, a tireless advocate for Catholicism, and a symbol of courage in the face of adversity.

JOHN OF DAMASCUS

BORN: c. 675, Damascus, Umayyad Caliphate

DIED: December 4, 749, Mar Saba, Byzantine Empire

FEAST DAY: December 4

PATRONAGE: Pharmacists, icon painters

SYMBOLS AND ATTRIBUTES: Quill, scroll

John of Damascus, also known as St. John Damascene, was a famed Christian theologian, monk, and hymnographer from the Byzantine Empire. His contributions to Christian thought and his defense of iconography in worship have left an indelible mark on the history of Christianity.

Born around 675 in Damascus, then part of the Umayyad Caliphate (the second rule of order after the death of Mohammad), John came from a Christian family. His father, Sergius, held a high-ranking position in the government and John received an excellent education, studying philosophy, theology, and other subjects. He also became fluent in Arabic and familiar with the Greek philosophical tradition.

After his studies, following in his father's footsteps, John began his career in the civil service. He held an official position at the court of the caliph. Around 726, however, John left his political career behind and embraced the monastic life. He entered the Monastery of St. Sabas near Jerusalem, where he devoted himself to prayer, contemplation, and writing.

John of Damascus became widely recognized for his theological works, which covered a broad range of topics. The most notable of these include *The Fount of Knowledge,* an attack on and critique of non-Christian and heretical movements, including Islam, and *An Exact Exposition of the Orthodox Faith.* This comprehensive systematic theology synthesized the teachings of earlier Church Fathers, including Gregory of Nazianzus, Basil the Great, and John Chrysostom, and became a cornerstone of Byzantine Christianity.

During John's lifetime, a significant theological and political controversy known as the Iconoclasm Controversy unfolded. Iconoclasts argued against the use of religious images, while defenders of icons, including John, vehemently supported their veneration. John penned numerous treatises and letters to defend icons, employing philosophical and theological arguments to substantiate their role in Christian worship. His writings shaped the theological underpinnings of the Iconodule movement.

John of Damascus's literary contributions extended beyond theology. He was also a prolific hymnographer, composing many liturgical hymns that are still sung in Eastern Orthodox churches today. His hymns, characterized by their theological depth and poetic beauty, enriched the worship experience and contributed to the further development of music in Byzantine worship.

John died in 749 and was laid to rest at the Monastery of St. Saba.

JOHN OF GOD

BORN: March 8, 1495, Montemor-o-Novo, Kingdom of Portugal
DIED: March 8, 1550, Granada, Kingdom of Spain
FEAST DAY: March 8

PATRONAGE: Hospitals, nurses, the sick, booksellers
SYMBOLS AND ATTRIBUTES: Heart, crown of thorns, alms

St. John of God, also known as João de Deus in Portuguese, was the founder of the Brothers Hospitallers. Born as João Cidade on March 8, 1495, in Montemor-o-Novo, Portugal, John moved to Spain with his family at the age of eight. In his early years, he served as a soldier in the army of Charles V, the Holy Roman Emperor, participating in various military campaigns and battles.

However, during a pilgrimage to Granada, Spain, in 1536, John experienced a profound religious conversion. Struck by remorse for his past life and moved by a sermon delivered by John of Ávila, he vowed to change his ways and dedicate himself to the care of the poor and the sick.

John began his ministry by tending to the sick and destitute in Granada and collecting and burying the abandoned bodies of the poor who had died. His actions earned him the nickname "John of God," and his reputation spread.

In 1539, John established a small hospital in Granada, which marked the foundation of the Order of the Brothers Hospitallers. This religious community focused on providing medical care and spiritual support to the sick and those in need. The hospital served as a refuge for the most vulnerable members of society, and John worked tirelessly to alleviate their suffering.

John of God's life of service ended on March 8, 1550. He was laid to rest in the chapel of the hospital he had established. In 1572, Pope Pius V formally recognized and approved John's order (officially named the Hospitaller Order of the Brothers of St. John of God). In 1690, Pope Alexander VIII canonized him as a saint, acknowledging his exceptional life of devotion and selflessness.

JOHN OF THE CROSS

BORN: June 24, 1542, Fontiveros, Kingdom of Spain

DIED: December 14, 1591, Úbeda, Kingdom of Spain

FEAST DAY: December 14

PATRONAGE: Contemplative life, mystical theology

SYMBOLS AND ATTRIBUTES: Cross, dove, crucifix, quill

Born Juan de Yepes y Álvarez in 1542 in Fontiveros, Spain, St. John of the Cross was a mystic and poet who played an important role in the Catholic Counter-Reformation. St. John's writings continue to inspire and challenge readers to this day, with his most famous work, *The Dark Night of the Soul*, being a pivotal text on the nature of mystical experience and the spiritual journey.

John entered the Carmelite order as a novice in 1563, at the age of twenty-one, in Medina del Campo, Spain. He took the religious name Juan de Santo Matía (John of St. Matthias). After completing his initial formation, he was ordained a priest in 1567. He continued his studies and began his work as a spiritual director and preacher.

In the same year, 1567, he met Teresa of Ávila, who was seeking to establish a reformed branch of the Carmelites. Impressed by John's earnestness, Teresa invited him to join her in her reform efforts. John quickly became her collaborator and supporter, and together they worked toward establishing the Order of Discalced Carmelites, a movement within the Carmelite order that advocated for a more contemplative and austere way of life.

In 1577, John was imprisoned by members of his own order who opposed the reforms he and Teresa had instituted. He was held for several months and subjected to physical and emotional abuse including lashing and flogging and being forced to live with very little light. He was consoled by God and remained committed to his beliefs. In 1578, he escaped from captivity, was nursed back to health by Teresa and her nuns, and continued to write and preach until his death in 1591.

John is often remembered for his spiritual writings of poetic and mystical beauty. His works emphasize the importance of detachment from worldly concerns and cultivating a deep interior life of prayer and contemplation.

Most notably, *The Dark Night of the Soul* describes the stages of a spiritual journey in terms of a metaphorical night. In the first stage, the "dark night of the senses," the individual begins to detach from worldly pleasures and experiences a sense of spiritual aridity. This is followed by the "dark night of the soul," in which a person experiences a deep sense of emptiness and abandonment by God. He emphasizes that this experience is a necessary part of the spiritual journey, as it purifies the soul and prepares it for an intimate encounter with God. The final stage, called the "divine union," is marked by an ineffable sense of love and union with God, which is beyond human understanding.

John's works have influenced Catholic theology, literature, philosophy, and psychology. His emphasis on the importance of the interior life and the pursuit of spiritual perfection has been explored by thinkers such as Martin Heidegger, who saw John's work as challenging the dominant rationalist and materialist paradigms of modern thought. John's poetry has also been widely read and celebrated, with figures like Salvador Dalí and T. S. Eliot acknowledging their debt to his work.

John of the Cross was canonized as a saint in 1726. (See Teresa of Ávila.)

JOHN PAUL II

BORN: May 18, 1920, Wadowice, Poland
DIED: April 2, 2005, Vatican City
FEAST DAY: October 22

PATRONAGE: World Youth Day
SYMBOLS AND ATTRIBUTES: Papal tiara, papal vestments, pastoral cross, World Youth Day logo

John Paul II was among the most influential popes in modern times and served as the head of the Catholic Church from 1978 until his death in 2005. He was noted for his efforts to improve relations between the Catholic Church and other faiths, his role in the fall of Communism in his native Poland, and holding both progressive and traditional Catholic views on various social issues.

Born Karol Józef Wojtyła in Wadowice, a small town in southern Poland, he was the youngest of three children. His father, Karol Wojtyła Sr., was a noncommissioned officer in the Polish army, and his mother, Emilia Kaczorowska, was a schoolteacher. Wojtyła's mother passed away when he was eight years old, and when he was twelve, his older brother Edmund died at age twenty-six.

Wojtyła excelled academically and in athletics, particularly soccer. He was an active member of the local theater group, which fostered his love of the arts. In 1938, he entered the Jagiellonian University in Kraków, studying philosophy and Polish literature. After the Nazis closed the university in 1939, Wojtyła continued his studies in secret, ultimately earning a theology degree a year after the end of World War II.

Ordained a priest on November 1, 1946, Wojtyła began serving as a chaplain to university students in Kraków. He earned a doctorate in theology in 1953. By 1958, he was appointed auxiliary bishop of Kraków, and in 1964, he became the archbishop. As archbishop, Wojtyła supported workers' rights, opposed government censorship, and fostered relations with leaders of the Orthodox and Jewish communities in Poland. Pope Paul VI named him a cardinal in 1967.

Wojtyła was elected pope on October 16, 1978, adopting the name John Paul II. He was the first non-Italian pope in 455 years and the first Polish pope. Well known for his charisma, he visited more than 129 countries, making him the most-traveled pope in history.

A vocal opponent of Communism, John Paul II's support for the Solidarity movement and his teachings on human dignity and freedom inspired resistance against dictatorial oppression. According to papal biographer George Weigel, John Paul II's visits to his native Poland and his support for the Solidarity movement provided moral and spiritual inspiration to the Polish people, weakening the Communist regime. He contends that John Paul II's courage in defending the rights of individuals was crucial in fostering a sense of hope and resistance among the people living under communist oppression.

John Paul II was shot on May 13, 1981, by Mehmet Ali Ağca, a Turkish mercenary, in St. Peter's Square. He survived the assassination attempt, eventually visiting his attacker in prison and forgiving him.

He was the first reigning pope to visit a synagogue and a mosque. John Paul II also sought to build relationships with other Christian denominations, including the Anglican and Lutheran Churches.

One of his significant contributions to Catholic teaching was his series of lectures known as "Theology of the Body," which discussed human sexuality, marital love, and the divine purpose of every person. An advocate for social justice, he opposed the death penalty and emphasized the importance of sustainable development. His encyclical *Centesimus annus* (1991) critiqued capitalism and socialism while calling for an economic system that upheld the dignity of all individuals.

John Paul II was passionately involved in the arts as a poet and playwright in his younger years. As pope, he continued to emphasize the importance and significance of art and culture in both the Church and broader society. Initiatives like World Youth Day, which gathered young Catholics from around the globe to pray, worship, and celebrate their shared faith, thrived under his guidance. Embracing modern technology, he advocated the use of the Internet for sharing the Good News of Jesus.

One of the longest-serving popes, John Paul II had a profound impact on the Catholic Church. Even in the face of declining health due to serious ailments, including Parkinson's disease, he championed a "new evangelization," urging Catholics to share their faith proactively with others. Pope Benedict XVI highlighted John Paul II's efforts against the "dictatorship of relativism," a notion that challenges the existence of objective truths or values.

John Paul II passed away on April 2, 2005. He was beatified by Pope Benedict XVI on May 1, 2011, and canonized by Pope Francis on April 27, 2014. During the canonization ceremony, Pope Francis praised John Paul II as the "pope of the family," emphasizing his devotion to the Virgin Mary, his deep spirituality, and his relentless drive for peace and reconciliation between spiritual brothers and sisters from all walks of life.

JOHN BAPTIST DE LA SALLE

BORN: April 30, 1651, Reims, Kingdom
of France

DIED: April 7, 1719, Rouen, Kingdom
of France

FEAST DAY: April 7

PATRONAGE: Teachers, educators

SYMBOLS AND ATTRIBUTES: Book, students

St. John Baptist de La Salle, also known as St. Jean-Baptiste de La Salle, was a French Catholic priest and educational reformer who lived from 1651 to 1719. He is known for his pioneering work in educating young people and establishing a new, democratizing model of schooling.

Born in Reims, France, in 1651, John Baptist de La Salle was the eldest of ten children of a wealthy family. He was educated by the Jesuits and was ordained at the age of twenty-seven. His first assignment was as a parish priest in a poor area of Reims, where over time he became deeply affected by the lack of learning among the poor children in his parish. He founded a school in his home and recruited other teachers to help him, developing new teaching methods and even writing textbooks tailored to his students' needs.

In 1679, John met Adrian Nyel, a layman and a prominent figure in the educational landscape of Reims. Nyel initially pursued the idea of opening schools for poor boys in Reims; John quickly became a key supporter and worked to further extend and enhance this initiative.

Nyel's can-do attitude was instrumental in helping John to recruit and form a community of dedicated teachers, which eventually evolved into the Institute of the Brothers of the Christian Schools. However, it was under de La Salle's visionary leadership and sustained efforts that the Brothers of the Christian Schools fully formed as a teaching order that was dedicated to the schooling of children from less privileged backgrounds. At the time, his school was one of the first to teach in the common language instead of Latin.

The de La Salle Brothers quickly grew in number, and John continued to develop new methods. He believed in the importance of teaching children valuable skills like reading, writing, and arithmetic alongside religious instruction. He also introduced the concept of teaching in the vernacular rather than in Latin so that students could more easily understand the material.

John Baptist de La Salle's methods were so successful that they were adopted by schools throughout France and beyond. He is credited with transforming education in France and making it more accessible to children from all backgrounds. His work was recognized by the Catholic Church, and he was canonized as a saint in 1900.

JOHN THE BAPTIST

BORN: c. 4 BC, Judea

DIED: c. 28–36 AD, Machaerus
(modern-day Jordan)

FEAST DAY: June 24 (birth), August
29 (beheading)

PATRONAGE: Baptism, birds, converts,
printer, tailors, booksellers, firefighters

SYMBOLS AND ATTRIBUTES: Lamb, shell, ax,
scroll, scallop shell, sackcloth, platter
with his head on it

St. John the Baptist is a prominent figure in Christianity and is known for his role as a prophet who foretold the coming of Jesus Christ. He is one of the most widely venerated saints in Christianity, and his influence extends beyond just religious contexts.

John the Baptist was born to Zechariah, a priest, and Elizabeth, a descendant of Aaron. According to the Gospel of Luke, John was born six months before Jesus Christ, and his mother was visited by an angel of the Lord (traditionally believed to be Gabriel), who foretold John's birth and his future role as a prophet (Luke 1:13–17).

John spent much of his life in the desert, living a simple and ascetic lifestyle. He dressed in camel's hair and ate locusts and wild honey (Mark 1:6). He preached a message of repentance and baptism for the forgiveness of sins, calling on people to turn away from their errant ways and prepare for the coming of the Messiah (Mark 1:4–5). According to the Gospel of John, John the Baptist identified Jesus as the Messiah when he baptized him in the River Jordan (John 1:29–34).

John's ministry attracted many followers, and many people were baptized by him in the River Jordan. He gained a reputation as a powerful and influential preacher, and though his message of repentance and salvation resonated with many, it attracted the attention of Jewish authorities who were suspicious of his teachings and his influence over the people. He spoke out against the corruption of the religious establishment and called for a return to the true teachings of God. He also publicly condemned King Herod Antipas's marriage to Herodias, which resulted in his arrest.

While John was in prison, during a feast held by King Herod, Herodias's daughter danced for the king, and in return, Herod promised to grant her any request. Prompted by her mother, she demanded John's head on a platter. Reluctantly, Herod honored the request, resulting in John's execution by decapitation (Matthew 14:3–11). John's death is commemorated on August 29, his feast day in the Catholic Church.

St. John the Baptist is the patron saint of the sacrament of Baptism. He is also the patron saint of many different groups and professions, including butchers and tailors, and of several countries, including Malta and Puerto Rico. His symbols include the lamb, which represents Jesus Christ as the Lamb of God (John 1:29), and a staff with a cross, which symbolizes John's role as a prophet and his message of repentance and salvation. He is sometimes depicted with his head on a platter.

JOHN THE DWARF

BORN: 339, Thebes, Egypt
DIED: 407, Scetes, Egypt
FEAST DAY: October 17

PATRONAGE: Those with dwarfism
SYMBOLS AND ATTRIBUTES: Monk's habit, prayer rope, stick, watering dry wood

St. John the Dwarf, also known as John Colobus or John the Short, is recognized as one of the Coptic Desert Fathers, a group of early Christian monks who sought solitude and spiritual enlightenment in the deserts of Egypt.

He was born in the middle of the fourth century in Thebes, Egypt. From a young age, he desired to dedicate his life to God. He joined a community of monks in the Egyptian desert and became a disciple of Abba Poemen, a prominent Desert Father.

He was known for his small stature, which earned him the nickname "the Dwarf" or "Colobus" in Greek, as well as for his extreme asceticism and humility. He practiced rigorous self-discipline, often going to great lengths to mortify his flesh and overcome his own weaknesses.

John's detachment from worldly possessions were evident in his way of life. He possessed only a few simple tools and garments and would perform menial tasks such as weaving mats to support himself and his fellow monks. He was also known for his gentleness, patience, and ability to offer wise counsel and guidance to those who sought it.

John the Dwarf's life and teachings greatly influenced the monastic tradition in Egypt and beyond. His example of self-denial, humility, and devotion to God inspired many other monks and followers of the Christian faith. He is venerated as a saint in the Coptic Orthodox Church.

JOHN THE EVANGELIST

BORN: c. 6 AD, Bethsaida, Galilee
DIED: c. 100 AD, Ephesus, Asia Minor
FEAST DAY: December 27

PATRONAGE: Love, loyalty, friendships, authors, burn victims, prophets
SYMBOLS AND ATTRIBUTES: Eagle, book, chalice with serpent

One of the twelve apostles of Jesus Christ, St. John the Evangelist is traditionally believed to be the author of the Gospel of John, the book of Revelation, and three New Testament letters bearing his name. He is also called the Beloved Disciple and is considered the closest of all the apostles to Jesus Christ; he is the only one of the original twelve who stands at the foot of the cross along with the three Marys at Christ's crucifixion.

Some scholars believe that John was born in Bethsaida, near the Sea of Galilee, and was the son of Zebedee, a fisherman, and Salome, the mother of James. Along with his brother James, John was called to be a disciple of Jesus, and the two became known as the

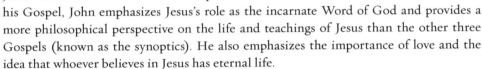

Sons of Thunder. The reason for this nickname is not explicitly mentioned in Biblical text, but it suggests that John and James had fiery or passionate temperaments and zealous natures. John was one of the three apostles who witnessed important events in Jesus's life, including the Transfiguration, the raising of Jairus's daughter, and the Agony in the Garden of Gethsemane.

John's Gospel, believed to have been written around 85–95, is known for its emphasis on the divine nature of Jesus Christ and his close relationship with God the Father. In his Gospel, John emphasizes Jesus's role as the incarnate Word of God and provides a more philosophical perspective on the life and teachings of Jesus than the other three Gospels (known as the synoptics). He also emphasizes the importance of love and the idea that whoever believes in Jesus has eternal life.

One of the best-known verses in John's Gospel is John 3:16, which states, "For God so loved the world that he gave his one and only Son, that whoever believes in him shall not perish but have eternal life." This verse is often quoted and is considered a cornerstone of Christian belief.

After the death and resurrection of Jesus, John played an influential role in the early Christian Church. He was present on the Day of Pentecost and was one of the apostles who performed miracles and healings in Jesus's name. Church tradition holds that John was the sole apostle who did not suffer a martyr's death, instead living to an advanced age.

In his later years, John is believed to have lived in Ephesus, present-day Turkey, where he founded and oversaw several Christian communities. He is also said to have been exiled to the island of Patmos by the Roman emperor Domitian, where he received the visions recorded in the book of Revelation.

John's book of Revelation, also known as the Apocalypse, is a prophetic and highly symbolic work. It presents a series of visions and revelations given to the evangelist while he was exiled to the island of Patmos. The book uses vivid imagery and symbolism to explore the cosmic conflict between the forces of God and the forces of evil, depicting the rise of the Antichrist, the persecution of Christians, the pouring out of divine wrath, the final judgment, and the establishment of God's kingdom on earth. Controversial to this day, the book not only impacted Christian thought but has inspired art, literature, and music for millennia.

John the Evangelist is venerated as a saint by the Catholic, Orthodox, and Anglican Churches. He is often depicted in art holding a chalice with a serpent, which symbolizes the story of his attempted poisoning and his triumph over the evil inside the cup (as recorded in the *Golden Legend*, a compilation of hagiographies assembled by Jacobus de Varagine in the thirteenth century). He is also shown with an eagle, representing the height of his spiritual insight and the soaring breadth of his Gospel message.

JOHN VIANNEY

BORN: May 8, 1786, Dardilly, Kingdom of France

DIED: August 4, 1859, Ars-sur-Formans, French Empire

FEAST DAY: August 4

PATRONAGE: Parish priests

SYMBOLS AND ATTRIBUTES: Scroll, cross

John Vianney, also known as the curé of Ars, was a French Catholic priest who lived primarily in the nineteenth century. He was the fourth of six children born to Matthieu Vianney and Marie Beluze in Dardilly, a village near Lyon, France, in 1786.

John Vianney's childhood was marked by the French Revolution, a period of intense political and social turmoil in France. During these uncertain times, he received religious instruction from his mother and showed a pronounced inclination toward the priesthood from an early age. However, the revolution disrupted his ability to pursue his plans.

In 1809, John was drafted during the Napoleonic Wars, but shortly thereafter fell ill and was unable to join his unit. During his recovery, the soldiers moved on, and when he was finally healthy enough to join, by some accounts, he became lost and could not locate them (some believe he intentionally avoided joining his unit due to his religious convictions). He sought refuge in the village of Les Noes, where a family took him in and where he taught local children as he bided his time until the authorities discovered him. He was eventually labeled a deserter, a severe crime during Napoleon's regime. However, an imperial decree was issued granting amnesty to all deserters, which enabled Vianney to return to his studies without the threat of military punishment.

John was ordained a priest on August 13, 1815. After serving briefly in another parish, he was assigned to the village of Ars-en-Dombes, a small and spiritually neglected community. Many of its residents had grown indifferent to their faith.

Dedicated to the pastoral care of Ars's people, Vianney emphasized the importance of prayer, Penance, and frequent participation in the sacraments. Known for his devout prayer life, he spent hours in the confessional, preached with endless energy, and was passionate about catechesis.

His reputation for holiness spread far and wide. Pilgrims traveled to Ars seeking his counsel and the sacrament of reconciliation. Vianney often devoted up to eighteen hours a day to hearing confessions. He possessed a unique charism of discernment, offering wise counsel and guiding many toward a deeper relationship with God.

Vianney's spiritual refinements were not confined to the confessional. He often sensed the presence of evil spirits and was known to engage in spiritual battles against these demonic forces, spending nights in prayer for his parishioners and the souls in his care.

John Vianney passed away on August 4, 1859, at the age of seventy-three. His funeral attracted thousands, including clergy, religious, and lay faithful from various backgrounds. He was canonized as a saint by Pope Pius XI on May 31, 1925.

POPE JOHN XXIII

BORN: November 25, 1881, Sotto il Monte, Kingdom of Italy

DIED: June 3, 1963, Vatican City

FEAST DAY: October 11

PATRONAGE: Papal diplomats, Second Vatican Council

SYMBOLS AND ATTRIBUTES: Papal vestments

Pope John XXIII was a pivotal figure in the Catholic Church during the twentieth century, serving as the 261st pope from 1958 until his death in 1963. Angelo Giuseppe Roncalli was born on November 25, 1881, in Sotto il Monte, Italy, to a devout family of farmers. His parents instilled in him a strong faith and a sense of responsibility toward others. Growing up in rural Italy, he developed a love for nature and a deep appreciation for the simplicity of life.

In his youth, Angelo displayed intellectual curiosity and a thirst for knowledge. He attended seminary in Bergamo, where he received a solid foundation in philosophy and theology. His studies continued at the Pontifical Roman Seminary in Rome, where he deepened his theological understanding and prepared for the priesthood. Throughout his life, he would embrace multiple callings and undertake various roles.

On August 10, 1904, at the age of twenty-two, Angelo was ordained as a priest in the Diocese of Bergamo, and in that same year he earned his doctorate in canon law. He was appointed a secretary of the bishop of Bergamo until 1914 and then served in World War I as a chaplain. In 1925, Angelo became a bishop and was appointed as the Apostolic Visitor to Bulgaria, marking the beginning of his lifelong pursuit of diplomatic solutions between nations and faiths.

During World War II, Angelo worked discreetly to aid prisoners of war, refugees, and displaced persons, regardless of nationality or religious affiliation. He was particularly concerned about the plight of Jewish people fleeing persecution in Nazi-occupied Europe. Throughout the war, Angelo collaborated with various diplomatic channels and local authorities to rescue Jews and provide them with the necessary documentation, shelter, and assistance to escape to safer locations. He issued baptismal certificates to Jews (the numbers range from hundreds to many thousands), which allowed them to find refuge in Christian institutions and avoid Nazi persecution. Angelo's efforts to aid Jewish refugees often required delicate negotiations and diplomatic maneuvers. He used his position as the Apostolic Delegate to intercede on behalf of Jewish individuals, seeking exit visas and safe passage. Angelo also worked closely with Jewish organizations, such as the World Jewish Congress, to facilitate rescue operations and protect those in danger. At the end of the war, he was appointed the Apostolic Nuncio of France.

In 1953, Pope Pius XII recognized Angelo's contributions, elevated him to cardinal, and appointed him patriarch of Venice. As the leader of the historic Venetian diocese, he continued to promote dialogue and understanding among different religious communities, earning the respect and admiration of many. On October 28, 1958, following the death of Pope Pius XII, Cardinal Angelo Roncalli was elected pope. Taking the name Pope John XXIII, he brought a fresh perspective and a pastoral approach to the papacy. His warm and jovial demeanor quickly endeared him to the Catholic faithful, who affectionately called him The Good Pope.

The most notable achievement of John XXIII's papacy was his decision to convene the Second Vatican Council (1962–1965), also known as Vatican II. The council aimed to address the challenges and opportunities facing the Catholic Church in the modern world. It sought to promote dialogue and engagement with other Christian denominations, improve relations with non-Christian religions, and address pressing social issues. Pope John XXIII firmly believed in the need for *aggiornamento*, a term he used to emphasize the Church's need for renewal and openness to change. Participants in Vatican II responded to this vision, resulting in significant reforms and transformations within the Church.

The council produced key documents such as the *Constitution on the Sacred Liturgy* (Sacrosanctum Concilium), the *Dogmatic Constitution on the Church* (Lumen Gentium), and the *Declaration on Religious Freedom* (Dignitatis Humanae), among others. Pope John XXIII's leadership during Vatican II had a lasting impact on the Catholic Church. By promoting dialogue and openness, he fostered a spirit of ecumenism, and engaged the Church in the modern world. His humble and approachable nature inspired many, earning him the reputation of a "pope of the people." Unfortunately, John XXIII would not live to witness the end of his council. In 1962, Pope John XXIII began experiencing stomach pain and discomfort. Initially, the cause of his ailment was uncertain, but it was diagnosed as stomach cancer.

Pope John XXIII remained resolute in his responsibilities. As the pope's condition worsened, he began experiencing severe pain, making it challenging to fulfill his duties. Nevertheless, he retained his optimism and sense of humor, frequently making light of his health issues to those around him.

On May 29, 1963, Pope John XXIII made his final public appearance, delivering a touching speech from the balcony of St. Peter's Basilica. During this "Urbi et Orbi" ("to the city and to the world") blessing, he conveyed his gratitude and love for the faithful, bestowing his apostolic blessing upon them. He received the last rites on June 2, 1963, and passed away on the evening of June 3, 1963, at eighty-one years old. Catholics and many others around the world grieved, mourning the loss of a revered spiritual leader who had reinvigorated and engaged the Catholic Church. Vatican II would continue under his successor, Paul VI.

Pope John XXIII's funeral occurred on June 6, 1963, and was attended by numerous heads of state, religious leaders, and thousands of mourners. The funeral Mass was celebrated in St. Peter's Basilica, and he was interred in the crypt below the basilica, resting beside other popes.

Though Pope John XXIII's papacy lasted only five years, his impact resonated long after his passing. Recognizing the enduring value of his contributions, Pope Francis canonized Pope John XXIII as a saint on April 27, 2014.

JOSAPHAT

BORN: c. 1580, Volodymyr, Volhynian Voivodeship, Crown of the Kingdom of Poland (modern-day Ukraine)
DIED: November 12, 1623, Vitebsk, Vitebsk Voivodeship, Polish–Lithuanian Commonwealth (modern-day Belarus)

FEAST DAY: November 12
PATRONAGE: Ukraine
SYMBOLS AND ATTRIBUTES: Palm branch, bishop's attire, cross

Josaphat was born in 1580 in the town of Volodymyr, which is in modern-day Ukraine. He was baptized John at birth and took the name Josaphat when he became a monk. He was ordained a priest in 1609 and became the archimandrite, or head, of the Vitebsk monastery in modern-day Belarus.

St. Josaphat, also known as Josaphat Kuntsevych, was a bishop and martyr who lived in the late sixteenth and early seventeenth centuries. Josaphat was committed to promoting unity between the Eastern and Western Churches, which had been separated since the Great Schism of 1054. He saw the unification as paramount to the renewal of the Church and the salvation of souls. He worked unremittingly to promote this cause, even though he faced opposition from members of his own Church who saw him as a traitor.

In 1614, Josaphat was appointed the bishop of Polotsk, also in modern-day Belarus. He continued his efforts to promote unity and also worked to reform the Church in his diocese. He was known for his simple lifestyle, devotion to prayer and fasting, and compassionate care for the ill and destitute.

Unfortunately, no good deed goes unpunished, especially when you're trying to repair a centuries-old rift between two powerful religious groups. In 1623, at the age of forty-three, he was attacked and killed by an angry mob who opposed his ecumenical work. His martyrdom was seen as a powerful witness to the importance of unity and reform in the Church, although it must be said that the Catholic and Orthodox Churches remain divided on certain theological issues to this day.

JOSEMARIA ESCRIVA

BORN: January 9, 1902, Barbastro, Spain

DIED: June 26, 1975, Rome, Italy

FEAST DAY: June 26

PATRONAGE: Ordinary life, laypersons, Opus Dei members, diabetes

SYMBOLS AND ATTRIBUTES: Cross, priestly attire, books (especially *The Way*), rosary

St. Josemaria Escriva was a prominent Spanish Catholic priest and theologian who is best known as the founder of the Prelature of the Holy Cross and Opus Dei, a Catholic organization that includes clergy and laypeople.

Josemaria Escriva de Balaguer y Albas was born in a devout Catholic family on January 9, 1902, in Barbastro, Spain. He showed early signs of intellectual curiosity, eventually pursuing studies in law at the University of Zaragoza. During his time at the university, he experienced a calling to the priesthood, and he entered the seminary. After completing his studies in philosophy and theology, Josemaria was ordained as a Catholic priest on March 28, 1925.

During his early years as a priest, Josemaria developed the spiritual foundations that would become the basis for Opus Dei, which translates to "Work of God." He believed that all individuals, regardless of their vocation, could strive for holiness and find God in their daily lives. This concept of "sanctification of work" became a central theme in his teachings and writings.

In 1928, Josemaria experienced a significant spiritual revelation that he interpreted as a direct message from God. According to his account, while praying in a chapel in Madrid, he received a vision of Opus Dei, which he understood to be a divine calling to build on his earlier revelations and establish an organization dedicated to promoting spiritual growth and the pursuit of holiness in ordinary life.

With the guidance of his spiritual director, Josemaria began to lay the foundations of Opus Dei that same year. Although the initial groundwork started in 1928, the path to official ecclesiastical recognition was gradual. Opus Dei was first granted a decree of praise by Pope Pius XII in 1947, affirming the Church's positive view of the organization and its mission. This was followed by final approval in 1950, solidifying its status within the Church. Pope John Paul II established Opus Dei as a personal prelature in 1982, a unique canonical status that reflects the organization's global presence and mission.

The organization aimed to provide spiritual formation and guidance to laypeople, emphasizing the integration of faith and work. Over time, Opus Dei grew and spread globally, gaining recognition from the Vatican and attracting followers from diverse backgrounds. Josemaria's approach to spirituality and his emphasis on sanctifying professional work, family life, and personal relationships was seen as innovative and transformative. His teachings and writings shaped Opus Dei's spiritual charism and philosophy.

He authored numerous books, including *The Way, Christ Is Passing By,* and *Furrow,* which provide practical advice and insights into pursuing holiness in various aspects of life. These works have been widely read and studied by Opus Dei members and have significantly impacted the organization's development.

His teachings and the establishment of Opus Dei attracted a devoted following, but they also faced criticism from various quarters. Some questioned the hierarchical nature of the organization, its perceived secrecy, and the level of control exerted by the leadership. Critics claimed that Opus Dei's emphasis on discipline and spiritual rigor could lead to excessive pressure and a sense of exclusivity among its members. Many also criticized the organization's use of corporeal mortification as a form of spiritual practice. There were also allegations of excessive financial influence and political maneuvering within the Catholic Church. Nonetheless, Josemaria remained driven in his mission.

In recognition of his spiritual contributions and the impact of Opus Dei (which has around 90,000 members today), Josemaria was canonized as a saint by Pope John Paul II on October 6, 2002. His canonization affirmed for his followers and the faithful his holiness and the validity of his spiritual teachings within the Catholic Church. Today, St. Josemaria Escriva's legacy inspires and guides millions of individuals worldwide as Opus Dei continues its mission of promoting personal sanctification and the integration of faith and work.

JOSEPH

BORN: c. Late 1st century BC
DEATH: c. Early 1st century AD
FEAST DAY: March 19 (St. Joseph's Day), May 1 (St. Joseph the Worker)

PATRONAGE: families, fathers, travelers, immigrants, home buyers and sellers, craftsmen, engineers, Catholic Church, Universal Church

SYMBOLS AND ATTRIBUTES: Carpenter's square, lily, staff, doves, holding Baby Jesus, Holy Family

St. Joseph, the Saint of Dreams and foster father of Jesus Christ and husband of the Virgin Mary, is described in the Gospels as a "just man." Though a relatively minor figure in the Gospels, he has been revered as a model of humility, obedience, and paternal love, making him a beloved figure in Christian tradition. His intercession has been sought by many of the faithful throughout the ages.

Joseph was a descendant of King David and a resident of Nazareth. Tradition holds that he was a carpenter by trade and that he played a significant role in the life of Jesus and in the fulfillment of Biblical prophecies.

According to the Gospel of Matthew, Joseph was engaged to Mary when he discovered she was pregnant. Initially, he planned to quietly divorce her to protect her from public shame. However, an angel appeared to him in a dream, explaining that the child Mary carried was conceived through the Holy Spirit, and Joseph should take her as his wife. The angel also directed Joseph to name the child Jesus, meaning "deliverer" or "rescuer," because he would save humankind from its sins.

Joseph faithfully obeyed the angel's message. He provided care and guidance to both Mary and Jesus throughout his life.

Joseph's most significant role was as a protector of the Holy Family. When King Herod sought to kill the infant Jesus, a divine messenger appeared to Joseph in a dream and told him to take Mary and Jesus and flee to Egypt. Joseph immediately obeyed. After Herod's death, the angel appeared to Joseph, instructing him to go back to Israel.

Various individuals have championed devotion to St. Joseph throughout history. One such figure was St. Teresa of Ávila, a Spanish mystic and writer of the sixteenth century, who held a deep devotion to St. Joseph and encouraged others to seek his intercession. Additionally, St. André Bessette, a Canadian religious brother, played an essential role in promoting St. Joseph's devotion by constructing St. Joseph's Oratory in Montreal and advocating for prayer to St. Joseph. Popes have also made significant contributions in this regard. Pope Pius IX officially declared St. Joseph as the patron of the Universal Church in 1870 and emphasized his importance in an encyclical. Likewise, Pope Leo XIII called for increased devotion to St. Joseph in his 1889 encyclical, emphasizing his virtues. Pope Francis, the current pope, has expressed a deep personal devotion to St. Joseph and proclaimed a "Year of St. Joseph" in 2020.

While his primary feast day is celebrated on March 19, Pope Pius XII introduced a supplementary commemoration in 1955: the Feast of St. Joseph the Worker, observed on May 1. (See Teresa of Ávila.)

JOSEPH CALASANZ

BORN: September 11, 1557, Peralta de la Sal, Spain
DIED: August 25, 1648, Rome, Italy
FEAST DAY: August 25

PATRONAGE: Catholic schools, schoolchildren
SYMBOLS AND ATTRIBUTES: Religious habit, children, book

St. Joseph Calasanz, also known as Joseph Calasanctius, was a Spanish Catholic priest and educator and is recognized today as the founder of the Piarist order (or the Order of Poor Clerics Regular of the Mother of God of the Pious Schools).

In 1592, at the age of thirty-five, Joseph moved to Rome in the hope of advancing his ecclesiastical career. He found support from Cardinal Marcoantonio Colonna, who appointed him as his theologian and entrusted him with spiritual guidance. In Rome, Joseph witnessed the plight of neglected and homeless children and became involved in charitable works. He joined the Confraternity of Christian Doctrine and started gathering children from the streets, offering them schooling.

After the disastrous flooding of the Tiber in 1597 that killed nearly two thousand people and created economic devastation, Joseph opened the first free public school in Rome, known as the Pious Schools, in 1600. This school provided education to poor children who had limited opportunities for learning. In addition, Joseph emphasized the moral and religious formation of his students. He focused on creating a safe and supportive learning environment for children, promoting a holistic approach that encompassed intellectual and spiritual development. His teaching methods became highly influential, and his Piarist order expanded to establish schools across Europe, including Italy, Spain, and Austria.

Pope Clement XIII canonized Joseph as a saint in 1769.

JOSEPH OF ARIMATHEA

BORN: 1st century BC, place unknown
DIED: 1st century AD, place unknown
FEAST DAY: March 29 (in some traditions)

PATRONAGE: Funeral directors, pallbearers, tin miners (in Britain)
SYMBOLS AND ATTRIBUTES: Holy Grail, shroud

Joseph of Arimathea was a wealthy member of the Sanhedrin, a secret disciple of Jesus, is one of the most beloved saints in Christian history and lore. He appears in all four of the Gospels of the New Testament. He is described in Luke as a good and righteous man, at odds with the Sanhedrin's decision to persecute Jesus. In John, he is revealed as a secret disciple of Jesus. In all accounts, he is connected to Jesus's burial. And though particulars may differ from story to story, Joseph went to Pontius Pilate after the crucifixion to ask him for Jesus's body. Pilate agreed. Joseph removed the crucified Jesus from the cross. He then wrapped Him in a linen cloth, and placed Him in a tomb owned by Joseph's family. His actions were significant because they fulfilled the prophecy that the Messiah would be buried in a rich man's tomb (Isaiah 53:9). They also demonstrated Joseph's commitment to Jesus and his willingness to publicly identify with Him, even though he had previously been a secret follower.

Despite his importance in the narrative of the crucifixion, Joseph fades from the Biblical record thereafter. However, his story does not end with the Gospel accounts. Over the centuries, a rich tapestry of folklore and legend has been woven around him.

Among the most famous of these legends is the story of the Holy Grail. In medieval European literature, the Holy Grail is often depicted as the cup, chalice, plate, bowl, or dish used by Jesus at the Last Supper, and is said to possess miraculous powers. The narrative of Joseph and the Grail dates back to Robert de Boron's poem "Joseph d'Arimathie" in the late twelfth or early thirteenth century. In the poem, Joseph receives the Grail from Jesus's Last Supper and uses it to catch Jesus's blood during the crucifixion. He is said to have brought the Grail to Britain and established the first Christian church at Glastonbury.

The association of Joseph with Glastonbury has led to numerous legends, including one in which Joseph planted his staff in the ground, blossoming into the Glastonbury Thorn, a tree that blooms twice a year.

In the British county of Cornwall, there are legends about tin mines owned by Joseph, supposedly used to support a trade connection between the eastern Mediterranean and Britain during the first century. While the existence of these mines can't be proven, the legends have been a part of Cornish and British folklore for centuries.

The story of Joseph and the Grail has influenced modern and contemporary pop culture, from Dan Brown's best-selling novel *The Da Vinci Code*, in which Joseph's association with the Holy Grail is a crucial plot element, to the adventure film *Indiana Jones and the Last Crusade* (1989), in which Joseph is said to have been the Grail's last known guardian before it found its way to the Knights Templar.

These contemporary interpretations often take considerable liberties with the character of Joseph and his story as told in the New Testament, usually emphasizing his role as the keeper of the Holy Grail. Yet whether through Biblical text, medieval legend, or modern storytelling, the figure of Joseph of Arimathea continues to captivate, embodying themes of faith, courage, and mystery.

Joseph died during the first century, and several places claim to be the true burial site, including the Abbey of Glastonbury in England and the Basilica of the Holy Sepulchre in Jerusalem. He is the patron saint of undertakers and funeral directors.

JOSEPH OF CUPERTINO

BORN: June 17, 1603, Cupertino, Apulia,
Kingdom of Naples

DIED: September 18, 1663, Osimo,
Papal States

FEAST DAY: September 18

PATRONAGE: Aviators, students, test
takers, astronauts

SYMBOLS AND ATTRIBUTES: Flying friar,
apple, lily

St. Joseph of Cupertino, also known as Giuseppe Maria Desa or Giuseppe da Copertino, was an Italian Catholic friar who lived during the seventeenth century. He is widely recognized for his remarkable mystical experiences, including levitation and ecstatic visions.

Joseph was traditionally believed to have been born in a stable on June 17, 1603, in the village of Cupertino, located in the southern region of Italy. His parents, Francesca and Felice Desa, were poor farmers, and Joseph was their third child. Joseph's father died before the child was born.

Growing up, Joseph was known for his pious nature and devotion toward Jesus. Although he was not a bright student and struggled with his studies, he desired to enter the religious life. Joseph faced challenges in joining religious orders because of his limited schooling and fits of ecstatic experiences. Initially, the Conventual Franciscan friars admitted him as a lay brother. However, Joseph's frequent spiritual trances made it difficult for him to carry out regular duties, leading to his dismissal. He then joined the Capuchin order but faced a similar outcome. Ultimately, a Franciscan convent near Cupertino welcomed him, first as a stable hand and finally as a member of the order.

His life was marked by extraordinary supernatural experiences that amazed those who witnessed them, famously, his ability to levitate, which frequently occurred during prayer or the celebration of Mass. He was said to rise from the ground and remain suspended in the air for an extended period, sometimes for hours. People would come from far and wide to witness this phenomenon and were often left awestruck.

Joseph's levitations were not the only mystical events that he experienced. He often experienced visions that lasted for hours. During these episodes, he would become unresponsive to external stimuli and was said to be completely absorbed in a divine reality.

Pope Clement XIII canonized Joseph of Cupertino as a saint in 1767. He is venerated as the patron saint of air travelers, pilots, and students taking exams.

JOSEPHINE BAKHITA

BORN: c. 1869, Olgossa, Darfur, Sudan

DIED: February 8, 1947, Schio,
Vicenza, Italy

FEAST DAY: February 8

PATRONAGE: Sudan, human
trafficking survivors

SYMBOLS AND ATTRIBUTES: Chains, cross

St. Josephine Bakhita is one of the most notable Black saints and the first Sudanese saint in history. She was born around 1869 in the Darfur region of Sudan, and endured a tumultuous early life marked by the horrors of slavery. Her birth name is lost to history.

When she was seven, Josephine was kidnapped by Arab slave traders while working in the fields near her home. After her abduction, Josephine was subjected to a grueling journey, being forced to walk long distances as part of the slave caravan heading toward El-Obeid, a major city in Sudan at the time. This treacherous trek exposed her to the harshness of slavery as she endured physical abuse, uncertain conditions, and the psychological torment of being separated from her family and everything she knew.

As a result of her traumatic experiences, the young girl forgot her birth name and was given the name "Bakhita," meaning "fortunate" in Arabic. During this time, she was forced to convert to Islam. She was sold and resold several times.

In 1883, Josephine Bakhita was purchased by an Italian official named Callisto Legnani. This marked a turning point in her life as she was taken to Venice, Italy, to live with the Canossian Sisters, a Catholic religious order. Under their compassionate guidance, Bakhita began to discover a sense of peace and security.

Bakhita's newfound freedom allowed her to embrace her Christian faith, and she decided to become a Catholic. In 1890, she was baptized and confirmed, taking the name Josephine Margherita Fortunata. Inspired by the charism and mission of the Canossian Sisters, Bakhita felt called to dedicate her life to serving others and spreading the message of God's love.

In 1896, Josephine Bakhita entered the novitiate of the Canossian Sisters in Schio, Italy. She embraced her vocation, striving to imitate the life of Jesus Christ through her acts of love, kindness, and selflessness. Her gentle and joyful disposition, coupled with her kindly and inspiring devotion to Jesus, touched the lives of those around her and drew others closer to the Church.

Following her profession of religious vows, Bakhita served in various capacities within the Canossian Sisters' convents, including as a cook, seamstress, and doorkeeper. Her humility and dedication to her duties further exemplified her commitment to a life of service and devotion.

Bakhita's health began to decline in her later years, and she suffered greatly. However, despite her physical suffering, she remained focused on Christ and expressed her desire to be united with God. Josephine Bakhita passed away on February 8, 1947, in Schio, Italy, leaving behind a legacy of compassion, forgiveness, and unwavering faith. She was beatified by Pope John Paul II in 1992 and canonized on October 1, 2000.

JUAN DIEGO

BORN: 1474, Cuautitlán, Aztec Empire (modern-day Mexico)

DIED: May 30, 1548, Mexico City, Viceroyalty of New Spain

FEAST DAY: December 9

PATRONAGE: Indigenous people, Americas

SYMBOLS AND ATTRIBUTES: Tilma with image of Our Lady of Guadalupe, roses

St. Juan Diego Cuauhtlatoatzin, commonly known as Juan Diego, was a sixteenth-century Nahua peasant who was central in one of the most significant religious events in Mexican history: the apparition of Our Lady of Guadalupe. His experiences shed light on the complex interplay between Indigenous culture and Spanish colonialism.

Juan Diego was born in a period of immense transition. By 1519, the Aztec Empire had expanded to its greatest extent. But the arrival of the Spanish that year ushered in profound change. As an adult, Juan Diego experienced the sweeping influences of Christianity on Indigenous societies, including his own Nahua people.

In 1531, a pivotal event occurred. While traversing Tepeyac Hill near Mexico City, Juan Diego reportedly encountered an apparition of the Virgin Mary. Speaking to him in Nahuatl, she said she desired that a church should be erected on that hill. He sought a sign of her genuineness, and the Virgin instructed him to gather roses—unexpected given the winter season—from the hillside. He gathered the roses, placing them in his tilma, a rudimentary cloak, so that he could carry them to the bishop. When he presented the roses to the bishop and the tilma was emptied, an image of the Virgin Mary, with Indigenous traits and encircled by light, miraculously appeared on the fabric.

The event and the ensuing Virgin of Guadalupe image resonated with the local community. The requested church was constructed, and the image became symbolic of the merging of Indigenous and Catholic identities in Mexico. The modern Basilica of Guadalupe, situated on the same site, attracts millions of global pilgrims yearly. The tale of Our Lady of Guadalupe holds enormous religious importance for Catholics around the world and is one of the most beloved devotions in the Church's history.

While scholars dispute the narrative's roots and meanings—some view it as a Spanish tool for Indigenous conversion, others as an authentic fusion of local beliefs and Catholic doctrine—Juan Diego's integral part in the story solidified his place in Mexican Catholicism. His significance was further acknowledged when Pope John Paul II canonized him in 2002, bestowing upon him the honor of being the first Indigenous saint of the Americas.

The narrative has inspired numerous artistic interpretations, from classic paintings to modern street art, emphasizing its cultural relevance. Prominent figures like Carl Anderson, the former Supreme Knight of the Knights of Columbus, have explored its wider societal impact, underscoring its messages of unity and optimism.

However, critiques persist, with claims of the story being used to overshadow Indigenous narratives or to establish a dominant Catholic perspective in Mexico. Regardless of these conflicting viewpoints, the narrative remains a cornerstone of Mexico's cultural and religious identity, representing cultural dialogue, adaptation, persistence, and the timeless essence of faith amid transformation.

JUDE

BORN: 1st century, place unknown
DIED: 1st century, place unknown
FEAST DAY: October 28
PATRONAGE: Desperate situations, lost causes, hospitals, Armenia

SYMBOLS AND ATTRIBUTES: Club, axe, medallion with face of Jesus, flame above head, ship

One of the twelve apostles of Jesus Christ, St. Jude is often referred to as Jude Thaddeus or Thaddeus to distinguish him from Judas Iscariot, who betrayed Jesus. Information about Jude in the New Testament is limited, and his exact relationship to Jesus is unclear.

According to tradition, Jude preached the Gospel after the death and resurrection of Jesus, traveling extensively to spread the teachings of Christianity. He is believed to have journeyed to Mesopotamia (modern-day Iraq) and Persia (modern-day Iran), where he faced persecution and opposition. Jude is known as the patron saint of desperate cases or lost causes, and he is often invoked by those seeking help in difficult or seemingly hopeless situations.

Jude's association with healing and desperate situations is reflected in the establishment of St. Jude Children's Research Hospital in the United States. This hospital, founded in 1962 by entertainer and comedian Danny Thomas, provides specialized medical treatment to children with cancer and other life-threatening diseases. Thomas was devoted to St. Jude and faced financial difficulties early in his career, leaving him unsure if he could support his family. Desperate, he prayed to St. Jude for guidance and vowed to build a shrine in his honor if he found success. Thomas's prayers were answered. Success followed.

St. Jude is often depicted in art with an axe, club, or medallion.

JULIA

BORN: c. early 5th century, Carthage or present-day Tunisia
DIED: c. 440, Corsica
FEAST DAY: May 23 or July 31

PATRONAGE: Torture victims, Corsica
SYMBOLS AND ATTRIBUTES: Palm branch, cross, chains

According to tradition, St. Julia, also known as Julia of Corsica, was born in either Carthage or present-day Tunisia. During her youth, pirates captured her and sold her as a slave to a pagan family, who brought her to Corsica. Tradition holds that she led a life of piety and devotion, serving her master with kindness and compassion. Julia's actions and unwavering faith eventually inspired those around her, and she was known for her virtuous character. However, her refusal to participate in pagan rituals and her open profession of Christianity angered her master, who subjected her to various forms of abuse.

Julia was eventually martyred for her faith. Accounts vary, but it is believed that she was either beheaded or thrown into the sea with a millstone tied around her neck. Her remains were discovered and enshrined in a church dedicated to her on the island of Corsica.

Julia has been revered throughout the centuries as a symbol of Christian faith, resilience, and purity. Her feast day is celebrated on May 23 in the Catholic Church and on July 31 in the Orthodox Church. She is the patron saint of Corsica and often depicted in religious art with a palm branch, and with the island of Corsica as a prominent attribute.

JULIE BILLIART

BORN: July 12, 1751, Cuvilly, Kingdom of France

DIED: April 8, 1816, Namur, United Kingdom of the Netherlands (modern-day Belgium)

FEAST DAY: April 8

PATRONAGE: Against poverty, bodily ills; sick people, educators, teachers

SYMBOLS AND ATTRIBUTES: Religious habit, cross

St. Julie Billiart was a French Catholic religious sister and the founder of the Institute of the Sisters of Notre Dame de Namur. She was born in Cuvilly, a small town in northern France.

From a young age, Julie showed a strong devotion to God, and despite her family's financial struggles, she was educated by the Benedictine nuns in nearby Amiens. However, at the age of twenty-two, after witnessing her father being shot, she was paralyzed by an unknown illness that left her bedridden for more than twenty years. She devoted herself to prayer and spiritual reflection, and she became known for her wisdom and spiritual guidance.

Despite her paralysis and confinement to bed, Julie displayed remarkable determination by teaching catechism to children in her village.

When a schismatic priest seized control of the local church, Julie staunchly refused to follow him and successfully rallied the entire village to do the same.

During Julie's time, the Catholic Church in France experienced significant turmoil. The political and societal shifts, especially during and after the French Revolution, led to divisions within the Church. Some priests, often referred to as schismatics, broke away from the authority of the pope and aligned themselves with revolutionary ideals. This presented faithful Catholics like Julie with a dilemma: follow these rebels and their newly established state church or stay loyal to the traditional teachings and risk persecution. Julie's refusal to align with the schismatic priest was not just a personal stand but a reflection of the broader religious tensions of her time. As a result, the authorities sought to silence her, leading Julie to flee and find refuge in hiding with the assistance of her friend, a wealthy woman named Françoise Blin de Bourdon.

In 1803, Julie had a vision in which she was called to create a religious order dedicated to the education of young girls. With the help of Françoise, she founded the Institute of Notre Dame in 1804. Named after Our Lady to honor the Virgin Mary and seek her intercession in their work, the institute aimed to provide support to girls from impoverished backgrounds, offering them opportunities for intellectual and spiritual growth.

Julie and Françoise devoted themselves to the establishment and growth of the institute. They worked to gather resources, recruit members, and develop a curriculum to meet the needs of the girls they served. The teachings focused on academic studies while fostering a solid foundation of faith and virtue.

The institute grew in popularity and influence, attracting young women who had the same passion for serving others and imparting knowledge. As the reputation of the Institute of Notre Dame spread, Julie and Françoise expanded their efforts beyond Amiens. They established fifteen Notre Dame convents throughout France, each dedicated to the mission of educating and caring for young girls in need.

JUNÍPERO SERRA

BORN: November 24, 1713, Petra, Mallorca, Kingdom of Spain

DIED: August 28, 1784, Mission San Carlos Borromeo, Italyo de Carmelo, Las Californias, New Spain (modern-day California, USA)

FEAST DAY: July 1

PATRONAGE: Vocations, Hispanic Americans

SYMBOLS AND ATTRIBUTES: Mission church, cross, Franciscan habit

Junípero Serra was a Spanish Franciscan friar and missionary best known for establishing missions during the Spanish colonization of Alta California, primarily present-day California.

He was born in 1713 in Petra, a small village on the island of Mallorca, Spain. His birth name was Miguel José Serra Ferrer. He came from a humble background, and his family belonged to the rural farming class. Junípero's parents, Antonio Nadal Serra and Margarita Ferrer, were devout Catholics.

At the age of sixteen, Serra entered the Franciscan order and took the name Junípero, inspired by the companion of St. Francis of Assisi, Brother Juniper. He joined the Lullian College in Palma, Mallorca, to pursue his studies in philosophy and theology, demonstrating extraordinary intellectual abilities and earning a reputation as a talented scholar.

Junípero later taught philosophy at Lullian College and was praised for his knowledge and oratory skills. In 1749, he was appointed to the University of Palma as a professor of theology, a position he held for several years. Junípero's academic career seemed promising, but he strongly desired to engage in missionary work and spread Christianity in the New World. He volunteered for the Franciscan missionary college in San Fernando, Mexico. His request was granted, and he set sail for Mexico in 1750. This marked the beginning of his journey to the Americas, where he would significantly impact California's history and development.

Upon arriving in Mexico, Serra was sent to the missionary college of San Fernando in Mexico City. There, he underwent further training and prepared for his missionary duties. Serra quickly became known for his religious zeal, dedication, and strong work ethic.

In 1752, he was appointed as the superior of the Sierra Gorda missions, a remote and challenging region inhabited by various Indigenous groups. He embarked on an arduous journey to the Sierra Gorda and began his missionary efforts among the Pame people. Junípero faced numerous hardships, including a lack of resources, harsh living conditions, and resistance from some Indigenous communities.

Junípero persevered in his mission to convert the Indigenous population to Christianity, learning the local languages, adapting to the Indigenous customs, and employing various strategies to attract converts. Junípero's efforts in the Sierra Gorda region resulted in the establishment of five missions, including Jalpan, Concá, and San Miguel.

During this period, Junípero also became involved in various aspects of mission administration. He served as a visiting inspector of the Franciscan missions in Mexico, ensuring their proper functioning and addressing any issues that arose. His dedication and leadership skills caught the attention of his superiors, who recognized his potential for greater responsibilities.

In 1768, Junípero received orders from the Franciscan authorities to join an expedition to establish missions in what is now Mexico. He embarked on the journey in early 1769 and arrived in the Baja peninsula, where he would lay the foundation for his subsequent missionary work in Alta California. Junípero would go on to found the first nine of more than two dozen California missions, including Mission San Diego de Alcalá, Mission San Carlos Borromeo de Carmelo (Carmel Mission), and Mission San Juan Capistrano.

His mission system aimed to convert the local population to Christianity, provide opportunities for learning, and introduce European agricultural techniques to the Indigenous people. Though successful for the Spanish at the time, over the years, this system had significant negative impacts on Indigenous populations, including the use of forced labor, cultural assimilation, and exposure to deadly European diseases.

Junípero Serra's efforts and leadership in establishing the California missions played a significant role in the Spanish colonization of California, and he is often considered the Father of the California Missions.

Junípero Serra's canonization by Pope Francis in 2015 generated significant debate and controversy, especially among Indigenous communities, due to the detrimental effects of Serra's mission system on Indigenous populations.

JUSTIN MARTYR

BORN: c. 100 AD, Flavia Neapolis (modern-day Nablus, West Bank)

DIED: c. 165, Rome, Italy, Roman Empire

FEAST DAY: June 1

PATRONAGE: Philosophers, apologists, lecturers

SYMBOLS AND ATTRIBUTES: Book, scroll

Justin Martyr, also known as St. Justin, was an early Christian apologist and philosopher who lived in the second century. He was born around the year 100 AD in Flavia Neapolis, an ancient city in Samaria (present-day Nablus, West Bank), in what was then the Roman province of Syria Palaestina. Justin is considered one of the most important figures in early Christian literature and apologetics.

Justin Martyr was initially influenced by various philosophical schools, including Stoicism, Aristotelianism, and Platonism. However, his search for philosophical truth led him to embrace Christianity. He is recognized as one of the first Christian thinkers to engage in dialogue with pagan philosophy and culture.

Justin Martyr is best known for his writings, particularly his two *Apologies* (Defenses) and *Dialogue with Trypho*. In his *Apologies*, Justin defended the beliefs and practices of Christianity against its critics and provided a rational defense of the Christian faith. He addressed Roman leadership, notably Emperor Antoninus Pius, appealing for tolerance and the recognition of Christianity as a legitimate religion.

Justin's *Dialogue with Trypho* is a philosophical and theological discourse between himself and a Jewish interlocutor named Trypho. In this work, Justin discusses the nature of Christianity and its relationship with Judaism, presenting Jesus as the fulfillment of Old Testament prophecies.

Justin Martyr's writings significantly influenced the development of Christian the-ology and apologetics. He emphasized the compatibility of faith and reason, seeking to show that Christianity was not an irrational or superstitious belief system. Justin also helped shape early Christian worship practices.

Justin Martyr's defense of Christianity came at a time when the religion faced per-secution and was often misunderstood by the Roman authorities and society. Around the year 165, during the reign of Emperor Marcus Aurelius, he was living in Rome and actively teaching and defending the Christian faith. This did not go over well with local authorities. He and several of his companions were arrested for promoting a false religion. They were brought before the Roman prefect, Junius Rusticus, who presided over their trial. Justin defended his beliefs and refused to renounce his faith in Christ. For this, he and his companions were beheaded.

Today, Justin Martyr is venerated as a saint in various Christian denominations, including the Eastern Orthodox Church and the Roman Catholic Church. His writings continue to be studied and appreciated for their insights into early Christian thought and their defense of the faith.

K

KATERI TEKAKWITHA

BORN: 1656, Ossernenon, Iroquois Confederacy (modern-day New York, USA)

DIED: April 17, 1680, Kahnawake, New France (modern-day Quebec, Canada)

FEAST DAY: July 14

PATRONAGE: Ecology, environment, loss of parents, Indigenous Americans, exiles

SYMBOLS AND ATTRIBUTES: Turtle (her clan symbol), lily, rosary, bird

St. Kateri Tekakwitha was an Indigenous woman who lived in the seventeenth century. She was the first Indigenous North American to be canonized a saint.

She was born in 1656 in a village near present-day Auriesville, New York. Her father was a Mohawk chief, and her mother was a Christian Algonquin woman captured in a raid and adopted into the Mohawk tribe. She was known for her quiet demeanor and spiritual inclinations from a young age.

When Kateri was around four years old, a smallpox epidemic swept through her village, which resulted in the death of her parents and younger brother. Although Kateri survived the illness, it left her with physical scars and weakened eyesight. As a result of the illness, she was often referred to as "Tekakwitha," which is believed to mean "she who bumps into things" or "she who puts things in order" in the Mohawk language.

Following the death of her family, Kateri was raised by her uncle, who became the chief of the tribe. Throughout her mourning, Kateri maintained a gentle and contemplative nature.

As Kateri grew older, she began to show interest in Christianity. This curiosity was likely influenced by the presence of Jesuit missionaries in the region, who would visit her village, instructing and catechizing the Mohawk people.

Kateri's decision to embrace Christianity caused tension within her community. Many tribal members opposed the spread of the foreign religion and viewed it as a threat to their traditional beliefs and way of life. Kateri remained steadfast in her desire to live a life dedicated to Christ. She secretly received instruction in the Catholic faith and, at the age of twenty, decided to be baptized, taking the name Kateri, in honor of St. Catherine of Siena.

Wanting to live out her faith more fully, Kateri eventually left her village and made an arduous journey to the Jesuit mission of St. Francis Xavier at Kahnawake, near Montreal, Canada. There, Kateri lived among other Indigenous converts. She dedicated herself to a life of prayer, penance, and service to others. Kateri's time in the mission allowed her to deepen her spiritual life and grow in her relationship with God.

Kateri's devotion to prayer was notable, spending hours in contemplation, seeking communion with the Divine, and offering intercessory prayers for others. She had a great love of the Eucharist. In addition to her devotion, Kateri Tekakwitha served others in the mission by caring for the sick, especially the elderly and infirm, showing compassion and tenderness in all that she did. Kateri's humility and willingness to assist those in need made her a beloved figure among the community. She was nicknamed "Lily of the Mohawks" as a nod to her purity and holiness.

Kateri Tekakwitha passed away on April 17, 1680, at the age of twenty-four. After her death, reports of miracles and healings associated with her intercession began to circulate. She was beatified by Pope John Paul II in 1980 and canonized as a saint by Pope Benedict XVI in 2012. (See Catherine of Siena.)

KATHARINE DREXEL

BORN: November 26, 1858, Philadelphia,
   Pennsylvania, USA
DIED: March 3, 1955, Bensalem Township,
   Pennsylvania, USA

FEAST DAY: March 3
PATRONAGE: Philanthropy, racial justice
SYMBOLS AND ATTRIBUTES: School,
   book, children

St. Katharine Drexel was an American heiress, philanthropist, and religious sister who dedicated her life to serving marginalized communities, particularly Indigenous and African Americans. She founded the Sisters of the Blessed Sacrament, a religious order devoted to advancing the intellectual and spiritual welfare of these communities, and she was known for her unwavering commitment to social justice.

Katharine was born to Francis Anthony Drexel and Hannah Langstroth on November 26, 1858, in Philadelphia, Pennsylvania. Her father was a wealthy banker and philanthropist. Her mother died five weeks after Katharine's birth.

Following her mother's death, Katharine's father married Emma Bouvier (an ancestor of Jacqueline Bouvier Kennedy Onassis), who became a loving and influential figure in the young girl's life. Emma instilled in her stepdaughter a deep sense of compassion and concern for those less fortunate.

Growing up, Katharine often witnessed her stepmother's charitable activities, including opening the family home to the poor and assisting the needy. These experiences instilled in Katharine a strong desire to make a positive impact on the lives of others.

From a young age, Katharine Drexel grappled with her life's purpose and contemplated how best to leverage her privileged position for the greater good. Her European sojourns, especially to Rome, introduced her to the Catholic Church's missionary endeavors and the service of religious orders to the underserved. In 1887, during one of her visits to the western United States, she was confronted by the dire circumstances of Indigenous Americans. Deeply moved, she channeled her family's wealth to champion their cause, establishing missions and schools to support them.

Heeding the Third Plenary Council of Baltimore's call set forth three years earlier, in 1884, Katharine and her sisters devoted themselves to missionary work.

Bolstered by her spiritual director, Bishop James O'Connor of Omaha, and with Pope Leo XIII's blessing, on February 12, 1891, Katharine committed to the monastic life. She took her vows, adopting the name Mother Katharine, and laid the foundation for the Sisters of the Blessed Sacrament. This order, under the guidance of the Sisters of Mercy in Pittsburgh, was singularly dedicated to uplifting Indigenous and African American communities.

In her lifetime, Mother Katharine spearheaded the establishment of numerous schools and missions. Among her notable contributions are the Xavier University in New Orleans, Louisiana—the first Catholic university in the United States for African Americans—and institutions like St. Michael Indian School in Arizona and the Holy Rosary Indian Mission in Montana.

In recognition of Mother Katharine's tireless work and impact in fostering care and education, she was beatified in 1988 by Pope John Paul II, who would later canonize her in 2000.

KILIAN

BORN: 640 Ireland

DIED: c. 689, Würzburg, Duchy of Franconia (modern-day Germany)

FEAST DAY: July 8

PATRONAGE: Rheumatism sufferers

SYMBOLS AND ATTRIBUTES: Sword, bishop's attire

Kilian, also known as Kilian of Würzburg, was a seventh-century Irish missionary. Born in Ireland, Kilian became a monk, then a bishop. Along with two companions, Colmán and Totnan, he was sent to evangelize the pagan territories of Franconia (modern-day Germany). They arrived in Würzburg, where Kilian began preaching the Christian faith and converting the locals. Kilian's mission faced opposition from Duke Gozbert, who was married to his brother's widow, a woman named Geilana, which violated the Church's laws on consanguinity. Kilian advised the duke to separate from his wife, but Geilana strongly opposed this. Tension ran high, and Kilian continued to preach the Gospel. One day when Duke Gozbert was away, Geilana sent soldiers to kill Kilian and his companions. They were beheaded in 689. The cult of Kilian multiplied following his martyrdom, and a cathedral was built in Würzburg in his honor. Today, he is revered as a symbol of courage, faith, and missionary work and is the patron saint of those who suffer from rheumatism.

KINGA OF POLAND

BORN: March 5, 1224, Esztergom, Kingdom of Hungary

DIED: July 24, 1292, Stary Sącz, Kingdom of Poland

FEAST DAY: July 24

PATRONAGE: Poland, salt miners

SYMBOLS AND ATTRIBUTES: Crown, salt mine, cross, Poland, Lithuania

Kunegunda Kinga, also known as St. Kinga of Poland, was a prominent figure in Polish history. She was born in 1224 in Hungary, and her father was King Béla IV of Hungary. Kinga was married off to Bolesław V the Chaste, the duke of Kraków and Sandomierz, as part of a political alliance between the two kingdoms.

Kinga is primarily remembered for her piety, charity, and dedication to religious life. After her husband's death in 1279, she devoted herself to a Christian life and became a nun. She entered the Poor Clare monastery in Stary Sącz, Poland, and lived there until she died in 1292.

Kinga supported numerous religious institutions, churches, and hospitals and was particularly concerned with the welfare of the poor and the sick.

Pope John Paul II canonized Kinga on June 16, 1999. She is often depicted holding a church or a small statue of a salt mine, as she is considered the patron saint of salt miners. Kinga's remains are enshrined in the Kinga's Chapel in her salt mine near Kraków.

L

LAWRENCE OF BRINDISI

BORN: July 22, 1559, Brindisi, Kingdom of Naples

DIED: July 22, 1619, Lisbon, Kingdom of Portugal

FEAST DAY: July 21

PATRONAGE: Brindisi, Italy

SYMBOLS AND ATTRIBUTES: Capuchin habit, crucifix

Also known as St. Lorenzo da Brindisi, St. Lawrence of Brindisi was an Italian Capuchin friar, theologian, scholar, and diplomat and is considered one of the great saints of the Counter-Reformation. He was born Giulio Cesare Russo into a family of Venetian merchants. Giulio was well educated, and from a young age, he displayed a natural gift for public speaking. Following his father's death, he continued his studies at St. Mark's College in Venice under the guidance of his uncle and joined the Capuchin Franciscan order when he was fifteen. He took the name Brother Lawrence and studied languages, becoming fluent in Italian, Latin, Hebrew, Greek, German, Spanish, and French.

Lawrence's reputation as a powerful and persuasive preacher grew, leading him to deliver Lenten sermons in Venice while still a deacon. At the age of twenty-three, he was ordained a priest, marking a significant milestone in his spiritual journey.

Pope Clement VIII recognized Lawrence's unique linguistic skills and appointed him to preach to the Jewish community in Rome. His fluency in Hebrew allowed him to connect with his audience and foster understanding between the two faiths.

Lawrence's contributions extended beyond his preaching. In 1599, he embarked on a mission to establish Capuchin monasteries in Germany and Austria, diligently striving to counteract the Protestant Reformation and reintroduce numerous individuals to the Catholic faith. He successfully founded friaries in Vienna, Prague, and Graz, leaving a lasting impact on the regions.

Lawrence's dedication to the Catholic cause reached its zenith when he became the imperial chaplain for the army of Rudolph II, Holy Roman Emperor. As tradition holds, he helped lead troops during the siege of Székesfehérvár in Hungary, armed only with a crucifix. His fearlessness and conviction inspired others to fight against the Ottoman Turks.

In 1602, Lawrence was elected as the vicar general of the Capuchin friars, a position of great honor and responsibility. He served as an advisor to his successors, offering his wisdom and guidance. Lawrence's commitment to the Catholic Church extended beyond his religious duties. He became a papal nuncio to Bavaria and Spain, working as a special envoy to resolve political and diplomatic matters.

Lawrence was also a prolific writer, covering many theological, exegetical, and spiritual topics. Some of his most notable works include his many sermons on a wide range of topics such as the lives of saints, theological teachings, moral exhortations, explanations of the Holy Mass, and reflections on Mary, her virtue, and her role in salvation history.

Lawrence died on his birthday, July 22, 1619. He was canonized as a saint by Pope Leo XIII in 1881 and named a Doctor of the Church.

St. Lawrence of Brindisi is often depicted in art wearing the brown robes of the Capuchin Franciscans, with a crucifix in one hand and a book in the other. His symbols include a pen and a quill, which represent his skills as a writer and theologian, as well as a sword, which symbolizes his efforts to defend the Church against its enemies.

LAWRENCE OF ROME

BORN: c. 225, possibly Heusca, Spain
DIED: August 10, 258, Rome, Italy,
    Roman Empire
FEAST DAY: August 10

PATRONAGE: Cooks, chefs, comedians
SYMBOLS AND ATTRIBUTES: Gridiron, palm
    branch, book

St. Lawrence, also known as Lawrence of Rome, was a deacon in the early Christian Church and was martyred for his faith during the reign of Emperor Valerian in the year 258.

Little is known about Lawrence's early life, but it is believed that he was born in Huesca, Spain, in the third century. He moved to Rome as a young man and became a deacon in the Church, even though Christianity was considered a crime punishable by death. Lawrence served as a trusted advisor to Pope Sixtus II, who was also his friend.

In 258, Emperor Valerian issued an edict ordering the execution of all Christian clergy. Pope Sixtus II was captured and beheaded, and Lawrence was left in charge of the Church's treasury. It is believed that the emperor demanded that Lawrence turn over all of the Church's wealth, but Lawrence refused, saying that the Church's true treasure was the poor.

The emperor was furious with Lawrence's defiance and ordered that he be executed by being roasted alive on a gridiron. Legend says that while Lawrence was being burned, he derided his executioners, famously saying, "Turn me over. I'm done on this side." He died a martyr's death on August 10, 258.

LAWRENCE RUIZ

BORN: c. 1594, Binondo, Manila
DIED: September 29, 1637,
    Nagasaki, Japan
FEAST DAY: September 28

PATRONAGE: Filipinos, the Philippines,
    immigrants, the poor
SYMBOLS AND ATTRIBUTES: Rope, palm
    branch, rosary

St. Lawrence Ruiz, also known as Lorenzo Ruiz, was a Filipino saint and martyr. He was born around 1594 in Manila, Philippines, during the time when the Philippines were under Spanish colonial rule. Lawrence Ruiz was a skilled calligrapher and a member of the Confraternity of the Holy Rosary.

In 1636, he was falsely accused of murder and sought refuge on a ship bound for Japan. However, unbeknownst to him, the country had closed its borders to foreigners, particularly Christians, who were facing persecution at the time. Upon arriving in Japan, Lawrence Ruiz and other Christians were arrested and subjected to interrogation and torture, in an effort to force them to renounce their faith. Lawrence refused. Alongside his companions, he was ultimately sentenced to death. On September 27, 1637, Lawrence Ruiz and his fellow martyrs were executed by hanging in Nagasaki.

Lawrence Ruiz is considered the first Filipino saint and the protomartyr of the Philippines. He was canonized by Pope John Paul II on October 18, 1987, in Manila.

LEO I

BORN: c. 400, Rome, Italy, Western Roman Empire

DIED: November 10, 461, Rome, Italy, Western Roman Empire

FEAST DAY: November 10

PATRONAGE: Papacy

SYMBOLS AND ATTRIBUTES: Papal vestments, chair, pastoral staff

St. Leo the Great, also known as Pope St. Leo I, was an influential bishop of Rome, serving as pope from 440 until his death. He is known for his work in defending the orthodox faith against various heresies and for his pastoral leadership during a time of great turmoil and upheaval in the Western Roman Empire.

Though little is known about his early life, he may have been born around 400 to parents of Tuscan heritage. During Pope Celestine I's papacy (r. 422–432), Leo was ordained as a deacon in Rome around 431. Pope Celestine I was known for his strong defense of orthodoxy and his involvement in resolving doctrinal controversies. Leo likely gained valuable experience and exposure to the workings of the Church, which would influence his own theological and administrative endeavors.

Leo's service under Pope Sixtus III (r. 432–440) was also significant. Pope Sixtus III is known for overseeing the construction of the Basilica of Santa Maria Maggiore in Rome and for his efforts to maintain the unity and orthodoxy of the Church. As a deacon under Pope Sixtus III, Leo served the Church in various capacities, gaining valuable insights into Church governance, theology, and pastoral care.

Upon the death of Pope Sixtus III, Leo was chosen as his successor and became the forty-fifth pope of the Catholic Church on September 29, 440.

As pope, Leo delivered a remarkable series of sermons that have come to be known as the Sermons of Leo the Great or the Ninety-Six Sermons. These sermons are considered some of the most influential and eloquent theological writings of early Christianity and cover a wide range of topics, including doctrinal matters, moral teachings, pastoral guidance, and interpretations of Scripture. These discourses emphasized the authority and primacy of the Holy See and the importance of unity within the Church. They also focused on Christology, the nature of Christ, and the mystery of the Incarnation.

One of the most important events of Leo's career involved a letter he sent to Flavian, the patriarch of Constantinople, in 449. The backdrop to this event was the Christological controversy surrounding the teachings of Nestorius, the former patriarch of Constantinople. Nestorius espoused a view suggesting a separation between Christ's divine and human natures, effectively denying the unity of Christ's personhood. This teaching raised concerns within the Church and threatened to divide the Christian community.

In response to the controversy, a Church council in 431, known as the Council of Ephesus was called, condemned Nestorius's teachings as heretical and affirmed the unity of Christ's person in the hypostatic union of his divine and human natures. However, the theological debates continued following the meeting and tensions escalated. Flavian found himself at the center of the controversy, and he sought support and guidance from Pope Leo I in Rome.

In 449, Leo I composed a letter known as the Tome of Leo or the Epistola Dogmatica. This letter, addressed to Flavian, articulated Leo's theological understanding of the Incarnation and the nature of Christ. He explained that in the mystery of the Incarnation, Jesus Christ is both truly God and truly man, without confusion or division. Leo's writings sought to provide clarity and precision on this crucial aspect of Christian doctrine.

Pope Leo I's missive was well received by Flavian but was challenged by others. Finally, at the Council of Chalcedon in 451, it was read and affirmed, ultimately upholding Leo's teachings and declaring them orthodox. The council condemned both Nestorius's teachings and the opposite extreme of Eutyches, who advocated for the absorption of Christ's humanity into his divinity.

The Tome of Leo became a significant theological document, contributing to the formulation of the Chalcedonian Creed, which solidified the orthodox Christological understanding of the faith while clarifying and affirming the Church's teachings on the nature of Christ and His Incarnation.

In 452, Pope Leo I shifted his focus to politics in an effort to prevent bloodshed. He courageously met with Attila the Hun as he and his army were on their way to invade Rome. The details of their conversation remain uncertain, but it is believed that Leo utilized diplomatic persuasion, appeals to Attila's conscience, and potentially even threats of divine retribution to convince him to withdraw his forces. Attila decided to spare Rome, and he retreated from Italy. Pope Leo I's intervention in preventing the sacking of Rome by Attila was celebrated as an extraordinary accomplishment, highlighting his leadership and influence, and it was lauded both within the Christian community and throughout the Roman Empire.

However, in 455, the Vandals, led by Geiseric, launched a devastating sack of Rome. The city suffered widespread looting and destruction, causing immense suffering and distress among its citizens. When Geiseric and his forces entered Rome, Leo I went out to meet him, urging him to spare lives and prevent further destruction. Geiseric agreed to some extent. Although the sack of Rome could not be fully prevented, Pope Leo negotiated with Geiseric to protect the lives of the inhabitants and prevent the mass killing and enslavement that often accompanied such sieges. Additionally, Leo I persuaded Geiseric to spare the ancient churches of St. Peter and St. Paul from destruction.

After the sack of Rome, Pope Leo I was vital in restoring order, providing aid to the victims, and rebuilding damaged churches and infrastructure. His efforts were instrumental in helping Rome recover from the devastating event.

Pope Leo I was canonized as a saint by the Catholic Church shortly after his death in 461 and was made a Doctor of the Church in 1754.

LONGINUS

BORN: 1st century AD, place unknown

DIED: 1st century, place unknown

FEAST DAY: March 15

PATRONAGE: Mantua, Italy

SYMBOLS AND ATTRIBUTES: Spear, helmet, eyes

What we know about St. Longinus, also known as St. Longinus the Centurion, comes primarily from the apocryphal gospel of Nicodemus.

In John 19:34, as Jesus hangs on the cross, an unnamed soldier—who came in later centuries to be called Longinus—thrust his spear into Jesus's side to ensure he was dead. Blood and water flowed out of the wound.

There is no further mention in the Bible, but according to the apocryphal gospel of Nicodemus, Longinus experienced spiritual transformation as he recognized the divine nature of Jesus at that moment. Tradition holds that Longinus then professed his faith, saying, "Truly this man was the Son of God."

After this event, Longinus converted to Christianity and left the military. He is believed to have become a monk in Cappadocia, an ancient region in present-day Turkey. Sometime thereafter, Longinus was martyred for his faith by beheading.

The lance associated with St. Longinus is commonly referred to as the "Holy Lance," the "Spear of Destiny," or the "Lance of Longinus." According to Christian tradition and medieval legends, the lance was believed to have acquired miraculous powers due to its contact with the body of Jesus. The lance was said to cure ailments, bring fertility, and protect against evil.

Over the centuries, various relics claiming to be the Holy Lance emerged, and many rulers and institutions sought to possess them. One of the most famous of these is the Hofburg Spear housed in Vienna, Austria. This artifact has been associated with Charlemagne and the Holy Roman Emperors and is now on display in the Imperial Treasury of the Hofburg Palace.

The Holy Lance gained further status during the Middle Ages as the "Spear of Destiny." It was believed that whoever possessed the spear would hold great power and authority. The spear became a symbol of divine right, and kings and conquerors sought to obtain it for their own purposes.

LOUIS AND ZÉLIE MARTIN

BORN: Louis, August 22, 1823; Zélie, December 23, 1831, France
DIED: Louis, July 29, 1894; Zélie, August 28, 1877, France

FEAST DAY: July 12
PATRONAGE: Married couples
SYMBOLS AND ATTRIBUTES: Wedding rings, roses, the Martin family

Louis and Zélie Martin were a French couple and parents of St. Thérèse of Lisieux, also known as The Little Flower. Both were devout Catholics, and influenced the spiritual formation of their children.

Louis Martin was born in Bordeaux, France, on August 22, 1823. He was a watchmaker by trade and a religious man; he considered becoming a monk but decided to pursue a family life instead. He married Zélie Guérin on July 13, 1858.

Zélie Martin, born Marie-Azélie Guérin on December 23, 1831, in Normandy, France, was a lacemaker before her marriage. She also had a strong faith and had thought to enter the religious life as a nun. However, due to her delicate health, Zélie was not able to pursue this vocation. Instead, she became a devoted wife and mother.

Louis and Zélie had nine children, four of whom died at a young age. The remaining five daughters all entered religious life, with the most famous being Thérèse, who became a Carmelite nun and a beloved saint and Doctor of the Church.

The Martins were known for their love and devotion to God, strong family bonds, and emphasis on simplicity and humility. Louis and Zélie influenced their children's spiritual development, fostering a deep love for God and encouraging their daughters to embrace a life of holiness.

Zélie died on August 28, 1877, and Louis passed away on July 29, 1894. They were both declared Venerable by the Catholic Church in 1994. On October 18, 2015, they were canonized together as saints by Pope Francis, making them the first couple in the history of the Church to be canonized together. (See Thérèse of Lisieux.)

LOUIS BERTRAND

BORN: January 9, 1526, Valencia, Crown of Aragon (modern-day Spain)

DIED: October 9, 1581, Valencia, Spain

FEAST DAY: October 10

PATRONAGE: Novitiate students in the Dominican order, Colombia, invoked during earthquakes and disasters

SYMBOLS AND ATTRIBUTES: Dominican habit, crucifix, a snake in a chalice

St. Louis Bertrand, also known as St. Louis Bertrán or St. Luis Bertrand, was a Spanish Dominican friar and missionary. In his early twenties, Louis entered the Dominican order, where he was ordained a priest and appointed professor of theology at the Dominican College of Valencia.

However, Louis's true calling was in missionary work. In 1562, he was sent to present-day Colombia, South America. Louis traveled extensively, preaching the Gospel, baptizing Indigenous people, and ministering to the sick and needy, and he is credited with numerous miraculous healings and conversions. He worked hard to defend the rights and dignity of the Indigenous people, advocating for their fair treatment and protection.

Louis's gentle, humble nature endeared him to the Indigenous communities he served. Many considered him a saint during his lifetime.

After seven years in South America, he returned to Spain in 1569 to further advocate for oppressed Indigenous communities. He became a spiritual advisor to many, including St. Teresa of Ávila, in Valencia. After years of tireless work, he fell ill and then died on October 9, 1581. His relics are enshrined in the Church of Santo Tomás and San Felipe Neri in Valencia.

Louis was canonized by Pope Clement X in 1671. He is often invoked as a protector against earthquakes due to his reputed ability to calm tremors during his missionary work. (See Dominic.)

LOUIS DE MONTFORT

BORN: January 31, 1673, Montfort-sur-Meu, Kingdom of France

DIED: April 28, 1716, Saint-Laurent-sur-Sèvre, Kingdom of France

FEAST DAY: April 28

PATRONAGE: Preachers, heralds of the Gospel

SYMBOLS AND ATTRIBUTES: Cross, rosary, book, Virgin Mary

St. Louis-Marie Grignion de Montfort was a French Catholic priest and an influential thinker and writer. He was born into a devout Catholic family in Montfort-sur-Meu, a town in Brittany, France, on January 31, 1673. His parents, Jean-Baptiste Grignion and Jeanne Robert, instilled in him a deep faith and love for the Church. At the age of twelve, Louis attended the Jesuit College in Rennes, where he displayed a particular devotion to the Blessed Virgin Mary, which would become a defining characteristic of his life and ministry.

After completing his studies, Louis embarked on his priestly formation and was ordained a priest in 1700. He initially served as a chaplain in a hospital in Nantes, where he dedicated himself to caring for the sick and the poor.

In 1703, in collaboration with Blessed Marie Louise Trichet, he co-founded the Daughters of Wisdom (or the Daughters of Divine Wisdom). This community, originally only a few sisters, was established to carry out various works of mercy, including teaching, nursing the sick, and serving the poor. In 1713 Louis also founded a separate group of priests, the Missionaries of the Company of Mary, who collaborated with the Daughters of Wisdom in their missionary and charitable endeavors locally and abroad.

Louis is best known for his writings on the Blessed Virgin Mary. His most famous work is *True Devotion to the Blessed Virgin Mary* (also known as *Treatise on True Devotion to the Blessed Virgin*), which outlines his teachings on Marian consecration and total consecration to Jesus through Mary. The book's central theme is the idea of "total consecration" to Jesus through Mary. Louis proposed that individuals should wholly and willingly give themselves to Mary, allowing her to guide and mold them in their journey toward Christ. According to Louis, Mary's role is not to replace Jesus but to lead individuals to Him more perfectly and securely. He believed that by consecrating oneself to Mary, one could better imitate her virtues, love Jesus more ardently, and grow in holiness.

His teachings and writings had a lasting impact on Catholic spirituality, and he is considered a significant figure in developing the Marian movement within the Church. St. Louis de Montfort was canonized as a saint by Pope Pius XII in 1947.

LOUISE DE MARILLAC

BORN: August 12, 1591, Le Meux, Kingdom
of France

DIED: March 15, 1660, Paris, Kingdom
of France

FEAST DAY: March 15

PATRONAGE: Social workers, widows,
disagreeable children

SYMBOLS AND ATTRIBUTES: Daughters of
Charity habit, cross

St. Louise de Marillac was a French Catholic saint known for her charitable work and contributions to the development of the Daughters of Charity, a religious congregation dedicated to serving the poor and marginalized. In 1613, she married Antoine Le Gras and had a son. However, her husband passed away in 1625, leaving Louise widowed and responsible for raising her child alone.

Louise was deeply committed to both her son and to serving others. She met Vincent de Paul, a French priest known for his works of charity, and became his collaborator and close friend. He had founded the Ladies of Charity, a community of women dedicated to serving the poor, sick, and needy. In 1633, Louise took some of Vincent's volunteers under her roof and trained and organized them for their work. This led to the development of the Daughters of Charity, a religious order instrumental in establishing hospitals, orphanages, and other charitable institutions throughout France.

Louise provided the sisters with spiritual guidance and practical skills necessary for their work. She emphasized the importance of humility, simplicity, and compassionate service, encouraging them to care for those in need with love and respect.

Louise was canonized as a saint by the Catholic Church in 1934. (See Vincent de Paul.)

LUCY OF SYRACUSE

BORN: 283, Syracuse, Roman Empire

DIED: 304, Syracuse, Roman Empire

FEAST DAY: December 13

PATRONAGE: The blind, martyrs,
authors, salespeople

SYMBOLS AND ATTRIBUTES: Eyes on a plate,
palm branch, lamp

St. Lucy of Syracuse, also known as St. Lucia, is a beloved and revered early Christian martyr. She was born in Syracuse, Sicily, in the late third century, during the reign of the Roman Emperor Diocletian.

According to tradition, she came from a noble Christian family. Her father died when she was young, and her mother, Eutychia, raised her. Lucy was known for her deep faith and commitment to Jesus Christ. She vowed to live in service to God and remain a virgin. She also gave her money and possessions to the poor and devoted herself to acts of charity.

However, Lucy's mother had arranged a marriage for her to a greedy pagan nobleman who thwarted her plans to aid those in need. When her mother fell seriously ill, Lucy convinced her mother to make a pilgrimage to the tomb of St. Agatha to pray for healing. Miraculously, Eutychia was healed.

Having thus demonstrated the power of God, Lucy asked her mother once again to allow her to distribute her dowry to the poor. Eutychia agreed, and the wealth was distributed accordingly. However, when news of this reached Lucy's betrothed, he became enraged, accused Lucy of being a Christian, and reported her to the Roman authorities.

Lucy was arrested, charged with being a Christian, and subjected to various tortures, all designed to force her to renounce her faith. She refused. The accounts of her martyrdom differ, but many versions report that her eyes were gouged out before she was ultimately executed by the sword.

St. Lucy is widely venerated as the patron saint of the blind and those with eye-related illnesses or vision problems. She is also invoked for protection against various afflictions, including diseases of the eye. (See Agatha.)

LUKE THE EVANGELIST

BORN: 1st century AD, Antioch
(modern-day Syria)
DIED: 1st century, Thebes, Greece
FEAST DAY: October 18

PATRONAGE: Artists, notaries, physicians, surgeons, students
SYMBOLS AND ATTRIBUTES: Winged ox or bull, physician's tools, book, quill

St. Luke the Evangelist, also known as Luke the Physician, holds a central position in the New Testament as one of the Four Evangelists. He was a trusted companion of the apostle Paul and the author of the Gospel of Luke and the Acts of the Apostles.

Luke, born in Antioch, Syria, in the early first century AD, was a Greek-speaking Gentile known for his exceptional literary skill. His Gospel reflects his erudition and eloquence. It is believed that Luke accompanied the apostle Paul on his second and third missionary journeys, offering him spiritual support during his imprisonment in Rome. Paul affectionately referred to him as "the beloved physician."

Luke's Gospel provides a comprehensive account of the life and teachings of Jesus Christ. It distinguishes itself in several ways from the other Gospels. Notably, it offers a detailed and extensive narrative of Jesus's birth, including the Annunciation, the

Visitation of Mary to Elizabeth, the Magnificat, and the Nativity scene with the shepherds. Through vivid descriptions, Luke paints a vibrant picture of the events surrounding Jesus's miraculous arrival.

Moreover, unlike the other Gospel writers, Luke directs his narrative specifically toward a predominantly Gentile audience. This emphasis underscores the universal nature of Jesus's message, highlighting God's inclusive love for all humanity.

Luke's Gospel also emphasizes the significant role of women in Jesus's ministry, giving prominence to their contributions within the narrative. Noteworthy examples include Mary, the mother of Jesus; Elizabeth, the mother of John the Baptist; Anna, the prophetess; and Mary Magdalene, whom tradition holds was one of Jesus's most devoted disciples.

Another distinctive aspect of Luke's Gospel is its focus on Jesus's compassion and mercy toward the marginalized and outcasts of society. It repeatedly emphasizes His teachings on love, forgiveness, and caring for others, calling all believers to extend compassion to those in need.

While parables can be found in other Gospels, Luke includes several unique ones that offer distinct spiritual lessons. The Parable of the Good Samaritan, the Prodigal Son, the Rich Man and Lazarus, and the Pharisee and the Tax Collector are just a few examples. Luke addresses issues of social justice and wealth disparities within these stories more explicitly than in other Gospel accounts, underscoring Jesus's teachings about caring for the poor, the importance of sharing possessions, and challenging the love of money.

Luke's Gospel also places significant emphasis on prayer. It depicts Jesus seeking solitude for contemplation and includes the Lord's Prayer, highlighting the role of prayer as foundational to one's spiritual path. Here, Jesus is not only an exemplar of devotional practice; he is also an instructor.

In addition to the Gospel, Luke is the author of the Acts of the Apostles, which chronicles the development of the early Christian Church. This book provides a detailed account of the disciples' teachings and miracles and records the spread of the Gospel from Jerusalem to other areas of the world.

St. Luke is honored as a saint in the Roman Catholic, Orthodox, and Anglican traditions and his symbol is a bull or winged ox. In art, he is often depicted near, or holding, an ox, suggesting his gentleness, or with a painting of the Virgin Mary, representing his emphasis on the importance of Mary in the life of Jesus. (See Paul.)

LYDWINE OF SCHIEDAM

BORN: March 18, 1380, Schiedam, County
of Holland (modern-day Netherlands)
DIED: April 14, 1433, Schiedam,
Burgundian Netherlands

FEAST DAY: April 14
PATRONAGE: Sickness, ice skaters,
multiple sclerosis
SYMBOLS AND ATTRIBUTES: Cross

Lydwine of Schiedam was a Dutch mystic and stigmatist who lived in the fourteenth and early fifteenth centuries. She is best known for her extraordinary spiritual experiences and the physical suffering she endured throughout her life. When she was a teenager she fell while ice skating and broke a rib. The injury did not heal properly and caused her great pain. Over time, her condition worsened, and she experienced a series of mysterious ailments and afflictions.

Lydwine's sufferings included severe chronic pain, loss of appetite, difficulty swallowing, and paralysis. She became bedridden and unable to move but maintained a deep faith and devoted herself to prayer, offering her suffering for the salvation of others. Many scholars today believe that Lydwine had developed multiple sclerosis.

In 1396, when Lydwine was around sixteen years old, she began to exhibit signs of the stigmata—the wounds of Christ's crucifixion appearing on her body. She reportedly bore the marks of the Crown of Thorns, the scourging, and the wounds of the nails in her hands and feet. The stigmata would periodically bleed and cause her immense pain. The wounds were said to emit a sweet fragrance, which was considered a sign of holiness.

Lydwine's stigmata attracted attention and drew pilgrims seeking her intercession and spiritual guidance. Her reputation for sanctity spread, and she became known as a living saint. After her death, her tomb in Schiedam became a popular pilgrimage site. In 1890, Pope Leo XIII beatified her, and in 1898, she was canonized as a saint by Pope Leo's successor, Pope Pius X.

St. Lydwine of Schiedam is considered the patron saint of the sick, chronically ill, and ice skaters. Her life and example continue to inspire people to find strength in the face of suffering and to offer their pain for the well-being of others.

M

MAGDALENE OF CANOSSA

BORN: March 1, 1774, Verona, Republic
of Venice

DIED: April 10, 1835, Verona, Kingdom
of Lombardy-Venetia

FEAST DAY: May 8

PATRONAGE: Canossian Daughters of
Charity, Canossian Sons of Charity

SYMBOLS AND ATTRIBUTES: Cross, crucifix,
children, religious habit

Magdalene of Canossa was an Italian Roman Catholic nun. She belonged to a noble family and was raised in a pious Catholic household. She is best known for founding the Canossian Daughters, officially known as the Daughters of Charity, Servants of the Poor, which she established in 1808 with the aim of providing education and assistance to the poor and disadvantaged, particularly in the aftermath of the Napoleonic Wars.

The Canossian Sisters focused on various charitable works, including running schools, orphanages, hospitals, and homes for the elderly. Under Magdalene's guidance, the congregation multiplied and expanded beyond Italy. Today, the Canossian Sisters serve in many countries.

Magdalene of Canossa is revered for her humility, compassion, and commitment to social justice. She was canonized as a saint by Pope John Paul II on October 2, 1988.

MALACHY

BORN: 1094–1095, Armagh, Kingdom
of Ireland

DIED: November 2, 1148, Clairvaux,
Kingdom of France

FEAST DAY: November 3

PATRONAGE: Ireland

SYMBOLS AND ATTRIBUTES: Bishop's
attire, book

St. Malachy, also known as Malachy O'Morgair or Maolmhaodhog ua Morgair in Irish Gaelic, was an influential Irish bishop who lived during the twelfth century. He was born in Armagh, Ireland, in 1094 or 1095. At age eight, he was sent to study with Abbot Imar O'Hagan, known for his strict discipline and deep spirituality. Malachy was ordained as a priest at the age of twenty-five and began his ministry as a monk at the Abbey of Bangor in County Down, where he was known for his adherence to the rules of monastic life and his devotion to the care of the sick and the poor. He became the abbot of the monastery, where he implemented reforms and brought the community back to a more exacting observance of monastic rule.

In 1132, Malachy was appointed archbishop of Armagh, the highest position in the Irish Church. At that time, the Church in Ireland was in a state of disarray, with many bishops and clergy leading lives of luxury and neglecting their pastoral duties. Malachy worked hard to reform the Church in Ireland, visiting parishes throughout the country and preaching about the importance of spiritual renewal and the need for bishops and clergy to live lives of holiness and service. He also established new monasteries and helped to rebuild churches and other religious institutions that had fallen into disrepair.

In 1139, Malachy embarked on a journey to Rome to meet Pope Innocent. On the way, he visited Bernard of Clairvaux. The two developed a strong bond of spiritual kinship as they shared a deep commitment to Church reform. Bernard would write a biography of Malachy, offering insight into the Irish saint's life and virtues and attesting to the depth of their friendship.

Malachy's visit proved to be of long-lasting significance for Ireland. He invited monks from Clairvaux to establish the first Cistercian monastery in Ireland, the Mellifont Abbey, in 1142. This abbey would become the motherhouse for other Cistercian monasteries in the country.

While Malachy may have been influential in helping to reform the Church in Ireland, he is perhaps best known today for the document commonly referred to as the *Prophecy of the Popes*. The prophecy is a list of brief Latin phrases, each supposedly describing a future pope. There are 112 phrases in all, starting with Pope Celestine II (elected in 1143) and ending with a pope referred to as "Peter the Roman," who is said to reign during a time of great tribulation that is leading to the end of the world. Each phrase is believed to correspond to a specific pope and is generally thought to describe some characteristic of that pontiff, or of the times during his papacy. For example, the phrase attributed to Pope John Paul II (1978–2005) is "*De labore Solis*," which means "of the labor of the sun" or "from the toil of the sun." Some interpreters believe this refers to John Paul II's extensive travels or his birth during a solar eclipse.

Malachy's life was cut short by illness, and he passed away on November 2, 1148, in Clairvaux, France, during a visit to the Abbey of Clairvaux. In a poignant closure to their friendship, it was reported that Malachy died in the arms of Bernard. Malachy's remains were transferred to Ireland and interred at Down Cathedral in Downpatrick.

Pope Clement III canonized Malachy on July 6, 1199. (See Bernard of Clairvaux.)

MARCELLINUS AND PETER

BORN: 3rd century, place unknown

DIED: 304, Rome, Italy, Roman Empire

FEAST DAY: June 2

PATRONAGE: Sufferers of infectious disease

SYMBOLS AND ATTRIBUTES: Cross, palm branch

Sts. Marcellinus and Peter were early Christian martyrs who lived in the third century during the persecution under Emperor Diocletian. Marcellinus, a priest, converted many to Christianity while Peter served the early Church as an exorcist, expelling evil spirits. After being arrested for being Christians, they converted their jailer and his family after a miraculous event. This act further angered authorities, and the two friends were forced to walk miles outside Rome, clear an area for their grave, and were beheaded in a forest.

Their legacy within the Christian community is evidenced by their mention in the Roman Canon of the Mass and the celebration of their feast day on June 2. Pope Damasus I honored them in the fourth century, and over the years, their burial site became a pilgrimage destination. Their relics, with a history of legendary travels and tales, are revered in places like Seligenstadt and Cremona Cathedral in Italy.

MARGARET MARY ALACOQUE

BORN: July 22, 1647, L'Hautecour, Kingdom of France

DIED: October 17, 1690, Paray-le-Monial, Kingdom of France

FEAST DAY: October 17

PATRONAGE: Devotees of the Sacred Heart

SYMBOLS AND ATTRIBUTES: Heart, image of Jesus revealing His Sacred Heart, nun's habit

St. Margaret Mary Alacoque was a French nun and mystic who played a significant role in the development of the devotion to the Sacred Heart of Jesus. Her mystical experiences, including visions of Jesus and conversations with Him, led her to promote a message of love, mercy, and compassion in the Catholic Church.

Margaret Mary was born on July 22, 1647, in the small village of L'Hautecour in Burgundy, France. She was the fifth of seven children of Claude Alacoque, a notary, and Philiberte Lamyn, a homemaker. When Margaret Mary was around eight years old, her father died, and shortly thereafter, Margaret Mary contracted rheumatic fever. Her family sent her to the Poor Clares, where she was bedridden for five years. There the nuns helped instill in her a love of prayer and devotion to the Eucharist.

At the age of twenty-four, she entered the Order of the Visitation of Holy Mary in Paray-le-Monial, a contemplative religious community known for emphasizing humility and devotion. Her life as a nun was difficult, as she was frequently ill and experienced many spiritual trials. During her time at the monastery, she began to experience mystical visions and conversations with Jesus.

Margaret Mary's first mystical experience occurred on December 27, 1673, when she prayed before the Blessed Sacrament. She saw a vision of Jesus, who showed her His heart, flames emanating from its crown. Jesus spoke to her: "Behold the Heart that has so loved me. Instead of gratitude, I receive from the greater part of mankind only ingratitude." For the next eighteen months, Margaret Mary had several more visions and conversations with Jesus. In these experiences, Jesus spoke to her about the importance of love, mercy, and compassion, and the need for the Church to promote these virtues. He also revealed his desire for a feast day to be established in honor of the Sacred Heart. Margaret Mary shared these experiences with her confessor, St. Claude de la Colombière, who believed in the authenticity of her visions and helped her to promote the devotion to the Sacred Heart.

While some within the Church were skeptical of her visions, Margaret Mary's message of love and devotion to the Sacred Heart slowly spread throughout France and Europe. Pope Clement XIII approved her devotion to the Sacred Heart; she was canonized a saint by Pope Benedict XV in 1920. She is often depicted in art in the presence of the Sacred Heart, dressed in her nun's habit.

MARGARET OF HUNGARY

BORN: January 27, 1242, Klis Fortress, Kingdom of Croatia

DIED: January 18, 1270, Budapest, Kingdom of Hungary

FEAST DAY: January 18

PATRONAGE: Fasting and prayer

SYMBOLS AND ATTRIBUTES: Dominican habit, lily, book

St. Margaret of Hungary was a medieval European princess and a member of the Árpád dynasty, which ruled the Kingdom of Hungary during that era. She was born on January 27, 1242, in the city of Klis, which is now in Croatia. Margaret was the daughter of King Béla IV of Hungary and Maria Laskarina, a Byzantine princess.

At a young age, Margaret was promised in marriage to the future Bohemian king, Ottokar II of Bohemia, as part of a political alliance. However, Margaret resisted this arrangement and, with her parents' consent, decided to dedicate her life to serving God instead. She took vows of chastity and entered a Dominican convent of Veszprém in Hungary. There, she continued to live a life of humility, prayer, and service to the needy.

A mystic and miracle worker, Margaret died at the age of twenty-eight on January 18, 1270. She was canonized as a saint by the Catholic Church and is often venerated as a model of Christian piety and devotion to God, particularly for her choice to forsake a royal marriage in favor of a life dedicated to religious service and charity.

MARÍA GUADALUPE GARCÍA ZAVALA

BORN: April 27, 1878, Zapopan, Jalisco, Mexico

DIED: June 24, 1963, Guadalajara, Jalisco, Mexico

FEAST DAY: June 24

PATRONAGE: Sick people, nurses, the Handmaids of St. Margaret Mary and the Poor

SYMBOLS AND ATTRIBUTES: Nun's habit, cross

María Guadalupe García Zavala, also known as Mother Lupita, was a Mexican Roman Catholic nun and a prominent figure in the history of the Catholic Church.

Mother Lupita dedicated her life to serving Mexico's poor, sick, and marginalized. From a young age, she expressed a strong desire to become a nun. In 1901, she co-founded the Congregation of the Servants of St. Margaret Mary and of the Poor (also known as the Handmaids of St. Margaret Mary and of the Poor) with Father Cipriano Iñiguez Martín del Campo.

As a member of the congregation, Mother Lupita was actively involved in various charitable endeavors, providing health care, education, and spiritual guidance to those in need, especially the impoverished and the ailing. Her efforts significantly contributed to the establishment and administration of hospitals, orphanages, and schools, particularly in Guadalajara.

During the Mexican Revolution (1910–1920), Mother Lupita risked her safety to care for wounded soldiers and civilians, often amid precarious situations. Her compassion, dedication, and selflessness earned her immense respect and love from the community.

In 1945, the Catholic Church officially recognized her congregation. The Handmaids of St. Margaret Mary and of the Poor received diocesan approval from the archbishop of Guadalajara, who acknowledged their religious charism and mission. This recognition paved the way for the congregation to continue their noble work and broaden their influence.

During her lifetime, Mother Lupita's contributions and impact were extensively acknowledged. Among the many honors she received, she was named a Dame of the Order of St. Sylvester by Pope Pius XII. Her reputation for holiness and service resonated beyond Mexico's borders, inspiring countless others to emulate her exemplary selfless love and unwavering devotion to the poor.

On April 24, 2004, Pope John Paul II beatified Mother Lupita, and Pope Francis canonized her on May 12, 2013. Today, she remains an influential figure in the Catholic Church, especially in Mexico, where her enduring legacy motivates countless individuals to champion justice, compassion, and the welfare of those less fortunate.

MARIA DI ROSA

BORN: November 6, 1813, Brescia, Kingdom of Lombardy-Venetia

DIED: December 15, 1855, Brescia, Kingdom of Lombardy-Venetia

FEAST DAY: December 15

PATRONAGE: Sick people, Handmaids of Charity

SYMBOLS AND ATTRIBUTES: Cross, nun's habit

Maria Crucifixa di Rosa, also known as St. Mary di Rosa, was an Italian Catholic nun. She was born in Brescia, Italy, and dedicated her life to the service of others, particularly the poor, sick, and marginalized.

During her early years, Maria worked as a teacher and actively participated in charitable activities. In 1836, she established a free school for girls in Brescia, providing education and vocational training to young women. Committed to her faith and inspired by the needs of society, she founded the Handmaids of Charity in 1840.

The Handmaids of Charity was a religious congregation dedicated to serving the sick and suffering. The sisters cared for the ill and dying in hospitals, nursing homes, and wherever they were needed. Maria emphasized the importance of compassion, humility, and self-sacrifice in their work. Under her leadership, the order expanded their services beyond Brescia, establishing houses in other parts of Italy and even reaching as far as Brazil.

Maria died on December 15, 1855, at the age of forty-two. She was canonized as a saint by Pope Pius XII on June 12, 1954.

MARIA GORETTI

BORN: October 16, 1890, Corinaldo, Kingdom of Italy

DIED: July 6, 1902, Nettuno, Kingdom of Italy

FEAST DAY: July 6

PATRONAGE: Youth, teenage girls, rape survivors, those struggling with forgiveness

SYMBOLS AND ATTRIBUTES: Lily, palm branch, white dress

Maria Goretti was a young Italian girl who became a symbol of purity, forgiveness, and courage due to her tragic martyrdom at the age of eleven. Her story continues to inspire millions of people worldwide.

Maria Goretti was born to poor farmers on October 16, 1890, in Corinaldo, Italy. When she was nine, her father died, leaving her mother, Maria, and her siblings to fend for themselves.

On July 5, 1902, while her mother was working in the fields, Maria was attacked by a twenty-year-old neighbor named Alessandro Serenelli. He attempted to rape her, but Maria bravely resisted and fought back, repeatedly telling her attacker that he was going to go to Hell for his actions. Enraged, Alessandro stabbed her repeatedly, causing grave injuries. Maria forgave her attacker, however, before succumbing to her wounds the following day, on July 6, 1902.

Initially, Alessandro Serenelli was sentenced to life in prison, but due to his young age, he was instead given thirty years in prison for her murder. While in prison, he underwent a spiritual transformation. He recounted having a vision of Maria, who smiled at him and handed him lilies, which burned his hands.

This experience led Alessandro to repent for his heinous crime and seek forgiveness. He wrote a letter to Maria's mother, pleading for her forgiveness, which she eventually granted.

Numerous reported miracles have been attributed to St. Maria Goretti. One notable case involved a young girl in Brazil who was gravely ill from a severe infection. Her parents fervently prayed to St. Maria Goretti for her healing; miraculously, she completely recovered.

Maria was canonized as a saint by Pope Pius XII in 1950. Alessandro attended Maria's canonization ceremony; he became a lay brother in a Franciscan monastery.

The feast day of St. Maria Goretti, celebrated on July 6, commemorates the anniversary of her death. She is widely regarded as the patron saint of youth, victims and survivors of rape, purity, and forgiveness and is invoked for protection against sexual assault and for the conversion of sinners. She is often depicted holding lilies, symbolizing her purity and virginity. Additionally, she is depicted with a palm branch, representing her martyrdom and triumph over sin and death. Some depictions also portray her with a knife, symbolizing the weapon used in her tragic murder.

MARIE MARGUERITE D'YOUVILLE

BORN: October 15, 1701, Varennes, New France

DIED: December 23, 1771, Montreal, Province of Quebec, British America

FEAST DAY: October 16

PATRONAGE: Widows, difficult marriages

SYMBOLS AND ATTRIBUTES: Gray habit, cross

St. Marie Marguerite d'Youville, often called the Gray Nun of Montreal, was born in Varennes, Quebec, into a prosperous family on October 15, 1701. Her early life was marked by hardships, including the loss of her father and her mother's subsequent remarriage to an unkind stepfather. At twelve, she joined a convent school in Montreal, finding solace and purpose as she delved deeply into her Catholic faith.

In 1722, Marguerite wed François d'Youville, a fur trader, alleged bootlegger, and scoundrel. The couple had six children, but only two reached adulthood. François's death in 1730 left twenty-nine-year-old Marguerite widowed and grappling with substantial debts. Nevertheless, she displayed resilience, settling these debts and caring for her children.

In 1737, Marguerite, a woman of deep faith, co-founded a mission to support Montreal's destitute. Starting with only a few members, the organization soon expanded as a result of their relentless commitment and fundraising. Despite their altruistic goals, they weren't immune to societal scorn. They were mockingly labeled "les grises," meaning both "the gray women" and "the drunken women"—an unkind reference to d'Youville's late husband's rumored illicit activities.

Yet, by 1744, their association evolved into an official Catholic religious order. Their philanthropic pursuits led them to assume the charter of Montreal's General Hospital in 1747. Even as they confronted immense challenges, such as massive debts and a catastrophic fire in 1765, d'Youville and her associates revitalized the institution. This tenacity earned them the affectionate title of the "Gray Nuns of Montreal," a reclamation of their earlier derogatory label. Their benevolent influence grew, and they became widely known simply as the "Gray Nuns," leaving a lasting legacy of kindness and fortitude.

The Gray Nuns of Montreal founded hospitals, orphanages, and schools and cared for prisoners and the elderly. Marguerite was celebrated for her humility and compassion, urging her sisters to treat everyone with dignity and respect.

Marie Marguerite d'Youville died on December 23, 1771. She was canonized by Pope John Paul II on December 9, 1990, and is the first Canadian to become a saint.

MARIE OF ST. IGNATIUS

BORN: March 30, 1774, Lyon, France
DIED: August 26, 1837, Lyon, France
FEAST DAY: February 3

PATRONAGE: Religious of Jesus and Mary
SYMBOLS AND ATTRIBUTES: Cross, nun's habit

St. Marie of St. Ignatius, born Claudine Thevenet, was a French Catholic nun and the founder of the religious congregation of the Religious of Jesus and Mary. She was born on March 30, 1774, in Lyon, France, and lived during the tumultuous period of the French Revolution.

As a young girl, Claudine witnessed the horrors and persecutions of the French Revolution, which affected her deeply. She developed a strong sense of compassion and a desire to alleviate the suffering of others. After the revolution, she dedicated herself to serving the poor and marginalized, particularly young girls and women who were victims of social unrest.

In 1818, Claudine founded the religious congregation of the Religious of Jesus and Mary (RJM) in Lyon. The congregation aimed to provide education and care for young girls and women, promoting their spiritual, intellectual, and social development. The RJM sisters opened schools, orphanages, and vocational training centers to empower girls and women, especially those from disadvantaged backgrounds.

Claudine took the religious name Marie of St. Ignatius after starting the congregation, placing great emphasis on the spiritual formation of her sisters and the importance of personal holiness in their work.

The legacy of Marie of St. Ignatius continues through the Religious of Jesus and Mary, which expanded its presence to various countries around the world. She was canonized as a saint by Pope John Paul II on March 21, 1993.

MARK THE EVANGELIST

BORN: c. 12 AD, Cyrene (near modern-day Libya)
DEATH: c. 68 AD, Alexandria, Egypt
FEAST DAY: April 25

PATRONAGE: Venice, lawyers
SYMBOLS AND ATTRIBUTES: Winged lion, book, quill

St. Mark the Evangelist is one of the four authors of the New Testament Gospels. A close companion of the apostle Peter, he was often called the "interpreter of Peter," and was appointed by the apostles to lead the church in Alexandria, Egypt.

St. Mark was born in the early first century AD. He was a relative of Barnabas and joined Paul and Barnabas on their first missionary journey. According to the Acts of the Apostles, Mark left the group in Perga and returned to Jerusalem, which caused a rift between Paul and Barnabas, as Paul felt that Mark was unreliable. However, Mark and Paul eventually reconciled, and he continued to travel with Paul on his journeys.

The Gospel of Mark, which is attributed to him, is the shortest of the four Gospels. Probably written sometime in the 60s AD, it is believed by some scholars to be based on the teachings of Peter (others reject this notion). Mark's Gospel emphasizes the humanity of Jesus and His miracles and strongly emphasizes the urgency of the coming of God's Kingdom.

In addition to his role as an evangelist and writer, Mark is traditionally remembered for his leadership of the church in Alexandria. Under his guidance, the church became a center of Christian learning and scholarship, and produced many influential early Christian writers, including Clement of Alexandria and Origen. Mark was martyred in that Egyptian city he called home, where he was dragged through the streets by Roman soldiers and eventually beheaded. His body was interred in the city, and a church was built over his tomb.

The symbol of St. Mark is the winged lion, which is said to represent his boldness in spreading the Gospel and his bravery in the face of persecution. The lion is also often depicted with an open book, symbolizing Mark's role as a writer of one of the Gospels. In addition, St. Mark is often depicted holding a papyrus, representing his role as a scribe in recording the teachings of Jesus and the apostles.

According to a tradition that dates back to the ninth century, the relics of St. Mark were believed to have been translated to Venice, Italy. During that time, Venice was a thriving maritime republic and an important center of trade. Two Venetian merchants named Buono da Malamocco and Rustico da Torcello traveled to Alexandria, Egypt, in the year 828. Their purpose was to retrieve the remains of St. Mark, which were held in high regard by the Christian community there.

Legend has it that the Venetians managed to smuggle the saint's relics out of the city by hiding them under layers of pork, which was considered unclean and undesirable to the Muslim guards inspecting the cargo. The plan succeeded, and the merchants returned to Venice with the sacred remains.

Upon their arrival in Venice, the relics were received with great enthusiasm and reverence. The doge (the chief magistrate of Venice) and the entire city greeted the artifacts with a grand procession. St. Mark's remains eventually were interred in the newly constructed St. Mark's Basilica, which became a central symbol of the city and a major pilgrimage site. Since then, St. Mark has been considered the patron saint of Venice. (See Peter.)

MARTHA

BORN: 1st century AD, Judea

DEATH: 1st century AD, Tarascon, France

FEAST DAY: July 29

PATRONAGE: Cooks, housekeeping, servants, innkeepers

SYMBOLS AND ATTRIBUTES: Dragon, keys, broom, ladle

St. Martha is a revered figure in the New Testament. According to tradition, she was born in Bethany, a small village near Jerusalem, and was the sister of Lazarus and Mary. She is often depicted as a hardworking, practical woman who was devoted to serving others, especially Jesus Christ.

Martha was present during the raising by Jesus of her brother Lazarus, but she is best known for a story recounted in the Gospel of Luke where Jesus visits her and her sister Mary at their home. While Mary sits at Jesus's feet and listens to Him teach, Martha stays busy preparing the meal. Irritated that Mary is not helping, Martha asks Jesus to rebuke her sister. Instead, Jesus gently reminds Martha that "Mary has chosen the better part," making the point that Martha would do well to focus on the spiritual rather than the temporal. This story has become a famous symbol of the tension between action and contemplation. Martha is often seen as an exemplar of the active life, while Mary represents the contemplative life.

Apart from this story, little else is known about Martha's life. According to tradition, she accompanied Mary and Lazarus to France, where they evangelized and converted many people. She is said to have died in France, and her relics were eventually enshrined in Tarascon, a town in the south of France.

MARTIN

BORN: c. 316, Savaria, Western Roman
Empire (modern Hungary)
DIED: November 8, 397,
Candes-Saint-Martin, Gaul
FEAST DAY: November 11

PATRONAGE: Soldiers, beggars,
wool-weavers, geese, alcoholics
SYMBOLS AND ATTRIBUTES: Goose, soldier
on horse sharing cloak with beggar

St. Martin, also known as Martin of Tours, was a Christian saint who lived in the fourth century. One of the best-known stories about Martin is the account of him sharing his cloak with a beggar. According to the legend, while Martin was still a soldier in the Roman army, he encountered a shivering beggar at the gates of the city of Amiens in France. Moved with compassion, Martin cut his military cloak in half with his sword and gave one half to the beggar. In a dream that night, he saw Jesus wearing the half cloak he had given away, an acknowledgment of his act of charity. This event is often depicted in art and has become a symbol of Martin's generosity and empathy.

Later in his life, Martin became a Christian and left the military to become a monk. He was eventually ordained as a bishop; significantly, he is credited for spreading Christianity throughout Gaul (modern-day France).

St. Martin is known for his ascetic lifestyle, humility, and dedication to monasticism and serving others. His feast day, known as Martinmas, is celebrated on November 11. It is observed in various countries and is often associated with harvest festivals, charitable acts, and tasting the season's new wine. St. Martin's legacy inspires many to live lives of compassion, generosity, and selflessness.

MARTIN DE PORRES

BORN: December 9, 1579, Lima, Viceroyalty of Peru, Spanish Empire
DIED: November 3, 1639, Lima, Viceroyalty of Peru, Spanish Empire
FEAST DAY: November 3

PATRONAGE: People of mixed race, Black people, barbers, public health workers, innkeepers
SYMBOLS AND ATTRIBUTES: Broom, crucifix, rosary, bread

St. Martin de Porres, also known as St. Martin of Charity, was a sixteenth-century Peruvian lay brother of the Dominican order. He is known for his selfless devotion to serving the poor and the sick, including African slaves, and for the numerous miracles attributed to him.

Martin was born in 1579 in Lima, Peru. His mother, Ana Velázquez, was a freed slave from Panama, while his father, Juan de Porres, was a Spanish nobleman who never recognized him as his son. Martin was therefore considered a mulatto, a person of mixed race (his mother was of African or possibly of Indigenous descent); as a result, he experienced discrimination and marginalization throughout his life.

At the age of fifteen, Martin became a lay helper at the Convent of the Holy Rosary in Lima, which was run by the Dominicans, where he was put in charge of menial tasks such as cleaning and cooking. However, he soon began healing the sick and caring for the poor. He also developed a life devoted to prayer, and displayed an intense devotion to St. Dominic, the founder of the Dominican order.

In 1603, at the age of twenty-four, Martin was admitted as a lay brother in the Dominican order, taking the vows of poverty, chastity, and obedience and becoming a full member of the religious community. He continued to serve as a cook, gardener, barber, and infirmarian, but his reputation as a miracle worker and a saintly person began to spread throughout Lima.

As a person of mixed race, he understood the struggles and discriminations faced by people of African heritage and the enslaved in colonial Peru. His experience growing up in poverty led him to have a deep compassion for the less fortunate. His work with the African slaves in Lima was significant. He used his position to serve these communities with kindness and charity, helping to provide them with food, medical care, and spiritual support. At times, St. Rose of Lima helped him with his mission.

PLATE V
Martin de Porres

Martin was known for his many miracles. One of his most famous was his ability to bilocate, that is, to be in two places simultaneously. According to several accounts, Martin would be seen by people in different parts of the city of Lima at the same time, sometimes performing miraculous healings or rescuing people from danger.

Martin was also said to have the gift of healing, and many people came to him seeking a cure for their illnesses or disabilities. He would often pray with them and apply a salve made from medicinal herbs, which was said to have miraculous properties. Many were healed through his intercession, and he became known as a patron of people suffering from bodily ills.

Martin de Porres died on November 3, 1639, at the age of fifty-nine. His funeral was attended by a large crowd of people who considered him a saint even before his death. His relics were venerated by the faithful, and many miracles continued to be attributed to his intercession.

In 1837, Martin was beatified by Pope Gregory XVI, and in 1962 he was canonized by Pope John XXIII, becoming the first Black saint in the Americas.

MARY

BORN: 18 BC, Judea

DIED: Assumed into Heaven 1st century after 33 AD, Jerusalem

FEAST DAY: Many feasts, including Assumption (August 15) and Immaculate Conception (December 8)

PATRONAGE: All humanity, mothers, young children, religious vocations, numerous cities and countries

SYMBOLS AND ATTRIBUTES: Blue mantle, stars, moon, snake under feet

Mary, also known as the Virgin Mary, the Blessed Virgin Mary, the Queen of Heaven, the Queen of Angels, the Queen of All Saints, and the Mother of God, is the mother of Jesus, wife to Joseph, and the most revered saint in all of Catholicism.

Mary's story is documented in the New Testament, particularly in the Gospels of Matthew and Luke. According to these accounts, Mary was a young Jewish virgin living in Nazareth, a town in the region of Galilee, during the first century AD. She was betrothed to a man named Joseph.

They had not yet consummated their marriage when Mary was visited by the angel Gabriel, who informed her that she would conceive a child by the power of the Holy Spirit and give birth to a son who would be called Jesus. While initially surprised and confused by this encounter, Mary humbly accepted the angel's message. She declared herself the handmaid of the Lord and praised God through her "Magnificat," her hymn of joy, for being chosen and blessed to carry the son of God within her. Mary then journeyed to see her cousin Elizabeth, who was pregnant with John the Baptist, a cousin of, and a harbinger for, Jesus. This encounter between cousins has come to be known as the Visitation.

When Mary's betrothed husband, Joseph, discovered her pregnancy, initially he planned to quietly divorce her. However, an angel appeared to Joseph in a dream. The angel reassured Joseph that the child was from the Holy Spirit, and instructed him to take Mary as his wife. He did. Shortly thereafter, Mary accompanied Joseph to Bethlehem to register for a census. Unable to find lodgings, Mary gave birth to Jesus in a stable. The birth of Jesus was accompanied by angelic announcements to shepherds in the fields, who came to worship the newborn Messiah, and a visit by the Magi, three wise men from the East, who brought gifts for the infant and his family.

After his birth, according to Jewish custom, Mary accompanied Joseph to present the infant Jesus in the Temple in Jerusalem. There they encountered Simeon, a devout man who had been waiting to see the Messiah. Simeon blessed them and prophesied about Jesus's future role as a light to the Gentiles and the glory of Israel. They also met the prophetess Anna, who recognized the child as the Messiah and praised God. Days later, an angel warned Joseph in a dream to flee to Egypt to protect the child from King Herod, who wanted to kill Jesus. Mary, Joseph, and Jesus escaped to Egypt and stayed there until Herod's death, when at last they returned to Nazareth in Galilee, where Jesus grew up as the "son of Joseph and Mary."

Mary does not appear again in the story of Jesus's life until the wedding at Cana, where she was instrumental in coaxing Jesus to perform His first public miracle: changing water to wine. She was also present at the crucifixion, and tradition holds that she experienced her son in His risen form after the resurrection. Mary was also with the apostles as they awaited Pentecost.

Over time, Mary assumed a prominent role in Christian history, tradition, and theology.

Mary is known as *Theotokos*, a theological title derived from the Greek words *Theos*, meaning "God," and *tokos*, meaning "bearer" or "one who gives birth." As Mother of God or God-bearer, Mary gave birth to someone who was both a human being and the Son of God. Jesus, as someone both fully human and fully divine, represents the affirmation of the belief in the Incarnation, which is the doctrine that Jesus is the Word of God made flesh. Because Mary is His mother, she can be rightly called the Mother of God.

The concept of Theotokos emerged as a response to theological debates and controversies in the early centuries of Christianity. Her title was affirmed at the Council of Ephesus in 431, where the Church officially recognized and declared Mary as Theotokos to counter the teachings of Nestorius, who denied Mary's divine motherhood. By acknowledging Mary as Theotokos, the Church affirmed her unique and exalted role in the salvation of humanity, recognizing her as the chosen vessel through whom God entered into the world and became incarnate as Jesus Christ.

PLATE VI
Mary

SAINTS, ANGELS & DEMONS

Outside of Christianity, Mary is also mentioned in the Quran, the central religious text of Islam. Islam acknowledges Mary, known as Maryam, as a pious and virtuous woman, honoring her as one of the greatest women in history. However, Islamic belief diverges from Christian doctrine regarding the nature of Jesus's birth, as Islam does not recognize the concept of virgin birth.

Within Catholicism, Mary is known as the Immaculate Conception, a belief that asserts that she was conceived without sin. The doctrine, one of only two infallible proclamations in all of Church history, teaches that Mary was conceived without original sin by a special grace and privilege granted by God. This belief emphasizes Mary's unique role as the Mother of Jesus, the sinless one and Savior of humanity. The Immaculate Conception is seen as a preparation for Mary to be a fitting vessel for the Incarnation of the Son of God. The doctrine's origins can be traced back to early Christian writings and devotion to Mary. However, the formal, infallible declaration of the Immaculate Conception was proclaimed by Pope Pius IX in 1854 through the papal bull *Ineffabilis Deus*, which states: "We declare, pronounce, and define that the doctrine which holds that the most Blessed Virgin Mary, in the first instance of her conception, by a singular grace and privilege granted by Almighty God, in view of the merits of Jesus Christ, the Savior of the human race, was preserved free from all stain of original sin, is a doctrine revealed by God and therefore to be believed firmly and constantly by all the faithful."

The second time the Church spoke ex-cathedra, or infallibly from the Chair of Peter, was the doctrine of the Assumption of Mary. This belief, also known as the Dormition of the Mother of God in Eastern Churches, states that at the end of her earthly life, the Virgin Mary was assumed, body and soul, into Heaven. It affirms that Mary did not undergo the decay of the body but was taken directly into Heaven, participating fully in the resurrection of Jesus Christ.

The Assumption of Mary does not appear in the Bible, which has led to heated theological discussions throughout the centuries. However, the belief has deep roots in the early Christian tradition and has been widely accepted by Catholics for hundreds of years. It was formally declared as an infallible dogma of the Catholic Church by Pope Pius XII on November 1, 1950, in his Apostolic Constitution Munificentissimus Deus.

Mary is also often called the Queen Mother because of her unique role as the mother of Jesus, who is seen as the eternal King. The title draws inspiration from the ancient Jewish tradition of the Gebirah, the Queen Mother in the Davidic Kingdom. In the Old Testament, the position of the Queen Mother was significant: she was the mother of the reigning king and held authority and influence, interceding on behalf of the people and advising the king.

The New Testament often draws parallels between the Davidic Kingdom and the Kingdom of God. Jesus, as a Son of David (the king of Israel) is seen as the fulfillment of the messianic prophecies and the eternal King of all creation. Therefore Mary, as the mother of Jesus, is seen as the Queen Mother in the Kingdom of God. Further, in Revelation 12:1, there's an image of a woman clothed with the sun, with the moon beneath her feet, and a crown of twelve stars on her head, which has traditionally been interpreted by Catholics as a representation of Mary, further reinforcing her title as queen.

Mary's unique closeness to Jesus and her role in his life and ministry make her a significant figure in the Church. She is believed to intercede for the faithful and is seen as a powerful advocate and mediator. Mary's exalted role as preeminent among the saints signifies her unique place in salvation history and her ongoing intercession in the life of believers.

Throughout the centuries, the faithful have encountered the Virgin Mary through numerous apparitions. Some of these include Our Lady of Guadalupe (1531, Mexico); Our Lady of Lourdes (1858, France); Our Lady of Knock (1879, Ireland); and Our Lady of Medjugorje (1981–present, Bosnia and Herzegovina).

Mary is also honored with various feast days and celebrations throughout the liturgical year, including: the Solemnity of Mary, Mother of God, on January 1, which celebrates Mary's role as the mother of Jesus and is observed on the octave day of Christmas, marking the beginning of the new calendar year; the Annunciation on March 25, commemorating the angel Gabriel's visit to Mary to announce that she would conceive Jesus by the power of the Holy Spirit; the Assumption of Mary on August 15; the Nativity of the Blessed Virgin Mary on September 8, which celebrates the birth of Mary, marking the beginning of her life and her significance in salvation history; and the Immaculate Conception on December 8.

MARY CLEOPHAS

BORN: 1st century, place unknown
DIED: 1st century, place unknown
FEAST DAY: April 24

PATRONAGE: Caretakers
SYMBOLS AND ATTRIBUTES: Often depicted at the crucifixion or resurrection scene

Mary Cleophas, also known as Mary Clopas, holds a significant place among the disciples of Jesus, earning her the esteemed title of one of The Three Marys. This collective name refers to a group of three women named Mary who feature prominently in the New Testament accounts of Jesus's crucifixion, burial, and resurrection. Though debated, Mary is believed to be the spouse of Clopas and the mother of two of Jesus's apostles, James the Less (also known as James the son of Alphaeus) and Joseph (or Joses).

The Gospel of John (19:25) attests to Mary's presence at the crucifixion of Jesus. In this poignant moment, she stands near the cross alongside Jesus's mother, Mary, exemplifying her unwavering devotion, making her an eyewitness to Christ's martyrdom. Matthew 27:56 portrays Mary Cleophas in the company of other women, including Mary Magdalene, immediately after Jesus's death. (See James the Less, Joseph.)

MARY FRANCIS OF THE FIVE WOUNDS

BORN: March 25, 1715, Naples, Italy

DIED: October 7, 1791, Naples, Italy

FEAST DAY: October 6

PATRONAGE: Naples

SYMBOLS AND ATTRIBUTES: Nun's habit, stigmata, crucifix, angel

Anna Maria Gallo, known as Mary Frances of the Five Wounds, was an Italian nun of the Third Order of St. Francis. She was born in 1715 in a seedy part of the Quartieri Spagnoli (Spanish Quarter) of Naples, possibly a red-light district known for its high crime.

At the age of sixteen, Anna refused an arranged marriage and sought to join the Franciscan Third Order. With the intervention of a friar, she gained permission from her father to enter the order and began living a devout life as a consecrated virgin within her family home. Anna took the religious name Mary Frances out of her devotion to the Blessed Virgin Mary and St. Francis of Assisi.

Mary Frances became known for her acts of charity, particularly in helping the poor of her neighborhood. She had a deep prayer life and spent long hours in meditation. She joined another Franciscan tertiary named Maria Felice, and they lived together, practicing a life of poverty and prayer. During this time, Mary Frances received the stigmata, the wounds of Christ. She bore these wounds patiently along with other physical afflictions and spiritual trials. She also had visions of the Archangel Raphael, who reportedly healed her of several ailments.

Mary Frances was buried in Naples's Franciscan Church of Santa Lucia al Monte. She was canonized by Pope Pius IX in 1867. (See Raphael.)

MARY MAGDALENE DE' PAZZI

BORN: April 2, 1566, Florence, Duchy of Florence

DIED: May 25, 1607, Florence, Grand Duchy of Tuscany

FEAST DAY: May 25

PATRONAGE: The sick

SYMBOLS AND ATTRIBUTES: Cross, crown of thorns, nun's habit

A Carmelite nun and mystic who lived during the sixteenth century, Mary Magdalene de' Pazzi was born Caterina de' Pazzi. Her upbringing was one of wealth and privilege. However, she had little desire for worldly possessions and demonstrated a deep religious inclination from a young age. When Caterina was nine, she was sent to a boarding school run by the Benedictine nuns in Florence. She learned to meditate by using the method of mental prayer, which would form the foundation of her spirituality.

At the age of fourteen, against the wishes of her family, who hoped she would marry, Caterina entered the Carmelite convent in Florence. Three years later, she was accepted as a novice, took the name Mary Magdalene, and committed herself fully to religious life.

Mary Magdalene is known for her intense mystical experiences, which began as a young woman and continued throughout her life. She underwent periods of ecstasy, rapture, and concentrated contemplation of the divine. Mary Magdalene practiced mortifications, notably wearing a crown of thorns, to identify with Christ's suffering and express penance.

Perhaps the most intense period of her mystical experiences began just a few days after she made her solemn profession of vows in 1584. For about forty days, she was almost constantly in a state of ecstasy, unable to attend to her normal duties in the monastery because of her intense spiritual experiences. Her fellow nuns documented her experiences as best they could, creating a valuable record of her mystical life.

One of the most notable mystical experiences involved a vision of Jesus taking her heart into His own Sacred Heart, promising to return it to her after she was purified of sin. This led to tumultuous spiritual desolation, and like many saints throughout their lives, she felt like Jesus had abandoned her. Though her spiritual hardships lasted five years, she continued to persevere in her faith. In 1590, at age twenty-four, the burdens of her soul were lifted, and she once again experienced profound spiritual consolations.

Mary Magdalene de' Pazzi died on May 25, 1607. She was beatified in 1626 and canonized a saint in 1669 by Pope Clement IX. She is often depicted in art with her Carmelite habit and holding a crucifix.

MARY MAGDALENE

BORN: 1st century, place unknown, possibly Magdala

DIED: 1st century, place unknown, possibly Magdala

FEAST DAY: July 22

PATRONAGE: Repentant sinners, women, apothecaries, perfumers

SYMBOLS AND ATTRIBUTES: Jar of ointment, skull, red egg, crucifix

Mary Magdalene, also known as Mary of Magdala, or the Magdalene, was a disciple of Jesus. She is thought to have been born in Magdala, a town in Galilee, in the first century AD.

According to the Gospel of Luke, Jesus had healed her of seven demons, and from then on, she became a devoted disciple and follower of His teachings. The Gospel accounts reveal that Mary Magdalene was one of the few people present at Jesus's crucifixion, standing near the cross with other women, including Jesus's mother, Mary. After His death, she witnessed his burial in a tomb belonging to Joseph of Arimathea.

In the Gospel of John, she was the first to witness the resurrected Jesus near the tomb. In this encounter, Jesus entrusted her with the message to go and inform the disciples about His resurrection, earning her the title "apostle to the apostles" (*apostola apostlolrum*) in early Christian tradition.

Over the centuries, various interpretations of Mary Magdalene's character and relationship with Jesus have emerged. In the medieval period, her image became conflated with that of a repentant prostitute, although this association is not found in the Biblical accounts. The identification of Mary Magdalene as such can be traced back to a sermon delivered by Pope Gregory I, also known as Gregory the Great, in the sixth century. Here he melded Mary Magdalene with the unnamed sinful woman who anointed Jesus's feet with oil and wiped them with her hair (Luke 7:36–50). Pope Gregory I suggested that the sinful woman was the same person as Mary Magdalene, even though the Biblical accounts do not make such a connection. This sermon significantly influenced subsequent interpretations of Mary Magdalene, particularly during the medieval period. Mary Magdalene as a penitent prostitute became a popular narrative in art, literature, and religious traditions. Modern Biblical scholarship, however, rejects this portrayal of Mary Magdalene, emphasizing her role as a devoted follower of Jesus.

Mary Magdalene is a central figure in the Gospel of Mary, an ancient and apocryphal text that is part of the Nag Hammadi Library, a collection of early Christian texts discovered in Egypt in 1945. The Gospel of Mary is believed to have been written in the second century, although the exact date and authorship are uncertain. The text is fragmentary, with portions missing, but it offers a glimpse into the early Christian community's thoughts and beliefs.

In the Gospel of Mary, Mary Magdalene emerges as a prominent disciple and a spiritual leader among Jesus's followers. She is depicted as having a deep understanding of His teachings and is shown engaging in dialogues with the other disciples, including Peter and Andrew. The text presents her as a wise and knowledgeable disciple who receives private revelations from Jesus and highlights her role as a teacher, imparting spiritual insights and guidance to the other disciples. The text also addresses issues of authority and conflicts within the early Christian community.

Mary Magdalene's story has given rise to numerous legends and folklore. According to one popular legend, after Jesus's ascension, Mary Magdalene traveled to the south of France, spreading the message of Christianity. Some believe she arrived in a boat without oars, guided only by divine intervention. Another tradition holds that Mary Magdalene traveled to Rome to tell Emperor Tiberius about Jesus's resurrection. To illustrate her point about life emerging from death, she picked up a hen's egg from the dinner table. As she described the resurrection, the egg miraculously turned red. Legends such as these contribute to the mystical and spiritual aura surrounding her.

Some traditions hold that Mary Magdalene spent the last years of her life as a hermit in a cave in Sainte-Baume, a mountain range in France. Pilgrims visit the grotto and hike the mountain to pay homage to her and seek spiritual inspiration. Her remains are believed to be housed in a sarcophagus at Sainte-Baume, and her head is buried elsewhere on the property.

St. Mary Magdalene's influence can be seen in art, music, and literature. Some notable works of art include Titian's *Penitent Magdalene*, which portrays her in a contemplative pose as a repentant sinner; Georges de La Tour's *The Magdalene with the Smoking Flame*, which emphasizes her devotion and spiritual illumination; Carlo Dolci's *The Penitent Magdalene*, showing her in deep sorrow and reflection; Artemisia Gentileschi's portrayal, which highlights her strength and empowerment; Francisco de Zurbarán's *Magdalene in Ecstasy*, capturing her mystical experiences; and Jean-Baptiste Jouvenet's *The Three Marys at the Tomb*, which depicts her astonishment at the empty tomb.

In music, Johann Sebastian Bach wrote a cantata in her honor. She was the inspiration for several musical compositions, including Sir George Dyson's choral work "Mary Magdalene," Heitor Villa-Lobos' opera *Magdalena*, Faye Wong's song "Mary Magdalene," John Dowland's lute song "St. Mary Magdalene's Lament," and alternative rocker PJ Harvey's song "Magdalene." These compositions touch upon themes of devotion, grief, spirituality, and personal transformation associated with Mary Magdalene's story, providing musical interpretations of her character and significance. She was also a central figure in Dan Brown's mega-bestseller, *The Da Vinci Code*, where the author scandalously proposed that Jesus and Mary were married.

St. Mary Magdalene is the patron saint of penitents, women, and hairdressers. She is also the patron saint of Vézelay, France, and La Madeleine, Paris. (See Gregory the Great.)

MARY OF THE CROSS MACKILLOP

BORN: January 15, 1842, Melbourne, Australia
DIED: August 8, 1909, North Sydney, Australia
FEAST DAY: August 8
PATRONAGE: Australia
SYMBOLS AND ATTRIBUTES: Crucifix, habit, book

The first Australian canonized as a saint and one of the country's most beloved figures, Mary of the Cross MacKillop was a Roman Catholic recognized for her tireless efforts in education and social work.

Born in 1842 in Fitzroy, Melbourne, Australia, she grew up in a devout family and developed a strong sense of faith from an early age. At the age of twenty-four, she co-founded the Sisters of St. Joseph of the Sacred Heart with the help of Father Julian Tenison Woods. The religious congregation aimed to serve poor and underserved communities, particularly in rural areas. Mary took her final vows to become a nun in 1869.

Mary and the Sisters of St. Joseph established numerous schools throughout Australia, focusing on areas with limited opportunities. They also opened orphanages and assisted those in need. Mary believed in the importance of empowering individuals through learning and dedicated her life to doing just that.

Mary faced numerous challenges and conflicts during her lifetime, encountering resistance and criticism from some clergy members, and was even excommunicated from the Catholic Church by her bishop for perceived insubordination. A year later, the bishop, on his deathbed, reversed his decision and apologized to Mary. From then on, she continued to work throughout Australia, including helping to better the lives of the Aborigines.

Mary passed away on August 8, 1909, in North Sydney, Australia, leaving a legacy as a compassionate educator and advocate for the disadvantaged. In 1995, she was beatified by Pope John Paul II, and on October 17, 2010, she was canonized as Australia's first saint by Pope Benedict XVI.

MARY SALOME

BORN: 1st century AD, Galilee
DIED: 1st century AD, unknown
FEAST DAY: October 22
PATRONAGE: Veroli, Italy

SYMBOLS AND ATTRIBUTES: Oftentimes depicted with the other women at the crucifixion or resurrection, thurible, red tunic

Mary Salome, also known as simply Salome, is mentioned in the New Testament alongside other women, including Mary Magdalene and Mary, the mother of James. In the Gospel of Mark (Mark 15:40), she is listed as one of the women who observed the crucifixion from a distance. The Gospel of Matthew (Matthew 27:56) describes a "Mary the mother of James and Joses," as well as "the mother of Zebedee's sons." Traditionally, this latter woman has been identified with Salome, suggesting she might be the mother of James and John, two of Jesus's disciples known as the Sons of Thunder (however, the text itself does not explicitly name her as Salome).

Salome is best known for her presence at Jesus's tomb after his crucifixion. According to the Gospel accounts, she, along with Mary Magdalene and Mary, the mother of James, went to the tomb early in the morning on the third day after Jesus's death. They discovered that the stone blocking the entrance had been moved aside and encountered an angel who informed them of Jesus's resurrection.

While the New Testament provides limited information about Salome, she is recognized as a devoted follower of Jesus and a witness to significant events in His life and ministry. Beyond the scant Biblical accounts, there is little historical information about her. The details of her life and role in early Christianity are primarily derived from religious traditions and interpretations of Biblical texts.

MATTHEW THE EVANGELIST

BORN: c. 1st century AD, Galilee

DIED: 1st century, Ethiopia

FEAST DAY: September 21

PATRONAGE: Accountants, bankers, tax collectors

SYMBOLS AND ATTRIBUTES: Winged man or angel, book

Matthew the Evangelist, also known as Levi, was one of the twelve apostles of Jesus Christ and the author of one of the Gospels of the New Testament. His role as an evangelist is foundational to Christian theology and the formation of the early Christian Church.

The name Matthew, derived from the Hebrew Mattityahu, signifies the "gift of Yahweh," which reflects Matthew's spiritual dedication to serving God's will. His alternate name, Levi, originates from his Jewish heritage, belonging to the Tribe of Levi, known for its religious and scholastic roles within the Jewish community.

Before his apostolic calling, Matthew worked as a tax collector for the Romans, during their occupation of Palestine in the first century AD. Some saw him as a traitor to his people, which makes his calling more extraordinary for Christians, as Matthew embodies Jesus's mission to call not the righteous but sinners to repentance (Mark 2:17). In the conversion of Matthew depicted in the synoptic Gospels (Matthew 9:9–13, Mark 2:14–17, and Luke 5:27–28), Jesus passes by the tax booth where Matthew is making his collections and says, simply, "Follow me." Matthew immediately leaves his old life behind and follows Jesus.

Matthew's Gospel, traditionally attributed to him, is a rich theological work. It was presumably written for a Jewish audience, as it consistently links the teachings of Jesus to Old Testament prophecies, establishing Jesus as the long-awaited Jewish Messiah. The Gospel opens with a genealogy of Jesus, tracing His lineage back to Abraham, further highlighting Jesus's Jewish heritage and fulfilling the Old Testament prophecy about the Messiah descending from the line of David.

The Gospel of Matthew also contains what has become known as the Five Discourses, and introduces the Sermon on the Mount, which encompasses significant teachings such as the Beatitudes, the Lord's Prayer, and various moral and ethical instructions.

As is true for other apostles, Matthew's death isn't explicitly recorded in the Bible. Early Church traditions propose different accounts, some suggesting natural death while others a martyr's death.

In iconography, St. Matthew is often depicted with a quill and a scroll or book, signifying his authorship of the Gospel. Sometimes he is shown accompanied by a winged man or angel, symbolizing the human lineage of Christ, which his Gospel elucidates.

MATTHIAS

BORN: 1st century AD, Judea
DIED: c. 80 AD, Jerusalem
FEAST DAY: May 14

PATRONAGE: Alcoholics, carpenters, sufferers of smallpox
SYMBOLS AND ATTRIBUTES: Halberd, axe

St. Matthias, sometimes called the thirteenth apostle, was chosen to replace Judas Iscariot, who betrayed Jesus and then died by suicide.

Though never mentioned in the Gospels, Matthias, whose name means "gift of Yahweh," was believed to be one of the seventy disciples of Jesus and was present with him from his baptism to his ascension. Matthias does, however, appear in the Acts of the Apostles (1:15–26). After Jesus ascended to Heaven, the remaining eleven apostles gathered to choose a replacement for Judas. They believed it necessary to maintain the number twelve, symbolizing the twelve tribes of Israel. As stated in Acts 1:21–22, the apostles wanted someone who had been with Jesus from the time of his baptism by John up to the ascension. They proposed two candidates, Joseph, called Barsabbas (also known as Justus), and Matthias. The apostles prayed and cast lots, and Matthias was chosen to become an apostle and take the place of Christ's betrayer.

Not much else is known about Matthias, but different traditions suggest he carried out missionary work in Ethiopia, where he was martyred, while others place his ministry and death in other regions such as the eastern Mediterranean. Another tradition tells he was stoned and beheaded in Jerusalem. Some believe that the relics of Matthias were brought to Rome by St. Helena. (See Helena.)

MAXIMILIAN MARY KOLBE

BORN: January 8, 1894, Zduńska Wola, Kingdom of Poland, Russian Empire
DIED: August 14, 1941, Auschwitz-Birkenau concentration camp, Poland
FEAST DAY: August 14

PATRONAGE: Drug addicts, families, journalists, prisoners
SYMBOLS AND ATTRIBUTES: Prison uniform, barbed wire, crucifix

St. Maximilian Mary Kolbe was a Polish Franciscan friar and martyr known for his selfless sacrifice during the Holocaust. He was born in Zduńska Wola, Poland, and was baptized with the name Rajmund (Raymond). He was the second son of a weaver and his wife, and his family was devoutly Catholic. Maximilian was devoted to the Blessed Virgin Mary from a young age. He joined the Franciscan order at the age of sixteen, taking the religious name Maximilian. He was ordained a priest in 1918 and went on to earn a doctorate in theology. In 1922, Maximilian founded the Militia Immaculata, a movement dedicated to the Virgin Mary and the conversion of sinners through her intercession.

The Militia Immaculata grew rapidly. In 1927, Maximilian founded a monastery in Niepokalanów, near Warsaw, which became one of the largest Franciscan friaries in the world. He also established a printing press to spread the message of the Militia Immaculata. Maximilian was also a prolific writer, publishing a number of books and articles on theology, philosophy, and the Catholic faith. Some of his notable works include *The Immaculata*, *The Knight of the Immaculata*, and *Mary: The Mother of Jesus and Our Mother*.

During World War II, Maximilian sheltered and protected Jewish refugees at the monastery at great risk to himself and his fellow friars. In February 1941, he was arrested by the Gestapo and interrogated. He was then sent to the Auschwitz concentration camp. There, he continued ministering to his fellow prisoners and secretly heard their confessions.

In July 1941, a prisoner escaped from the camp, and as punishment, the Nazis selected ten prisoners to be starved to death. One of the men chosen was Franciszek Gajowniczek, who cried out for his wife and children. Maximilian, moved with compassion, offered to take Gajowniczek's place. The offer was accepted, and Maximilian was thrown into a starvation cell with nine other prisoners. There Maximilian led the men in prayer and sang hymns to lift their spirits. After two weeks, Maximilian was one of only a few prisoners still alive, only to be killed with a lethal injection of carbolic acid on August 14, 1941.

Maximilian was beatified by Pope Paul VI in 1971 and canonized by Pope John Paul II in 1982. His feast day is celebrated on August 14, the day of his death.

MECHTILD

BORN: c. 1210, Magdeburg, Holy Roman Empire

DIED: c. 1282/1294, Helfta, Holy Roman Empire

FEAST DAY: November 19

PATRONAGE: Writers

SYMBOLS AND ATTRIBUTES: Cup, book, quill

Also known as Mechtildis of Hackeborn, Mechtild was a thirteenth-century mystic who hailed from the noble Hackeborn family in Germany. She was devoted to her faith from the time she was young and entered the convent of Helfta, also known as the Abbey of St. Mary, when she was just seven years old. This abbey was part of the Cistercian order and was known for its strict adherence to the Rule of St. Benedict.

Mechtild had several mystical experiences and visions during her life, which she recorded in her most notable work, *Liber specialis gratiae* (Book of Special Grace). This book is a collection of her visionary experiences and theological insights. Mechtild's visions often revolved around the themes of the Divine Love and the Passion of Christ, emphasizing the importance of personal purity, prayer, and devotion.

Some believe that Mechtild inspired a character in Dante's "Purgatorio," part of his *Divine Comedy*. In the poem, Dante encounters a mysterious woman named Matelda after ascending a mountain with seven terraces representing purification. While the name suggests a connection to a warrior-countess of Tuscany, the character's traits don't support this. Interestingly, Mechtild's *Liber specialis gratiae* describes a similar seven-terraced mountain for purification. Since Mechtild's work was well known in Dante's Florence and their writings have similarities, it's possible Dante's Matelda was influenced by St. Mechtild's spiritual ideas.

Mechtild's impact goes beyond her mystical writings. She took on key roles in the Helfta community, first as prioress and then as sub-prioress. Her leadership and commitment to monastic life uplifted and inspired others, leading to the abbey's spiritual growth.

Mechtild died leaving behind a thoughtful spiritual and literary legacy. Her works continue to be studied and revered by theologians, scholars, and those seeking spiritual guidance. The Cistercian order and the wider Christian community recognize her as a saint, celebrating her feast day on November 19.

MEINRAD

BORN: c. 797, possibly near Reichenau
Island, (modern-day Germany)
DIED: January 21, 861,
Einsiedeln, Switzerland

FEAST DAY: January 21
PATRONAGE: Switzerland, hospitality
SYMBOLS AND ATTRIBUTES: Ravens,
monk's habit

St. Meinrad was a monk and hermit who lived primarily during the ninth century. Born in the region of Swabia, in present-day Germany, around the year 797, he entered the Benedictine monastery of Reichenau as a young man, where he received his education and training. Seeking a life of solitude and prayer, he moved to the region of Switzerland and settled in a remote area known as the Etzel forest.

In the Etzel forest, Meinrad established a hermitage and lived a life of prayer, contemplation, and manual labor. He dedicated himself to asceticism and prayer, and his reputation for holiness and wisdom attracted many people who sought his spiritual guidance and counsel.

According to the legend, two ravens began visiting him in the forest, bringing bread that they placed at his feet. Grateful for their assistance, he would bless the bread brought by the ravens and share it with them. The ravens would patiently wait for their portion, and it is said that they only touched the bread once Meinrad permitted them to do so. The legend represented the harmony between humans and nature as well as Meinrad's unquestioning trust in God's provision.

In 861, two thieves came to Meinrad's hermitage seeking treasure. Realizing that he had nothing of material value, they became enraged and beat him to death. The story tells that Meinrad forgave his attackers before he died.

After his martyrdom, Meinrad's hermitage became a pilgrimage site, with many people coming to honor his memory and seek his intercession. A chapel was built on the site, which developed into the Abbey of Einsiedeln, one of Switzerland's most important Benedictine monasteries.

Meinrad is venerated as the patron saint of hospitality and the Swiss Alps. His life and martyrdom serve as an inspiration for those seeking a life of devotion, solitude, and spiritual reflection.

MONICA

BORN: c. 331, Tagaste, Roman North Africa (modern-day Algeria)

DIED: 387, Ostia, Roman Empire

FEAST DAY: August 27

PATRONAGE: Wives, mothers, difficult marriages, conversion of relatives

SYMBOLS AND ATTRIBUTES: Tears, praying, crucifix

Known also as Monica of Hippo, St. Monica was the mother of St. Augustine of Hippo. She was born in Tagaste, present-day Algeria, around the year 331. She came from a Christian family, and her parents raised her with a strong Christian foundation. However, during her youth, she married a pagan named Patricius, who held a high position in society but had a volatile temper.

Monica remained immutable in her faith during her marriage and became known for her prayerfulness and charitable works. She was concerned about the spiritual well-being of her family, particularly her son Augustine, who had become involved with the Manichaean sect during his time in Carthage in Northern Africa. Manichaeism was a religious movement founded by the Parthian prophet Mani in the third century (in modern-day Iran). It integrated aspects of Zoroastrianism, Christianity, and Gnosticism, presenting a dualistic worldview that saw the universe as a battleground between the forces of light and darkness.

Monica and many Christians saw the Manichaeans as heretics. For many years, she fervently prayed for her son's spiritual awakening, and sought the guidance of influential Christian figures, such as Bishop Ambrose of Milan. Her perseverance and intercessory prayers were eventually rewarded when Augustine embraced Christianity and became arguably the most influential theologian in Christian history. Monica's life and role as a mother are vividly portrayed in the book *Confessions* by her son, St. Augustine.

Confessions, an autobiographical work by Augustine, is considered one of the most important texts in Western literature and a foundational work in Christian theology. In this book, Augustine reflects on his life, intellectual journey, and spiritual transformation. Monica is depicted as a central figure in Augustine's life, a deeply religious woman with a fervent faith in God. He highlights her unwavering devotion and her persistent prayers for his conversion.

Monica is venerated as the patron saint of wives, mothers, and difficult marriages, and her life inspires many believers who face similar struggles in their own families. (See Augustine of Hippo.)

MOSES THE BLACK

BORN: c. 330, Ethiopia

DIED: 405, Egypt

FEAST DAY: August 28

PATRONAGE: Nonviolence, Africa

SYMBOLS AND ATTRIBUTES: Monk's habit, chain

Moses the Black, also known as Moses the Ethiopian or Moses the Robber, was a fourth-century hermit and martyr. Originally a slave in Egypt, Moses was known for his violent and criminal behavior as a leader of a gang of thieves. One day, while fleeing from the authorities, he sought refuge in a monastery in the desert. There, he experienced a profound conversion and decided to leave behind his former life of crime.

Moses embraced a life of repentance and became a monk, dedicating himself to prayer, asceticism, and spiritual discipline; from then on, he exhibited deep humility, obedience, and self-control. Over time, he became renowned for his wisdom and spiritual insight. Moses is believed to have said, "Sit in your cell, and your cell will teach you everything," which emphasized the importance of solitude and introspection in the monastic life. He is venerated for his beliefs in nonviolence and racial harmony.

N

NEOT

BORN: 9th century, England

DIED: c. 877, Cornwall, England

FEAST DAY: July 31

PATRONAGE: Fish

SYMBOLS AND ATTRIBUTES: Fish, well

According to legend, St. Neot may have been related to King Alfred the Great of England and helped to heal the ruler when he fell ill during a hunting expedition. He was renowned for his ascetic lifestyle and devotion to prayer and study. He performed numerous miracles, including healing the sick, raising the dead, and taming wild animals, and he attracted many followers who sought his guidance and spiritual wisdom. He would also commune with angels.

St. Neot's Well, nestled in a serene and picturesque setting near the village of St. Neot in Cornwall, England, is steeped in legends tied to the life of the saint. One of the most enduring tales tells of the monk's daily ritual: he would offer prayers and then take just one fish from the well (or sometimes a pond), and even though there were only three fish, in the water their number never diminished, always miraculously replenishing.

After his death, Neot was buried in his monastery, and his relics became objects of veneration. It is believed that his body experienced *osmogensia*, or the odor of sanctity. His tomb reportedly became a site of miraculous healings, and his reputation as a saint grew over time. Several churches in Cornwall are dedicated to him, and his memory is honored by local communities.

NEREUS

BORN: 1st century AD, place unknown

DIED: 1st century AD, Rome, Italy

FEAST DAY: May 12

PATRONAGE: Friendship

SYMBOLS AND ATTRIBUTES: Palm of martyrdom, sword, angels

St. Nereus was a Christian martyr who lived during the first century AD in Rome. Not much is known about his life, but according to tradition, he and a companion named Achilleus were members of the Roman army and personal bodyguards to Emperor Domitian's niece, Domitilla. Loyal servants, Nereus and Achilleus converted to Christianity shortly after Domitilla and her fiancé did. Some legends tell of how the two soldiers were baptized by St. Peter himself. As Christians, the brothers refused to participate in a pagan sacrifice and were subsequently arrested and brought before the emperor. Refusing to renounce their faith, they were tortured and martyred.

Though lesser-known saints today, Nereus and Achilleus seem to have been highly revered in the fourth century. Statues of them were discovered in the Catacombs of Domitilla that were excavated in the middle of the nineteenth century. Two of the 140 statues that adorn St. Peter's Square in Rome are of the brothers. (See Achilleus.)

NICHOLAS

BORN: c. 270, Patara, Lycia, Roman Empire
DIED: December 6, 343, Myra, Lycia,
   Roman Empire
FEAST DAY: December 6

PATRONAGE: Children, sailors, merchants,
   the falsely accused
SYMBOLS AND ATTRIBUTES: Bishop's attire,
   three gold balls, ship

St. Nicholas, or Nicholas of Myra, also known in some cultures as Santa Claus, is one of the most beloved of all Catholic saints.

Born around 270 in Patara, a city in what is now Turkey, Nicholas came from a wealthy Christian family and was raised in a devout household. Following the death of his parents, Nicholas inherited their fortune, which he utilized to assist the less fortunate and those in need. His benevolent acts and generosity earned him a reputation for being compassionate and selfless. One legend concerns a poor man who couldn't afford dowries for his three daughters, which meant the young women would go unmarried and be forced into lives of prostitution. In order to avoid such a fate, Nicholas secretly placed bags of gold inside their stockings, which were drying by the fireplace. This act of charity is believed to have inspired the tradition of hanging stockings filled with gifts and treats by the fireplace, a custom observed in many cultures during the Christmas season.

Little else is known about Nicholas's early life, but it is believed that in the fourth century he served as the bishop of Myra, a city in present-day Demre, Turkey. He was known for defending Christian orthodoxy during the tumultuous times of the Roman Empire's persecution of Christians. He suffered imprisonment and endured various hardships due to his staunch beliefs. Nicholas died on December 6, 343. He was buried in the church of Nicholas in Myra; the church served as a pilgrimage site, attracting numerous devotees who sought the saint's intercession. According to various accounts and legends, the bones of Nicholas exuded a fragrant oil.

Over the centuries, the veneration of Nicholas spread throughout Europe, and his reputation as a protector of children, sailors, and those in need grew. Numerous churches and cathedrals were dedicated to him, and his popularity as patron saint extended to various professions and countries.

The stories and legends surrounding St. Nicholas eventually evolved into Santa Claus or Father Christmas, celebrated in many cultures as a bringer of gifts during the Christmas season. Though the evolution of St. Nicholas into the Jolly Old Elf was gradual and multifaceted, it began in the decades after the Protestant Reformation in the sixteenth century, a time when the veneration of saints and religious practices came under attack. As a result, some Protestant regions abandoned the celebration of St. Nicholas altogether. However, the figure of St. Nicholas continued to live on in various forms. In some areas, he became known as Christkind or the Christ Child, who delivered gifts to children. In other areas, St. Nicholas merged with other local figures or pagan traditions.

One significant influence on the transformation of St. Nicholas into Santa Claus came from Dutch settlers in North America. The Dutch had a tradition of celebrating the feast of St. Nicholas (Sinterklaas) on December 6. Over the years, this holiday began to meld with similar traditions in other parts of the world. In later traditions, Sinterklaas would arrive on a steamboat from Spain, accompanied by his companion, Black Peter (Zwarte Piet). Dutch immigrants brought this tradition to America, where it gradually took on a life of its own.

In the nineteenth century, the American Santa Claus emerged from a blend of Dutch Sinterklaas traditions and British Christmas customs. Clement Clarke Moore's 1823 poem, "A Visit from St. Nicholas," and Thomas Nast's 1860s illustrations in *Harper's Weekly* shaped the modern Santa image, featuring his red suit, North Pole workshop, and the naughty or nice list. As the commercialization of Christmas grew in the twentieth century, Santa's popularity spread worldwide, symbolizing generosity and kindness.

NICODEMUS

BORN: End of the 1st century BC, Galilee
DIED: Middle of the 1st century, Judea
FEAST DAY: August 3

PATRONAGE: Students, undertakers and pallbearers
SYMBOLS AND ATTRIBUTES: Meeting Christ at night, phylacteries, scroll, quilt

Also known as Nicodemus the Pharisee, St. Nicodemus is a Biblical figure who appears in the Gospel of John, one of the four canonical Gospels in the New Testament. His encounters with Jesus shed light on important aspects of Christian theology, particularly the concept of spiritual rebirth through Baptism.

Nicodemus is featured in two key passages in Scripture. In John 3:1–21, he visits Jesus by night, acknowledging Him as a teacher from God, and engages in a conversation about the necessity of being "born again" or "born from above" to enter the kingdom of God. Jesus explains the importance of spiritual rebirth through water and the Spirit, alluding to the concept of Baptism. In John 7:45–52, Nicodemus makes a brief appearance when he defends Christ before the Pharisees and the chief priests, who are passionately discussing the arrest and condemnation of Jesus. He points out the principle of giving a person a fair hearing before passing judgment. Nicodemus makes his final appearance in chapter 19, where he joins Joseph of Arimathea in preparing the body of Jesus for burial. Together, they wrap Jesus's body in linen cloths with spices, adhering to Jewish burial customs, demonstrating their reverence and respect for the crucified Messiah.

Nicodemus's encounters with Jesus, though brief, highlight important theological themes, including the need for spiritual transformation, the importance of Baptism in Christian faith, and the hope of life everlasting. His nighttime conversation with Jesus is where Jesus famously says, "For God so loved the world that He gave His only Son, so that everyone who believes in Him may not perish but may have eternal life" (John 3:16).

NOËL CHABANEL

BORN: February 2, 1613, Saugues, France
DIED: December 8, 1649, Nottawasaga River, New France
FEAST DAY: October 19

PATRONAGE: Missionaries to the Huron people
SYMBOLS AND ATTRIBUTES: Palm branch, cross

Noël Chabanel was one of the North American Martyrs. He entered the Jesuit order in 1630 and was sent to New France (now Canada) in 1643 to work with the Huron people.

Noël faced considerable challenges during his time in New France. He struggled to adapt to local customs and food, and to learn the Huron language. Even so, he vowed never to leave the mission. However, Noël's life was cut short under mysterious circumstances. After the martyrdom of fellow Jesuits and the capture of the Huron mission of St. Jean by the Iroquois, Chabanel was traveling to another mission when he disappeared on December 8, 1649. He is believed to have been killed by an angry Huron who suspected the Jesuits of conspiring with the Iroquois.

NORBERT

BORN: c. 1080, Xanten, Holy Roman Empire
DIED: June 6, 1134, Magdeburg, Holy Roman Empire
FEAST DAY: June 6

PATRONAGE: Childbirth
SYMBOLS AND ATTRIBUTES: Crosier, monstrance

Norbert, also known as Norbert of Xanten, was a prominent figure in the Catholic Church during the twelfth century. He was born around 1080 in Xanten, a town located in the Holy Roman Empire, now part of Germany. Norbert came from a noble family and was well educated. After completing his studies, he embarked on a career in the clergy, though he was unwilling to give up the worldly and aristocratic lifestyle. His attitude changed dramatically when, in 1115, a bolt of lightning struck near him while he was riding his horse during a thunderstorm. He was thrown to the ground and almost died. This near-death experience led Norbert to reassess his life and commit himself fully to God.

Inspired by his newfound spiritual awakening, Norbert renounced his former way of life and embraced a more ascetic and contemplative existence. He became a wandering preacher dedicated to spreading the message of repentance and religious reform. In 1120, he was ordained a priest.

In 1121, Norbert founded the Norbertine order, also known as the Premonstratensians. This religious order combined aspects of monastic life with an active apostolate, emphasizing pastoral work and the reform of the clergy. The Norbertines followed the Rule of St. Augustine and focused on communal life, poverty, and the pursuit of holiness while serving the surrounding community.

Norbert's influence extended beyond the establishment of the Norbertine order. He became an advisor to popes and bishops, advocating for reform within the Church and working toward unity and reconciliation between different religious leaders. Norbert mediated and promoted dialogue during the Investiture Controversy, a conflict between the papacy and secular rulers over the appointment of bishops.

St. Norbert died on June 6, 1134, and was canonized by Pope Gregory XIII in 1582. His legacy lives on through the Norbertine order, which continues to flourish via numerous abbeys and priories throughout the world.

OLAF

BORN: c. 995, Ringerike, Norway
DIED: July 29, 1030, Stiklestad, Norway
FEAST DAY: July 29

PATRONAGE: Norway, kings, difficult marriages
SYMBOLS AND ATTRIBUTES: Sword, axe, crown, model of a church

St. Olaf, also known as Olaf II Haraldsson, was a medieval Norwegian king who played a significant role in the Christianization of Norway. He was born around 995 and reigned as the king of Norway from 1015 until his death in 1030.

Olaf was born into royalty, the son of King Harald Grenske of Norway, and spent his early years as an explorer and adventurer. He was baptized into Christianity around 1010. When he was still a young man, he returned to his homeland in 1015 after the death of his father. He embarked on a mission to unite the country under his rule and spread the faith. He was successful in establishing a centralized government and converting many Norwegians to Christianity, often through forceful means.

During his reign, Olaf faced opposition from local chieftains who resisted his efforts to centralize power. He engaged in several military campaigns to assert his authority, both within Norway and against neighboring kingdoms, launching expeditions against territories such as the Orkney Islands, the Hebrides, and parts of Sweden, all with the aim of extending his authority and securing Norway as a dominant regional power. His military successes and his strong Christian faith earned him a reputation as a powerful, devout ruler.

Olaf's reign ended in 1030 when he was defeated in the Battle of Stiklestad by a coalition of local rulers who opposed his reign. Olaf was killed in the battle, and his body was initially buried in an unmarked grave. However, stories of miracles associated with his remains began to spread, including healing the wounded, restoring sight to the blind, and defeating an enormous sea creature singlehandedly, leading to the veneration of Olaf as a saint.

Olaf's life is narrated in various sagas, notably in Snorri Sturluson's *Heimskringla*, a compilation about Norwegian kings that mixes historical events with legendary tales, and paints a vivid picture of Olaf's achievements and miraculous deeds. Beyond his spiritual importance, Olaf became a symbol of Norwegian independence and national pride, particularly during times when Norway was under foreign rule. Today, his legend continues to shape Norwegian literature, art, and culture.

Olaf was officially canonized as a saint in 1164 by the Catholic Church, and his shrine at the Nidaros Cathedral in Trondheim, Norway, became an important pilgrimage site. Today, Olaf is considered the patron saint of Norway, and his legacy continues to hold cultural and historical significance in the country.

OLYMPIAS

BORN: c. 360, Constantinople, Byzantine Empire
DIED: 408, Nicomedia, Byzantine Empire
FEAST DAY: December 17

PATRONAGE: Poor
SYMBOLS AND ATTRIBUTES: Alms, deaconess's attire, cross,

Olympias, also known as Olympias the Deaconess, was a prominent figure in early Christianity during the fourth and fifth centuries. She was born in Constantinople around the year 360 and belonged to a noble and influential family. Olympias became a widow at a young age, but instead of remarrying, she devoted herself to a life of asceticism and dedicated her resources to the Church, becoming a deaconess in the Church, where she cared for the poor, ministered to the sick and the marginalized, and supported the clergy.

Olympias had a close relationship with John Chrysostom, the archbishop of Constantinople, who regarded her as a trusted confidante and advisor. However, their association led to conflicts and political controversies, as Chrysostom faced opposition from powerful individuals within the Church and the imperial court. As a result of her loyalty to Chrysostom, Olympias was subjected to persecution and mistreatment.

When John Chrysostom was banished from Constantinople, Olympias was stripped of her possessions and subjected to physical abuse and eventual exile. Olympias died in 408, likely due to the mistreatment she endured.

Her feast day is December 17 and her memory is honored as one of 140 statues that adorn St. Peter's Square in Vatican City. (See John Chrysostom.)

OSCAR ARNULFO ROMERO Y GALDÁMEZ

BORN: August 15, 1917, Ciudad Barrios, El Salvador

DIED: March 24, 1980, San Salvador, El Salvador

FEAST DAY: March 24

PATRONAGE: The Americas, persecuted Christians, El Salvador

SYMBOLS AND ATTRIBUTES: Priestly attire, crucifix

St. Oscar Arnulfo Romero y Galdámez, often referred to as Oscar Romero, was a Salvadoran Roman Catholic bishop who was assassinated in 1980 while celebrating Mass in his home country. He was an outspoken advocate for the rights of the poor, which earned him the moniker "The Voice of the Voiceless." Oscar's life and legacy are celebrated and remembered around the world, particularly for his unwavering commitment to social justice and his struggle against oppression and inequality.

Oscar was born on August 15, 1917, in the town of Ciudad Barrios, located in the eastern part of El Salvador. He was the second of seven children born to Santos Romero and Guadalupe de Jesús Galdámez. His father worked as a telegraph operator, and his mother was a homemaker.

Oscar grew up in a modest household and experienced the challenges faced by the working class in El Salvador. His family struggled financially, and this upbringing instilled in him a deep empathy for the poor and marginalized, and greatly influenced his commitment to social justice and liberation theology.

From a young age, Oscar showed an intense devotion to his Catholic faith. He served as an altar boy in his local parish and felt a calling to the priesthood. In pursuit of his vocation, he entered the seminary in San Miguel, a city in eastern El Salvador, at thirteen. Oscar continued his studies at the national seminary in San Salvador, where he received a licentiate in theology.

In 1942, at the age of twenty-four, Oscar was ordained a priest in the Diocese of San Miguel. He then served as a parish priest in several towns and rural areas and gained a firsthand understanding of the challenges faced by the poor as he witnessed the social inequalities and injustices prevalent in Salvadoran society.

His dedication and pastoral work earned him respect and recognition within the Catholic Church. In 1966, Oscar was appointed as the secretary of the Bishops' Conference of El Salvador, a role that allowed him to engage with national issues and contribute to the Church's response to the pressing social problems of the time.

In 1970, he was appointed as an auxiliary bishop of San Salvador; in 1977, he became archbishop. During this time, El Salvador was plagued by a brutal military dictatorship and faced significant social and political violence and unrest. The country was marked by widespread poverty, economic inequality, and human rights abuses committed by state forces as well as paramilitary death squads associated with right-wing factions.

As the archbishop of San Salvador, Oscar used his position and platform to denounce the violence and call for an end to the suffering of the poor and marginalized. He delivered powerful sermons and pastoral letters that condemned the government's repression and highlighted the plight of the oppressed.

Oscar's vocal opposition to the regime and his demand for justice made him a target for those who sought to maintain the status quo. On March 24, 1980, while celebrating Mass at the Chapel of Divine Providence in San Salvador, Oscar Romero was assassinated by a single gunshot to the heart. The perpetrator was a member of a right-wing death squad, widely believed to have had connections to elements within the Salvadoran government. Oscar's death spurred international outrage and brought greater attention to the ongoing violence and human rights abuses in El Salvador.

After his martyrdom, Oscar Romero became an inspirational figure within the Catholic Church and among activists and advocates for social justice worldwide. His life and work have inspired numerous books, films, and documentaries, highlighting his commitment to the poor and marginalized in El Salvador and beyond. One notable film, *Romero* (1989), starring Raul Julia in the title role, chronicles the life and martyrdom of the archbishop.

Oscar's legacy has also influenced the development of liberation theology, a movement within the Catholic Church that emphasizes social justice, the preferential option for the poor, and the importance of political activism in pursuit of a more just society. His life and work exemplify the transformative power of faith when combined with a commitment to human rights.

After a thorough investigation, the Vatican recognized a miracle attributed to the intercession of Oscar, leading to his beatification on May 23, 2015. The miracle involved Cecilia Flores, who, after an emergency cesarean section, fell into a coma due to an infection and internal bleeding, with her kidneys nearing failure. Doctors doubted her survival. Devastated, her husband, Alejandro Rivas, recalled his late grandmother's faith in Romero. Finding a prayer card with Romero's image in his grandmother's Bible, Rivas prayed for his intervention. Miraculously, Flores recovered from her illness.

In 2018, Pope Francis canonized Oscar Romero, further solidifying his place in the history of the Church and the global struggle for the rights of the least among us. His feast day is celebrated on March 24, the anniversary of his assassination.

P

PASCHAL I

BORN: 8th century, Rome, Italy
DIED: February 11, 824, Rome, Italy
FEAST DAY: February 11

PATRONAGE: Eucharistic conferences
SYMBOLS AND ATTRIBUTES: Papal vestments, keys of St. Peter

Pope Paschal I was the bishop of Rome from January 25, 817, until his death on February 11, 824. He was born in Rome and spent his early years as a monk at the monastery of St. Stephen and served in the papal chancellery.

Paschal I's papacy began during a period of upheaval in the region. The Carolingian Empire dominated Western Europe, and the papacy was increasingly under its influence, though Pope Paschal I maintained a degree of independence while he focused on pastoral and theological issues.

One significant aspect of his papacy was his devotion to the cult of the saints and his commitment to the construction and renovation of churches and monasteries. This included transferring the remains of many saints to new locations, a practice known as translation. He rebuilt three basilicas, including the Basilica of Santa Prassede.

Pope Paschal I also had to navigate tricky relationships with the political powers of his time, notably the Carolingian emperor Louis the Pious and his son Lothair. Paschal was implicated in a conspiracy against Louis, resulting in the Frankish Empire losing papal territory.

There were other significant controversies associated with his papacy, including conflicts with the Frankish bishops about his practice of translating saints' relics. He also faced accusations of blinding and murdering two bishops.

In 823, Pope Paschal I welcomed several political refugees from the Carolingian court who had been involved in a failed rebellion against Emperor Louis the Pious. This group included a bishop named Theodore and his companion Leo, who were accused of supporting the uprising.

In accepting these individuals into Rome, Pope Paschal I likely hoped to assert the independence of the papacy from the Carolingian empire and to underline the traditional idea of Rome as a city of refuge. However, this move was regarded as a political threat by the emperor.

After the refugees arrived in Rome, they mysteriously died. Some historical accounts suggest that they were assassinated, potentially at the behest of Emperor Louis. However, other sources lay the blame at the feet of Pope Paschal I himself. Emperor Louis the Pious ordered an investigation into the matter.

Pope Paschal I was subsequently accused of being complicit in their deaths, but he insisted on his innocence. There is a common belief that Emperor Louis deposed Pope Paschal I at a council in 824. However, historical records do not confirm this. Despite the tension between them, Carolingian emperors like Louis did not have the authority to remove popes from their position as some later rulers did. Despite these controversies, Pope Paschal I was canonized in the sixteenth century.

PATRICK

BORN: c. 385, Britain
DIED: c. 461, Ireland
FEAST DAY: March 17
PATRONAGE: Ireland and numerous locations, engineers, paralegals, excluded people, for protection against snakes

SYMBOLS AND ATTRIBUTES: Shamrock, snakes, bishop's attire, harp, crosier, the color green

Patrick, also known as the Apostle of Ireland, is the patron saint of Ireland and one of the most popular saints in the world. What is known about him blends fact and legend.

He was born around 385 in Roman Britain, now believed to be in modern-day Scotland or Wales. His birth name was Maewyn Succat, and he was of British descent.

When Patrick was sixteen, he was abducted by Irish pirates and taken to Ireland as a slave. He was imprisoned for several years and forced to work as a shepherd. Patrick turned to Christianity as a way to alleviate his hardships, and he developed a deep faith in God.

According to his writings, during his captivity, he had a vision in which he heard a voice urging him to escape and return to his homeland. Eluding his captors, Patrick returned to Britain and reunited with his family, and subsequently traveled to Gaul (modern-day France) to pursue religious studies. He spent several years in Gaul, possibly at the monastery of Lerins or under the tutelage of Germanus of Auxerre, where he received theological training and was ordained as a bishop.

After his time in Gaul, Patrick heeded what he believed to be a divine calling to return to Ireland. His mission was to bring the message of Christianity to the people of Ireland, among whom he had been enslaved earlier in his life. Patrick considered himself a chosen instrument of God, guided by a duty to spread the Gospel and convert the Irish people.

Around 432, Patrick arrived in Ireland as a missionary. He faced significant challenges in his work, as Ireland was still primarily a pagan society with a rich tradition of druidic practices. Nonetheless, Patrick fearlessly preached the Gospel, converted many Irish people to Christianity, and established numerous churches and monasteries throughout the land.

St. Patrick's writings primarily consist of two attributed documents, although many scholars believe followers of Patrick wrote them. The *Confession* is an autobiographical work in which he shares his personal journey, including his upbringing, enslavement in Ireland, escape, and subsequent mission as a bishop. It highlights his deepened faith during captivity and his reliance on divine guidance. The "Letter to the Soldiers of Coroticus" passionately denounces the actions of Coroticus, a warlord who enslaved Patrick's converts. This missive defends the Irish Christian community and reveals Patrick's strong moral convictions. Both writings offer insights into his life, mission, and religious beliefs, providing a historical and spiritual understanding of his challenges, commitment to Christianity, and efforts in Ireland. While their authorship is debated, they remain significant in comprehending Patrick's life and impact.

Patrick's commitment to his mission and his efforts to combat pagan rituals and beliefs played a vital role in the Christianization of Ireland. He also incorporated existing pagan symbols and practices into Christianity, making it more relatable for the Irish people. For instance, he celebrated Easter with bonfires, inspired by the festival of Ostara, a spring equinox celebration.

Patrick's life is intertwined with legend. Among the most famous tales is his use of the shamrock—a three-leafed clover—to elucidate the doctrine of Holy Trinity to the Irish. By demonstrating how three separate leaves form a single clover, he aimed to convey the idea of one God in three persons: Father, Son, and Holy Spirit. Another legend credits Patrick with driving snakes out of Ireland. While fasting atop a hill believed to be Croagh Patrick in County Mayo, he was purportedly attacked by snakes. Patrick then chased them into the sea, ridding Ireland of the slithering creatures. This story is often interpreted as symbolizing the rise of Christianity over pagan beliefs or the banishment of evil from the land.

Whether or not the legends are true, the influence of Patrick's missionary work in Ireland is widely recognized. His death is believed to have occurred on March 17, around 461. This date became St. Patrick's Day, an important feast celebrated in Ireland and by people of Irish descent worldwide.

PAUL

BORN: c. 5 AD, Tarsus, Roman Empire
DIED: c. 64–68 AD, Rome, Italy
FEAST DAY: June 29 (with Peter)

PATRONAGE: Writers, publishers, tentmakers, evangelists
SYMBOLS AND ATTRIBUTES: Sword, book, three springs of water

Paul, originally named Saul, was born in Tarsus in modern-day Turkey. His letters suggest that he came from a devout Jewish family and was a Roman citizen, an uncommon status among Jews at that time, indicating his family's higher social standing or unique circumstances. Paul was educated by Gamaliel, a noted Pharisee scholar, who provided him with a deep grounding in Jewish law.

He was initially a persecutor of the early Christian Church. He was present at the martyrdom of Stephen as depicted in the Book of Acts. Stephen was one of seven men chosen to be deacons in the early Church in Jerusalem. He attracted the attention of the Sanhedrin, the Jewish religious council, who eventually convicted him of blasphemy. Stephen was expelled from the city and stoned to death. Notably, those who witnessed this event placed their garments at the feet of a man known as Saul, suggesting his potential involvement, albeit indirectly, in Stephen's martyrdom.

Saul sought and received permission from the Jewish high priest to journey to Damascus to arrest any followers of "the Way," a name for early Christianity, and bring them back to the city for trial. It was on this journey that Saul had a life-altering encounter with the risen Christ, which sparked his conversion.

As Saul approached Damascus, a light from Heaven suddenly flashed around him. He fell to the ground and heard a voice saying, "Saul, Saul, why are you persecuting me?" When Saul asked who was speaking, the voice responded, "I am Jesus, whom you are persecuting" (Acts 9:3–5). Struck blind by the experience, Saul was led into Damascus by his companions. For three days, he neither ate nor drank and remained without sight.

Meanwhile, in Damascus, a disciple named Ananias received a vision from Jesus. In it Christ instructed him to go to a man of Tarsus named Saul. Ananias was initially reluctant, but the Lord comforted him, saying that Saul had been chosen to "carry my name before Gentiles, kings, and the children of Israel" (Acts 9:15).

Ananias went to the blind man, laid his hands on him, and prayed for healing and restoration. Scales fell from Saul's eyes and miraculously he regained his sight. He was then baptized and regained his strength after eating.

Post-conversion, Saul took the name Paul, and he turned from persecuting followers of Jesus to becoming one of the most influential leaders in the early Christian Church, proclaiming the Gospel and interpreting the life of Christ for those who would listen. While this name change is not explained in the Bible, it is generally thought to represent Saul's profound inner transformation and radical change of heart.

Paul's teachings center on the belief that Jesus is the Christ, the Son of God, who died and was resurrected to redeem humankind from their sins. He highlighted the power and significance of grace, a divine gift that humans cannot earn by their own merits. He also formulated the doctrine of justification by faith, which asserted that individuals are justified, or made right with God, not through acts, such as obeying the Mosaic Law, but through faith in Jesus Christ.

Paul wrote a considerable share of the New Testament (estimates range from 28 to 50 percent), including the letters (epistles) to the Romans, Corinthians, Galatians, Ephesians, Philippians, Colossians, and Thessalonians, as well as the personal letters to Timothy, Titus, and Philemon. His letters, intended to teach, reprimand, and encourage the early Christian communities, are the earliest Christian documents on record and are of immense value for understanding the early Church.

Paul's missionary journeys took him across the Mediterranean world, from Asia Minor to Greece, possibly as far as Spain, and finally to Rome. In each place, he sought to spread the message of the Gospel, often facing severe opposition. The Book of Acts records these travels, although some discrepancies exist between Paul's own accounts in his letters and the narrative presented in Acts.

Historically, Paul's impact cannot be overstated. His contribution to Christian theology and his role in spreading Christianity beyond the Jewish community significantly shaped the course of Western history. He is regarded as a critical figure in the transition of Christianity from a minor Jewish sect to a global religious tradition.

While the New Testament does not provide an account of Paul's death, early Christian tradition holds that Paul was martyred in Rome during the reign of Emperor Nero, who ruled from 54 AD to 68 AD. The details of his death come to us from various early Christian writings and traditions outside of the canonical New Testament.

According to these accounts, Paul was arrested and brought to Rome, where he was kept under house arrest for some time, as mentioned in the final chapters of the Book of Acts. During the Neronian persecutions—a significant wave of violence against Christians initiated by Nero after the Great Fire of Rome in 64 AD—Paul was arrested again.

It is traditionally held that Paul, being a Roman citizen, was afforded a quicker, less painful, and more humane execution by beheading rather than the more brutal methods such as crucifixion used for noncitizens.

The apocryphal work known as the Acts of Paul, which dates back to the second century, documents the longstanding tradition surrounding his death and elaborates on the narrative by describing a miraculous event wherein milk, rather than blood, is said to have emanated from Paul's severed neck. This extraordinary occurrence is interpreted as a symbol of his exceptional purity and sanctity.

Paul's purported burial place is now marked by the Basilica of St. Paul Outside the Walls in Rome, one of the four major papal basilicas. (See Stephen.)

PAUL CHŎNG HASANG

BORN: 1795, Korea

DIED: September 22, 1839, Korea

FEAST DAY: September 20

PATRONAGE: Korea

SYMBOLS AND ATTRIBUTES: Cross, Korean attire (hanbok and gat)

Paul Chŏng Hasang was born into a devout Catholic family. His father, Augustine Jeong Yak-Jong, and his nephew, John Jeong Yak-Yong, were some of the earliest individuals to convert to Catholicism in Korea. When Paul was seven years old, his father and older brother, authors of the first catechism in Korea, known as Jugyo Yoji, were martyred for their faith. Despite facing persecution and losing their property, Paul's family never wavered in their dedication to their faith.

As he matured, Paul Chŏng Hasang became an assistant to a government official. As part of his work, he made several trips to Beijing, where he appealed to the city's bishop, requesting a diocese and more priests for Korea. His efforts paid off, and a diocese was indeed established in Korea, largely thanks to his persistence.

Deepening his commitment to the faith, Paul furthered his studies in Latin and theology under the mentorship of Bishop Laurent-Marie-Joseph Imbert. However, when a renewed wave of anti-Catholic sentiment surged, Paul was captured. In the face of brutal torture, he chose martyrdom over renouncing his beliefs. He was executed at the age of forty-five.

The Roman Catholic Church commemorates the Korean Martyrs, including Paul Chŏng Hasang, with a memorial on September 20. In 1984, Pope John Paul II canonized 103 of these martyrs, recognizing their sacrifice and unwavering devotion to the Catholic faith. Paul Chŏng Hasang's life serves as a testament to the resilience and dedication of early Korean Catholics.

PAUL MIKI

BORN: c. 1562, Settsu, Osaka, Japan
DIED: February 5, 1597, Nagasaki, Japan
FEAST DAY: February 6

PATRONAGE: Japan
SYMBOLS AND ATTRIBUTES: Cross, Japanese attire

St. Paul Miki was a Japanese Roman Catholic priest and martyr who is among the Twenty-Six Martyrs of Japan, a group of Catholics who were executed by crucifixion on February 5, 1597, at Nagasaki.

Born around 1562, Paul was a native of Tounucumada, Japan, and the second son of a noble Samurai family of the Sanuki Province. His father, Miki Handayu, was an administrator (daimyo) of the castle in Harima Province. As a young boy, he was educated by the Jesuits in Azuchi and Takatsuki.

Paul joined the Society of Jesus, inspired by the work of missionaries like Francis Xavier, who brought Catholicism to Japan. He became the first native-born Japanese Jesuit priest and did so while there was intense religious and political tension in Japan. Toyotomi Hideyoshi, the de facto ruler of Japan, had initially tolerated the practice of Christianity, but his stance grew increasingly hostile, culminating in the persecution of Christians.

In 1597, Paul and twenty-five others were arrested for being Christians. These individuals came to be known as the Twenty-Six Martyrs of Japan. The group consisted of three Japanese Jesuits, six Spanish Franciscans, and seventeen Japanese laypeople. They were taken to Nagasaki, a city that had become a center for Catholic missionary activities.

Upon arrival in Nagasaki on February 5, they were crucified on a hill, and spears were thrust through their bodies. This area has become known as the Holy Mountain, or Nishizaka Hill, and is a pilgrimage site in Japan.

During his execution, Paul reportedly delivered a sermon from his cross, forgiving his executioners and professing his faith. His last words declared that there was no other way to paradise except the Christian path.

Paul Miki and his companions were canonized by Pope Pius IX in 1862. They are collectively known as the Twenty-Six Martyrs of Japan, and their feast day is celebrated on February 6.

In Japan, he is known as a symbol of the Christian tradition in the country and a martyr who died for his faith. His life and death reflect the difficulties early Christian missionaries and converts faced in Japan.

PAUL OF THE CROSS

BORN: January 3, 1694, Ovada, Italy
DIED: October 18, 1775, Rome, Italy
FEAST DAY: October 20

PATRONAGE: Hungary
SYMBOLS AND ATTRIBUTES: Black religious habit, crucifix, Passionist sign

Paul of the Cross, or Paul Daneom, was a prominent Italian mystic, preacher, and the founder of the Passionist Congregation. He is considered one of the great saints of the Catholic Church, known for his deep devotion to the suffering of Christ.

He was born in Ovada, a town in the region of Liguria, Italy. His parents, Luke Daneo and Anna Maria Massari, were devout Catholics who instilled in their children a strong faith and love for God. From a young age, Paul showed a remarkable inclination toward spiritual life and was known for his deep faith and contemplative nature.

At nineteen, he experienced a spiritual awakening during a retreat, which led him to dedicate his life to the service of God and the Church. He felt a calling to establish a religious order devoted to meditating on the Passion of Christ and spreading devotion to it. He was ordained a priest and began his mission of preaching and promoting the message of Christ's suffering and redemption.

Between 1720 and 1725, Paul of the Cross founded the Congregation of the Passion, also known as the Passionists. The congregation's focus was to imitate Christ's Passion, his suffering and death, through prayer, austerity, and preaching. The members of the order, known as Passionist Fathers, took vows of poverty, chastity, and obedience and wore a black habit with the distinctive emblem of a heart and three nails with the words *Jesu XPI Passio,* which means Passion of Christ in Greek and Latin.

Paul of the Cross spent his life preaching missions, promoting devotion to the Passion, and guiding the members of his congregation. His legacy as a saint and founder of the Passionists continues to inspire many in these modern times. In 1867, Paul of the Cross was canonized by Pope Pius IX, officially recognizing his sanctity and his significant contributions to the Catholic Church.

POPE PAUL VI

BORN: September 26, 1897, Italy

DIED: August 6, 1978, Italy

FEAST DAY: September 26

PATRONAGE: Archdiocese of Milan and the Second Vatican Council

SYMBOLS AND ATTRIBUTES: Papal vestments

St. Pope Paul VI, whose birth name was Giovanni Battista Enrico Antonio Maria Montini, served from 1963 to 1978 as the 262nd pope of the Roman Catholic Church. Born on September 26, 1897, he left a significant mark on the Church during an era of social, political, and religious changes. Perhaps the most defining aspect of his papacy was overseeing the majority of the Second Vatican Council (1962–1965), which was initiated by his predecessor, St. Pope John XXIII. This council ushered in pivotal reforms in Catholic liturgy, ecclesiology, and the Church's relationship with other religions.

In 1968, Pope Paul IV released his influential encyclical *Humanae vitae* (On Human Life), which affirms, among other official teachings, the Church's stance against artificial contraception. While this document remains a point of contention within the Church, Paul VI was unwavering in upholding traditional teachings.

Beyond his administrative decisions, he was a pioneer in ecumenism and interfaith dialogue. Notably, he became the first reigning pope to travel by airplane, undertaking impactful journeys such as his pilgrimage to the Holy Land. During a trip made in 1965, he and Patriarch Athenagoras I of Constantinople met in Jerusalem, which represented a monumental step toward Christian unity. The same year, he became the first pope to visit the United States. While there, he delivered a passionate address emphasizing global peace to the United Nations General Assembly.

However, his tenure was not without challenges. Paul VI survived two assassination attempts, with a particularly dramatic episode occurring during his 1970 visit to the Philippines, when a man disguised as a priest tried to stab him.

After his passing in 1978, the Church recognized his significant contributions and began his cause for canonization. Pope Francis formally beatified him in 2014 and canonized him as a saint in 2018. Today, St. Pope Paul VI's legacy is his dedication to modernizing the Church while maintaining fidelity to its core teachings.

PAULINUS OF NOLA

BORN: c. 354, Bordeaux, Gaul

DIED: June 22, 431, Nola, Italy

FEAST DAY: June 22

PATRONAGE: Bell makers

SYMBOLS AND ATTRIBUTES: Bishop's vestments, crosier

A Roman poet and a bishop, St. Paulinus of Nola began his career as a lawyer and held high positions in the Roman Empire, including governor of Campania in Italy.

However, his life took a transformative turn when he encountered the teachings of St. Ambrose of Milan, which led him to convert to Christianity. Fueled by his newfound faith, Paulinus abandoned his secular pursuits and embraced a life of asceticism and devotion to God.

In 395, Paulinus was ordained as a priest and eventually became the bishop of Nola, a city in present-day Italy. As a bishop, he dedicated himself to promoting his flock's spiritual and material welfare. He was particularly known for his acts of charity and generosity, using his considerable wealth to aid the poor and support various charitable causes.

He was also a gifted poet and writer and composed numerous hymns and poems that celebrated the life and teachings of Jesus Christ and other saints. His literary works shaped the development of Christian poetry and hagiography.

One of his most prized works is the *Carmina*, a collection of poems and hymns that have survived through the ages. These writings exemplify his deep spirituality and offer profound insights into the Christian faith. Through his art, Paulinus conveyed the beauty and richness of Jesus and Christian teaching to both the clergy and the laity.

Paulinus is also often associated with the introduction of bells in Christian services and devotion. Tradition holds that Paulinus used bells to call the faithful to worship. He commissioned and cast a large bronze bell for this purpose, which he called a *campanas* after his hometown. He also used handbells, which came to be known as nola bells. While many scholars contest this story, Paulinus is still considered the patron saint of bell makers.

Paulinus died in 431. La Festa dei Gigli, or the Festival of the Lilies, is a famous Italian festival held yearly in Nola to celebrate Paulinus. The story behind the festival is tied to a legend about the devoted saint. According to tradition, Paulinus sold himself into slavery to the Barbarians to secure the release of a Nola resident. When he was eventually freed, the people of Nola greeted him with lilies. The lilies became a symbol of Paulinus, and the festival reenacts his triumphant return.

The most spectacular part of the festival is the procession of the *gigli*, which are huge obelisks that are handcrafted and beautifully decorated. There are eight *gigli*, each representing a different artisan guild and another one representing a boat, symbolizing the journey of St. Paulinus. About 120 men carry the structures, called *paranza*, through the city streets in a carefully choreographed parade that can take the entire day. The carrying of these enormous structures is a display of devotion and strength, accompanied by music, dancing, and much celebration. La Festa dei Gigli takes place on the Sunday following June 22, though the festival's preparation begins months in advance and involves the entire community. (See Ambrose of Milan.)

PERPETUA

BORN: c. 182, place unknown
DIED: March 7, 203, Carthage
FEAST DAY: March 7 (with St. Felicitas)

PATRONAGE: Mothers
SYMBOLS AND ATTRIBUTES: Palm branch, cross, angels

St. Perpetua, also known as St. Perpetua of Carthage, was an early Christian martyr who lived in the second century. Born in the Roman city of Carthage, which is now modern-day Tunisia, Perpetua was a young noblewoman and a convert to Christianity. She was married and had an infant son.

In 203, Perpetua and several other Christians were arrested and imprisoned for their refusal to renounce their faith. Perpetua kept a diary during her imprisonment, which is known as *The Passion of St. Perpetua, St. Felicitas, and Their Companions.* In her diary, she documented her experiences and the events leading up to her martyrdom.

Perpetua and her companions were eventually sentenced to death and thrown into the arena to be attacked by wild animals during a public spectacle. According to various accounts, she and her companions courageously met their impending deaths and even comforted one another during their final moments.

PETER

BORN: 1st century AD, Bethsaida
DIED: c. 64 AD, Rome, Italy
FEAST DAY: June 29 (with Paul)

PATRONAGE: Fishermen, locksmiths, popes, bakers, bridge builders, those suffering fever or foot problems
SYMBOLS AND ATTRIBUTES: Keys, inverted cross, fish

St. Peter, originally named Simon, is one of the twelve apostles of Jesus Christ and a central figure in the Christian tradition. As one of Jesus's closest disciples, he is "the rock" upon which Christ built His church; he served at the Catholic Church's first pope.

Simon, a fisherman, first encountered Jesus by the Sea of Galilee. As recounted in the Gospels, Jesus saw Simon and his brother Andrew casting their nets into the sea and invited them to join his ministry with the words: "Come, follow me, and I will make you fishers of men" (Matthew 4:19). Simon immediately left his nets and followed Jesus, marking the start of a profound spiritual journey from laborer to spiritual leader.

Jesus would change Simon's name to Peter, a move that held great significance. In Greek, the name is Petros, meaning "rock." During a conversation in Caesarea Philippi, Jesus asked the Apostles who they thought He was. Peter answered, "You are the Messiah, the Son of the living God" (Matthew 16:16). Jesus responded, "And I tell you that you are

Peter, and on this rock I will build my church, and the gates of Hades will not overcome it" (Matthew 16:18). This name change signifies Peter's foundational role in the establishment of the early Church and his unwavering faith in Jesus.

St. Peter's close relationship with Jesus is evident in the numerous pivotal moments he shared with the Messiah. From the miracle at the Sea of Galilee where Peter, wavering between faith and doubt, attempted to walk on water toward Jesus only to sink beneath the waves, to the awe-inspiring Transfiguration where he, along with James and John, witnessed Jesus in His divine form on a mountaintop (Matthew 17:1–9). At the Last Supper, it was Peter who passionately claimed he would never betray Jesus, despite Christ's prophecy that he would deny Him three times before dawn (Matthew 26:33–35). This prophecy came to pass after Jesus's arrest. When Roman soldiers arrested Jesus, Peter came to His defense, drew a sword and sliced off the ear of Malchus, a servant of the high priest. Jesus, however, reproached Peter and restored the servant's ear. In the hours ahead, Peter, who had been a defender of his earlier in the night, denied knowing Jesus three times, just as Jesus had predicted, leading to deep remorse and marking the lowest point in Peter's journey as a disciple. After Jesus's resurrection, Peter reaffirmed his love for Him three times. This act of restoration mirrored his three denials, signifying Peter's forgiveness and restoration.

This series of events underscores Peter's unique position in Jesus's inner circle. His very human experiences of doubt and faith highlight the transformative nature of his discipleship under Jesus, and set the stage for his subsequent leadership in the early Christian community.

Beyond the Gospels, Peter emerged as a leader in the early Christian community in Jerusalem. His leadership is prominent in the Acts of the Apostles. After the ascension of Jesus, when Jesus returned to Heaven after his resurrection, Peter took charge of the apostolic community in Jerusalem. He was a key figure on the Day of Pentecost, when he delivered a powerful sermon that led to the conversion of about three thousand souls (Acts 2:14–41). Furthermore, he performed miracles in Jesus's name and faced persecution for his faith. Peter's vision of a sheet with unclean animals, as recounted in Acts 10, led to the pivotal decision to admit Gentiles into the early Christian community without requiring them to adhere to Jewish ceremonial laws.

There are several post-Biblical legends and traditions associated with St. Peter. Perhaps the best-known is his crucifixion in Rome under Emperor Nero. Christian tradition maintains that Peter was indeed martyred in Rome during the reign of Emperor Nero, around 64–68 AD. It is believed that Peter requested to be crucified upside down, feeling unworthy to die in the same manner as Jesus. Additionally, St. Peter's Basilica is traditionally believed to be built over the site of Peter's burial.

Another legend, popular during the Middle Ages, tells of how Peter fled persecution in Rome in the years after Christ's death and resurrection and was met with a vision of Jesus heading into the city. When Peter asked, "Quo vadis, Domine?" (Latin for "Where are you going, Lord?"), Jesus replied that He was going to Rome to be crucified again. This encounter prompted Peter to return to the city and face his martyrdom.

St. Peter's influence on the Catholic Church is immeasurable. He established the Church in Rome and served as its first bishop, hence, its first pope, laying the foundation for the papacy and establishing the authority of the Church. His leadership and teachings have shaped the beliefs and practices of the Catholic Church to this day.

Peter shares his feast day with St. Paul on June 29, and he is often depicted in art holding the keys of Peter, the emblem of the papacy of the Catholic Church.

PETER CANISIUS

BORN: May 8, 1521, Nijmegen, Duchy of Guelders

DIED: December 21, 1597, Fribourg, Switzerland

FEAST DAY: December 21

PATRONAGE: Germany, Catholic press

SYMBOLS AND ATTRIBUTES: Book, pen

Also known as Peter Kanis or Petrus Canisius, Peter Canisius was a Dutch Jesuit priest (the first for the order), theologian, and Doctor of the Church. He was born in the Netherlands, and was the eldest son of a wealthy merchant family. He joined the Society of Jesus in 1543 and was instrumental in the Counter-Reformation, a period of Catholic renewal in response to the Protestant Reformation.

Peter Canisius advocated Catholic education and helped establish colleges, universities, and schools throughout Europe. He believed that education could combat the spread of Protestantism and revitalize the Catholic faith.

He was a prolific writer and theologian, producing numerous works, including catechisms, spiritual treatises, and sermons. His most notable contribution was his *Catechismus minor,* a concise and accessible catechism that became immensely popular and was translated into several languages. This catechism served as a fundamental tool for educating both clergy and laity about the foundations of the Catholic faith. He wrote several other works, including the *Summa doctrinae Christianae* and the *De Maria Virgine.*

Peter Canisius was an active participant in the Council of Trent, a significant ecumenical council that addressed the challenges of the Protestant Reformation. He was central in formulating the council's decrees and actively promoting their implementation throughout Europe. During the sessions of the council, Peter Canisius engaged in theological debates and discussions, providing intellectual arguments and offering insights on matters related to doctrine, liturgy, and discipline. His contributions helped give shape to the council's decrees and resolutions, which aimed to address the issues raised by Protestant reformers while reaffirming and clarifying Catholic teachings.

Pope Pius XI canonized Peter Canisius as a saint on May 21, 1925. He is revered as the patron saint of the Catholic press, Catholic schools, and the Catholic laity.

PETER CHANEL

BORN: July 12, 1803, France
DIED: April 28, 1841, Futuna, Wallis and Futuna
FEAST DAY: April 28

PATRONAGE: Oceania
SYMBOLS AND ATTRIBUTES: Palm of martyrdom

St. Peter Chanel was a French missionary and martyr. He was born in 1803 in the village of La Potière, France, and was the fifth of eight children. At a young age, he developed a deep love for God. He studied at a local seminary and was ordained a priest in 1827.

In 1831, Peter was sent as a missionary to the island of Futuna, which is now part of the French territory of Wallis and Futuna in the South Pacific. The island's Indigenous population was resistant to Christianity. Peter, however, was undeterred. He began preaching the Gospel and was initially successful in converting some of the islanders to Christianity. Although he was vehemently opposed by the island's ruler and his supporters, Peter continued his mission work and even baptized the chief's son. This did not go over well, and in 1837, Peter was beaten and speared by a group of islanders. He died as a martyr to his faith. The Church recognized Peter Chanel's faith and dedication to his mission, and he was canonized as a saint in 1954. He is considered the first martyr of Oceania.

PETER CLAVER

BORN: June 26, 1580, Spain
DIED: September 8, 1654, Cartagena, New Granada
FEAST DAY: September 9

PATRONAGE: African missions, enslaved people
SYMBOLS AND ATTRIBUTES: Ship, chains, anchor

Peter Claver was a Jesuit priest dedicated to serving the oppressed and marginalized during the seventeenth century.

Born in 1580, in Verdu, Catalonia, Spain, Peter grew up in a devout Catholic family that instilled in him a strong faith and a sense of compassion for others. In 1602, Peter joined the Society of Jesus, studying philosophy and theology in Spain. In 1615, he was ordained a priest. Shortly after his ordination, he expressed a deep desire to serve as a missionary in the New World, particularly in the Spanish colonies of the Americas.

In 1616, Peter arrived in Cartagena, Colombia, which was one of the largest slave-trading ports at that time. Here, he would dedicate most of his life to the welfare of enslaved African people, earning him the title "Apostle of the Slaves." Peter was appalled by the inhumane treatment and conditions under which the slaves were transported, bought, and sold.

Peter chose to live among the slaves, ministering to their spiritual and physical needs. He would meet slave ships as they arrived in the port, often being the first person to greet the enslaved individuals who had endured the arduous journey. Peter would go on board, providing medical care, food, and water to those sick and dying, showing them compassion and love.

Fluent in several languages, including Spanish, Portuguese, and African dialects, Peter preached the Gospel and passionately denounced the injustices of slavery, speaking out against the dehumanization of the African people. Peter believed that all human beings were created in the image of God and deserved to be treated with dignity and respect.

His unrelenting dedication to improve the lives of the enslaved extended beyond the port. Peter would visit the slave markets and plantations, teaching and baptizing those who were willing to embrace Christianity. Facing opposition from both slave traders and plantation owners, he remained committed to justice and equality.

Peter's ministry extended beyond his work with the enslaved. He also cared for the sick and destitute in Cartagena, often visiting hospitals and jails and ministering to the needs of patients and prisoners. He wrote many letters over the years, though many of them have been lost. In these missives, he describes his experiences ministering to the people and his struggles with the slave traders and plantation owners. He also writes about his own spiritual journey and his devotion to the Catholic faith. His letters offer a vivid picture of life in the Spanish colonies and the hardships faced by those caught in the disgusting net of slavery.

PETER DAMIAN

BORN: c. 1007, Ravenna, Italy

DIED: February 21/22, 1072, Faenza, Italy

FEAST DAY: February 21

PATRONAGE: Reformers, writers

SYMBOLS AND ATTRIBUTES:
Cardinal's vestments

Peter Damian was one of the most influential figures of the eleventh-century Church. He was born into a noble family but faced early hardship, losing both his parents by age five. He was entrusted to the care of his older brother, who treated him harshly and denied him a proper education. However, Peter Damian's intellect and determination prevailed, and he pursued his studies with the help of another brother, displaying exceptional academic abilities.

In his early adulthood, he became drawn to the ascetic and contemplative life. He joined the Benedictine order at Fonte Avellana, where he devoted himself to a life of prayer, meditation, and rigorous self-discipline, sometimes including self-mortification. His dedication to the monastic life eventually led him to become one of the leading figures in monastic reform.

A prolific theologian and philosopher, his writings and teachings, including *The Life of St. Romuald*, the founder of the Camaldolese order, and his *Letter to the Hermitage*, which emphasized the value of solitude, prayer, and self-denial in the pursuit of holiness, shaped theological thought and influenced subsequent Church reform movements. One of his most notable works, *The Book of Gomorrah*, addressed clerical immorality and advocated for stricter adherence to celibacy and moral purity within the clergy. It was the first medieval text to condemn sexual sins, including homosexuality.

Moreover, Peter Damian was a pivotal figure in the Gregorian Reformation of the eleventh century. This movement, named in honor of its champion, Pope Gregory VII, sought to cleanse the Catholic Church from the stain of simony—the transactional sale of spiritual positions—and to reinforce the pope's overarching authority within the Church.

Peter Damian's dedication to a more virtuous Church made him address significant issues of misconduct and misuse of power within the papacy. In acknowledgment of his commitment to bettering the Church, he was appointed cardinal-bishop of Ostia. Nonetheless, Peter chose to stay true to his monastic roots, prioritizing his spiritual pursuits and writings over residing in a diocese. He was canonized as a saint by Pope Leo XII in 1823 and is revered as a Doctor of the Church. (See Gregory the Great.)

PHILIP

BORN: 1st century AD, Galilee

DIED: c. 80 AD, Hierapolis, Phrygia (modern-day Turkey)

FEAST DAY: May 3

PATRONAGE: Hatters, pastry chefs

SYMBOLS AND ATTRIBUTES: Cross, loaves of bread, spear

Philip, one of the original twelve apostles of Jesus Christ, hailed from Bethsaida, like Peter and Andrew. Traditionally believed to have been a disciple of John the Baptist, he was among the earliest to hear Jesus's call, "Follow me."

His presence in the Gospels is marked by significant interactions. In John's Gospel, it's Philip who introduces Nathanael (also known as Bartholomew) to Jesus, showcasing his evangelistic spirit. When faced with feeding a crowd of 5,000, Jesus turned to Philip, inquiring where they could procure bread, testing his faith and insight. During the Last Supper, Philip sought clarity from Jesus about knowing God the Father. In response, Jesus emphasized that knowing Him was akin to knowing the Father; in essence, God and Jesus were one and the same.

Post-ascension, Philip disappears from Biblical narratives, but early Christian traditions suggest a robust legacy. The historian Eusebius (c. 260–340) cites Polycrates, bishop of Ephesus, claiming Philip shone as one of the great lights of Asia (modern-day Turkey) and met martyrdom at Hierapolis. Tradition holds that his remains found their final resting place in Rome's Basilica of the Twelve Apostles.

His feast day was traditionally celebrated on May 1, but in the modern Roman Catholic calendar, it's celebrated together with St. James the Less on May 3. (See John the Baptist, James the Less.)

PHILIP NERI

BORN: July 21, 1515, Florence, Italy
DIED: May 26, 1595, Rome, Italy
FEAST DAY: May 26

PATRONAGE: Rome, Italy, United States Army Special Forces, comedians, artists, writers

SYMBOLS AND ATTRIBUTES: Fire, lily, book

St. Philip Neri is often known as the Apostle of Rome and played a pivotal role in the Catholic Church during the Counter-Reformation.

Philip's mother passed away when he was very young. He was educated by the Dominicans of San Marco, specializing in philosophy and theology. Facing financial difficulties, his father sent Philip to stay with a prosperous relative in San Germano, with the hope that Philip would eventually inherit the family business.

However, in San Germano, Philip experienced a mystical conversion. He decided to abandon his potential career and dedicate his life to God. He moved to Rome in 1533, where he began working as a tutor while pursuing further studies.

Philip was known for his joyfulness, humor, and love of music, art, and good conversation, which he saw as ways of experiencing God's creation. His style of spirituality, characterized by balance and joy, was a counterpoint to the rigorous austerity often associated with religious life during the Counter-Reformation. He also had mystical visions.

In 1544, while in the catacombs of San Sebastiano, he underwent a transformative spiritual experience. He envisioned a ball of fire entering his chest, which he believed was a manifestation of the Holy Spirit. This encounter not only affected him spiritually but is also said to have physically enlarged his heart. Tradition suggests that merely thinking of Christ would cause Philip's heart to palpitate and induce perspiration.

Philip's unwavering faith and charisma attracted followers, and with some companions, he began to work with the sick, the poor, and the prostitutes of Rome. His ministering to the city's marginalized people earned him the nickname "Apostle of Rome." During this time, he met and befriended Ignatius of Loyola, the founder of the Jesuits. In 1551, Philip was ordained a priest. Possibly inspired by Ignatius's Jesuit order, Philip founded a society of secular clergy known as the Congregation of the Oratory. This was not a religious order in the traditional sense because members did not take vows nor did they live in a communal setting. Instead, they dedicated themselves to prayer, preaching, and providing spiritual direction to those who made their way to them. The Oratory was notable for its flexibility and adaptation to the needs of the people of that time.

Philip Neri passed away on May 26, 1595. It was said that after he died, it was discovered that his heart had indeed doubled in size, to the point that it had broken two of his ribs. His cause for canonization was opened in 1612; he was beatified by Pope Paul V in 1615 and canonized by Pope Gregory XV on March 12, 1622. (See Ignatius of Loyola.)

PHILOMENA

BORN: c. 291, Corfu, Greece
DIED: c. 304, Rome, Italy
FEAST DAY: August 11 (unofficially)

PATRONAGE: Infants, babies, children
SYMBOLS AND ATTRIBUTES: Anchor, arrow, palm branch

St. Philomena is a beloved but controversial figure in the Catholic Church. She is believed to have been a Greek princess martyred at the age of thirteen during the reign of the Roman Emperor Diocletian in the fourth century. However, the first historical account of Philomena dates back only to the early nineteenth century, nearly 1,500 years after her supposed death.

In 1802, an intact tomb was discovered and opened in the Catacomb of Priscilla on the Via Salaria in Rome. Inside, the remains of a young woman were found, and due to the symbols of a lily (purity), a palm branch (martyrdom), arrows (trials and tribulations), an anchor (hope and fidelity), and a lance (instruments of torture), it was inferred that these were the relics of an early Christian martyr. An inscription reading "Peace be to you, Philomena" led to the identification of the remains as those of a martyr named Philomena.

News of the archeolgical discovery spread, and various miracles were soon associated with the area. The most influential of these reports came from John Vianney, the curé of Ars, who claimed that Philomena had interceded in various prayer requests at the time.

The veneration of St. Philomena spread rapidly. In 1837, Pope Gregory XVI authorized her public veneration, making her the only person recognized as a saint solely based on miraculous intercessions, as no historical evidence of Philomena's life existed. Her feast day was established as August 11.

However, in the 1960s, the Roman Catholic Church became more rigorous in its criteria for sainthood and removed Philomena from the calendar of saints, as her existence could not be historically verified. It should be noted that this did not "de-canonize" her, as such a thing is not possible, but rather it removed her feast from the universal Church calendar. In spite of this move, she continues to have a popular following among some Catholics, especially in Italy. (See John Vianney.)

PHOEBE

BORN: 1st century AD, place unknown
DIED: 1st century AD, place unknown
FEAST DAY: September 3

PATRONAGE: Women leaders, hospitality
SYMBOLS AND ATTRIBUTES: Scroll, cross, diakonos (deacon) vestments

Phoebe is a deaconess and a benefactor to Paul, as described in Romans 16:1–2, "I commend to you our sister Phoebe, a deacon of the church in Cenchreae. I ask you to receive her in the Lord in a way worthy of his people and to give her any help she may need from you, for she has been the benefactor of many people, including me."

Although the term *deaconess* can have various interpretations, it suggests that Phoebe held a position of service and leadership within the Christian community. She was the only woman in the New Testament to hold that title. She is recognized for her generosity and support toward Paul and others in their ministry endeavors. Paul specifically requests the Romans to extend hospitality to her, indicating that she likely carried Paul's letter to the Romans and would require assistance upon arrival.

PIO OF PIETRELCINA

BORN: May 25, 1887, Pietrelcina, Italy
DIED: September 23, 1968, San Giovanni Rotondo, Italy
FEAST DAY: September 23

PATRONAGE: Civil defense volunteers, adolescents, stress relief
SYMBOLS AND ATTRIBUTES: Stigmata, brown Franciscan habit, rosary

St. Pio of Pietrelcina, also known as Padre Pio, was born Francesco Forgione in Pietrelcina, Italy, on May 25, 1887. He was the fourth of nine children in a poor farming family. At the age of fifteen, he entered the Capuchin friars, taking the name Pio in honor of Pope Pius X, who reigned at the time. Pio was ordained in 1910. He was drafted into World War I in 1915 and discharged for health reasons. In 1916, he moved to the convent of San Giovanni Rotondo in southern Italy, where he would reside until his death in 1968.

Padre Pio was known to possess the gift of discernment of spirits, or the ability to distinguish between the influence of God, the influence of evil spirits, and the influence of the human spirit. Hence, he could read people's hearts and minds, knew detailed information about individuals he'd never met, and offered spiritual advice that was eerily accurate and specific to a person's situation. He often knew the sins of penitents who came to him for confession before they even mentioned them. For many, this was a sign that Pio embodied a supernatural awareness. As such, Pio was a popular confessor, hearing the confessions of hundreds of people each day. He also held a special devotion to St. Michael. According to Fr. Sean Connolly: "Padre Pio was deeply devoted to the Sanctuary of St. Michael atop Mount Gargano and would often direct penitents to climb the mountain to petition the Archangel's intercession in their battle against sin."

In addition, Padre Pio was one of the most famous stigmatics—bearers of the marks of the stigmata, the wounds received by Christ at his crucifixion—in the history of the Catholic Church.

According to Padre Pio, he first experienced the stigmata in private on September 20, 1918, while praying in the choir loft of the Church of Our Lady of Grace in San Giovanni Rotondo. Padre Pio reported having a vision of Jesus, after which he noticed wounds in his hands and feet and a wound on his side. Unlike most stigmatics, Padre Pio's wounds allegedly never healed, remaining open and bleeding for fifty years until his death.

His stigmata became a source of significant controversy, with some suggesting that the wounds were self-inflicted or psychosomatic. The Vatican, initially skeptical, conducted several investigations into the phenomenon and, in 1920, two years after the appearance of the stigmata, imposed sanctions that prohibited him from celebrating Mass publicly or responding to letters from the faithful. However, these sanctions were lifted in 1933, and Pio was allowed to resume public religious activities.

Padre Pio went to great lengths to cover his wounds, wearing fingerless gloves on his hands and keeping his feet covered as well. The wounds are said to have produced a robust and distinct odor, described as floral by some witnesses, a phenomenon known in Catholic mysticism as the "odor of sanctity."

Throughout many investigations, a definitive explanation for Padre Pio's stigmata has yet to be universally accepted. For many of his devotees, they were and remain a sign of his profound, personal union with Jesus Christ. Padre Pio himself seldom spoke of the stigmata except to his spiritual advisors, and he requested that after his death all photographs and descriptions of the wounds be destroyed. Nevertheless, the stigmata became one of the most recognized aspects of his life and ministry.

Pio was also supposedly able to bilocate, a miraculous phenomenon in which an individual is present in two places at the same time. There were many reports of him appearing to people in need in various parts of the world while he was known to be at the friary in San Giovanni Rotondo, Italy. One notable example involves an incident during World War II. Allied pilots claim they saw an image of a monk in the sky over San Giovanni Rotondo. The pilots said that this figure prevented them from dropping their bombs. When they visited the town, they reportedly recognized the monk as Padre Pio. In another instance, Padre Pio was said to have bilocated to the bedside of a dying girl in Milwaukee. The girl's mother had written to Padre Pio asking him to pray for her daughter. When she was shown a photograph of Padre Pio, the girl identified him as the man who had sat at her bedside.

Padre Pio died on September 23, 1968. More than a hundred thousand people attended his funeral. He was beatified on May 2, 1999, by Pope John Paul II, who had met the monk when he was young; the pope declared him a saint on June 16, 2002.

St. Pio of Pietrelcina is considered the patron saint of civil defense volunteers and is also sometimes prayed to for stress relief and January blues. His intercession is often sought by those who struggle with various forms of emotional difficulty, reflecting his own life of suffering and his deep compassion for the suffering of others.

PIUS I

BORN: 1st century AD, Aquileia, Italy

DIED: 155, Rome, Italy

FEAST DAY: July 11

PATRONAGE: Protectors of doctrine

SYMBOLS AND ATTRIBUTES: Papal vestments, cross

Pius I, also known as Pope Pius I, was a significant figure in early Christianity and served as the bishop of Rome from approximately 140 to 155. He is recognized as the tenth successor of St. Peter.

Pius I was likely born in Aquileia, a city located in modern-day Italy. During his pontificate, Pius grappled with a burgeoning heretical movement, excommunicating prominent Gnostics like Marcion while also witnessing the teachings of stalwart Catholic figures like St. Justin in Rome. The *Liber pontificalis,* a book of papal biographies from St. Peter to the fifteenth century, sheds light on Pius's ecclesiastical decisions, highlighting his stance on baptizing Jewish Christian converts, though the intricacies of this decree remain ambiguous.

Pius is sometimes credited with founding two churches in Rome—the titulus Pudentis and titulus Praxedis. However, historical scrutiny suggests these churches likely emerged in the fourth century, potentially succeeding early Christian meeting places.

St. Pius I's exact date of death is uncertain, but it is believed to have occurred around 155. He was buried in the Catacombs of Callixtus in Rome, which became a famous site of Christian burial and veneration. (See Justin Martyr, Peter.)

PIUS V

BORN: January 17, 1504, Bosco, Italy

DIED: May 1, 1572, Rome, Italy

FEAST DAY: April 30

PATRONAGE: Malta

SYMBOLS AND ATTRIBUTES: Papal vestments, Dominican habit, crucifix

Pius V served as pope during the Counter-Reformation. Born Antonio Ghislieri on January 17, 1504, in the Italian region of Lombardy, he entered the Dominican order at a young age, taking the religious name Michele Ghislieri. Throughout his studies, he exhibited exceptional theological acumen, eventually becoming a professor of theology in Bologna and in Rome. His knowledge of Scripture and the writings of the early Church Fathers earned him a reputation as a distinguished Bible scholar and theologian.

In 1556, Michele was appointed the inquisitor of Como to combat heresy and promote orthodoxy. As an inquisitor, his primary task was investigating and suppressing heretical activities and preserving Catholic doctrine and unity. His zealous efforts and remarkable organizational skills caught the attention of Pope Pius IV, who recognized his talents and appointed him a cardinal around 1557. As a cardinal, Michele continued to defend Catholic doctrine and played an essential role in the deliberations of the Council of Trent, a critical ecumenical council that sought to address the theological and disciplinary challenges facing the Church.

Upon the death of Pope Pius IV in 1565, Cardinal Ghislieri was elected as his successor, taking the name Pope Pius V. As pope, he was known for his austere lifestyle, humility, and prioritizing the needs of the poor and marginalized.

One of the most significant contributions of Pius V was his effort to enforce the reforms mandated by the Council of Trent. He issued the Roman Catechism, which provided clear and comprehensive instructions on Catholic doctrine and practice. He also revised the Roman Missal, promulgating the Missale Romanum in 1570, which standardized the celebration of the Mass throughout the Latin Church.

Pius V defended Catholicism against external threats and actively supported the Catholic states of Italy and Spain during the Battle of Lepanto in 1571, which resulted in a significant victory against the Ottoman Empire.

Tradition holds that, before the battle, Pius V prayed the rosary. To celebrate this victory and to give thanks to God and the Blessed Virgin Mary, he established the Feast of Our Lady of Victory, later renamed the Feast of Our Lady of the Rosary.

Controversy marred his papacy, however, and he is often remembered for his maltreatment of Jews during the Inquisition.

PIUS X

BORN: June 2, 1835, Riese, Italy

DIED: August 20, 1914, Rome, Italy

FEAST DAY: August 21

PATRONAGE: First communicants, pilgrims

SYMBOLS AND ATTRIBUTES: Papal vestments, cross

St. Pius X served as the 257th pope from 1903 until his death in 1914. Born Giuseppe Melchiorre Sarto on June 2, 1835, in the town of Riese, Venetia, in what is now Italy, he came from a humble background and was the second of ten children.

His early years were marked by his strong faith and academic abilities, which helped him pursue a career in the priesthood. After completing seminary studies, he was ordained a priest in 1858. He then served in various pastoral roles, displaying a deep devotion to the spiritual well-being of his parishioners.

His dedication and theological acumen caught the attention of Church authorities, leading to his appointment as the bishop of Mantua in 1884. During his time as bishop, he implemented several reforms, emphasizing the importance of catechism, fostering spiritual renewal, and promoting a greater understanding of the liturgy.

In 1903, upon the death of Pope Leo XIII, Giuseppe Melchiorre Sarto was elected as his successor, assuming the papal name Pius X. His pontificate was characterized by an unwavering commitment to upholding traditional Catholic teachings and practices amid the challenges of modernism.

Pius X sought to combat the influence of modernist ideas within the Church, which he believed undermined the authority of the Church's teachings. In 1907, he issued the encyclical *Pascendi Dominici gregis*, which condemned modernism as a grave error and called for its suppression. He also helped to bolster the office that would become the Congregation for the Doctrine of the Faith, to ensure orthodoxy in theological matters.

Recognizing the liturgy's significance in fostering the faithful's spiritual life, Pius X implemented substantial reforms in this area. In 1903, he issued the motu proprio "Tra le Sollecitudini," which sought to restore the sacredness and dignity of the liturgy, emphasizing Gregorian chant, active participation of the laity, and the use of Latin.

Pius X was also deeply concerned about the moral and spiritual welfare of children. He lowered the age for receiving First Holy Communion from between ten and fourteen years old to seven, encouraging children to participate in the Eucharist at the beginning of their lives. This proclamation, which came to be known as the Pius X Decree, aimed to foster a lifelong devotion to the Eucharist among the faithful.

A strong advocate for peace and justice, he condemned the exploitation of workers and supported labor reforms to improve their conditions. He also actively promoted ecumenical relations, seeking unity among Christians and fostering dialogue with other faith traditions.

St. Pius X passed away on August 20, 1914, leaving behind a lasting legacy. His efforts to preserve the integrity of Catholic doctrine, restore the beauty of the liturgy, and promote the spiritual well-being of the faithful continue to inspire and shape the Catholic Church to this day. In 1954, he was canonized as a saint by Pope Pius XII for his exemplary holiness and meaningful impact on the Church.

POLYCARP

BORN: c. 69, Smyrna, Roman Empire

DIED: c. 155, Smyrna, Roman Empire

FEAST DAY: February 23

PATRONAGE: Earaches

SYMBOLS AND ATTRIBUTES: Book, bishop's vestments

Polycarp, also known as Polycarp of Smyrna, was an influential figure in early Christianity. Born around 69, he lived during a critical period in the development of the Christian faith and played a significant role in preserving its teachings.

His exact birthplace is uncertain, but it is widely believed that he was born in Smyrna, an ancient city located in present-day Turkey. He is often referred to as a disciple of the apostle John, which highlights his close connection to the early Christian community and the apostolic tradition.

The earliest mention of Polycarp comes from a letter written by Ignatius of Antioch, another prominent figure in early Christianity. Ignatius addressed a letter to Polycarp, commending him for his faith and encouraging him to continue his work in shepherding the Church.

As Polycarp grew in prominence, he became the bishop of Smyrna, a position he held for several decades. He was known for his outstanding leadership and pastoral care, overseeing the spiritual well-being of the Christian community in Smyrna and its surrounding regions.

According to historical accounts, during the reign of the Roman emperor Marcus Aurelius, Polycarp was urged by the authorities to renounce his faith in Christ and offer sacrifices to the Roman gods. He vehemently refused and was subsequently arrested.

During the trial, Polycarp remained firm in his commitment to Christ, refusing to recant his beliefs. The proconsul threatened him with torture and death, but Polycarp remained resolute. Tradition holds that he uttered the famous words, "Eighty-six years I have served Christ, and He has never done me any wrong. How can I blaspheme my king who saved me?"

In 155, Polycarp was martyred by being burned at the stake. His courage in the face of persecution inspired many early Christians, and his memory has been venerated throughout the centuries.

Polycarp's influence extended beyond his lifetime. He wrote a letter known as the Epistle of Polycarp, which has been preserved as an important early Christian text. The letter, also referred to as the Letter to the Philippians, was written around the middle of the second century and addressed to the Christian community in Philippi in Greece. It stands as one of the earliest extant writings in Christian literature and holds great historical and theological significance, as it provides insights into the beliefs, practices, and challenges faced by early Christians. The letter reflects Polycarp's pastoral concern for the Philippians and his desire to encourage and instruct them in their faith. In it, he writes on various topics of importance to the early Christian community, emphasizing the need for unity and harmony within the Church, urging the Philippians to live following the teachings of Christ, and stressing the importance of love, humility, and obedience as essential virtues for believers.

Polycarp also addresses issues related to moral conduct and the pursuit of righteousness, encouraging the Philippians to live virtuously by avoiding sin and following the example of Christ. He emphasizes the significance of good works and exhorts them to be diligent in their Christian walk.

The Epistle of Polycarp references the New Testament, affirms the divinity of Jesus Christ and emphasizes the role of faith, underscores the importance of Church leadership, and offers valuable insights into early Christian teachings and challenges in the second century.

It is worth noting that apart from the Epistle of Polycarp, other writings attributed to him, such as a letter to the Romans and a collection of his own teachings, have not survived to the present day. These additional works, while lost to history, are mentioned in other Christian writings suggesting Polycarp's importance in helping to shape Christian thought. (See Ignatius of Antioch.)

PRISCA

BORN: 3rd century, place unknown
DIED: c. 270, Rome, Italy
FEAST DAY: January 18

PATRONAGE: Prisoners
SYMBOLS AND ATTRIBUTES: Palm of martyrdom, lion

During Emperor Claudius's reign, Christianity was deemed a threat to the Roman Empire and consequently outlawed. Christians faced brutal punishment, including torture and death, if they refused to renounce their faith. Prisca was among these early Christian martyrs. She was arrested for her beliefs and brought before the emperor, who demanded that she renounce her faith. She refused.

As punishment, Prisca endured various tortures. She was thrown to a lion in the Colosseum, but miraculously, the beast refused to attack her. She was subjected to starvation, which didn't break her spirit. And she was burned alive, but the flames did not affect her. Eventually, she met her fate when she was beheaded.

St. Prisca is the patron saint of pottery, young girls, and water. Depictions of her often portray her with a lion, symbolizing her encounter in the Colosseum, and sometimes holding a palm branch, a symbol of her martyrdom.

PRISCILLA AND AQUILA

BORN: 1st century, place unknown
DIED: 1st century, place unknown
FEAST DAY: July 8

PATRONAGE: Love and marriage
SYMBOLS AND ATTRIBUTES: Tent, book of Acts, cross, palm branch

Priscilla and Aquila were a married couple who played a significant role in the early Christian movement. Their story is depicted in the New Testament, primarily in the Book of Acts and the Epistles of Paul.

Priscilla and Aquila were Jewish, tentmakers by trade, and hailed from Rome. However, around the year 49 AD, and according to Acts 18:2, Emperor Claudius ousted all Jews from Rome; Priscilla and Aquila fled to Corinth, where they met the apostle Paul.

The couple is portrayed as close friends and supporters of Paul. Their shared trade (tentmaking) would have been an initial point of connection, and they also shared a profound commitment to the Christian faith. After meeting in Corinth, the couple traveled with Paul to Ephesus, where they continued their ministry.

In Ephesus, the couple instructed Apollos, an eloquent speaker, on the teachings of Jesus. When the Jews were allowed back into Rome, Priscilla and Aquila returned, and their home became one of the meeting places for the Christian community. Paul often mentions them with fondness and respect in his letters, commending them for their service to the Christian community and stating that they risked their own lives for his.

Over the years, Priscilla and Aquila have come to be seen as the embodiment of evangelization and partnership in the spreading of the Christian message. They are equally mentioned and never separated from one another. Intriguingly, Priscilla's name often precedes Aquila's in early writings about the saints, which was unusual for the times, suggesting she may have been the more prominent of the two.

PROTASE AND GERVASE

BORN: 1st century, place unknown

DIED: 2nd century, Milan

FEAST DAY: June 19

PATRONAGE: Milan, haymakers,

SYMBOLS AND ATTRIBUTES: Sword, palm branch

St. Protase, also known as Protasius, is an early Christian martyr and saint. According to Christian tradition, he was the son of St. Vitalis and the twin brother of St. Gervase, also known as Gervasius. Both Protase and Gervase were believed to have been martyred for their Christian faith during the persecutions initiated by the Roman emperors in the early centuries of Christianity.

Since the story of their martyrdom is not well documented in early Christian writings, much of what is known comes from later sources and hagiographic traditions. Nevertheless, the brothers are venerated particularly in the Roman Catholic and Eastern Orthodox traditions.

Their relics were said to have been discovered by St. Ambrose, the bishop of Milan, in the fourth century. Following this discovery, the Basilica of Saints Gervase and Protase in Milan was dedicated to them. They are invoked in the Roman Canon of the Mass, and their feast day is celebrated on June 19 in the Roman Catholic liturgy.

QUINTIN

BORN: 3rd century, place unknown

DIED: c. 287, Saint-Quentin, France

FEAST DAY: October 31

PATRONAGE: Chaplains, locksmiths

SYMBOLS AND ATTRIBUTES: Sword, dove, usually depicted as tortured

What we know about St. Quintin comes primarily from *The Golden Legend*, a medieval compilation of hagiographies written by Jacobus de Voragine. Quintin was a third-century martyr believed to have been born in Rome, Italy, of noble lineage, during the reign of Emperor Decius, around the year 250. He went to preach the Gospel in Gaul (modern-day France), arrived in Amiens, and began spreading the Christian faith, converting many to Christianity.

However, his efforts drew the attention of the local authorities, particularly the Roman governor, Rictiovarus, who was a fierce persecutor of Christians. Rictiovarus arrested Quintin and subjected him to various tortures.

The Golden Legend describes how Quintin was beaten, whipped, and had his limbs dislocated. Throughout this ordeal he refused to renounce Christianity and miraculously continued to preach the Gospel and convert others, even from his prison cell. The story recounts a miraculous incident in which an angel appeared to Quintin, healing his wounds and giving him strength. This encounter further emboldened Quintin in his resolve to face martyrdom.

Finally, Rictiovarus ordered Quintin to be beheaded. According to the legend, as Quintin knelt before the executioner, an angel carried his soul to Heaven before the blade touched his neck.

Following his martyrdom, Quintin's remains were reportedly buried in the region where he was executed, which became the city of Saint-Quentin in France. The town became a place of veneration and pilgrimage for Christians seeking the saint's intercession.

Over time, Quintin's cult grew, and he became widely revered as a patron saint for those suffering with physical illnesses, especially those related to paralysis. Numerous miracles were attributed to his intercession, including one where a woman possessed by an evil spirit was brought to the tomb of Quintin. As soon as the possessed woman reached the shrine, she was freed from the tormenting spirit, and her sanity was restored.

QUIRINUS

BORN: 1st century, Rome, Italy
DIED: c. March 30, 116, Rome, Italy
FEAST DAY: April 30

PATRONAGE: Animals, knights, soldiers, Neuss, invoked against the plague, smallpox, and gout
SYMBOLS AND ATTRIBUTES: Military attire, armor, sword, hawk, palm branch

According to tradition, Quirinus served as a Roman officer or jailer during the reign of Emperor Hadrian in the second century. Pope Alexander I, the leader of the early Christian community in Rome, was imprisoned during this time. Quirinus is said to have been so impressed by the pope's commitment to his faith and the miracles he performed in prison that he converted to Christianity. His daughter Balbina converted as well after a miracle involving the chains that once imprisoned St. Peter. As a new believer in Jesus, Quirinus was dismissed from his position and persecuted by his former friends and allies. He was martyred for his faith, but the exact circumstances of his death are uncertain. (See Balbina of Rome.)

R

RAYMOND NONNATUS

BORN: 1204, Portell, Catalonia, Spain
DIED: August 31, 1240, Cardona, Spain
FEAST DAY: August 31

PATRONAGE: Childbirth, pregnant women, midwives
SYMBOLS AND ATTRIBUTES: Cardinal's hat, monstrance, padlock over his lips

Raymond Nonnatus was a thirteenth-century member of the Mercedarian order. Born in the year 1204 in the region of Catalonia, Spain, he hailed from the noble Despuig family. The epithet "Nonnatus" comes from the Latin phrase *non natus*, meaning "not born." This title was attributed to Raymond because he was delivered by cesarean section after the death of his mother.

Raymond Nonnatus dedicated his life to the service of God and joined the Order of Mercy, also known as the Mercedarians or the Order of Our Lady of Mercy for the Redemption of Captives. This religious order focused on helping Christians who were held captive by the Moors during the thirteenth century. Raymond demonstrated immense bravery and selflessness in his mission to negotiate the release of prisoners. His efforts were centered on the regions of Spain and North Africa, where he faced significant risks and challenges to carry out his work. He would gather funds and resources to ransom the prisoners, using his own life as ransom if needed.

His exceptional holiness and dedication to rescuing captives earned him a reputation as a saint. Pope Alexander VII canonized him in 1657, officially recognizing his sanctity. His feast day is celebrated annually on August 31, honoring his life, example, and intercession. He is the patron saint of pregnant and expectant women. He is often depicted with a padlock on his lips, in reference to a legend regarding the Moors lancing his mouth and locking it shut so he was unable to preach.

RAYMOND OF PENYAFORT

BORN: c. 1175, Spain
DIED: January 6, 1275, Barcelona, Spain
FEAST DAY: January 6

PATRONAGE: Lawyers, canonists
SYMBOLS AND ATTRIBUTES: Book, pen, angels, a cape used as a boat and a sail

St. Raymond of Penyafort was a Spanish Dominican friar and lawyer who made significant contributions to the development of canon law. His life was characterized by deep commitment to the Catholic faith, devotion to the Virgin Mary, and passion for helping others.

He was born into a noble family in Penyafort, Catalonia. He studied law at the University of Bologna, eventually returning to Barcelona to become a lawyer. Years later, he felt a strong call to religious life and joined the Dominican order at the age of thirty-seven.

As a Dominican friar, Raymond dedicated himself to preaching, teaching, and the study of theology and canon law. He became a highly venerated scholar and was appointed the official compiler of the Decretals of Pope Gregory IX, which comprised a collection of Church laws and regulations. His work on the Decretals helped to establish a more unified and organized system of canon law, which has had a lasting impact on the Catholic Church even to this day.

In addition to his legal work, Raymond significantly impacted moral theology. His *Summa de casibus poenitentiae* (Summary Concerning the Cases of Penance) was a manual for confessors, providing guidance on moral and ethical issues that might come up in the confessional. This work was innovative, as it systematically approached moral theology on a case-by-case basis, helping to standardize confession practices across the Church. Its influence extended far beyond its time, impacting the Church's approach to confession and penance and contributing significantly to the development of moral theology as a field of study.

Italian artist Tommaso Dolabella's painting of Raymond illuminates a famous legend about the saint. Prevented from leaving Majorca by the angry king, Raymond attached his black cape (part of his Dominican garb) to a stick to create a makeshift sailboat, and the winds of God blew him across the sea to safety.

St. Raymond died at the age of one hundred, after a life spent serving God and his fellow human beings. He was canonized by Pope Clement VIII in 1601.

RENÉ GOUPIL

BORN: May 15, 1608,
  Saint-Martin-du-Bois, France
DIED: September 29, 1642, Ossernenon,
  New France

FEAST DAY: October 19
PATRONAGE: Anesthetists
SYMBOLS AND ATTRIBUTES: Palm branch,
  cross, head wound

Also known as Renatus Goupil, René Goupil was a French lay missionary and martyr of the early seventeenth century. Born near Angers, France, in 1608, René Goupil was a skilled surgeon and a devout Catholic. He had a strong desire to serve God and bring the message of Christianity to the Indigenous peoples of North America.

René joined the Society of Jesus, commonly known as the Jesuits. In 1640, he embarked on a journey to New France (now Canada) as a lay missionary, accompanying the Jesuit missionaries who were establishing missions among the Huron-Wendat people.

Upon arriving in New France, René dedicated himself to serving the Indigenous population, tending to their physical and spiritual needs. As a skilled surgeon, he used his medical expertise to provide healing and care. Alongside his missionary work, he energetically studied the Huron language and culture to effectively communicate the teachings of Christianity.

During his time in New France, René encountered various hardships and challenges. The region was rife with territory tensions, intertribal conflicts, and disease, and yet he remained dedicated to his mission and committed to his Christian faith.

In 1642, René was captured by the Mohawk Iroquois tribe after he was caught making the sign of the cross on the heads of the tribe's children. The Iroquois tortured René, who refused to renounce his faith and continued to profess his loyalty to Jesus Christ.

On September 29, 1642, René was martyred by the Iroquois, who inflicted a mortal blow to his head with a tomahawk. His martyrdom and unwavering commitment to the Christian faith earned him the status of a saint in the Catholic Church. René Goupil is regarded as one of the North American Martyrs, a group of eight Jesuit missionaries who were murdered while spreading Christianity in the New World. They share a feast day, October 19, as a testament to their faith and devotion to God.

RITA OF CASCIA

BORN: 1381, Roccaporena, Italy
DIED: May 22, 1457, Cascia, Italy
FEAST DAY: May 22

PATRONAGE: Impossible causes, marital problems, abuse victims
SYMBOLS AND ATTRIBUTES: Roses, thorns, crucifix

Rita of Cascia was an Augustinian nun who lived in the fourteenth and fifteenth centuries. Along with St. Jude, she is revered in the Catholic Church as the patron saint of impossible causes. She is also the patron saint of abused women and marital problems. She was born Margherita Lotti in Roccaporena, near Cascia in central Italy in 1381, a time of great social unrest, political instability, and religious conflicts. The Papal States, where St. Rita lived, faced several challenges, including the Western Schism, which divided the Catholic Church into rival factions.

At a young age, Margherita expressed a desire to become a nun. However, following the custom of the time, she was married off at approximately the age of twelve to a man named Paolo Mancini. Her husband was abusive, but Rita exhibited great patience, love, and virtue, despite his abuse. She remained a faithful wife and bore two sons, Giangiacomo Antonio and Paolo Maria.

In 1410, Paolo was murdered, and her two sons vowed to avenge his death. Rita, fearing that her sons would commit a grave sin, prayed fervently for their souls to be saved. She also prayed for God to take her sons' lives before they could carry out their revenge. Both of her sons died shortly afterward, and Rita was left alone and grief-stricken.

It was then that she decided to enter the convent of the Augustinian nuns in Cascia. She was initially turned away. Undeterred, Rita prayed for three days and three nights, asking God to help her enter the convent. On the third night, she had a vision of St. John the Baptist, St. Augustine, and St. Nicholas of Tolentino, leading her to the convent and opening the door. Shortly thereafter, she was admitted by the Augustinians.

Rita spent the rest of her life in the nunnery, where she lived a life of prayer, penance, and devotion to God. She became known for her mystical experiences, which included communicating with angels, visions, ecstasies, and stigmata. She also experienced a thorn from Christ's crown of thorns on her forehead, which caused her great pain and suffering.

Tradition holds that for the last four years of her life, Rita lived only on the Eucharist. She died on May 22, 1457, at the age of seventy-six. After her death, her body was found to be incorrupt and exuded a sweet fragrance. Her relics are housed in the Basilica of St. Rita in Cascia, Italy, which serves as a pilgrimage site for devoted Catholics. Since her death many miracles have been attributed to St. Rita's intercession, including the healing of illnesses, the conversion of sinners, and the restoration of peace in families. Her prayers are sought by those facing difficult and impossible situations, particularly in the realms of marital problems, family conflicts, and abusive relationships.

St. Rita's life exemplifies the virtues of forgiveness, love, and perseverance. She is often depicted with a crown of thorns, a crucifix, or a wound on her forehead, symbolizing her identification with the sufferings of Christ. She was beatified by Pope Urban VIII in 1627 and canonized by Pope Leo XIII on May 24, 1900.

ROBERT BELLARMINE

BORN: October 4, 1542, Montepulciano, Italy

DIED: September 17, 1621, Rome, Italy

FEAST DAY: September 17

PATRONAGE: Catechists, catechumens, canonists

SYMBOLS AND ATTRIBUTES: Book, quill, cardinal's attire

St. Robert Bellarmine was an Italian Jesuit, cardinal, and an important theologian during the Counter-Reformation.

Born in Montepulciano, Italy, Bellarmine joined the newly founded Society of Jesus, or the Jesuits, in 1560 and was ordained a priest a decade later. As a promising scholar, he taught at the University of Louvain in Belgium before moving to the Roman College in Rome. He served as spiritual director to Aloysius Gonzaga, who would become a saint. Among his numerous theological writings, his three-volume *Disputations on the Controversies of the Christian Faith against the Heretics of This Time* stands out for its defense of Catholic beliefs against Protestant arguments. In 1605, he was elected to head the Vatican Library.

Beyond his scholarly pursuits, Bellarmine was a fervent defender of papal authority. During an era rife with political and religious tensions, he contended against the divine right of kings, arguing that monarchs did not possess overarching authority, particularly in faith matters. Bellarmine was also involved in pivotal debates about the relationship between science and faith. Perhaps most notably, he engaged in dialogue about the heliocentric theory, which proposed that the Earth orbits the Sun, and even met with the prominent scientist Galileo Galilei, who had proposed this theory. Significantly, Bellarmine unapologetically upheld the traditional view that Scripture should be the primary authority on matters of faith and morals. Yet he also granted that if the heliocentric theory were proven correct, the Church would be obliged to reevaluate its interpretation of the Scriptures in question.

Bellarmine's significant contributions to the Church were recognized when he was beatified in 1923, canonized in 1930, and declared a Doctor of the Church by Pope Pius XI in 1931. (See Aloysius Gonzaga.)

ROMUALD

BORN: c. 951, Ravenna, Italy

DIED: June 19, 1027, Val-di-Castro, Italy

FEAST DAY: June 19

PATRONAGE: Monastic life

SYMBOLS AND ATTRIBUTES: Monk's habit, model of a church

St. Romuald, also known as Romuald of Ravenna, was a tenth-century Italian monk and founder of the Camaldolese order. Born into a noble family in Ravenna, Italy, around 951, Romuald was destined for a career in the military. However, after watching his father take a man's life in a duel, Romuald became disillusioned with the world and decided to become a monk.

Romuald began his religious life at the Abbey of Sant'Apollinare in Classe but left after a few years to lead a solitary life as a hermit. He spent several years living in various caves and forests in Italy, devoting himself to prayer and penance.

Around 1005, Romuald founded the Camaldolese order, which combined the eremitic (solitary) and cenobitic (communal) monastic traditions. Monks lived together in hermitages, leading a collective existence while also dedicating substantial time to solitary prayer and contemplation. Romuald's rule for the order included strict observances of silence, manual labor, fasting, and abstinence.

Throughout his life, Romuald was known for his austere lifestyle and strict adherence to St. Benedict's Rule. He also had a reputation as a visionary and was repeatedly attacked by demons, which he combated through prayer and fasting. In Peter Damian's biography of St. Romuald, several miracles are attributed to the monk, including exorcising a possessed man and healing the blind.

ROQUE GONZÁLEZ

BORN: November 17, 1576,
Asunción, Paraguay
DIED: November 15, 1628, Caaró, Brazil
FEAST DAY: November 17

PATRONAGE: Posadas, Argentina, and
Encarnación, Paraguay
SYMBOLS AND ATTRIBUTES: Priest's attire,
Indigenous people, heart pierced with
an arrow

Also known as Roque González de Santa Cruz, Roque González was a Jesuit missionary and martyr who worked to spread Christianity in South America during the seventeenth century. He hailed from a noble family and studied theology and philosophy. At twenty-eight, he joined the Jesuit order and began missionary work in a region known as the Guayrá, which encompassed parts of present-day Brazil, Paraguay, and Argentina. There he established several missions, including the prominent mission of San Ignacio Guazú. These missions served as centers for religious instruction, agriculture, and crafts, providing a way of life that integrated Christian teachings with the traditional Guaraní culture.

One of the most significant aspects of Roque González's missionary work was his love of the Guaraní people. Roque sought to understand their language, culture, and way of life, meeting the people where they were instead of demanding them to embrace who he was.

Roque González and his fellow Jesuits faced numerous challenges in their missionary work, including resistance from some Indigenous groups and opposition from exploitative colonial authorities and settlers. On November 15, 1628, while working at the mission to install a new church bell, González was attacked and killed by a group of warriors from the Mbyá. His body, along with that of a fellow Jesuit, was dumped in the church, which was then burned to the ground.

St. Roque González was beatified by Pope Pius XI on January 28, 1934, and canonized as a saint by Pope John Paul II on May 16, 1988. He is venerated as one of the Martyrs of South America, a group of Jesuit missionaries who gave their lives for their faith during the evangelization of the continent.

ROSA VENERINI

BORN: February 9, 1656, Viterbo, Italy
DIED: May 7, 1728, Rome, Italy
FEAST DAY: May 7

PATRONAGE: Schoolgirls and young women
SYMBOLS AND ATTRIBUTES: Book, nun's habit

Born in Viterbo, Italy, in 1656, Rosa Venerini was an Italian Roman Catholic nun and educator. She is recognized as the founder of the Religious Teachers Venerini, who helped to establish free public school education in Italy.

Rosa dedicated her life to God from an early age and entered the Dominican Monastery of St. Catherine when she was twenty years old. She devoted her life to the teaching and spiritual formation of young girls and women, which was sorely lacking in the early eighteenth century.

She began by gathering young girls in her home in Viterbo to instruct them on religion and academics, including reading and math. She expanded her efforts and established schools for girls in various towns and cities across Italy. Rosa formed the Religious Teachers Venerini, which provided quality learning to girls and trained teachers to carry out this mission. The congregation grew rapidly, and its members, known as the Venerini Sisters, continued establishing schools throughout Italy and eventually in other parts of the world (the first such school in the United States opened in 1909).

Pope Benedict XVI canonized Rosa Venerini as a saint on October 15, 2006. She is remembered for her commitment to empowering girls and women through knowledge and faith.

ROSE OF LIMA

BORN: April 20, 1586, Lima, Viceroyalty of Peru
DIED: August 24, 1617, Lima, Viceroyalty of Peru
FEAST DAY: August 23

PATRONAGE: Indigenous people of Latin America, embroiderers, florists, gardeners, those suffering from family problems
SYMBOLS AND ATTRIBUTES: Jesus child, crown of roses, crown of thorns

St. Rose of Lima was a seventeenth-century Peruvian saint and mystic who lived a life of extreme austerity and penance. She was the first person born in the Americas to be canonized as a saint by the Catholic Church.

Rose was born on April 20, 1586, in Lima, Peru, to Gaspar de Flores and Maria de Oliva. She was baptized Isabel Flores de Oliva but was given the name Rose by her family for her delicate beauty, as well as a mysterious event in her infancy when a servant reported seeing the baby's face transform into a rose. At the age of eleven, she was confirmed and officially adopted the name Rose.

Rose was a devout Catholic from an early age and spent much of her time in prayer and contemplation. During her childhood, Rose admired Catherine of Siena, and as a result started fasting and performing secret penances. Disturbed by her own beauty, she cut off her hair, rejected suitors, and devoted herself to contemplating the Blessed Sacrament.

When Rose was a teenager, her family fell on hard times, and she began to work as an embroiderer to support them. She soon became known for her skill and earned enough money to support her family while still devoting herself to a life of prayer and penance. In addition to her work, Rose also spent long hours praying and fasting, often depriving herself of food and sleep to better commune with God.

Her dedication caught the attention of Dominican friars, but her father forbade her from becoming a nun. Instead, she joined the Third Order of St. Dominic while continuing to live at home with her parents. At twenty, she took a vow of perpetual virginity, slept only two hours a night, and wore a silver crown resembling the Crown of Thorns, concealing it with a veil she always wore. She often gave away her earnings to those in need and would care for the sick in her own home. She also worked with Martin de Porres, assisting slaves brought to Lima from Africa.

It was said that Rose often battled with Satan and would call on her guardian angel for help. She died after a long illness at the age of thirty-one. She was buried in the Church of San Domingo, where her tomb became a popular site of pilgrimage. She was canonized as a saint by Pope Clement X in 1671, becoming the first person born in the Americas to be honored in this way.

One of her symbols is a crown of thorns, which represents her devotion to Christ and her willingness to suffer for Him and symbolizes her practice of mortification and self-discipline. (See Catherine of Siena, Martin de Porres.)

ROSE PHILIPPINE DUCHESNE

BORN: August 29, 1769, Grenoble, France

DIED: November 18, 1852, St. Charles, Missouri, USA

FEAST DAY: November 18

PATRONAGE: Perseverance amid adversity

SYMBOLS AND ATTRIBUTES: Cross, school, map, Indigenous Americans

St. Rose Philippine Duchesne, also known as Mother Duchesne, was known for her missionary work in the United States. Born in Grenoble, France, she belonged to a devout family deeply committed to their faith.

Growing up, Rose was influenced by the religious environment within her household, which instilled in her a strong desire to dedicate her life to God. At the age of eighteen, she entered the Visitation order, an order of nuns known for their contemplative spirituality and dedication to the education of young girls. Despite her initial inclination toward a cloistered life, in 1804, answering the call to missionary work, Rose joined the newly established Society of the Sacred Heart. In 1818, at forty-nine, she embarked on her missionary journey to the United States.

She arrived in New Orleans and soon began her work in the Louisiana Territory, looking to bring learning and faith to the Indigenous people and establishing a school in St. Charles, Missouri, in 1818.

Rose faced numerous challenges during her missionary endeavors. She encountered linguistic barriers, as she had to learn the languages of the Potawatomi and other tribes to communicate with them effectively. Additionally, she endured harsh living conditions, often facing extreme weather and limited resources.

She became known as the Woman-Who-Prays-Always among the Potawatomi people due to her constant prayer and devotion, and she continued her work in the United States until her death on November 18, 1852, in St. Charles, Missouri. She was canonized as a saint by Pope John Paul II on July 3, 1988, in recognition of her significant contributions to the spread of Catholicism in the United States and her commitment to educating young girls and Indigenous communities.

S

SCHOLASTICA OF NURSIA

BORN: c. 480, Nursia, Italy

DIED: c. 543, Monte Cassino, Italy

FEAST DAY: February 10

PATRONAGE: Nuns, convulsive children, invoked against storms and rain

SYMBOLS AND ATTRIBUTES: Dove, book, crosier

Information about Scholastica of Nursia's life is limited, and much of what is known about her comes from the writings of St. Gregory the Great in his *Dialogues*, a collection of biographies of prominent Christian figures. According to these accounts, Scholastica was born into a noble family around 480 in Nursia, Italy. Notably, she was the twin sister of St. Benedict of Nursia, the founder of the Benedictine order, with whom she was raised.

Like her brother, Scholastica devoted herself to God and embraced a life of prayer and spiritual discipline. While Benedict established the monastic community at Monte Cassino, Scholastica founded a convent for women in Plombariola not far from her brother's monastery. As the first abbess of this community, she was paramount in nurturing the spiritual lives of the women under her care.

One of the best-known stories about Scholastica comes from a meeting between her and Benedict. As the story goes, the two siblings would meet once a year to discuss matters of faith and spiritual issues. On one occasion, they had a particularly passionate discussion about the contemplative life. As the discussion continued late into the night, Scholastica, recognizing that their time together was drawing to a close, began to fervently pray for God to prolong their meeting.

In response to her prayer, a severe storm suddenly erupted, preventing Benedict from leaving their meeting place. He exclaimed, "God forgive you, sister! What have you done?" To this, Scholastica replied, "I asked you, and you refused. I asked my God, and He listened. Go now, if you can; leave me, and return to your monastery." Recognizing the significance of this event as a sign from God, Benedict stayed with Scholastica, and they continued their spiritual discussions until the following morning. (See Benedict of Nursia, Gregory the Great.)

SEBASTIAN

BORN: c. 256, Narbonne, Gaul
DIED: c. 288, Rome, Italy
FEAST DAY: January 20
PATRONAGE: Soldiers, archers, athletes, those with disabilities, those suffering from plague

SYMBOLS AND ATTRIBUTES: Arrows, depicted tied to a post, sometimes with an angel

St. Sebastian was a third-century Roman martyr. Little is known about Sebastian's origins, but it is believed he was born in Narbonne, Gaul (modern-day France), or possibly Milan around 256.

A member of a noble family, Sebastian eventually joined the Roman army, rose through the ranks, and became a captain in the Praetorian Guard under Emperor Diocletian's rule. Despite his high position in the Diocletian empire, which persecuted Christians, Sebastian secretly professed his Christian faith and fervently supported his fellow believers, offering them solace, encouragement, and aid during the emperor's reign. He

PLATE VII
Sebastian

converted numerous soldiers and members of the Roman elite to Christianity through his teachings and personal example. However, his clandestine activities were not hidden for long; eventually, he was outed as a Christian.

When Sebastian refused to renounce his beliefs, Diocletian ordered his execution. Accounts of Sebastian's martyrdom differ in their specific details, but the most commonly accepted version describes him being shot with arrows by a group of archers. Miraculously, he survived the ordeal through the protection of angels and was found alive by a pious Christian named Irene, the widow of the martyr Castulus.

Irene tended to Sebastian's wounds and nursed him back to health. Once he regained his strength, Sebastian confronted Diocletian again, openly criticizing his persecution of Christians. This audacity led to Sebastian's second arrest, and this time, he was mercilessly beaten to death with clubs. The year of his death is commonly believed to be around 288, though some sources suggest 286.

St. Sebastian's martyrdom made him an iconic figure in Christian iconography and devotion. He is often depicted tied to a tree or post, with arrows piercing his body, symbolizing the torture he endured. Over the centuries, Sebastian became a highly venerated saint, with numerous churches, chapels, and artworks dedicated to him. Throughout history, he has been depicted in various works of art. Notable examples include Andrea Mantegna's *The Martyrdom of Saint Sebastian,* Sandro Botticelli's *Saint Sebastian,* José de Ribera's *Martyrdom of Saint Sebastian*, and Georges de La Tour's *Saint Sebastian Tended by Saint Irene.* In modern times, alternative rock band R.E.M.'s music video for "Losing My Religion" invokes Sebastian, and features an androgynous figure tied to a tree, pierced with arrows.

His intercession is sought by those facing physical afflictions, including diseases, plagues, and accidents. (See Castulus.)

SIMEON

BORN: 1st century BC, place unknown
DIED: 1st century AD, place unknown
FEAST DAY: February 3

PATRONAGE: Zadar, Croatia
SYMBOLS AND ATTRIBUTES: Holding the Baby Jesus

Also known as Simeon the Righteous or Simeon the God-receiver, Simeon lived in Jerusalem at the time of Jesus's birth. He is a significant figure in the narrative of the infant Jesus, as recorded in Luke 2:25–35. The Holy Spirit had revealed that Simeon would not die until he saw the Messiah. Led by the Spirit, he went to the temple where Mary and Joseph brought Jesus in fulfillment of the customary rituals to present the firstborn male child to the Lord.

When Simeon saw Jesus, he took the baby in his arms and gave praise to God. He uttered a prayer known as the Nunc Dimittis or the Song of Simeon. The song is recorded in Luke 2:29–32 and expresses Simeon's joy and fulfillment in encountering the Messiah. In his words, Simeon refers to Jesus as "a light for revelation to the Gentiles, and the glory of your people Israel."

Simeon's prophetic words foreshadowed Jesus's role as the Savior for the Jewish people and all nations. Simeon recognized the significance of the holy birth before him and proclaimed that God's salvation had arrived in the person of this child. Simeon's prophecy to Mary also warned that "a sword will pierce your own soul too" (Luke 2:35), foreshadowing her sorrow at Jesus's crucifixion.

Simeon's encounter with Jesus is celebrated as the Feast of the Presentation of Jesus at the Temple, or Candlemas. This event is observed on February 3, forty days after Christmas, to commemorate the moment Jesus was presented in the Temple and recognized as the fulfillment of the Old Testament prophecies. Simeon is regarded as a symbol of faithful expectation of God's promises.

Simeon's song is used liturgically in various Christian churches, including the Catholic Church, the Eastern Orthodox Church, and the Anglican Communion, and is usually sung or recited during evening prayer or at the end of a service.

SIMEON STYLITES THE ELDER

BORN: c. 390, Sis, Cilicia

DIED: September 2, 459, near Aleppo, Syria

FEAST DAY: September 1

PATRONAGE: Ascetics

SYMBOLS AND ATTRIBUTES: Pillar, scroll

St. Simeon Stylites the Elder, also known as Symeon the Stylite or Simeon the Pillar-Saint, was a Christian monk known for his extreme form of asceticism and his life spent atop a pillar. He is regarded as one of the most remarkable and iconic figures of early Christian monasticism.

Simeon Stylites was born around the year 390, in Sis, Cilicia (in present-day Turkey). At a young age, he decided to devote his life to God and joined a monastery. However, he soon felt called to embrace a more solitary and rigorous form of asceticism.

In pursuit of his spiritual goals, Simeon chose to live atop a pillar, also known as a stylos or column. The first pillar he erected was about six feet high, but he gradually increased the height of subsequent pillars over the years. His chosen location for pillar-dwelling varied throughout his life, but most notably, he spent considerable time near the city of Aleppo in modern-day Syria.

Simeon's ascetic practice was characterized by extreme self-denial, self-mortification, and a commitment to solitude and prayer. He would spend days, months, and eventually years atop these structures, exposed to the elements and living a life of remarkable austerity.

Simeon's pillar was narrow, giving him minimal space to stand, sit, or sleep. He would adopt various postures during his devotions, including standing with outstretched arms, kneeling, or bowing in prayer. He endured severe physical hardships during his time on the pillar, such as exposure to extreme temperatures, insect bites, and the constant risk of falling.

Simeon attracted many admirers and disciples who sought his wisdom, blessings, and prayers. People from all walks of life would visit him, seeking spiritual guidance and miraculous healings. Simeon would offer counsel and encouragement to those who approached him, even from the heights of his pillar.

Simeon Stylites's reputation as a holy man spread far beyond the regions where he lived. His ascetic practice and pillar-dwelling were seen as extraordinary and awe-inspiring acts of devotion and self-sacrifice.

St. Simeon Stylites the Elder died on September 2, 459, after spending thirty-seven years atop his final pillar. His body was carefully brought down and interred in a monastery, which became a place of pilgrimage for centuries, inspiring believers to embrace a life of prayer, simplicity, and detachment from worldly concerns.

SIMON

BORN: 1st century AD, place unknown

DIED: c. 65 AD, Persia

FEAST DAY: October 28 (with St. Jude)

PATRONAGE: Curriers, tanners

SYMBOLS AND ATTRIBUTES: Boat, cross, saw

Simon, also known as Simon the Zealot, is one of the twelve apostles chosen by Jesus Christ. In the lists of the twelve apostles found in the Gospels of Matthew, Mark, and Luke, Simon is mentioned as "Simon the Zealot" or "Simon, who was called the Zealot." The term *zealot* is believed to refer to a political movement of Jewish revolutionaries who advocated for the liberation of Israel from Roman occupation through militant means.

Apart from being identified as a Zealot, there is no additional information about Simon's life or specific teachings in the New Testament. Various traditions arose over the years. According to some accounts, Simon the Zealot preached the Gospel in Egypt, Cyrenaica (a region in modern-day Libya), and Persia. Another tradition associates him with preaching in Britain. He may or may not have been martyred. One tradition holds that he was crucified, while another suggests he was sawed in half, and another suggests he died peacefully in his sleep. In Islamic tradition, Simon is recognized among the twelve apostles and is believed to have been sent to preach the faith to the Berbers outside of North Africa. He shares his feast day with St. Jude, who may have been his companion as he evangelized after Jesus's resurrection. (See Jude.)

STANISLAUS

BORN: c. 1030, Szczepanów, Poland
DIED: April 11, 1079, Kraków, Poland
FEAST DAY: April 11

PATRONAGE: Poland, moral order
SYMBOLS AND ATTRIBUTES: Bishop's vestments, crosier, sword

Stanislaus was the bishop of Kraków, Poland, who lived in the eleventh century. Born in the town of Szczepanów, Poland, around the year 1030, Stanislaus displayed exceptional intellectual capabilities from an young age, affording him the opportunity to pursue his studies at various centers of learning, including the Bishop's School in Gniezno and the University of Paris. Upon completing his education, Stanislaus returned to Poland and was ordained as a priest. His theological knowledge and virtuous character soon caught the attention of Bishop Lambert of Kraków, who appointed him as a canon and preacher at the Kraków Cathedral. Stanislaus's sermons were known for their eloquence, intellectual depth, and profound spiritual insight, earning him admiration and respect among both clergy and laypeople.

In 1072, following the death of Bishop Lambert, Stanislaus was appointed bishop of Kraków, a position he held until his martyrdom. As a bishop, he focused on reforming the clergy, advocating for strict adherence to canonical norms, and promoting moral and spiritual renewal within the Church. His efforts extended beyond the ecclesiastical realm, as he also became involved in matters of governance, often challenging the actions of the ruling monarch.

In 1079, Stanislaus confronted King Bolesław II for his tyrannical behavior and mistreatment of the Polish people and excommunicated him, a bold act considering the political power wielded by the monarch. This action earned Stanislaus the admiration of the Polish populace, who saw him as a champion of justice and a defender of the oppressed.

King Bolesław, however, viewed Stanislaus's actions as an affront to his authority and ordered his soldiers to execute the bishop. The exact details of his martyrdom vary in different historical accounts, but it is widely believed that he was slain, possibly hacked to death or stabbed repeatedly, while celebrating Mass in the Church of St. Michael in Kraków. His martyrdom occurred on April 11, 1079.

Following his death, Stanislaus became a symbol of Polish national identity, revered for his unwavering commitment to justice and his courageous stand against tyranny. His cult grew rapidly, and Pope Innocent IV canonized him as a saint in 1253. His feast day is celebrated on April 11, commemorating his martyrdom.

STANISLAUS KOSTKA

BORN: 1550, Rostkowo, Poland

DIED: 1568, Rome, Italy, Papal States

FEAST DAY: November 13

PATRONAGE: Novices, Jesuit students, broken bones

SYMBOLS AND ATTRIBUTES: Lily, cross, rosary, Jesus

Stanislaus Kostka was a young Polish novice who lived in the sixteenth century. Born in Rostkovo near Prasnysz, Poland, in 1550, Stanislaus was a remarkable figure whose short life left an indelible mark on the hearts of many.

Coming from a prominent family, Stanislaus was the second child of John Kostka, a senator of the Kingdom of Poland, and Margaret de Drobniy Kryska, a member of the influential Palatine family. His upbringing was characterized by a rigorous emphasis on discipline and virtue, shaping him into a young man of exceptional piety, modesty, and temperance.

According to scholar Francis van Ortroy, Stanislaus and his older brother, Paul, received their early education at home, where their parents instilled in them the values of religious devotion and obedience. Subsequently, they were sent to the Jesuit college in Vienna, where Stanislaus's amiable nature and cheerful disposition endeared him to his peers.

In Vienna, Stanislaus joined the Congregation of St. Barbara, a group comprising fellow students from the Jesuit college who sought to deepen their spiritual lives. It was during this time that Stanislaus claimed to have had a series of divine encounters with St. Barbara, who brought two angels to administer the Holy Eucharist to him during a severe illness. These mystical experiences only fueled his dedication to his faith and reinforced his desire to lead a life of sublime devotion.

Stanislaus's dedication to Christ strained relations with his elder brother, Paul, leading to many confrontations. Resolving to join the Jesuits, Stanislaus left Vienna, a decision Paul would have to justify to their parents. Braving a perilous journey to Rome and depending on strangers for aid, Stanislaus reached the city on October 25, 1567. Despite obstacles and pursuit from his family, he gained entry to the novitiate of St. Andrew under St. Francis Borgia. However, after nearly a year of study and service, he developed a severe illness. When Stanislaus became aware that he was going to die, he composed a poignant letter to the Blessed Virgin Mary. In it he asked her to call him to the afterlife, where he could join her in celebrating the glorious anniversary of her Assumption, the time when she was taken body and soul into Heaven.

On August 15, 1568, on the very feast day of the Assumption of Mary, Stanislaus passed away while praying. He was seventeen years old. In his final moments, it was reported that his face radiated serenity, bearing witness to the deep love he had for Jesus and Mary. The news of his passing quickly spread throughout the city, and people from all corners flocked to venerate his remains and seek relics.

Recognizing his remarkable sanctity, the Catholic Church beatified Stanislaus in 1605 and canonized him on December 31, 1726. His brother Paul was in attendance for his beatification. Today, Stanislaus Kostka is celebrated as a beloved saint in Poland, with many religious institutions selecting him as the patron saint of their novitiates.

Depictions of Stanislaus in art vary, reflecting the diverse aspects of his spiritual journey. He is often portrayed as a youth receiving Holy Communion from the hands of angels or cradling the Infant Jesus, who has been bestowed upon him by the Virgin Mary. (See Barbara.)

STEPHEN

BORN: c. 1st century AD, Jerusalem
DIED: c. 34 AD, Jerusalem
FEAST DAY: December 26

PATRONAGE: Deacons, bricklayers, builders, stonemasons, headaches

SYMBOLS AND ATTRIBUTES: Stones, palm branch, deacon's vestments

Known also as the Protomartyr, St. Stephen is considered the first martyr of Christianity. According to the Book of Acts, he was a disciple of Jesus and was one of the first deacons appointed by the early Christian community in Jerusalem.

He was known for performing great wonders and signs in the name of Christ, which drew the attention of certain individuals who falsely accused Stephen of blasphemy against Moses and God. The Book of Acts recounts that Stephen delivered a powerful defense of his faith before the Jewish council, known as the Sanhedrin, accusing the council of resisting God. Stephen's speech enraged the members of the council, who took him outside the city walls of Jerusalem and stoned him to death. As he was being martyred, Stephen had a vision and saw Jesus standing at the right hand of God. In the midst of his suffering he called out, "Lord Jesus, receive my spirit." Stephen then prayed for forgiveness for his persecutors, echoing Jesus's words on the cross: "Lord, do not hold this sin against them."

In Acts 7:58, the witnesses to the stoning of Stephen placed their garments at the feet of a Pharisee named Saul, implying that Saul was not directly involved in the act of stoning, but he was present and consented to Stephen's execution. This event would mark a pivotal moment in Saul's life, eventually leading to his conversion and transformation into the apostle Paul. (See Paul.)

STEPHEN OF HUNGARY

BORN: c. 975, Esztergom, Hungary
DIED: 1038, Székesfehérvár, Hungary
FEAST DAY: August 16

PATRONAGE: Hungary, kings, masons, stonecutters, invoked after a child has died

SYMBOLS AND ATTRIBUTES: Crown, orb, scepter, double cross

St. Stephen of Hungary, also known as Stephen I or Stephen the Great, holds an important place in the history of Hungary and the Christian faith. Born around the year 975, he was the son of Grand Prince Géza and Sarolt, a member of the ruling house of the Magyars. Stephen's birth occurred when the Hungarians were transitioning from a nomadic, pagan society to a Christian one.

Stephen's early years were marked by political instability and power struggles within the Hungarian kingdom. Following his father's death, Stephen ascended to the throne in the year 997, becoming the first king of Hungary at the age of twenty-two. Stephen's reign was characterized by a series of reforms and initiatives aimed at consolidating his power and establishing a stable government. He also sought to promote the Catholic Church as the dominant religious institution within his kingdom. To accomplish this, Stephen brought in missionaries from various regions, most notably from Germany and Italy, who were instrumental in converting the Hungarian population. He founded several bishoprics, established monasteries, and worked to develop a network of churches throughout the country.

During Stephen's reign, he navigated external challenges, notably conflicts with neighboring states and invasions from nomadic tribes. His military and diplomatic efforts, however, fortified Hungary as a Christian kingdom, fostered European alliances, and earned papal recognition as the Apostolic King of Hungary.

St. Stephen's dedication to the Christian faith and his country, and his efforts to promote the Church's influence in Hungary, led to his veneration as a saint. He is celebrated as the patron saint of Hungary, and his feast day is August 16, though Hungarians celebrate the placing of his relics in Buda on August 20. Stephen's legacy as a ruler, statesman, and advocate for Christianity in Hungary continues to be remembered and revered to this day.

SYLVESTER I

BORN: c. 3rd century, place unknown

DIED: 335, Rome, Italy

FEAST DAY: December 31

PATRONAGE: The chivalric order called the Militia Aurata, or "of the Golden Spur"

SYMBOLS AND ATTRIBUTES: Papal vestments

St. Sylvester I was the bishop of Rome from 314 to 335. During that time, the Church faced significant challenges and transformations. One of the most notable events leading up to his papacy was the Edict of Milan in 313, issued by Constantine and Licinius, which granted religious tolerance to Christians. This edict effectively ended the persecution of Christians, marking a major turning point for the Church.

According to traditions and legends, Sylvester's close association with Emperor Constantine played a significant role in the history of Christianity. While the details of their relationship are unclear, it is believed that Sylvester had a considerable influence on the emperor's decision to legalize and support Christianity.

Although Sylvester was not physically present at the Council of Nicaea due to his old age, he played an essential role in its proceedings, especially through his legates. The council aimed to address prevailing theological issues, notably the Arian heresy (that held that Jesus was not equal to God), eventually formulating the Nicene Creed, which affirmed the divinity of Jesus Christ and set forth a theological foundation for orthodox Christianity. Sylvester I's support for the council's teachings, and his influence on its outcome, contributed to establishing orthodoxy and preserving the Church's doctrinal unity.

In art, Pope Sylvester I is often depicted wearing papal vestments, including the tiara or papal crown, a symbol of his authority as pope.

T

TABITHA

BORN: 1st century AD, Judea

DIED: 1st century AD, Joppa

FEAST DAY: October 25

PATRONAGE: Tailors, dressmakers

SYMBOLS AND ATTRIBUTES: Cross, needle and thread

Tabitha, also known as Dorcas, was a disciple of Jesus Christ who lived in the town of Joppa (part of modern-day Tel Aviv). She was known for her acts of charity and her skill in making garments for the widows in her community. Tabitha is mentioned in Acts 9:36–42.

According to the Biblical account, Tabitha became ill and died. Her fellow believers prepared her body for burial and laid her in an upper room. When they heard that the apostle Peter was nearby in the town of Lydda, they sent two men to him, urging him to come to Joppa. Peter came and, after praying, commanded Tabitha to rise, and she was restored to life. This miraculous event led many people in the area to learn more about the teachings of Christ and the power of God working through the apostles.

TERESA OF ÁVILA

BORN: March 28, 1515, Ávila, Spain
DIED: October 4, 1582, Alba de
   Tormes, Spain
FEAST DAY: October 15

PATRONAGE: Lacemakers, Spanish Catholic
   writers, people ridiculed for their
   devotion, and sick people
SYMBOLS AND ATTRIBUTES: Book, quill,
   arrow-pierced heart, flaming heart, dove

A Spanish mystic, writer, and reformer, Teresa of Ávila, also known as St. Teresa of Jesus, was born Teresa Sánchez de Cepeda y Ahumada in Gotarrendura, Spain. She is considered one of the most significant figures in Christian mysticism and an influential personality during the Counter-Reformation.

She was the third child of Don Alonso Sánchez de Cepeda, a successful wool merchant, and Dona Beatriz Davila y Ahumada. Teresa was a pious child who, at the age of seven, began to feel a strong calling to religious life. She was deeply affected by the death of her mother when she was fourteen years old, leading her to adopt a deeper devotion to the Virgin Mary, who served as her spiritual mother. She found solace in prayer and began practicing acts of penance and self-mortification.

Teresa received her early instruction from Augustinian nuns, who taught her the fundamentals of the Catholic faith. She exhibited a keen intellect and a love for learning, showing particular interest in religious texts and literature. Her father had an extensive library, which allowed her access to a wide range of spiritual and secular writings. During her adolescence, Teresa came across several mystical texts that radically influenced her spiritual outlook, including *The Third Spiritual Alphabet* by Francisco de Osuna, which explored the practice of contemplative prayer and the stages of spiritual growth. This text sparked a desire within Teresa to pursue an even deeper spiritual life.

Around the age of twenty, Teresa entered the Carmelite Monastery of the Incarnation in Ávila. Teresa took her monastic vows but initially struggled with maintaining a consistent prayer life, finding it challenging to focus her mind on God. Teresa sought guidance from experienced spiritual directors within the monastery and persevered.

PLATE VIII
Teresa of Ávila

During her years in the monastery, Teresa had numerous mystical experiences and encounters with God, including visions, locutions (hearing divine voices), ecstasies, and a vision of Hell. She was also known to experience ecstasy and rapture during prayer. These mystical states involved a profound sense of union with God, during which she felt lifted out of her physical body and immersed in divine contemplation. Teresa described these experiences as moments of intense joy or spiritual intoxication. One of the best-known spiritual experiences associated with Teresa is the transverberation of her heart. It happened in 1559, when, during prayers, Teresa received a powerful vision in which an angel appeared before her. The heavenly messenger held a fiery golden spear and pierced her heart, causing intense spiritual pain and ecstatic feelings of love. This experience symbolized her penetrating union with God's love and her willingness to suffer for Jesus.

As a nun, Teresa was committed to a life of poverty, simplicity, and contemplative prayer. She believed that the Carmelite order had strayed from its intended purpose with its increasing wealth and lax observance of the original rules. Inspired by her own spiritual experiences and a desire to return to the primitive ideals of the order, she sought to establish a community that embraced a stricter adherence to poverty, humility, and contemplative practices. In 1562, with the support of influential individuals, Teresa established her first Discalced Carmelite monastery in Ávila, Spain. Named St. Joseph's Monastery, it became the prototype for subsequent foundations. The monastery followed a more austere way of life, emphasizing solitude, silence, and deep prayer.

Teresa's reform movement gained momentum as more individuals, both men and women, embraced her vision. She collaborated with John of the Cross, who shared her commitment to reforming the Carmelite order. Together, they established numerous Discalced Carmelite monasteries throughout Spain.

Teresa faced opposition from some Carmelite superiors, who considered her reforms disruptive and divisive, and the wider Church questioned the legitimacy and methods of the Discalced Carmelites. But in time, Pope Gregory XIII formally approved the Discalced Carmelites as a separate branch of the Carmelite order in 1580. Their reforms revitalized the order and emphasized the importance of prayer, simplicity, and contemplation in pursuing spiritual growth. Today, the Discalced Carmelites continue to thrive as a distinct branch within the Carmelite family.

Teresa was also a prolific writer. Her writings reflect her deep understanding of spiritual life and her personal experiences with God, emphasizing the importance of interior prayer, detachment from worldly distractions, and the pursuit of humility and self-knowledge. Her works, such as *The Way of Perfection*, and her autobiographical masterpiece, *The Life of Teresa of Jesus*, provide valuable insights into the nature of divine union and the path to spiritual perfection.

The Interior Castle, also known as *El castillo interior* or *Las moradas* in Spanish, is one of Teresa of Ávila's most famous and influential works. Written in 1577, it is a spiritual guide-book that explores the journey of the soul toward a fusion with God, using the metaphor of a magnificent castle with seven interior mansions, each representing a different stage of spiritual development. Emphasizing self-awareness, humility, and divine surrender, it champions contemplative prayer and virtue cultivation. A cornerstone in Christian mysticism, this guide confronts challenges, temptations, and blessings on the spiritual path, enlightening countless souls in their pursuit of the divine. It remains a pivotal resource for those seeking a deeper understanding of the soul's journey toward God.

Pope Gregory XV canonized St. Teresa in 1622, and in 1970, Pope Paul VI named her a Doctor of the Church. As the first woman to receive this title, it underscores the significance of her teachings and the profound influence of her spiritual legacy. (See Joseph, John of the Cross.)

TERESA OF CALCUTTA

BORN: August 26, 1910, Skopje, Ottoman Empire
DIED: September 5, 1997, Calcutta, India
FEAST DAY: September 5

PATRONAGE: World Youth Day, missionaries, doubters
SYMBOLS AND ATTRIBUTES: Blue-trimmed sari, rosary

St. Teresa of Calcutta, born Agnes Gonxha Bojaxhiu on August 26, 1910, in Skopje, now the capital of North Macedonia, was a Catholic nun, missionary, and Nobel Peace Prize winner celebrated for her lifelong service to the poor and the sick. Known as Mother Teresa, she was the youngest of three children of Nikola and Dranafile Bojaxhiu, Albanian Catholics. Her father was a businessman and rights activist.

Agnes was deeply religious from a young age, and by the time she was twelve, she felt a calling to missionary work. She joined an Irish Catholic order known as the Sisters of Loreto at eighteen, adopting the name Sister Mary Teresa. In 1929, she was dispatched to Calcutta, India, to teach at a convent school. In 1944, she ascended to the role of head-mistress, at which time, in line with the convent's traditions, she began to be addressed as "Mother."

Mother Teresa was profoundly affected by the abject poverty she witnessed in Calcutta. In 1948, she was granted permission to leave the convent and establish her own mission. Notably, she began donning a sari, its white fabric with blue borders soon becoming an emblematic representation of her and her mission.

Mother Teresa's Missionaries of Charity, founded in 1950, were dedicated to serving the "poorest of the poor." Starting with a mere thirteen members, the order provided the needy food, shelter, and medical care, especially in Calcutta's dire streets. Over time, the Missionaries of Charity expanded their reach; now there are more than 4,500 sisters in 133 countries, diversifying into areas like education, orphanages, and care for the mentally ill.

In 1965, Pope Paul VI awarded the Decree of Praise to the Missionaries of Charity, and global acknowledgment came in 1979 with the Nobel Peace Prize for Mother Teresa's compassionate service to humanity.

During the 1980s' HIV/AIDS pandemic, Mother Teresa swiftly responded. Recognizing the stigma associated with the disease, she initiated the Gift of Love Hospice in Calcutta, catering specifically to those afflicted. Alongside physical care, she sought to combat societal prejudice and champion the dignity of every patient. She also played a pivotal role during the Ethiopian famine in 1984, visiting refugee camps and bringing the crisis to the attention of the public so as to mobilize international aid. In the United States, she spoke out strongly against abortion and other societal concerns.

Throughout her life, Mother Teresa undertook numerous journeys worldwide, spreading her message of love and service. These tours, often marked by her visits to places affected by poverty, natural disasters, or war, showcased her commitment to alleviating suffering wherever it existed. In 1982, during the Siege of Beirut, she brokered a temporary cease-fire between the Israeli army and Palestinian guerrillas to evacuate thirty-seven children from a hospital. In another significant journey, she traveled to Armenia in 1988 after a devastating earthquake, providing support and comfort to the survivors. Each of her tours, from visiting the famine-stricken regions of Africa to aiding the radiation victims of Chernobyl, cemented her reputation as a global ambassador of goodwill and compassion, demonstrating the universal applicability of her mission.

Over the years, Mother Teresa found herself in the company of world leaders, including Pope John Paul II, President Ronald Reagan, Soviet Union leader Mikhail Gorbachev, British prime minister Margaret Thatcher, Romanian dictator Nicolae Ceauşescu, Cuban leader Fidel Castro, and India's prime minister Indira Gandhi, each meeting a testament to her growing global stature. Her interactions often transcended political and ideological boundaries and focused on forging collaborations for the betterment of humanity. One of the most iconic meetings was with Princess Diana in the 1990s. The women, both committed to charitable causes, were often pictured together during Diana's visits to India, uniting in their mission to highlight and address societal ailments. Their shared dedication to the sick and impoverished created a bond between them, leading to numerous joint charitable ventures. Mother Teresa's discussions with leaders, be it with presidents, prime ministers, or royalty, always revolved around advocating for peace, understanding, and support for the less fortunate, making her not just a spiritual guide but also a global diplomat of charity and compassion.

Mother Teresa died on September 5, 1997, at eighty-seven. While she was revered for her dedication to the impoverished, some critiques centered on the quality of care by the Missionaries of Charity and their perceived emphasis on palliative care over systemic poverty alleviation. Proponents argue that these critics miss the point—that her main contribution was to offer love and dignity to society's marginalized, affirming their worth in their final moments.

Though many would call her a living saint during her lifetime and a woman close to God, Mother Teresa struggled with her faith during her long years of service. Her book *Come Be My Light*, edited by her advocate and postulator for her cause for sainthood Brian Kolodiejchuk and published posthumously in 2007, offers a poignant glimpse into the extraordinary inner life of this dedicated nun. Within these pages, we see a woman characterized by an unwavering commitment to serving the poorest of the poor, yet she also grappled with profound inner struggles. Through her letters and writings, Mother Teresa reveals a spiritual darkness that surrounded her for much of her life, a deep sense of isolation, and an unrelenting longing for a closer connection with God. These intimate revelations humanize a revered figure and stand as a testament to the complex nature of faith and the indomitable spirit of a woman who, despite her own doubts and turmoil, continued to be a beacon of hope and compassion to the world's most vulnerable. Her legacy remains one of unmatched selflessness and service, which is epitomized in these words attributed to her: "We can do no great things, only small things with great love."

She was canonized as a saint by Pope Francis in 2016, who called her "a generous dispenser of divine mercy," a woman whose "mission to the urban and existential peripheries remains for us today an eloquent witness to God's closeness to the poorest of the poor." Two posthumous miracles cemented her path to sainthood. The first involved Monica Besra, a woman from West Bengal who experienced an unexplained healing from an abdominal tumor after praying to Mother Teresa. The second was Marcilio Andrino from Brazil, whose miraculous recovery from a severe brain infection is attributed to Mother Teresa's intercession. Her feast day is September 5, and she is officially venerated as the patron saint of the Missionaries of Charity. She is endeared to millions around the world.

THÉRÈSE OF LISIEUX

BORN: January 2, 1873, Alençon, France
DIED: September 30, 1897, Lisieux, France
FEAST DAY: October 1

PATRONAGE: Missionaries, florists, aviators, tuberculosis sufferers, homeless
SYMBOLS AND ATTRIBUTES: Roses, crucifix, child Jesus, Carmelite habit

Thérèse of Lisieux, also known as St. Thérèse of the Child Jesus and the Holy Face, is widely regarded as one of the most beloved saints of the modern era. She is affectionately known as The Little Flower.

Born Marie-Françoise-Thérèse Martin on January 2, 1873, in Alençon, France, she was the youngest of nine children born to Louis and Zélie Martin. Her parents were devout Catholics who lived a life of faith and virtue. Both Louis and Zélie had initially considered religious life themselves but chose instead to marry and raise a family. They ran a successful lace-making business and provided a loving and nurturing environment for their children.

Thérèse's early years were marked by the positive influence of her family's faith. Her parents instilled a deep love for God and taught the importance of prayer and devotion. They often read stories about the lives of saints and shared the richness of the Catholic faith with their children.

However, tragedy struck four-year-old Thérèse when her mother, Zélie, died of breast cancer. This event deeply impacted Thérèse. It was said by her family that she suddenly became acutely aware of the reality of suffering and the brevity of human life. Following her mother's death, the family moved to Lisieux to be closer to relatives and to seek a fresh start.

In Lisieux, Thérèse formed a deep bond with her four older sisters, Pauline, Marie, Leonie, and Celine, who would join her in religious life. Together, they created a "spiritual childhood" in their home, imitating the lives of saints and nurturing their love for God.

On Christmas Eve 1886, Thérèse experienced a powerful moment of grace, which she referred to as her "Christmas miracle." During Midnight Mass, she saw a statue of the Infant Jesus smile at her, and she felt a profound presence of God's love. This experience had a transformative effect and ignited within her a burning desire to devote her life entirely to God.

Inspired by the lives of missionaries and martyrs, Thérèse aspired to become a saint and to offer her life for the salvation of souls. She longed for the religious life and sought admission to the Carmelite monastery at the age of fourteen. However, due to her young age, she was not accepted at that time.

Undeterred by the initial rejection, Thérèse persisted in her desires; she was granted permission to enter the Carmelite monastery in Lisieux on April 9, 1888, a few months after her fifteenth birthday. She took the religious name Sister Thérèse of the Child Jesus and the Holy Face. Her life as a Carmelite nun was characterized by deep love for God, and commitment to practicing what she called The Little Way—her belief that holiness was not reserved for those who accomplish great deeds but could be attained by anyone, regardless of their position or abilities. She saw herself as a "little soul" in the eyes of God and believed that even the most minor acts performed with love and devotion could have profound spiritual significance. Thérèse's Little Way revolved around finding God's presence in life's ordinary and mundane experiences. Whether it was sweeping the floor, smiling at a fellow sister, or enduring suffering with patience, Thérèse saw each moment as a chance to draw closer to God.

Thérèse wrote extensively in her personal journals, capturing her spiritual insights, reflections, and prayers. These writings, compiled after her death, formed the basis of her autobiography, *Story of a Soul*. This work, widely read and influential, recounts Thérèse's childhood, spiritual awakening, and life as a Carmelite nun. It delves into the depths of her inner being, revealing her love for God, her desire for holiness, and her longing for intimacy with Jesus, whom she called her Divine Spouse. Thérèse shares her spiritual insights, reflections, and the struggles she encountered along her journey and writes extensively about her devotion to the Holy Face of Jesus and her desire to console Him for the offenses committed against Him. She also reveals her longing to offer herself as a sacrifice to God's merciful love, embracing suffering and trials as a means of participating in Christ's redemptive work.

Story of a Soul was initially distributed privately among the Carmelite community. However, after Thérèse died in 1897, her sister, Pauline, recognized the manuscript's spiritual value and sought to have it published. The first edition of *Story of a Soul* was published in 1898.

The book quickly became popular with readers worldwide. It has been translated into numerous languages and continues to be read and studied by people today seeking spiritual guidance.

Thérèse was canonized as a saint by Pope Pius XI on May 17, 1925, only twenty-eight years after her death. In 1997 Pope John Paul II declared her a Doctor of the Church, the youngest person to hold such a title. She is venerated as the patron saint of a wide range of causes and groups, including missions, aviators, florists, people with AIDS, and those suffering from tuberculosis. Devotion to St. Thérèse has spread globally, and many churches, shrines, and religious communities have been dedicated to her. Her feast day, October 1, is celebrated by Catholics worldwide.

THOMAS AQUINAS

BORN: c. 1225, Roccasecca, Kingdom of Sicily

DIED: March 7, 1274, Fossanova, Papal States

FEAST DAY: January 28

PATRONAGE: Academics, apologists, theologians, book sellers, philosophers, scholars, students, the Catholic university, and the Dominican order

SYMBOLS AND ATTRIBUTES: Sun on chest, chalice, monstrance, book, model of a church

Thomas Aquinas, also known as Thomas of Aquino, stands as a towering figure in thirteenth-century theology and philosophy. Born in Roccasecca, Italy, around 1225 or 1226, Thomas came from a prominent aristocratic family. His parents, Landulf, the count of Aquino, and Theodora, a noblewoman, greatly influenced his early learning and upbringing. At age five, Thomas began his schooling at the Benedictine monastery of Monte Cassino, where he received his initial instruction in the liberal arts, subjects that encompassed grammar, rhetoric, logic, arithmetic, geometry, astronomy, and music. Thomas displayed an exceptional aptitude and an insatiable curiosity, which set him apart from his peers. Recognizing his talent, his parents sent him to the University of Naples to pursue further studies.

In 1243, Thomas decided to join the Dominican order against the wishes of his family, who had expected that he would pursue a life in the Benedictine tradition, which at the time held more prestige and influence. This move caused a strain on his relationship with his family, so much so that his brothers kidnapped him and held him captive for a year in an attempt to dissuade him from his religious vocation. When the family realized that Thomas would not change his mind, they accepted his decision.

After completing his initial studies in Naples, Thomas moved to Paris to study under the celebrated philosopher Albertus Magnus. During this time, Thomas encountered the works of the Church Fathers, particularly the writings of Augustine of Hippo, which greatly influenced his theological thinking. He also studied the works of Jewish philosopher Maimonides and Islamic scholars Avicenna and Averroes. He became captivated by the writings of Aristotle, particularly his emphasis on rational inquiry and the pursuit of knowledge through observation and analysis.

Thomas saw Aristotle's philosophy as a powerful tool that could be harmoniously integrated with Christian theology. Aristotle's ideas about causality, substance, potentiality, and natural law, among others, provided Thomas with a comprehensive philosophical vocabulary that he could utilize in his theological and intellectual endeavors. Thomas's comprehensive moral theory was grounded in reason, a theory that bridged the gap between the humans and the Divine. Furthermore, Aristotle's emphasis on the importance of empirical observation and analysis influenced Thomas's approach to theology. He argued that reason, guided by faith, could illuminate certain truths about God and the divine order.

Albertus recognized Thomas's exceptional intellect and assigned him to teach at the University of Paris, where Thomas also began

writing. His most significant work, known as the *Summa theologiae* or the *Summa theologica*, is considered a masterpiece of medieval theology, comprising a comprehensive examination of theological topics synthesizing Christian doctrine and Aristotelian philosophy. Although Thomas could not complete the *Summa theologiae* before his death, the work remains a testament to his intellectual prowess and is still influential in Christian theology.

Apart from the *Summa*, Thomas authored numerous other treatises, including commentaries on Aristotle's works, Biblical commentaries, philosophical treatises, and disputed questions. Some notable works include *De ente et essentia* (On Being and Essence), *De veritate* (On Truth), and *Summa contra Gentiles* (A Summa against the Gentiles).

He has been called the Angelic Doctor due to his personal virtue as well as for his affinity for angelology and his exploration of heavenly beings in his theological writings. Thomas dedicated considerable attention to the topic, drawing from Scripture, the Church Fathers, and his own philosophical reflections. His comprehensive treatment of angelic nature, hierarchies, and functions would impact Church teachings for centuries to come.

Toward the end of his life, Aquinas underwent a series of mystical experiences that impacted him profoundly, and he stopped writing altogether, declaring that all his works seemed like "straw" compared to the divine reality he had experienced.

St. Thomas Aquinas died on March 7, 1274, and was canonized as a saint in 1323 by Pope John XXII. He was recognized as one of the greatest theologians and philosophers in the history of Christianity. His approach to theology, characterized by rigorous logical analysis and synthesis of philosophical concepts, became a hallmark of academic thought. His methodology and intellectual framework laid the groundwork for subsequent scholastic theologians and philosophers.

Beyond his unparalleled influence on Catholic thought, his writings have left an indelible impact on broader Christian theology. Many Protestant and Orthodox theologians, philosophers, and scholars from all walks of life have engaged with Aquinas's works, drawing inspiration from his insights.

THOMAS BECKET

BORN: c. December 21, 1119 or 1120, Cheapside, London, England

DIED: December 29, 1170, Canterbury, Kent, England

FEAST DAY: December 29

PATRONAGE: Secular clergy, the Archdiocese of Portsmouth

SYMBOLS AND ATTRIBUTES: Sword (sometimes through the head), miter, pallium

Thomas Becket, also known as Thomas à Becket or Thomas of Canterbury, was a prominent figure in medieval Christian history. Born in London in 1119 or 1120, he would become the archbishop of Canterbury, serving as a key spiritual and political figure in twelfth-century England.

Thomas's early life was marked by privilege and prestige. He received an excellent education and entered the service of Theobald of Bec, the archbishop of Canterbury, who recognized the young man's intellectual potential, and appointed him as his personal secretary. Through this position, Thomas gained valuable experience and built connections within the Church.

Thomas and King Henry II first became acquainted during their early years, likely in the 1150s, when both were rising in prominence. Thomas, known for his intelligence and administrative skills, caught the attention of Henry, who recognized his potential and appointed him as his chancellor in 1155. As chancellor, Becket served as Henry's trusted advisor and played an indispensable role in the administration of the kingdom.

The friendship between Thomas and Henry blossomed during their time together. They shared a close bond, often engaging in leisure activities together and enjoying each other's company. His friendship with Henry granted him access to wealth, power, and influence.

In 1162, Henry nominated Thomas to be the archbishop of Canterbury, the highest ecclesiastical position in England. This appointment was part of Henry's efforts to strengthen his control over the Church and the clergy. However, once Thomas assumed his role as archbishop, he underwent a significant transformation.

As archbishop, Thomas took his responsibilities seriously and became a zealous advocate for the Church's independence from secular authority. This put him at odds with the king, who desired to exert control over the clergy and bring them under royal jurisdiction. The conflict between Thomas and Henry escalated over time, driven by clashes over legal and political matters, including the rights and privileges of the Church and the Crown.

One notable event that intensified the conflict was the Council of Clarendon in 1164, where Henry II attempted to assert royal authority over the Church. Thomas initially agreed to the king's demands but retracted his consent, fearing the erosion of the Church's independence.

In response to Thomas's resistance, Henry made several attempts to intimidate and control him, which led Thomas to flee to France, seeking the protection of King Louis VII. During his exile, Thomas maintained his stance against the encroachment of secular authority on the Church and engaged in diplomatic efforts to rally support from the papacy and other European leaders.

In 1170, after years of strained relations, a reconciliation was attempted. Thomas returned to England, hoping to find a resolution to his conflict with Henry. However, tensions remained high, and on December 29, 1170, four knights loyal to King Henry interpreted his expressed frustration with Thomas as a command to assassinate him. They confronted Thomas in Canterbury Cathedral and, as he refused to yield to their demands, he was brutally murdered.

The Christian world was shocked by this turn of events, and Thomas was immediately hailed as a martyr and saint by many. His tomb in Canterbury became a popular pilgrimage site, and numerous miracles were attributed to his intercession. In 1173, just three years after his death, Thomas was canonized by Pope Alexander III.

The murder of Thomas Becket had repercussions on the relationship between Church and state in medieval England. It underscored the significance of ecclesiastical independence and the limits of royal authority, leaving a lasting impact on the development of religious and political institutions in the country.

THOMAS MORE

BORN: February 7, 1478, London, England
DIED: July 6, 1535, Tower Hill, London, England
FEAST DAY: June 22

PATRONAGE: Politicians, lawyers, civil servants
SYMBOLS AND ATTRIBUTES: Chancellor robe and collar, cross, scroll

Thomas More was a prominent statesman, lawyer, philosopher, author, and eminent figure in English history. He was born on February 7, 1478, in London, England, studied at St. Anthony's School in London, and attended Oxford University, where he immersed himself in classical languages, literature, and philosophy. After completing his studies, Thomas pursued a legal career. His intellectual prowess, eloquence, and integrity gained him recognition, leading to various prestigious positions within the English government.

Thomas's rise to prominence in the court of King Henry VIII began in the early 1500s. As a humanist scholar and a devout Catholic, Thomas caught the attention of the king. His wit, intelligence, and erudition made Thomas a charming guest at the king's informal gatherings and in the intellectual circles at court.

In 1518, Thomas was appointed as a member of the Privy Council, the king's advisory body, which further solidified their friendship and raised Thomas's stature in society. Henry, who valued Thomas's legal acumen and wise counsel, entrusted him with various diplomatic missions, both at home and abroad. In 1529, Thomas More succeeded Thomas Wolsey as lord chancellor of England, the first layperson to hold this title. As lord chancellor, Thomas was the king's trusted secretary, presided over the House of Lords, and was one of the most powerful men in the kingdom.

However, Thomas's friendship with the king faced significant strain when Henry sought an annulment of his marriage to Queen Catherine of Aragon, a request that directly challenged More's deeply held religious belief in the indissolubility of marriage. As a result, he could not support the annulment, which he considered a violation of Church doctrine.

As Henry's pursuit of the annulment intensified so that he could marry Anne Boleyn, Thomas' opposition grew more pronounced, refusing as he did to compromise his conscience or bend his principles to accommodate the king's desires. This irreconcilable conflict ultimately led to a breakdown in their relationship and a divergence in their paths. Thomas chose to resign from his position as lord chancellor in 1532, unwilling to endorse what was mounting to be a separation from the Catholic Church and the establishment of the Church of England.

Henry married Anne on January 25, 1533. In September of that year she gave birth to their daughter Elizabeth, and the following year, the Act of Succession made Anne Boleyn's children with Henry the legitimate heirs to the throne and required all subjects to take an oath acknowledging the act's provisions. Thomas's refusal to attend Anne Boleyn's coronation and of the Act of Succession led to his arrest and trial for treason. During his time in prison, he composed several notable works, including *A Dialogue of Comfort against Tribulation,* demonstrating his resilience and unwavering faith.

On July 6, 1535, Thomas was martyred by beheading. His final words before he was executed were, "I die the king's faithful servant, but God's first."

Thomas is widely regarded as a champion of religious freedom, the rule of law, and conscience rights. His most famous work, *Utopia,* is a philosophical treatise that critiques contemporary society while presenting an idealistic vision of a just and egalitarian culture. Thomas's writings and unwavering adherence to his principles have continued to inspire generations of Catholics, scholars, and philosophers.

In recognition of his influence and enduring legacy, Thomas More was beatified in 1886 and canonized as a saint by Pope Pius XI in 1935. His feast day serves as a reminder of his exemplary life, his martyrdom for the sake of conscience, and his unwavering commitment to God, his faith, and his country.

THOMAS THE APOSTLE

BORN: c. 1st century AD

DIED: c. 72 AD, present-day Tamil Nadu, India

FEAST DAY: July 3

PATRONAGE: Architects, builders, construction workers, the blind, Christians in India

SYMBOLS AND ATTRIBUTES: Carpenter's square, spear, lotus flower

Often referred to as Doubting Thomas, Thomas, one of the twelve apostles chosen by Jesus Christ for his earthly ministry, was a significant figure in the New Testament. He was likely born in Galilee and was probably a fisherman before his call to apostleship. Thomas was frequently known as Didymus in the Gospels, which translates to "the twin" in Greek, though the identity of his twin remains unknown.

In the story of the death of Lazarus in the Gospel of John, Thomas demonstrates courage and defiance as he rallies his fellow apostles to join Jesus in returning to Judea, even under the threat of stoning. "Let us also go, that we may die with him," Thomas proclaims. His unwavering loyalty to Jesus portrays a man of great strength and devotion. This moment humanizes the apostle and makes even more compelling his best-known appearance later in the same gospel when Thomas expresses his doubt about Jesus's resurrection.

When the other disciples inform Thomas that they've seen Jesus resurrected, Thomas is skeptical. He says he will believe it only if he can personally see and touch Jesus's wounds. Jesus appears and invites Thomas to do just that, whereupon the Doubter exclaims in awe, "My Lord and my God!" Jesus rebukes His old friend, saying, "Because you have seen me, you have believed; blessed are those who have not seen and yet have believed" (John 20.24–29).

Following Jesus's ascension, tradition holds that Thomas embarked on missionary journeys to propagate Jesus's teachings to various regions, including Parthia and Persia (both in modern-day Iran), and finally to India, where he is believed to have founded a Christian community and performed numerous miracles.

The Acts of Thomas, a noncanonical Christian text from the third century, recounts Thomas's deeds the East, including his baptism of the local king and the founding of churches. The text also provides the earliest account of Thomas's martyrdom, asserting he was executed in India, either by spearing or stoning. In 1945, writings that came to be known as the Gospel of Thomas were discovered among a group of texts known as the Nag Hammadi library in Egypt. Unlike the four canonical gospels of the New Testament—Matthew, Mark, Luke, and John—which all provide narrative accounts of the life, death, and resurrection of Jesus, the Gospel of Thomas does not follow the same format. Instead, the Gospel of Thomas is a collection of 114 sayings attributed to Jesus, some of which closely mirror phrases found in the canonical Gospels, while others are unique to this work. It opens with the lines, "These are the hidden words that the living Jesus spoke. And Didymos Judas Thomas wrote them down." This opening implies that the contents of the text are secret teachings or wisdom passed from Jesus to the apostle. The precise origins of the Gospel of Thomas are still debated among scholars. Some believe it to have been written as early as the first century AD, making it contemporary with the books of the New Testament. Others argue that it was written in the early to mid-second century and consider it a Gnostic text.

St. Thomas's symbols are derived from his life and martyrdom, including a spear signifying his death in India, a carpenter's square referring to a legend of him building a palace, and his depiction with a twin (often Jesus) as he was known as Didymus, meaning "twin." He is also depicted in art with a book or scroll, common emblems for apostles, and sometimes shown touching the resurrected Christ's wounds, referring to the famous Biblical episode where his skepticism was challenged.

TIBURTIUS

BORN: 3rd century, place unknown

DIED: 3rd century, Rome, Italy

FEAST DAY: August 11

PATRONAGE: Martyrs

SYMBOLS AND ATTRIBUTES: Palm of martyrdom

St. Tiburtius, also known as St. Tiburtius of Rome, was a Christian martyr who lived during the early Christian era. He is often closely associated with his friend and fellow martyr St. Castulus.

According to Christian tradition, Tiburtius and Castulus were Roman citizens who embraced Christianity. They were apprehended for their faith during the persecutions under the Roman emperor Diocletian. While the accounts of their martyrdom vary from different sources, it is generally believed that they were executed for their refusal to make sacrifices to the Roman gods. One story tells how Tiburtius miraculously walked unharmed through fire before being beheaded. The feast day commemorating Tiburtius is observed on August 11. (See Castulus.)

TIMOTHY

BORN: c. 17 AD, Lystra

DIED: c. 97 AD, Ephesus

FEAST DAY: January 26

PATRONAGE: Stomach and intestinal disorders

SYMBOLS AND ATTRIBUTES: Bishop's attire, staff

Timothy was the first bishop of Ephesus and a close companion of the apostle Paul. It is believed that Timothy was born in Lystra, a city in the Roman province of Galatia, around the first century AD. Timothy's mother, Eunice, was a Jewish woman who had embraced the Christian faith, while his father was a Greek, possibly a Gentile.

Timothy's encounter with the apostle Paul is documented in the book of Acts in the New Testament. During his second missionary journey, Paul visited Lystra and recognized Timothy's potential as a leader. Impressed by Timothy's character and commitment to the faith, Paul chose him as a companion and took him under his wing as a protégé.

However, because Timothy's father was Greek and he had not allowed his son to be circumcised, Paul faced a dilemma. Circumcision was not required for salvation or faith in Jesus Christ, as Paul strongly emphasized throughout his teachings. However, Timothy's uncircumcision could have hindered their ministry among Jewish communities, where adherence to Jewish customs and traditions was expected. Timothy willfully agreed to be circumcised so that he might more effectively engage with the Jewish people he and Paul would encounter during their travels.

Timothy became Paul's trusted disciple and coworker, accompanying him on various missionary journeys and serving as an emissary to different Christian communities. It is believed that Timothy received formal ordination as a minister and was appointed the first bishop of Ephesus, a prominent city in Asia Minor. He was involved in overseeing the local Christian community, teaching and preaching the Gospel, and providing pastoral care. Paul's first epistle to Timothy, written around 63 AD, contains valuable instructions and advice for Timothy in his leadership position.

Throughout Paul's letters, we gain insights into Timothy's character and the challenges he faced. He was described as a young man with a genuine faith, a gentle spirit, and a sincere love for others. However, he also struggled with timidity and anxiety, which prompted Paul to encourage him to be strong, courageous, and faithful in his ministry.

Timothy's association with Paul was not without difficulties. They encountered opposition and persecution, and confronted false teachings and heresies that threatened the early Christian community. Paul's second epistle to Timothy, written near the end of Paul's life, expresses his deep affection for Timothy and urges him to remain steadfast in the face of adversity.

According to tradition, Timothy continued his ministry in Ephesus even after Paul's martyrdom. He became the city's first bishop and was known for his diligent efforts to combat false teachings and promote sound doctrine within the Church. Eventually, Timothy himself suffered martyrdom, although specific details about his death are not recorded in Biblical accounts. A fourth-century text, however, describes Timothy's execution by a group of pagans when he refused to pray to the goddess Diana. (See Paul.)

TITUS

BORN: 1st century AD, place unknown

DIED: 96 AD, Gortyn, Crete

FEAST DAY: January 26

PATRONAGE: United States Army Chaplain Corps

SYMBOLS AND ATTRIBUTES: Scroll, bishop's attire

St. Titus was a companion and disciple of the apostle Paul. He was a Greek Gentile, and his exact birthplace remains unknown, but it is believed that he came from Antioch.

The first Biblical mention of Titus is in Galatians 2:1–3. Here Titus became a key figure in the argument about whether Gentile converts to Christianity need to observe the Mosaic law and be circumcised. Paul used Titus as a test case, and his acceptance by the Jerusalem community without circumcision became a significant precedent in the early Christian community. It helped to show that the new covenant established through Jesus Christ was open to all, regardless of ethnicity or previous religious background.

Paul sent Titus on several sensitive missions, including one to Corinth to help resolve the Church's difficulties there. Titus accomplished this mission and initiated a collection for the poor in Jerusalem. The Epistle to Titus reveals that Paul left Titus in Crete with the directive to appoint elders in every town. This task was quite challenging given the notorious reputation of the Cretans, who were often violent against Christians.

It is believed that Titus rejoined Paul when the apostle was in custody in Rome. Sometime thereafter, Titus returned to Crete, where he served as bishop until he died at an old age. His life as a peacemaker, missionary, and trusted companion of Paul reminds Christians of the importance of loyalty, wisdom, and courage when sharing and living the Gospel. (See Paul.)

V

VALENTINE

BORN: c. 226, Terni (modern-day Italy)
DIED: c. February 14, 269, Rome, Italy
FEAST DAY: February 14
PATRONAGE: Lovers, engaged couples, beekeepers, people with epilepsy, protection against plague

SYMBOLS AND ATTRIBUTES: Roses, birds, bishop with a disabled or epileptic child, bishop with a rooster

St. Valentine was a third-century priest in Rome and is remembered as the inspiration for the modern-day holiday Valentine's Day. Despite his cultural significance, relatively little is known about the historical St. Valentine, and many aspects of his life remain shrouded in mystery.

During the third century, Roman emperor Claudius II issued a ban on marriage among young people. It was believed that unmarried soldiers, unburdened by wives and families, would make more committed, focused soldiers. In defiance of this edict, Valentine performed marriages in secret. When this was discovered, he was arrested. The emperor allowed Valentine the opportunity to recant his faith. The priest refused, and he was flogged and beheaded by Roman authorities.

There is also a popular legend that tells the story of how Valentine, while in prison awaiting execution, healed the blind daughter of his jailer. On the eve of his death, he is said to have penned a farewell note to the girl, signing it "from your Valentine," a phrase that is still in use today.

Other accounts suggest that Valentine might have been a bishop in Terni, Italy, who was martyred in Rome. These discrepancies have led some scholars to speculate that the St. Valentine of Valentine's Day may be a composite of separate individuals.

Valentine was believed to have been executed on February 14, 269. In 496, Pope Gelasius I declared February 14 to be St. Valentine's Day, which over time became associated with love and romance. This is thought to be due to the timing of the celebration, which coincides with the old pagan fertility festival of Lupercalia, as well as the start of the mating season of birds in England.

St. Valentine is recognized as a saint in the Roman Catholic Church, the Anglican Communion, and the Lutheran Church. However, because of the scarcity and inconsistency of historical evidence about his life, the Roman Catholic Church removed his feast day from the General Roman Calendar in 1969, though he is still officially recognized as a saint.

The figure of St. Valentine is an example of how history, mythology, and cultural traditions can intertwine over time to create a figure of significant cultural and religious importance. Even with the uncertainties and variations in his story, his association with love and devotion remains a powerful symbol recognized worldwide.

VERONICA GIULIANI

BORN: December 27, 1660, Mercatello sul Metauro, Italy
DIED: July 9, 1727, Città di Castello, Italy
FEAST DAY: July 9

PATRONAGE: Mystics
SYMBOLS AND ATTRIBUTES: Crucifix, crown of thorns, heart in her hand, stigmata

Born as Ursula Giuliani in Mercatello, Italy, St. Veronica Giuliani was an Italian Franciscan mystic and saint. At the age of seventeen, she entered the Capuchin Poor Clares convent in Città di Castello, taking the name Sister Veronica.

Veronica Giuliani was known for her intense spiritual experiences, including visions, ecstasies, and mystical encounters with Jesus and the Virgin Mary. She had a deep devotion to the Passion of Christ and experienced the stigmata, the wounds of Christ's crucifixion, on her own body. Veronica Giuliani displayed a strong commitment to prayer, penance, and self-mortification throughout her life. She was known for her humility, obedience, and love for others, even amid physical and spiritual sufferings. She held various positions of responsibility within the convent and became the abbess of the monastery in Città di Castello in 1716.

Pope Benedict XVI noted that Veronica Giuliani's literary output was extensive, encompassing a wide range of genres such as letters, autobiographical reports, and poems. Nevertheless, her diary is the primary and most valuable resource for understanding her thoughts and beliefs. This remarkable journal, begun in 1693, consists of approximately 22,000 meticulously handwritten pages that provide an intimate glimpse into her cloistered life spanning over thirty-four years.

St. Veronica Giuliani's pious example and teachings greatly influenced those around her. She was recognized for her practical nature and holiness during her lifetime and was venerated as a living saint by many people. She died on July 9, 1727, and was canonized by Pope Gregory XVI on May 26, 1839.

VERONICA

BORN: 1st century AD, Judea
DIED: 1st century AD, Judea
FEAST DAY: July 12
PATRONAGE: Photographers, laundry workers

SYMBOLS AND ATTRIBUTES: Cloth with the face of Jesus (often referred to as the "Veil of Veronica")

Although her name does not feature in the Bible, St. Veronica, also known as Veronica of Jerusalem, is a notable figure in Christian tradition, which narrates a poignant encounter between her and Jesus Christ as He made His way to Calvary, the site of His crucifixion.

The story, as depicted in the sixth Station of the Cross, a sacred devotion that follows Jesus as He travels to His crucifixion, describes Veronica, moved by deep compassion, stepping forward from the crowd to offer Jesus a cloth to clean His face, then streaked with sweat and blood. After Jesus accepted her gesture of compassion and used the fabric, an image of His face miraculously imprinted itself onto the material. This miraculous imprint is known as the Veil of Veronica or the Sudarium.

The name "Veronica" is considered to be derived from the Latin words "vera" (meaning "true") and "icon" (meaning "image"), thereby symbolizing the "true image" of Christ.

Venerated as a saint in the Catholic Church, St. Veronica is celebrated annually on her feast day, July 12.

VICTOR I

BORN: c. 140, North Africa
DIED: c. 199, Rome, Italy
FEAST DAY: July 28

PATRONAGE: Unknown
SYMBOLS AND ATTRIBUTES: Papal vestments, bread

Pope Victor I, also known as Victor of Rome, was an important figure in early Christianity. He served as the bishop of Rome and the supreme pontiff of the Catholic Church from approximately 189 to 199. Historical records regarding Pope Victor I are limited, but one significant account comes from the writings of St. Irenaeus of Lyons, a prominent early Church Father and theologian. According to Irenaeus, Victor I was originally from North Africa, specifically, the region of modern-day Tunisia.

His tenure as pope occurred during a critical period in the development of Christianity that was marked by theological controversies and the expansion of the Church. Victor I faced several challenges during his papacy, most notably the Quartodeciman controversy. This theological dispute revolved around the date of Easter and whether it should be celebrated according to the Jewish Passover or on a fixed Sunday. Some Christian communities, particularly those in Asia Minor, continued to observe Easter based on the Jewish calendar, while others followed the fixed Sunday tradition. Pope Victor I, seeking to establish a unified practice, exerted significant influence in favor of the Sunday observance and issued a letter to the Asian bishops urging them to conform.

This controversy led to strained relations between the Roman Church and the Asian bishops, particularly Polycrates of Ephesus, who vehemently defended the Quartodeciman practice. Victor I initially threatened to excommunicate the Asian churches over this controversy.

A strong and sometimes intimidating leader, he actively engaged in ecclesiastical affairs, maintained correspondence with various Christian communities, and made decisions concerning the sacraments of Baptism and Penance. He also helped to popularize Latin, which would become the official language of the Church.

St. Pope Victor I is recognized for his defense of orthodoxy and his efforts to maintain unity among the early Christian communities. While the exact details of his death are uncertain, it is believed that he died around 199. His feast day is celebrated on July 28 in the Roman Catholic Church. (See Irenaeus.)

VINCENT DE PAUL

BORN: April 24, 1581, Pouy,
Gascony, France
DIED: September 27, 1660, Paris, France
FEAST DAY: September 27

PATRONAGE: Charities, hospitals,
volunteers, prisoners, horses
SYMBOLS AND ATTRIBUTES: Children,
heart, flames

St. Vincent de Paul was a French Catholic priest and humanitarian. He was born in Pouy, Gascony, France, and educated by the Cordeliers, a Franciscan order in Dax, then ordained in 1600. As a young man, while traveling by sea, he was captured by Turkish pirates and sold into slavery in Tunis. A persuasive faith-filled speaker, Vincent converted his captor to Christianity and escaped in 1607. Upon his return to France, he deepened his commitment to the Church through further studies in Avignon and Rome. Vincent was appointed a chaplain to Queen Marguerite of Valois and was subsequently granted the Abbey of Saint-Léonard-de-Chaume to pastor.

At this time, his charitable work began in earnest, focusing initially on the parish of Clichy near Paris. Guided by his spiritual connection with Madame de Gondi, a wealthy benefactor, Vincent initiated missions to assist the poor on her and her husband's estates. These efforts led to the establishment of charities to aid those in need.

Vincent also began to minister to convicts and was appointed the royal almoner, or distributor of alms to prisoners, by King Louis XIII. He worked hard to improve their conditions. He also established hospitals in Marseilles.

Vincent de Paul's dedication culminated in the foundation of the Congregation of the Mission (Vincentians or Lazarists), committed to spreading the Church's teachings and assisting the needy. Additionally, he founded the Daughters of Charity, a religious institute devoted to serving the needy, known for their distinctive headdress and apron. Vincent's work extended to orphans, the elderly, and anyone needing shelter and employment. His efforts reached beyond France, including endeavors to free enslaved Christians in Barbary.

Vincent's vision for the Congregation of the Mission was to also provide spiritual guidance and support to those in rural areas, where access to religious services and schooling was often limited. The Vincentians helped to form priests, while establishing seminaries for clerics, ensuring that they were well-prepared to serve their communities. The order continues to be active today, operating in various parts of the world, carrying forward St. Vincent de Paul's mission of service and compassion.

Vincent was canonized in 1737 by Pope Clement XII.

VINCENT FERRER

BORN: January 23, 1350, Valencia, Spain

DIED: April 5, 1419, Vannes, France

FEAST DAY: April 5

PATRONAGE: Builders, construction workers, plumbers, fishermen

SYMBOLS AND ATTRIBUTES: Dominican habit, wings, pulpit, trumpet, book

Vincent Ferrer, also known as Vincent of Valencia, was a Dominican friar and preacher during the fourteenth and fifteenth centuries. He was born into a devout Christian family. His father, William Ferrer, served in the court of King Alfonso IV of Aragon, and his mother, Constantia Miguel, was a woman of remarkable faith. From a young age, Vincent showed extraordinary intelligence and a deep interest in religious matters. He pursued his education at the University of Lleida; at the age of 18, he joined the Dominican order and was later sent to Barcelona to complete his studies. He then began teaching at Lleida, a city in western Catalonia, and then returned to Barcelona, where he gained fame for his accurate predictions regarding the timely arrival of grain ships during a famine.

In the following years, Vincent became an advisor to Cardinal Pedro de Luna, who became the antipope Benedict XIII. He served as a confessor and apostolic penitentiary to Benedict XIII in Avignon, France. This position arose after Benedict's irregular election as a rival pope in 1394. Vincent declined all the honors and offices Benedict XIII offered him, including the cardinalate, choosing instead to focus on his preaching and spiritual work.

According to Matthew Bunson, during a French siege of Avignon in 1398, Vincent contracted an illness and almost died. During his convalescence, he underwent a miraculous healing following a vision in which he saw Jesus, St. Dominic, and St. Francis of Assisi. In this spiritual encounter, he was instructed to go forth beyond the land he knew as home and spread the Word of God. However, Benedict XIII initially resisted Vincent's departure from Avignon due to the political and military battles at the time. Finally, around 1399, Benedict granted permission for Vincent, who was known for eloquence and passionate delivery, to embark on a preaching tour across Western Europe.

One of the defining characteristics of Vincent Ferrer's preaching was his emphasis on eschatology, or the study of the end times and the Second Coming of Christ. He believed that the world was nearing its final stages and that repentance and spiritual renewal were of utmost importance. Vincent's sermons were marked by a sense of urgency, calling upon people to turn away from sin and embrace God's grace. He became known as the Angel of Judgment, or the Angel of the Apocalypse for his sermons on the end times, which reflected the religious and social climate of his time. The fourteenth and fifteenth centuries witnessed various challenges, including the aftermath of the Black Death, political instability, and religious divisions. Vincent's preaching provided a sense of hope and direction in a tumultuous era, offering guidance on navigating the dire present while looking forward to the promise of eternal life.

In Spain in 1410, Vincent Ferrer was appointed as one of the nine judges tasked with deciding the succession to the crown of Aragon. King Ferdinand I, also known as Ferdinand the Just, was ultimately chosen as the successor, ruling from 1412 to 1416.

Vincent Ferrer's reputation as a miracle worker also contributed to his prominence. Numerous accounts describe him as healing the sick, raising the dead, and performing other extraordinary deeds. These miracles along with his persuasive preaching earned him a widespread following, leading to his unofficial recognition as a saint shortly after his death, which occurred on April 5, 1419, in Vannes, France. In 1455, Pope Callixtus III canonized Vincent Ferrer, officially recognizing him as a saint of the Catholic Church. He is often depicted in religious art holding a crucifix and a trumpet, symbolizing his role as a herald of the Second Coming.

VITUS

BORN: c. 290, Sicily
DIED: c. 303, Lucania, Italy
FEAST DAY: June 15

PATRONAGE: Actors, comedians, dancers, dogs, people with epilepsy, oversleeping, protection against lightning, protection against snake bites
SYMBOLS AND ATTRIBUTES: Rooster, palm branch, kettle

St. Vitus, also known as St. Guy, was a Christian martyr who lived in the third century. He is considered one of the Fourteen Holy Helpers. According to tradition, Vitus was born in Sicily to a noble Christian family. Early in his life, he embraced his faith and became known for his virtue and dedication to God. To escape Diocletian persecution, Vitus, his tutor Modestus, and his nurse Crescentia fled Sicily and eventually ended up in Rome, a city not known for religious tolerance. There, they continued openly professing their faith and converting many people to Christianity. This drew the ire of the Roman authorities, and Vitus, Modestus, and Crescentia were arrested and brought before the prefect of Rome.

Vitus and his companions remained firm in their devotion to Christ. Legends recount that while in prison, Vitus healed the sick and performed miracles. The Roman prefect, unable to break his spirit, eventually ordered the execution of the young man and his companions. Various accounts claim that Vitus was martyred by being thrown into a boiling cauldron of oil or by being fed to the lions in an amphitheater.

After his death, Vitus's popularity grew and he was venerated by many. Devotees were known to dance around his statue, a ritual later termed the St. Vitus Dance. This term was later used to describe a neurological disorder that caused involuntary movements.

Vitus became revered as a patron saint of dancers, actors, and those suffering from epilepsy, nervous disorders, and snake bites. His relics were said to have been transferred to various locations, including Sicily, where they were enshrined in a church dedicated to him. The veneration of St. Vitus spread throughout Europe, particularly in Germany, where numerous churches and chapels were dedicated to him. Over time, St. Vitus became associated with various legends and miracles, with accounts of his intercession providing healing and protection.

WENCESLAUS

BORN: c. 907, Prague, Bohemia
(modern-day Czech Republic)
DIED: September 28, 935, Stará
Boleslav, Bohemia

FEAST DAY: September 28
PATRONAGE: The Bohemian people
SYMBOLS AND ATTRIBUTES: Lance,
crown, armor

A revered figure in Christian history, St. Wenceslaus, also known as St. Václav, was born into the Přemyslid dynasty around 907. He was raised under the guidance of his esteemed paternal grandmother, Ludmilla. His father, Duke Vratislaus I, a devout Catholic, passed away, and Wenceslaus assumed the throne of Bohemia when he was thirteen. Because of his age, Wenceslaus's pagan mother, Drahomira, reigned for her son. She was a brutal ruler, so much so that around 924, Wenceslaus overthrew her to take back control of his kingdom.

Wenceslaus's reign was marked by his commitment to upholding his father's values, promoting Christianity as the state religion, and fostering peace within his kingdom. He worked to improve the spiritual and moral well-being of his subjects. He founded churches, supported clergy, and promoted learning, aiming to spread the message of Christianity and cultivate a just and prosperous society.

In addition to his religious pursuits, Wenceslaus demonstrated a strong sense of justice and compassion. He was known for his charitable acts and generosity toward the poor, earning him a reputation as a protector of the weak and vulnerable.

However, Wenceslaus's commitment to righteousness and efforts to unify Bohemia drew the ire of his younger brother Boleslaus. In 935, Boleslaus and his deposed mother conspired against Wenceslaus and orchestrated his assassination. Wenceslaus was murdered while on his way to morning prayers on September 28, 935. He is widely celebrated for his virtues and regarded as a national hero by the Czech people.

St. Wenceslaus is prominently featured in the Christmas carol "Good King Wenceslas." The song narrates a fictional account of St. Wenceslaus and his page braving harsh winter weather to help the poor on St. Stephen's Day (December 26). He is also often depicted in artworks, stained glass windows, and statues. These depictions typically show him as a noble, devout figure, often accompanied by symbols such as a crown, a cross, or the Czech coat of arms. His relics were enshrined in the Church of St. Vitus in Prague, which became a significant pilgrimage site. The feast day of St. Wenceslaus is celebrated on September 28, the anniversary of his martyrdom. (See Stephen.)

Z

ZECHARIAH

BORN: 1st century BC
DIED: c. 1st century AD
FEAST DAY: September 23

PATRONAGE: Fatherhood, grandparents, bishops
SYMBOLS AND ATTRIBUTES: Book, scroll

St. Zechariah, also known as St. Zachariah, is the father of St. John the Baptist and the husband of St. Elizabeth. In the Gospel of Luke, he is depicted as a righteous man and devout priest. After years of yearning for a child, the angel Gabriel appeared to him and Elizabeth, who were in their old age at the time, and informed them that they would have a child and would name him John. Zechariah responded to the heavenly messenger with disbelief, and as a consequence, Gabriel rendered him mute for doubting God's plan. This condition lasted until the birth of his son. When he confirmed that the child would be named John, his speech was restored. (See Elizabeth, John the Baptist.)

ZITA

BORN: 1212, Lucca, Italy

DIED: 1272, Lucca, Italy

FEAST DAY: April 27

PATRONAGE: Domestic servants, lost keys, homemakers, waiters, waitresses

SYMBOLS AND ATTRIBUTES: Wheat, bread, keys

St. Zita, also known as Santa Zita or St. Sitha, was a humble and devout Christian who lived during the thirteenth century in Lucca, a city in modern-day Italy. Born in 1212, she dedicated her life to serving God and others, particularly through her commitment to domestic work and charity.

She worked as a domestic servant in the household of the Fatinelli family, where she gained a reputation for extraordinary virtue. She performed daily duties with exceptional care and devotion, and her work was often accompanied by acts of charity toward the poor and marginalized. Her deep faith and unwavering commitment to her vocation made her an exemplary model of Christian service.

She became famous through her miracles, including instances of multiplying food for the hungry and healing the sick. She could also communicate with angels, and routinely asked for their assistance. One story tells of an occasion when Zita was preparing bread for the household. As she began kneading the dough, angelic beings appeared to her and assisted in the task, kneading the dough themselves, allowing her to complete the baking quickly and effortlessly.

After she died in 1272, her reputation as a woman of sanctity grew, and she was officially canonized by Pope Innocent XII in 1696.

St. Zita is often invoked as the patron saint of domestic servants. Her example serves as an inspiration for those who labor in humble and often overlooked roles, reminding them of the inherent dignity and value of their work. Her life also emphasizes the importance of integrating faith into everyday life and finding spiritual fulfillment in even the most ordinary tasks.

ZYGMUNT GORAZDOWSKI

BORN: November 1, 1845, Sanok, (modern-day Poland)

DIED: January 1, 1920, Lwów, Poland (modern-day Lviv, Ukraine)

FEAST DAY: January 1

PATRONAGE: Sisters of St. Joseph

SYMBOLS AND ATTRIBUTES: Priestly vestments, crucifix

According to Pope Benedict XVI, St. Zygmunt Gorazdowski was a priest of immense dedication and compassion. Serving in various parishes, he was devoted to his pastoral responsibilities and the welfare of his community. This commitment was most evident during a devastating cholera outbreak in Wojnilow, during which Gorazdowski tended to the ailing and the deceased. In addition to his pastoral duties, he authored and disseminated religious materials to guide and educate his parishioners while pioneering numerous apostolic initiatives to aid the marginalized and impoverished.

In 1877, he embarked on a monumental spiritual and humanitarian endeavor at the Parish of St. Nicholas in Lviv, dedicating four decades of his life to its service. Under his leadership, the parish saw the establishment of various institutions, each tailored to the specific needs of the community: a refuge and soup kitchen for the destitute, specialized health-care facilities, and schools for the underprivileged. To ensure the sustainability and expansion of these charitable efforts, Gorazdowski founded in 1884 the Congregation of the Sisters of St. Joseph. Often called the "father of the poor and priest of the homeless," Zygmunt passed away in Lviv on January 1, 1920, leaving a legacy of altruism and faith-driven service.

He was beatified by Pope John Paul II in 2001 during the pope's visit to Ukraine. Pope Benedict XVI canonized Zygmunt Gorazdowski as a saint in the Roman Catholic Church on October 23, 2005.

ANGELS

Angels, according to the Catechism of the Catholic Church, are "spiritual, non-corporeal beings" who serve as intermediaries between the Divine and humanity. The word *angel* comes from the Greek *angelos*, which means "messenger." Angels appear throughout the Bible. They exist at the dawning of creation, serve and worship God, aid humankind, and stand triumphant at the end of time. They exist as part of a heavenly hierarchy. Many saints, from St. Augustine to St. Denis the Areopagite, have written about this hierarchy, setting forth different interpretations of its composition.

Though the Catholic Church has no official teaching on the ranks, St. Gregory the Great believed that the hierarchy comprised nine orders of angels. St. Thomas Aquinas "divides the angels into three hierarchies, each containing three orders. Their proximity to the Supreme Being serves as the basis of this division" (*Catholic Encyclopedia*). The first and highest order comprises Seraphim, Cherubim, and Thrones; the middle order consists of Dominions, Virtues, and Powers; while the lowest order encompasses Principalities, Archangels, and Angels (including guardian angels).

SERAPHIM

Seraphim are considered the highest order of angels. The name derives from the Hebrew word *saraph*, which means "to burn" or "fiery one." The Seraphim are often depicted as six-winged beings, with two wings covering their faces, two covering their feet, and two used for flying. As the name implies, they are associated with the element of fire, which is thought to symbolize their intense love for God.

The first mention of the Seraphim in the Bible appears in the book of Isaiah, where the prophet describes his vision of these heavenly and enigmatic figures. In this vision, the Seraphim are seen encircling the throne of God. They call out to each other, "Holy, holy, holy is the Lord of hosts; the whole earth is full of his glory!" (Isaiah 6:3). This verse has been used by scholars to support the idea that the Seraphim are the angels closest to God and that their purpose is to praise His name.

Although the Seraphim are often depicted in art as peaceful creatures, their intense love and devotion to God makes them intimidating and awe-inspiring, or as the poet Rainer Maria Rilke writes in the *Duino Elegies*, "terrifying." And yet they have a deep love of and concern for humanity. Tradition holds that they are sent by God to guide individuals on their spiritual journey. In the book of Revelation, the Seraphim are depicted holding bowls of incense, which are said to represent the prayers of the saints, suggesting that the Seraphim are intimately involved in the spiritual lives of believers, helping to lift up their prayers and bring them to God as offerings. In addition, the element of fire, with which the Seraphim are associated, also serves as a metaphor for the concept of purification. In the same way that intense heat can burn away impurities, leaving behind only what is pure and holy, the Seraphim help to purify and cleanse the souls of believers, enabling them to become more holy and therefore closer to God.

CHERUBIM

Cherubim rank as the second highest order of angels. Traditionally, Cherubim are associated with wisdom and guardianship. Although the concept of the Cherubim originates in Jewish Scripture, their role and symbolism have become part of the Catholic faith.

The term *Cherubim* derives from the Hebrew *kerub,* meaning "to bless." In Jewish Scripture, Cherubim are portrayed as winged creatures that serve as spiritual sentinels. They make their initial appearance in Genesis. After the expulsion of Adam and Eve from the Garden of Eden, God stationed Cherubim wielding flaming swords to guard the path to the Tree of Life.

Cherubim appear as two intricately crafted golden figures adorning the lid of the Ark of the Covenant, referred to as the "mercy seat." The two Cherubim face each other, their wings unfurled overhead, providing a protective canopy over the Ark. In the book of Kings, Solomon's temple is said to have housed grand Cherubim statues within its innermost sanctuary. However, the physical depiction of Cherubim in the Hebrew Bible is not always as clear-cut as in these two examples. Some Scriptures present Cherubim as winged beings drawing divine chariots, as in the visions of the prophet Ezekiel. In these revelations, they each possess four faces—human, lion, ox, and eagle—and are integrated into an intricate visionary tableau that includes wheels, fire, and the divine throne.

In Catholicism, Cherubim are frequently linked to wisdom and knowledge. In art they have been popularly rendered as cherubs—plump, rosy-cheeked infants with wings. This endearing interpretation, markedly different from the majestic Biblical Cherubim, gained traction during the Renaissance. Theologically, Cherubim stand as guardians of the divine presence, and, as such, they symbolize God's sanctity, grandeur, and the profound chasm between the heavenly and human realms. Their placement in sacred spaces and their presence during pivotal Biblical events underscore the significance of divine encounters.

THRONES

The Thrones, the "many-eyed ones," are the third-highest order of angels (after the Seraphim and the Cherubim). The name comes from the Greek *thronos,* which means "seat" or "throne," reflecting their role as divine judges responsible for upholding God's justice in the world. They are often depicted as holding the books of judgment or the scales of justice. The Thrones also act as intermediaries between God and the lower angels, conveying divine messages and carrying out God's will. As St. Thomas Aquinas writes, "They are bearers of God and wholly capable of undertaking all that is divine."

One of the most iconic depictions of the Thrones comes from the book of Ezekiel in the Hebrew Bible. In Ezekiel's vision these heavenly beings are metaphorically depicted as "wheels within wheels"—a symbol of their connection to the ever-turning will of God and its ability to move in all directions. In the apocryphal book of Enoch, the Thrones, otherwise known as the *ophanim*, are described as wheels with many eyes, symbolizing their all-seeing nature and spiritual insight; these angelic beings are responsible for maintaining divine order in the universe and guiding the movement of heavenly bodies and celestial events.

DOMINIONS

The Dominions are believed to be the fourth-highest order of angels and are often depicted holding a scepter or a staff, which symbolizes their authority. The name Dominions comes from the Latin *dominus*, which means "lord" or "master." The Dominions are associated with leadership and governance, and are sometimes referred to as "Dominations," "Lordships," or "Potentates."

In Catholic tradition, the Dominions are mentioned in Colossians 1:16: "For by Him all things were created, in Heaven and on earth, visible and invisible, whether thrones or dominions or rulers or authorities—all things were created through Him and for Him." Though little is known about this order, they are often acknowledged as the regulators of the lower orders of angels; their role is to ensure that the lower angelic ranks fulfill their heavenly duties.

VIRTUES

Virtues, sometimes also referred to as Strongholds, are associated with the idea of moral excellence and the strengthening of faith. Virtues comes from the Latin *virtus*, which means "moral excellence." As divine warriors and intermediaries, they are responsible for maintaining the natural order of the cosmos, and for helping believers strengthen their faith. In Hebrew tradition they are sometimes referred to as *Hashmallim*, angelic beings associated with the element of electricity or amber-like substances, and are mentioned in Ezekiel's vision of God's throne.

According to sixth-century Christian theologian Pseudo-Dionysius the Areopagite, the Virtues govern and direct the movements of heavenly bodies, including stars, planets, and other celestial entities. In the medieval worldview, celestial bodies were believed to influence events and phenomena on Earth. Along with their role in guiding heavenly bodies, the Virtues are also thought to oversee the laws governing the natural elements, the seasons, and the cycles of nature. They are also seen as the guardians of God's moral order and often are invoked for guidance and protection in matters of moral, ethical decision-making. As celestial agents in charge of governing nature and carrying out supernatural events, they are also associated with the working of miracles.

POWERS

The Powers, often termed Authorities or Potestates, are a lower, though still commanding, order of angels. Derived from the Greek *dynamis*, meaning "strength," the Powers are the sixth-highest angelic rank. Their primary role is to shield humanity from evil; unsurprisingly, then, they are typically portrayed as sword-wielding, shield-wearing warriors.

Within Catholic tradition, the Powers are synonymous with spiritual warfare. They act as divine agents to combat evil forces, thus becoming symbols of God's strength. Consequently, they are invoked during prayers for protection, strength, and courage, and most especially during spiritual battles. Exorcists often rely on the Powers to assist them in casting out demons.

Despite their warrior-like depiction, the Powers are believed to have deep compassion for humans. God often dispatches them to safeguard individuals during spiritual endeavors. The Powers represent God's protective dedication to humanity. In Romans 8:38, Paul writes, "For I am convinced that neither death nor life, neither angels nor demons, neither the present nor the future, nor any powers, neither height nor depth, nor anything else in all creation, will be able to separate us from the love of God that is in Christ Jesus our Lord." Here, "powers" is mentioned among the list of spiritual entities and circumstances, but even though they have a formidable nature, they cannot separate believers from the love of God in Christ Jesus.

PRINCIPALITIES

The seventh order, the Principalities, are considered guardian angels of institutions, nations, and rulers. Their task is to carry out the orders given to them by the Dominions, then dispense these orders to the Archangels and Angels below them. Sometimes considered protectors of religions, the Principalities closely monitor the moral and spiritual direction of human communities such as the Church, and oversee large groups of people.

ARCHANGELS

Archangels may refer to two different types of angels. Commonly, they are members of the second-to-lowest order of angels. They are nevertheless powerful celestial beings who act as messengers to and guardians of humans. The term *Archangel* comes from the Greek *archē,* meaning "chief" and *angelos,* meaning "messenger" or "angel." Some theologians and exorcists believe that the term *Archangel* means that they're the most powerful angels ever created and oversee all angelic orders.

Archangels are called upon in prayers for guidance, protection, and support during challenging times. The New Testament mentions the word *archangel* twice. In 1 Thessalonians 4:16, Paul comforts the Thessalonians, addressing their worries about the fate of the dead prior to Jesus's return. The moment Christ returns from Heaven, marked by the call of the Archangel and the sound of God's trumpet, will herald the resurrection of those who have died in Him. The second reference is in Jude 1:9, where the Archangel Michael is discussed: "But when the archangel Michael, contending with the devil, was disputing about the body of Moses, he did not presume to pronounce a blasphemous judgment, but said, 'The Lord rebuke you.'" This text intentionally tackles apostasy and false teachings (the verse alludes to an event from a Jewish apocryphal text called the Assumption of Moses). In this instance, the Archangel guards humanity's moral character through example: "Judge not lest you be judged."

The Catholic Church acknowledges the names of only three Archangels: Michael, Gabriel, and Raphael. The Eastern Orthodox Church recognizes four additional Archangels: Uriel, angel of light and wisdom; Selaphiel, angel of prayer and devotion; Jegudiel, angel of mercy and benevolence; and Barachiel, angel of blessings and prosperity. Though some scholars believe that the Archangels Michael and Gabriel are of a higher ranking, they are included here as they are most often associated with the rank of Archangel.

MICHAEL

St. Michael the Archangel is a significant figure in various religious traditions, including Christianity, Judaism, and Islam. His name, which means "Who is like God?" reflects his unwavering loyalty and obedience to the Almighty. He is often depicted as a mighty winged figure clad in armor and carrying a sword. Though he never lived as a human being, the angel Michael, along with Gabriel and Raphael, is considered a saint in Catholicism as well as in some other Christian denominations.

In the Hebrew Bible, particularly in the book of Daniel, Michael is mentioned in several passages, highlighting his role as a powerful and protective figure. In Daniel 10:13, the prophet Daniel has a vision of an angelic being who is delivering a message. During this encounter, the angel mentions that he was delayed by the "prince of the kingdom of

PLATE IX
Michael

Persia" and that only the assistance of Michael enabled him to break free so that he could make his way to Daniel. This reference suggests that Michael plays a significant role in overcoming spiritual opposition to deliver God's message, not just for human beings but for other angelic beings, too.

In Daniel 12:1, Michael is depicted as "the great prince" who stands up for God's people during a time of distress: "At that time shall arise Michael, the great prince who has charge of your people. And there shall be a time of trouble, such as never has been since there was a nation till that time." These passages present Michael as a heavenly figure who defends and supports God's faithful against spiritual adversaries. His presence symbolizes divine protection, assistance, and victory over opposition and evil forces.

In addition, Michael appears in the Talmud, where he is described as one of the angels who aided Abraham in his discussions with the wicked King Nimrod. According to the tradition, Nimrod sought to challenge Abraham's belief in the one true God, and Michael supported Abraham in his responses to Nimrod's inquiries. In this Jewish text, Michael is described as one of the angels who stands in the presence of God and receives divine knowledge. The Talmud also mentions Michael alongside other angelic figures like Gabriel, Uriel, and Raphael.

Michael's prominence increased in Christian traditions, particularly Roman Catholicism and the Eastern churches, where he is entrusted with significant tasks in the divine hierarchy, including leading God's army of angels against the forces of darkness. According to Christian beliefs, Michael is a central figure in the war in Heaven described in the book of Revelation (Chapter 12:7–9). He led the faithful angels in battle against the rebellious angel Lucifer (often identified as either Satan or the devil) and cast Lucifer and his followers out of Heaven. This event is commonly referred to as the "Fall of the Angels" or the "War in Heaven." Michael's victory over the forces of evil solidified his status as the heavenly champion and the patron saint of soldiers and warriors.

Michael is also associated with other notable events and figures in Christian tradition. According to the book of Jude, Michael fought the devil over the burial of Moses's body. In some narratives, Archangel Michael appears to Constantine the Great on a number of occasions, including as a vision of the Angel in a dream. This encounter led to the conversion of a pagan shrine into a Christian sanctuary known as the Michaelion, which is located just outside Istanbul. The Church also celebrates on May 8 the feast of The Apparition of St. Michael. This special day commemorates several visitations by the Archangel to the bishop and some of the inhabitants at Mount Gargano in Southern Italy between 492 and 496. Miracles followed, including a spent arrow that defied physics, victory in a local battle, and protection during a time of pestilence.

According to some accounts, Michael appeared to St. Francis in a vision and guided him in his spiritual journey and mission to rebuild the Church. Joan of Arc claimed that Michael instructed her to support Charles VII of France, the Dauphin, during the

Hundred Years War to help him reclaim his rightful throne. St. Padre Pio, a twentieth-century Italian priest and mystic, is also said to have had mystical experiences with Michael, who defended and protected him from demonic attacks.

In Islam, Michael, known as Mikail, is considered one of the Archangels, along with Jibril (Gabriel), Israfil, and Azrael. Each Archangel has distinct duties and responsibilities assigned by Allah. Mikail is the angel of mercy entrusted with significant tasks in Islamic belief. While the Quran doesn't mention Mikail by name, Islamic tradition upholds his importance based on Hadith, which are sayings and actions of the Prophet Muhammad. The Hadith literature references Mikail's role particularly in overseeing the distribution of sustenance as well as blessings and provisions from Allah to all creatures on Earth. These duties include providing rain, fertility, and sustenance in accordance with Allah's divine plan. Mikail is regarded as a devoted servant of Allah, faithfully carrying out His commands and acting as an intermediary between Allah and humanity to ensure the implementation of divine decrees.

Michael has attracted a devoted following throughout history, with numerous churches, chapels, and monasteries dedicated to his honor. The veneration of Michael was especially prominent in medieval Europe. Several grand cathedrals, including Mont-Saint-Michel in France and Michael's Mount in England, were constructed in his honor.

In the modern era, devotion to Michael remains strong, especially in Catholicism where he is revered as a powerful intercessor and a symbol of God's strength and victory over evil. He is an angel of justice and guardian of the Church.

St. Michael's feast day is celebrated on September 29. This day, when the Catholic Church also honors the Archangels Gabriel and Raphael, is collectively known as the Feast of the Archangels or the Feast of Saints Michael, Gabriel, and Raphael. Michael's feast day is November 8 in many Eastern churches.

GABRIEL

The angel Gabriel holds significant importance in the Abrahamic faiths of Judaism, Christianity, and Islam. Gabriel is the angel of revelation, mercy, Annunciation, and resurrection.

In the Old Testament, Gabriel is not explicitly mentioned by name, but some scholars believe Gabriel may be associated with certain anonymous angels who appear in various passages. In the book of Daniel (Daniel 8:15–26; 9:20–27), an angel, traditionally believed to be Gabriel, provides Daniel with interpretations of visions and prophecies. In the book of Zechariah (Zechariah 1:7–17; 2:1–13; 5:1–11), there are references to various angelic beings who deliver messages; Gabriel is believed to be one of these divine couriers.

In the Talmud, Gabriel is mentioned in a discussion of celestial beings as one of the angels who stands on the left side of God's throne. The Midrash, a collection of rabbinic commentaries on the Hebrew Bible, also contains references to Gabriel. In Midrash Tadshe (Genesis Rabbah 32:5), Gabriel offers divine guidance and support to Hagar, the mother of Abraham's son Ishmael.

In the New Testament, Gabriel heralds the Annunciation of the birth of Jesus. In the Gospel of Luke, Gabriel first appears to the elderly Zechariah to announce the miraculous conceiving of John the Baptist, his son, with his wife, Elizabeth. He then appears to the Virgin Mary, Elizabeth's cousin, and informs her that she will conceive a child by the Holy Spirit and give birth to the Son of God.

In Islamic tradition, Gabriel is known as Jibril. Considered one of the most important angels, he is believed to have been entrusted with the revelation of the Quran to the Prophet Muhammad. According to Islamic teachings, Gabriel appeared to Muhammad over a period of twenty-three years, delivering the divine messages that form the basis of the Islamic faith.

In Christian art, the Archangel Gabriel is often depicted as a majestic, radiant figure extravagantly adorned with dramatic wings and wearing luxuriant, flowing robes. He is typically shown holding a lily, a sign of purity, or a trumpet, which symbolizes his role as a messenger and his announcement of important news, such as the Annunciation to the Virgin Mary. Famous artworks featuring Gabriel include Leonardo da Vinci's *Annunciation* and Sandro Botticelli's *Cestello Annunciation*. John Milton's epic poem *Paradise Lost* portrays Gabriel as one of the Archangels in Heaven who, as a loyal messenger of God, participates in significant events such as the War in Heaven and the expulsion of Adam and Eve from the Garden of Eden.

Gabriel's feast day is commemorated on September 29 in the Catholic Church, where he is regarded as the patron saint of messengers, postal workers, and telecommunications workers. He is also known as a patron of diplomats, ambassadors, and those involved in peace negotiations, and is considered a patron of clergy members, priests, and religious vocations because of his association with divine announcements.

RAPHAEL

Raphael is an angel of great prominence in the Jewish, Christian, and Islamic traditions. His name means "God heals" or "He who heals" in Hebrew.

Raphael is featured prominently in the Book of Tobit, a canonical Biblical text in the Roman Catholic and Orthodox Christian traditions; however, the Book of Tobit is considered apocryphal by Protestants and Jews. In this colorful narrative, Tobit, an Israelite from the tribe of Naphtali, was exiled to Nineveh in Assyria. Despite his circumstances,

Tobit remained devout, even after he became blind from bird droppings falling into his eyes. Tobit was known for burying the dead against the king's decree, which led to his persecution.

At the same time, in a different city, a young woman named Sarah suffered torment at the hands of a fiendish demon named Asmodeus. This evil spirit had killed each man she married, seven in total, on their wedding night, preventing the consummation of her marriages.

Tobit wants to retrieve a sum of money he left in trust in a distant city. He sends his son, Tobias, to undertake this task. To help Tobias on this journey, God sends the Archangel Raphael, who disguises himself as a relative of Tobit, a man named Azarias.

Early in their journey, while Tobias is washing his feet in the river, a large fish tries to swallow his foot. Under Raphael's instruction, Tobias catches the fish and removes its heart, liver, and gallbladder, preserving them for later use. Upon reaching their destination, Raphael introduces Tobias to Sarah and arranges their marriage. Raphael suggests using the fish's heart and liver to drive away the demon that has been tormenting Sarah. Tobias and Sarah pray, burn the fish's organs, and exorcise the devil, whom Raphael binds in an Egyptian desert. Upon returning home, under Raphael's guidance, Tobias applies the fish's gallbladder to Tobit's eyes, which cures his father's blindness.

After these miraculous events, Raphael reveals his true identity to Tobit and Tobias. He explains that he was sent by God to help them in their mission and tells them that God heard and remembered their prayers, alms, and good deeds. Raphael admonishes Tobit and Tobias to proclaim the wondrous deeds of God, after which he returns to Heaven.

The story, famous throughout the centuries, emphasizes faith, holiness, and the intercession of angels. Raphael's role as a guide, healer, and protector is instrumental in exemplifying divine intervention in the lives of the faithful.

Raphael also appears in the book of Enoch, a noncanonical text but a well-known pseudepigraphic work. Enoch provides an elaborate narrative about the fallen angels, known as the Watchers, and their offspring, the Nephilim. In this series of stories, Raphael confronts the demon Azazel, who led humans astray by teaching them various forbidden arts, including warfare and the use of cosmetics. Raphael is tasked with binding Azazel, casting him into darkness, and burying him beneath jagged rocks in the desert to ensure that he will remain there until the final judgment. Following the corruption brought about by the Watchers, Raphael also plays a role in healing the Earth from the damage done by Satan and his minions.

While Raphael is not explicitly mentioned in the Quran, many Islamic scholars identify him with the angel Israfil (also Israfel). In Islamic eschatology, Israfil is the angel who will blow the trumpet to announce the Day of Judgment.

In art, Raphael is often depicted holding a staff, representing his role as a healer and guide, or a fish, which refers to the intervention he made on behalf of Tobias. Raphael is recognized as the patron of travelers, persons who are blind, health-care workers, and matchmakers. He is often invoked for matters related to healing. His feast day is celebrated on September 29, along with the Archangels Michael and Gabriel.

URIEL

Uriel, whose name translates to "God is my light," is considered an Archangel in many faith traditions. While he is not explicitly mentioned in the Hebrew Bible, Jewish mystical and apocryphal traditions recognize him as an angel of wisdom, enlightenment, and prophecy. Similarly, while Uriel is absent from the Christian canonical Scriptures, his existence is acknowledged in various apocryphal texts, including the book of Enoch, where he is identified as one of the chief Archangels and is portrayed as the angel of thunder and awe. Some traditions hold that Uriel was the angel who warned Noah of the flood, and that he was the angelic being who inspected the door frames of the Israelites for blood during the inaugural Passover.

Uriel is venerated in the Anglican Church, most especially on the feast of the Archangels. In Orthodox iconography, Uriel is often depicted wielding a flaming sword, symbolizing the flame of truth, in his right hand, and clutching a crystal orb, which represents divine clarity or wisdom, in his left.

SELAPHIEL

Selaphiel is one of the seven Archangels recognized in the Eastern Orthodox Christian tradition. He is typically depicted in a posture of humility, in a deep bow, with his face and eyes downcast, and engrossed in prayer. This position starkly contrasts with the more assertive or combative stances often attributed to angels like Michael, who is frequently shown brandishing a sword.

Selaphiel's unusual posture conveys reverence, submission, and devotion. The pose reminds the faithful of the gravity and importance of prayer, indicating that even heavenly beings demonstrate utmost respect and earnestness when communicating with God. Based on its Hebrew etymology, Selaphiel's name decisively derives from *Selah*, which means "to pray," and *El*, meaning "God." As such, Selaphiel's name encapsulates his primary role: "The Prayer of God" or "One Who Prays to God." Within this role, he isn't just an angel who communicates with God; he is the patron and protector of prayers and of those who pray. He is also an advisor and motivator, spiritually prompting believers to engage more deeply in the Almighty.

JEGUDIEL

Jegudiel, also known as Jehudiel or Yehudiel, is one of the seven Archangels in certain Christian traditions, especially within the Eastern Orthodox Church. His name means "Praise of God" or "Laudation of God." Archangel Jegudiel is often depicted holding in his right hand a golden crown, symbolizing the reward for successful spiritual labor, and, in his left hand, a three-pronged whip, representing the need for spiritual discipline and diligence. As the patron of all those who work, he encourages and guides the faithful in their tasks and duties. He is also invoked for counsel and direction in making difficult decisions, as well as for fortitude needed to overcome obstacles in one's spiritual journey.

BARACHIEL

Barachiel, also spelled Barakiel or Barchiel, is recognized as one of the seven Archangels in the Eastern Orthodox Church. The name "Barachiel" is often translated as "Blessing of God." Barachiel is invoked for God's divine favor in various aspects of life. In iconography, he is often depicted holding a white rose against his chest, symbolizing the blessings from God. He is also sometimes portrayed with rose petals scattered on his cloak, or holding a basket of bread, representing the blessings of children. Barachiel is considered the chief of the guardian angels.

ANGELS

As the lowest order of angelic beings, angels are responsible for carrying out God's tasks on Earth. In Catholic tradition, they were created by God and are commonly understood to have three primary roles: worshipping and praising God; acting as messengers or intermediaries between God and humans; and serving as guardians and guides for earthly individuals. Often depicted as winged beings, angels, like their other celestial comrades, are immortal. They are endowed with knowledge and can understand spiritual truths more deeply than humans. However, they do not possess the fullness of divine knowledge, and therefore depend on God for revelation, nor are they privileged to enjoy the corporal experience.

GUARDIAN ANGELS

Guardian angels provide protection and guidance for individuals. The belief in an invisible, spiritual agent dates back to the time of early Mesopotamian civilizations like the Babylonians and Sumerians.

The Catholic Church offers specific teachings about guardian angels that are rooted in Scripture. In Exodus, God promises Moses: "I am sending an angel ahead of you to guard you along the way and to bring you to the place I have prepared" (Exodus 23:20). In the New Testament, Jesus underscores their importance: "In heaven, the angels of these little ones always see the face of my Father" (Matthew 18:10, ESV).

As outlined in the *Catechism of the Catholic Church* (CCC), each human is enveloped by the diligent care of these angels throughout life: "Beside each believer stands an angel as protector and shepherd leading him to life" (CCC 336). This sentiment was echoed by early Church figures including St. Basil and St. Jerome, who emphasized the special bond between souls and their guardian angels.

The belief in angels was solidified during the Lateran Council of 1215. Though not exclusively about guardian angels, the council reaffirmed the genuine existence of the angelic realm and its bond with humanity.

Guardian angels are seen as guiding forces leading believers to Heaven. St. Thomas Aquinas's teachings suggest that only the lowest tier of angels are designated guardians, and every soul, not just the baptized, receives such protection. This protection is not absolute, however: guardian angels can influence our senses and imagination but not directly our will.

They remain with souls even in the afterlife, though their roles change once that soul arrives in Heaven. St. Aloysius Gonzaga taught that a guardian angel accompanies the departing soul, helping it face God's judgment confidently. If a human soul moves on to to Heaven, it enters into the communion of saints, praising God along with the angels.

AVENGING ANGELS

Avenging angels are celestial beings believed to carry out God's justice. Though they are not a formal part of Catholic doctrine in the way saints or Archangels are, their existence is inferred from various scriptural passages in which angels act as agents of divine retribution. This is clearly seen in Exodus, where an angel of the Lord is described as passing over Egypt and striking down the firstborn child in every Egyptian household as the last of the ten plagues sent by God to convince Pharaoh to release the Israelites from slavery. Avenging angels are also sent to Sodom and Gomorrah to execute judgment on the cities' wicked inhabitants.

In the eschatological book of Revelation, warring angels play a significant role in the events of the end-times, where angelic beings pour out bowls of God's wrath upon the Earth. In addition, the mysterious figures known as the Four Horsemen of the Apocalypse—Pestilence (sometimes called Conquest), riding a white horse; War, riding a red horse; Famine, riding a black horse, and Death, riding a pale horse—who appear at the opening of the Seven Seals, which ushers in the Apocalypse, may be forms of avenging angels that herald the end of the world.

FOUR ANGELS

The Four Angels are the four angelic beings that stand at the corners of the Earth, as is detailed in Revelation 7:1: "After this, I saw four angels standing at the four corners of the earth, holding back the four winds of the earth to prevent any wind from blowing on the land or on the sea or on any tree."

Though the angels are not named, some people believe that Michael, Gabriel, Raphael, and Uriel (an angel not mentioned in the Christian canon) are the four who stand as compass points to protect creation on the north, south, east, and west sides of the world.

DEMONS

Demons, as conceived in various religious, mythological, and cultural traditions, represent malevolent supernatural entities often believed to oppose the Divine and afflict humanity. These spiritual and sometimes monstrous beings span diverse civilizations and historical periods, encompassing a range of attributes and roles, but typically are seen as agents of chaos, disorder, and spiritual corruption.

The term *demon* is derived from the ancient Greek word *daemon*, signifying a spirit or divine power. In the context of early Hellenic traditions, daemons could be benevolent or malicious intermediaries between gods and mortals, playing pivotal roles in influencing human fates. Over centuries, especially with the rise of Christianity, the term's connotation evolved, predominantly leaning toward the malevolent beings recognized in contemporary belief.

Beyond ancient Greece, tales of malevolent spirits or entities resonate across various cultures. Ancient Mesopotamian civilizations harbor stories of wicked spirits seeking to deceive or harm the living. In Islamic traditions, the jinn, or spirits occupying a separate realm from humans, can affect worldly events, displaying beneficial and malefic attributes and echoing certain aspects of the Christian understanding of demons.

In the Old Testament, there are references to *shedim* (often transliterated as "sedim" or "sheds"). This Hebrew word, שׁדִים (shedim), is translated as "demons" or "evil spirits" in some contexts. The exact origins of the term are debated, but it's generally accepted that the term *shedim* has connections to the Akkadian *shēdu*, which refers to protective deities, often depicted in bull form. However, in the Hebrew Bible, the word has negative connotations.

Within Christian theology, demons are often understood as fallen angels who, led by Satan, rebelled against God and were subsequently cast out of Heaven. These exiled entities then became adversaries of humanity, seeking to lead souls astray from righteousness. The New Testament of the Bible frequently portrays encounters between Jesus Christ and individuals possessed or influenced by demons. These narratives underscore Jesus's divine authority, as He consistently exorcises and rebukes these spirits, highlighting the ongoing cosmic battle between good and evil.

In contemporary interpretations, the belief and understanding of demons vary. While some view them as symbolic representations of inner human struggles or societal ills, others maintain a literal belief in their existence and influence, as does the Catholic Church. Demons have also been subjects of exploration in psychology, literature, and popular culture, showcasing humanity's enduring fascination with and struggle to comprehend the darker aspects of the spiritual realm and the unknown.

ABADDON

Abaddon, or Apollyon, known as the Angel of the Bottomless Pit, is a powerful, wretched demon in the Judeo-Christian tradition. Often portrayed as a destroyer and the angel of death, he features prominently in the book of Revelation as the king of the abyss. In Revelation 9:11, during the account of the fifth trumpet, a celestial body descends from the sky and receives the key to unlock the abyss. From this pit, a horde of locusts emerges to torment those who do not have the seal of God on their foreheads.

In Hebrew, Abaddon originates from the root word *abad*, meaning "to perish" or "to be lost." Abaddon is often rendered in English as "Destruction." The Greek term *Apollyon* is derived from the verb *apollymi*, which means "to destroy" or "to kill," leading to its translation as The Destroyer. Both demonic names are used in Revelation 9:11, indicating the demon's existence in Jewish, Greek, and Roman cosmology.

The Biblical book of Job cites Abaddon as a realm of the dead and a place of devastation. Similarly, Psalms evoke its imagery as a domain of darkness. Beyond canonical texts, Gnostic and apocryphal texts delve deeper into Abaddon's role as a demonic enforcer. Some narratives place him as the warden of the abyss who is responsible for imprisoning malevolent spirits and fallen angels, while others state that he was a dark force present at the resurrection of Jesus Christ.

Traditionally, Abaddon is envisioned as an intimidating entity having the body of a locust and the lethal tail of a scorpion. He has been occasionally linked with the Biblical demon Azazel, an outcast from Heaven reputed to have introduced humanity to weapons and dark arts. In contemporary interpretations, Abaddon has been seen both as a symbolic embodiment of human malevolence and as a tangible preternatural force in apocalyptic literature. Popular culture has adopted and reimagined him; notable appearances include the television series *Supernatural*, where he emerges as a formidable demon with apocalyptic ambitions, and in video games like the Diablo series, where he is cast as the Lord of Destruction. Tim LaHaye and Jerry B. Jenkins incorporated the figure of Abaddon (Apollyon) in book number five of their best-selling Left Behind series.

AHRIMAN

Ahriman, also known as Angra Mainyu, is a central figure in Zoroastrianism, which is one of the world's oldest monotheistic religions, originating in ancient Persia, modern-day Iran. In this religion, Ahriman is the evil spirit, the destructive force that counteracts the divine, good spirit known as Ahura Mazda. The religion emphasizes a dualistic cosmology of a battle between the forces of good and evil.

The Zoroastrian concept of dualism has been suggested by some scholars to have influenced later religious traditions, including Judaism, Christianity, and Gnostic religions. The parallels between Ahriman and the Judeo-Christian belief in Satan or the devil are notable. Both are seen as opposing forces to a supreme deity. Both tempt humans and try to lead them from the righteous path. Both are associated with the forces of chaos, destruction, and evil. However, it's important to note that any historical evidence linking Zoroastrianism's Angra Mainyu/Ahriman and the Judeo-Christian Satan is speculative.

Outside of the Judeo-Christian tradition, Rudolf Steiner, a writer, philosopher, and early-twentieth-century founder of anthroposophy, which is a spiritual synthesis of esotericism, theosophy, and individual insights, constructed a multifaceted cosmology of belief involving two opposing forces embodied in the demons of Lucifer and Ahriman. Steiner depicts Lucifer as an illuminating entity that draws humans toward excessive self-centeredness, subjectivity, and ethereal detachment, while Ahriman and his demonic forces lure humanity toward materialism, overreliance on technology, and stagnant thinking. Some believe that humanity's overreliance on TV, computers, and social media is evidence of Ahriman's demonic control over the souls of modern people.

ASHTAROTH

Ashtaroth, also known as Astaroth or Ashtoreth, is a formidable demon associated with lust, seduction, and corrupting human sexuality. She is sometimes depicted as a beautiful woman capable of captivating and ensnaring victims with her charms; those who fall under her spell are doomed to a life of debauchery and sin. Meanwhile, Ashtaroth delights in human suffering and degradation.

The origins of Ashtaroth can be traced back to ancient Near Eastern mythology, where the demon was known as Astarte, a Phoenician fertility goddess who was worshipped in various forms across the region. The Bible mentions Astarte (Ashtaroth or Ashtoreth) several times as a pagan deity worshipped by the Canaanites and other neighboring peoples. Before entering the Promised Land, the Israelites were cautioned against adopting local worship practices, as noted in Deuteronomy 7:1–5, which explicitly warned against intermarriage and serving foreign gods. Despite such warnings, the allure of local deities persisted, with Israel's drift toward the worship of Baal and Ashtoreth. These deviations were exemplified by King Solomon, who, influenced by his foreign wives, worshipped Ashtoreth and other deities, which led to God's proclamation that Solomon's kingdom would be torn from his lineage, but not during his lifetime. It would happen during the reign of Solomon's son (1 Kings 11:9–13). Future rulers like King Hezekiah and King Josiah sought to rectify Solomon's idolatry, implementing reforms to eradicate such practices.

As the centuries passed, the image of Ashtaroth evolved from that of a pagan goddess to a demonic male figure associated with sin and temptation. In the Middle Ages, Ashtaroth was often depicted in Christian artwork as a monstrous creature with a hideous head, sometimes of a goat, and having the wings of a bat and the tail of a serpent.

Ashtaroth is explicitly mentioned in Act IV of the sixteenth-century play *Doctor Faustus* by Christopher Marlowe. In a subplot, Benvolio, aided by Frederick and Martino, schemes to kill Faustus for humiliating him. In retaliation, Faustus summons several demons, including Ashtaroth, to torment and punish Benvolio. With the help of Ashtaroth and the others, Faustus transforms Benvolio's head into that of an ass. Centuries later, Ashtaroth would be referenced on the silver screen in the 1971 Disney classic *Bedknobs and Broomsticks*. In this film, the "Star of Astoroth" is a magical talisman that is used in England to help defeat Nazi invaders in World War II.

ASMODEUS

Asmodeus, a demon of lust, temptation, and destruction, is a malevolent spirit mentioned in various religious traditions, including Judaism, Christianity, and Islam.

One notable depiction of Asmodeus is found in the apocryphal book of Tobit, which tells the story of a man named Tobit and his son Tobias. In the story, Tobias is instructed by his father to travel to a distant land to collect a debt owed to him. Along the way, Tobias is accompanied by the Archangel Raphael, who disguises himself as a human and helps Tobias overcome various obstacles, including Asmodeus himself. In the story, Asmodeus is depicted as a mighty demon who has killed the seven husbands of a young woman named Sarah. Tobias is eventually able to defeat Asmodeus through exorcism, binding the demon in a desert away from humans.

In the Talmud and other Jewish writings, Asmodeus, sometimes considered the "king of demons," is associated with various stories and legends. One of the most famous involves the capture of the demon by King Solomon. In other Jewish folklore, Asmodeus was originally a prince of demons who served under the command of the demon king, Samael. He was said to have been responsible for tempting King Solomon, one of the wisest and most powerful kings in ancient Israel. According to legend, Asmodeus was able to seduce Solomon's wife and corrupt his kingdom, leading to his eventual downfall.

In Christian tradition, Asmodeus is a fallen angel who rebelled against God. He is often associated with the sin of lust and is said to tempt humans to engage in immoral acts. In some Christian writings, Asmodeus, along with other powerful demons such as Lucifer, Beelzebub, and Leviathan, is identified as one of the seven princes of Hell.

In Islamic tradition, Asmodeus, known as Ashmadia or Asmadai, is considered a powerful demon responsible for tempting humans into committing adultery and fornication. He is said to have the ability to take on various forms and manipulate humans into fulfilling their desires, even if those desires are harmful or immoral.

Asmodeus was associated with the Loudun possessions, which took place in the seventeenth century in the small town of Loudun, France, and involved a group of Ursuline nuns who claimed to be possessed by demons. The alleged possessions led to a series of exorcisms, public spectacles, and, ultimately, in 1634, the trial and execution of a local priest named Urbain Grandier. Grandier was accused of bewitching the nuns, making a pact with the devil, and sending demons to possess them. During the exorcisms, several demons' names were said to have been identified as possessing the nuns, with Asmodeus being among the most prominent. Aldous Huxley's *The Devils of Loudun* offers a detailed account and analysis of these events.

In Collin de Plancy's *Dictionnaire infernal,* an influential demonological encyclopedia first published in the nineteenth century, the illustration of Asmodeus shows him as a creature with the torso of a man, the legs of a rooster, the tail of a serpent, and three heads—one of a sheep, one of a man, and one of a bull. Plancy's Asmodeus, who rides a lion with dragon wings, is one of the more iconic representations of this demon and has influenced many subsequent portrayals in contemporary folklore.

AZAZEL

Azazel, a fallen angel associated with war and the deception of cosmetics, has been depicted in various sources as a formidable figure of evil. With seven serpent heads, fourteen faces, and twelve wings, Azazel is a powerful lord of Hell and a seducer of humans.

This demon is notably featured in Leviticus in the Old Testament. Here, God instructs Moses and Aaron to sacrifice two goats for the atonement of sins. One goat is for God. The other, designated "for Azazel," is sent into the wilderness. Although the precise interpretation of this passage is the subject of constant debate by religious scholars, Azazel is thought by some to symbolize the menacing forces of chaos and malevolence; offering a scapegoat temporarily pacifies these dark forces. The Mishnah, the collection of Jewish oral traditions, further details this sacrifice during Yom Kippur, suggesting that the sacrificed goat brings appeasement, and the Azazel goat signifies the acts of atonement made during this holy period.

The book of Enoch depicts Azazel as a leader of the Watchers, fallen angels who took human wives, resulting in the Nephilim, or violent giants who wreaked havoc on Earth.

In Islamic tradition, Azazel is known as Iblis, a jinn, or spirit made of "smokeless fire." When Iblis refused to bow to Adam, he was expelled from Paradise. Despite this, he was granted reprieve until Judgment Day and is allowed to tempt and lead them astray.

Medieval iconography often portrayed Azazel as goatlike, linking him to witchcraft and diabolism. As Christianity expanded in Europe, local traditions and deities were labeled heretical and linked with the devil. Azazel's goatlike image became synonymous with these fears. Witches, thought to be devil worshippers, were thought to form sinister pacts for supernatural powers with such entities as Azazel. Such beliefs fueled witch hunts, leading to accusations, trials, and executions, more often than not of women.

BAAL

Baal, an ancient deity in the Canaanite pantheon, is mentioned numerous times in the Old Testament. Considered a demon by Jews and Christians alike, the name Baal originates from Northwest Semitic languages. It translates to "lord" or "owner" and was used to denote various pagan gods in the ancient Near East.

Within Hebrew tradition, Baal's mention frequently emerges in contexts portraying the Israelites' oscillation between the worship of Yahweh and the allure of the Canaanite gods, with Baal often symbolizing the latter. This religious tension is a recurring theme that sheds light on the spiritual struggles of the Israelites, and Yahweh's response to them. The book of Judges, for instance, narrates episodes wherein the Israelites worship Baal, leading to their subsequent subjugation by enemies as a form of divine retribution. In other words, worship a demon and you'll have Hell to pay.

The most renowned Biblical account involving Baal is found in the first book of Kings, where the prophet Elijah confronts the prophets of Baal on Mount Carmel. This dramatic event ends with Yahweh manifesting His power by sending down fire, thereby highlighting His supremacy over the lesser god. This narrative is set against the backdrop of King Ahab's reign with the concurrent patronage of Baal by his wife, Jezebel. The couple is notorious for their attempts to establish Baal worship in Israel, and for their persecution of Yahweh's prophets.

The prophet Hosea likens Israel's intermittent devotion to Baal and other gods to marital unfaithfulness, depicting Israel's relationship with Yahweh metaphorically as a spousal bond wherein turning to other gods was equivalent to adultery. Another notable episode occurs in the book of Numbers, where the Israelites, while encamped at Shittim, worship Baal of Peor, which leads to a divine plague.

BAPHOMET

Baphomet is a demonic figure that, notably, does not appear in the Bible but emerged during the Middle Ages. This entity has been depicted in various ways across different eras, influenced by diverse groups and individuals. Over time, interpretations of Baphomet have evolved, giving rise to myriad representations and symbolisms.

During the Templar Trials of the fourteenth century, the Knights Templar, a formidable medieval Christian military order, faced accusations of heresy. Some confessions, likely extracted under torture, alluded to the worship of an entity named Baphomet. Descriptions of the demon ranged from a multiheaded idol to a bearded figure or even a cat. Given the circumstances under which these confessions were made, their veracity is highly debatable.

The nineteenth century brought about a great interest in the occult. French occultist Eliphas Lévi presented a detailed depiction of Baphomet in his book from the 1850s, *Dogme et rituel de la haute magie*. Lévi's version was a winged humanoid with a goat's head, possessing attributes of both genders. This Baphomet held aloft his opposing arms tattooed with the words *Solve* and *Coagula*, meaning "dissolve" and "coagulate," an alchemical idea on breaking something down and giving it new life, and sported a torch between its horns and a forehead pentagram.

By the twentieth and twenty-first centuries, Baphomet had been adopted and adapted by various modern occult and satanic groups. Many drew inspiration from Lévi's representation. The Satanic Temple, for instance, introduced a Baphomet statue with two awestruck children looking up in wonder at the demon as a counterpoint to the Ten Commandments monuments in certain US public spaces. In pop culture, Baphomet has been portrayed as a figure of magic, mayhem, and malevolence in movies, books, and music.

BEELZEBUB

Beelzebub, also known as Beelzebul or Belzebuth, a Philistine god and powerful demon in the Judeo-Christian tradition, embodies decay, darkness, and malevolence. He is often referred to as the prince of demons, surpassed only by Satan in terms of might and dominance. Historically, the name Beelzebub has roots in an ancient Canaanite deity, Baal. The transition from Baal to Beelzebub can be linked to the Hebrew term *Ba'al Zebub* translating to "lord of the flies." This moniker was meant to be derogatory, inferring decay and contamination, given that flies were commonly drawn to the sacrifices presented to Baal.

Within the New Testament, references to Beelzebub highlight his reputed capacity to exorcise other demons. Such mentions illustrate the ancient belief in Beelzebub's authority over demonic realms, ranking him among one of the most powerful spirits in Hell. This is demonstrated in the synoptic Gospels when Pharisees, religious leaders at the time, leveled an accusation against Jesus, accusing him of casting out demons by the power of Beelzebub. Jesus, they believed, was in league with the devil. In response, Jesus clarifies that a kingdom divided against itself is destined to fall, underscoring that casting out demons serves as a spiritual gift and a tangible manifestation of the kingdom of God.

Outside of the Judeo-Christian tradition, however, this well-documented demonized version of Beelzebub represents a significant departure from his original depiction in Canaanite beliefs. Early texts indicate Baal was revered for his dominion over fertility, storms, and agriculture, and was often symbolized with a thunderbolt in his grasp, which suggests that his image had been distorted, evolving from a revered deity to a feared demon as religious paradigms shifted. Nevertheless, Baal was regarded as an idol by Jews and Christians, and the allusion to him as the "lord of the flies" further suggests that this foreign deity held dominion over insects swarming around excrement.

Literary works like John Milton's *Paradise Lost* present Beelzebub as a shrewd seducer and one of the chief fallen angels who served as a trusted adviser to Satan. When Satan first wakes up in Hell after being expelled from Heaven, Beelzebub is at his side. In William Golding's *The Lord of the Flies*, a gripping narrative unfolds as a group of British boys find themselves marooned on a desolate island. As their descent into chaos and violence ensues, they become ensnared by a chilling idol: a severed pig's head impaled on a makeshift spear, which they dub the "Lord of the Flies." This grotesque effigy symbolizes the evil and darkness lurking within the recesses of human nature, offering a stark portrayal of their gradual moral deterioration.

BEHEMOTH

Behemoth appears in the Bible and in Jewish folklore as an imposing demon often recognized as the counterpart to Leviathan, a female demonic monster of the seas and according to folklore one of three monsters created on the fifth day of creation. The Hebrew word *behemoth* (תומהב) is the plural form of *behemah* (המהב), signifying "beast" or "animal," as seen in the Bible (Job 40:15–24), where it describes a formidable creature symbolizing great strength. Although the origins of Behemoth are unclear, it seems that his story begins in Near Eastern mythology, possibly inspired by the Babylonian god Marduk, who is central to the Babylonian creation myth, known as the "Enuma Elish." According to this epic, Marduk emerged as the supreme deity by defeating the chaotic sea goddess Tiamat in a great battle. This victory established Marduk as the ruler of the cosmos.

In Jewish tradition and folklore, Behemoth is reputed to be a malevolent demon associated with chaos and destruction. According to one Midrashic tradition, along with Leviathan and Ziz (a demon associated with birds or flight), Behemoth was created on the eve of the Sabbath. Some interpret this unholy trinity as symbolizing the power of earth, sea, and air. The Talmud describes Behemoth as a massive creature so large that its shadow can cover an entire city. According to some Jewish legends, the messiah will slay Behemoth, Leviathan, and other evil forces at the end of days.

In Christian tradition, Behemoth is often interpreted as a symbol of the earthly powers of evil that drive tyrants and despots. Some scholars have suggested that Behemoth represents the Roman Empire in first-century Palestine.

The demon is prominent in the work of eighteenth-century poet and visionary William Blake. Blake's poem "The Tyger," from his collection *Songs of Experience*, is thought to reference the robust, sinewy forces of Behemoth and the demon Leviathan. In Blake's view, Behemoth is associated with the dark, violent forces of nature and the destructive power that tyrannical rulers and institutions can unleash. In his illustrations of the book of Job, Blake depicts Behemoth as a fearsome creature with fiery eyes and a powerful, muscular body. The beast is often shown surrounded by flames and smoke, symbolizing the chaos and destruction that it represents.

In modern times, Behemoth has become a popular subject in literature and popular culture. Philosopher Thomas Hobbes's follow-up to *Leviathan* is titled *Behemoth*, a book on the English civil wars and the abuse of power. Behemoth is also a character in Stephen King's The Dark Tower series. Behemoth has been featured in video game series like Final Fantasy and Bayonetta, and in role-playing games like Dungeons and Dragons. (See Leviathan, Ziz.)

BELIAL

Belial, spelled as Beliar in some texts, is a term that originates in the Hebrew Bible and translates to "worthless" or "lawless." It was used in the Old Testament to characterize individuals as wicked or of no value. By the intertestamental period, the time between the close of the Old Testament and the beginning of the New Testament, Belial began to be personified, particularly in Jewish lore, as a distinct demonic entity or representation of the devil. This transformation is later evident, for example, in St. Paul's Second Letter to the Corinthians, where he explicitly mentions Belial and juxtaposes the demon with Christ: "What harmony is there between Christ and Belial? Or what does a believer have in common with an unbeliever?"

Belial is mentioned in the Dead Sea Scrolls, a collection of Jewish texts discovered in the mid-twentieth century near the Dead Sea and the ancient settlement of Qumran. Belial's significance in the Dead Sea Scrolls is primarily as a symbol of evil, wickedness, and lawlessness. He is often portrayed as an adversary or opponent of God and righteousness in the Scrolls, and is associated with darkness, deceit, and rebellion against God's will. Belial is often contrasted with the Sons of Light or the Children of Righteousness, God's faithful followers. The conflict between the Sons of Light and the Sons of Belial is a recurring theme in some of the Scrolls.

Belial's appearances in the Scrolls highlight the forces of evil and corruption that the religious community at Qumran faced during their lifetime.

Belial is often compared to Ahriman, a demon in Persian mythology.

DAGON

Dagon was a god worshipped by the Philistines, and considered a false god or demon by the Hebrews of the Old Testament. It is believed the Dagon's name is based on the Semitic root *dag* meaning "little fish," as he is often depicted as a "fish-man," with the upper-body of a human and the lower half like a fish. And yet his name has generated various theories regarding its origins. Some scholars propose links to words like "grain" and "cloudiness," and the interpretation of Dagon as a fish god has been discredited by contemporary scholars. Alternative theories suggest that his name may have roots in a pre-Semitic language of inland Syria, aligning with the linguistic complexity of the region.

In ancient Mesopotamian religions, Dagon was sometimes revered as a "father of gods." He was often associated with Shalash, a Mesopotamian goddess, although her presence in Dagon's cult varied regionally. His offspring included Hadad (god of storms) and possibly Hebat (goddess of fertility).

In the Judeo-Christian Bible, Dagon is mentioned in the narrative of Samson that appears in Judges. After the Philistines capture Samson, they bring him to Dagon's temple in Gaza to showcase their victory. In a climactic moment, Samson prays for strength and, with a final push, collapses the temple's pillars, leading to his own death and the demise of numerous Philistines. Another significant passage can be found in 1 Samuel 5. Here, following their seizure of the Ark of the Covenant, the Philistines placed it in Dagon's temple in Ashdod. The next day, to their astonishment, the statue of Dagon was seen prostrated before the Ark. After restoring the statue to its former position, they discovered the following day that it had fallen once again. This time, the head and hands broke off and were found lying on the ground at the threshold of the temple. Additionally, 1 Chronicles 10:8–10 notes that after Saul and his sons were killed on Mount Gilboa, the Philistines displayed in the temple of Dagon Saul's head and armor as trophies.

Centuries after its ancient origins, twentieth-century writer H. P. Lovecraft, a master of horror and weird fiction, integrated Dagon into his Cthulhu Mythos. Within Lovecraft's intricate universe, Dagon stands as a formidable cosmic entity: a monstrous sea deity that melds human, fish, and frog characteristics and overshadows many of the other dark creatures in his lore.

LEGION

Legion is a demon of the New Testament and the central figure of one of Jesus's public exorcisms. The story of Legion appears in three variations in the three synoptic Gospels: Mark, Matthew, and Luke, with Mark offering the most detailed account. The narrative tells of a possessed man who lived among tombs and was so strong that chains and shackles could not restrain him. When Jesus arrived in the area, the possessed man ran toward him and fell at his feet. Jesus commanded the demon to leave the man, and the demon replied ominously, "My name is Legion, for we are many." Jesus proceeded to expel numerous demons from the man, sending them into a nearby group of pigs (viewed as unclean animals by the Jewish people), which then rushed into the sea and drowned. The local residents, made fearful by the events, asked Jesus to leave, but the healed man expressed a desire to accompany Jesus. In Matthew, the story unfolds in the Gadarenes, with two demon-possessed men, in contrast to Mark's solitary figure. While the demons are unnamed in this story, they are exorcised to the pigs, which drown, leading the towns-people to request Jesus's departure from the area. Luke's version, set in the Gerasene region, mirrors Mark's telling of just one possessed man. Here, after the demons are cast into pigs, Luke tells of a mixed reaction to Jesus's miracle by the local citizenry.

During the time of Jesus, the term *legion* was understood as a Roman army unit comprising around 5,000 soldiers. The Roman Empire's legions were symbols of authority and the pervasive presence of the Roman government throughout the regions it conquered, including Judea.

By naming themselves Legion, the demons not only highlighted their vast number but also made a not-so-subtle reference to the oppressive power of Rome. This association accentuated Jesus's role as a liberator from spiritual oppression as well as a figure of hope in the face of earthly oppressors.

The story of Legion has been interpreted in many ways over the years. Some scholars see it as a literal account of demon possession, while others view it as a metaphorical representation of mental illness or societal oppression.

LEVIATHAN

Leviathan is a mythical demonic sea creature. In Jewish folklore, the Leviathan is an enormous monster that dwells in the depths of the ocean, while in Christianity, the name sometimes represents Satan, the embodiment of chaos and destruction.

According to Talmudic writings, Leviathan is one of the three monsters that were created on the fifth day of creation. The other two are Behemoth, a land animal, and Ziz, a giant bird. Leviathan, considered to be the most fearsome and powerful of these three creatures, is associated with the primordial waters of creation and represents the forces of chaos that existed before God created the world. Some scholars suggest that Leviathan symbolizes the chaos within each of us; the struggle to control this chaos is a central theme of Jewish spirituality.

In the book of Job, Leviathan is described as a creature that is nearly invincible, with impenetrable scales and a fiery breath that can set the sea ablaze. Isaiah 27:1 asserts that God's wrath will "punish Leviathan the fleeing serpent . . . Leviathan the twisting serpent; and he shall slay the dragon that is in the sea." Here, Leviathan is referred to in a prophetic context, symbolizing destructive forces or entities that God ultimately will defeat.

In Christian traditions, Leviathan is frequently portrayed as a demon or a fallen angel, representing Satan or the forces of evil. In Christian demonology of the Middle Ages, Leviathan was often depicted as a serpent or dragon from the book of Revelation, with seven heads and ten horns, representing the seven deadly sins and possibly an inversion of the Ten Commandments. This image of Leviathan as a monstrous creature symbolizes the dangers of temptation and the importance of resisting these forces to maintain a virtuous life. Leviathan is sometimes depicted in art as being defeated by the Archangel Michael.

In modern times, Leviathan continues to be a popular figure in literature and pop culture. Herman Melville's *Moby-Dick* is one of the most famous literary works that mentions Leviathan. In this classic novel, the monstrous whale Moby-Dick is compared to the demon, as both creatures represent the unfathomable power of the natural world. Leviathan also appears in Jules Verne's *20,000 Leagues under the Sea* as a fearsome sea monster that the protagonists must confront and defeat. (See Behemoth, Ziz.)

LILITH

Lilith is an enigmatic figure from Jewish mythology. The earliest mention of her in Jewish texts comes from the Babylonian Talmud, written between the third and fifth centuries. In the Talmud, Lilith is portrayed as a seductive demon who seeks to harm men and babies. She is said to have been created at the same time as Adam but chose to leave the Garden of Eden rather than be subservient to a man. In later Jewish folklore, Lilith is often depicted as a succubus: a beautiful but demonic long-haired, winged woman who lures men with her charms and then either kills them or steals their souls.

Despite the negative associations with Lilith, many see her as a positive figure and a role model for modern women. Some feminist interpretations of Lilith see her as a symbol of female empowerment and resistance against patriarchal norms. In modern Wiccan and pagan traditions, Lilith is often invoked as a goddess of sexual liberation and feminine power. Some feminist theologians have also reclaimed Lilith as a symbol of female resistance and empowerment, arguing that her story represents the struggle of women to assert their own autonomy and reject patriarchal control.

LUCIFER

Lucifer is a demon of light. His name originates from the Latin words *lux* (light) and *ferre* (to bring), which translates to "light-bringer" or "morning star." Historically, the term referred to Venus, a planet of striking brightness in the night sky. Different Bible translators employed the word *Lucifer* not only for Venus but also for the morning light, the zodiac signs, and the dawn.

The king of Babylon was metaphorically referred to as Lucifer in Isaiah 14:12–15, highlighting his prominence during his reign: "How you are fallen from heaven, O Morning Star, son of Dawn! How you are cut down to the ground, you who laid the nations low!" The High Priest Simon, son of Onias in Sirach 50:6–7, was referred to as Lucifer due to his outstanding virtue. Moreover, the term *Lucifer* was applied to represent Heaven's grandeur and even to represent Jesus Christ as an indication of the true illumination of our spiritual existence.

Biblical scholar Anthony Maas associates the name of Lucifer with the interpretation of the Hebrew noun *helel,* which means, in some dialects, "to lament." It is believed that when writing the Latin translation of the Bible, St. Jerome drew on these origins, and associated Lucifer with a chief angel who laments over his lost radiance, which was once as bright as the morning star. This interpretation is crucial in the Christian narrative, where Lucifer is not seen as the devil's real name but instead signifies the angel's lamentable fallen state.

The context of Isaiah 14:12, which exclaims, "How you are fallen from heaven, O Morning Star, son of Dawn!" is a critique of the king of Babylon's arrogance. Yet, with translations like that of St. Jerome, the name began to represent a once-illustrious angel who plummeted from grace. Early Christian theologians expanded on this, visualizing the story of Lucifer as the leader of an angelic rebellion.

In St. Augustine's seminal work *City of God*, the theologian argues that Lucifer, once a mighty angel, though he had been created good, chose to deviate from the divine through an act of arrogance and will. The narrative of the devil's fall thus serves as a poignant illustration of the potential perils of free will: A once-noble angel transformed into an enemy of creation not by design but by decision. Here Lucifer emerges not merely as a fallen angel but as the foremost among them, often dubbed the "prince" of the fallen. His rebellion set a precedent, prompting a host of angels to forsake their divine allegiance, culminating in a cosmic rift between the realms of light and darkness. This portrayal accentuates Lucifer's pivotal role in ushering evil into the world. Later, literary masterpieces such as Dante's *The Divine Comedy* and Milton's *Paradise Lost* further reinforced the tale of Lucifer's hubris, insurrection, and subsequent fall.

Over time, the name Lucifer would conflate with Satan, though some modern-day exorcists and demonologists see the two as distinctly separate entities. (See Jerome, Satan.)

MAMMON

Mammon, which comes from the Aramaic *māmōn*, meaning "riches" or "property," is a demon associated with wealth and materialism. He first appears in the New Testament, in the Gospel of Matthew, when Jesus says, "No one can serve two masters. Either you will hate the one and love the other, or you will be devoted to the one and despise the other. You cannot serve both God and mammon." In this context, Jesus may be referring to Mammon as a minor god or a personification of wealth and greed. The name nevertheless underscores the dangers of materialism and how greed and avarice can lead to division.

In later Christian tradition, especially during the medieval period, Mammon began to be personified as a demon or a god of wealth and greed. This transformation was part of the broader tendency to classify various vices and sinful tendencies as demonic entities. In Jacques Collin de Plancy's *Dictionnaire infernal*, he is depicted as a covetous troll-like figure.

According to Gustav Davidson, St. Gregory of Nyssa believed Mammon was also the demon Beelzebub (also known as the Lord of the Flies). And though he is not named in Dante's *Divine Comedy*, the wolf-like god known as Plutus, who rules over the fourth circle of Hell set aside for those whose sin is avarice, is thought to be an embodiment of Mammon.

In some demonology circles, Mammon is also believed to be an infernal ambassador to England.

MOLOCH

Moloch is the demon of child sacrifice. In the Old Testament, this evil entity is the harrowing embodiment of idolatry, representing the very antithesis of Israelite worship and values. Venerated by the Ammonites and several other Canaanite tribes, Moloch was not merely another deity in the pantheon of ancient gods but was uniquely associated with disturbing rituals. Central to this worship was the devilish ritual of immolating innocent children in a hollow bronze statue of the god.

Moloch's name became synonymous with extreme apostasy and spiritual degradation in the Biblical narrative. The Old Testament does more than condemn the worship of this deity (as it would all gods beyond the One True God); it expresses a deep revulsion for the inhumane practices associated with him. The book of Leviticus, in its stern mandates found in chapter 20:2–5, not only denounces such rituals but also decrees the gravest of punishments for its practitioners, be they Israelite or foreigner in the land. The judgment against Moloch throughout Biblical texts underscores the depth of abhorrence felt toward the god and his worship, positioning him as an emblematic figure of heathenish idolatry and moral depravity.

In the book of Acts, the apostle Stephen strongly rebukes Jewish leaders for their devotion to false gods, using the chilling example of Moloch to drive home the sinfulness of idolatry.

Moloch's wickedness extends beyond Biblical references. In Greek myths, Moloch finds parallels with Cronus, the god notorious for devouring his children to thwart prophecies of his own dethronement. The Romans drew similar associations, linking Moloch with Saturn, another deity with a grim appetite for his progeny.

NEPHILIM

The Nephilim are mysterious figures referenced in the Hebrew Bible, specifically in the book of Genesis. Genesis 6:1–4 delineates their association with the "sons of God" and "daughters of humans," though the exact nature of this relationship remains the subject of scholarly and theological debate. Drawing from some ancient Jewish writings and the noncanonical book of Enoch, one interpretation suggests that the Nephilim are the offspring of fallen angels (demons) and human women. Another idea suggests that the Nephilim resulted from the union between the godly descendants of Seth, Adam and Eve's third son, and the cursed lineage of Cain. A further perspective interprets the "sons of God" as referring to ancient rulers or kings, implying that the Nephilim were a line of esteemed monarchs or warriors. Additionally, certain Biblical passages such as Numbers 13:33 describe the Nephilim as being of substantial size, which has led to their association with giants.

PAZUZU

An ancient Assyrian demon, Pazuzu was the embodiment of the southwest wind and commanded an army of wind demons. He played a dual role, being both a harmful, demonic wind—the bringer of plague—and a protector against other demons, particularly safeguarding pregnant women and mothers from nefarious forces. He is depicted as a grotesque combination of bird, scorpion, and serpent. People performed rituals, cast spells, and created artifacts to secure his protection. Pazuzu's presence in Mesopotamian culture dates back to the Early Iron Age. Visual representations of him can be found from the eighth century BC, while textual references date to the seventh century BC. A statue of Pazuzu appears as a focal point in William Peter Blatty's 1971 novel *The Exorcist* (and its subsequent film adaptation), which was inspired by the real-life exorcism of Roland Doe that took place in St. Louis, Missouri, in 1949.

UNCLEAN SPIRITS

Unclean spirits are referenced predominantly in the Bible's New Testament; they denote demonic or evil entities believed to afflict individuals in various ways. These spirits are depicted as malevolent forces, sometimes possessing humans and causing physical or spiritual disturbances. Their origin, while not exhaustively detailed within the Scriptures, is often intertwined with Christian theological interpretations, suggesting that an individual may be possessed by a impure angel or demon who once rebelled against God under the leadership of Satan.

One of the most pronounced themes surrounding unclean spirits in the Gospels is the authority Jesus Christ holds over them. Throughout His ministry, Jesus encountered numerous individuals possessed or tormented by these spirits. His ability to exorcise and command these spirits was a testament to His divine authority and a powerful sign of the commencement of God's Kingdom on Earth.

The effects of these spirits on people varied widely. While some individuals were rendered mute, others exhibited signs of epilepsy, and still others displayed moral or behavioral aberrations. Not every ailment or sickness was attributed to these spirits, as is underscored by the Gospels providing clear demarcation between what were believed to be naturally occurring illnesses and demonic possessions. The healing of Peter's mother from fever and restoring a man's ability to walk at the pool of Bethesda are seen as miracles over naturally occurring ailments and diseases, not as afflictions brought on by possession.

Some of the most notable exorcisms of unclean spirits in the Gospels are:

- The Man with an Unclean Spirit in Capernaum (Mark 1:21–28; Luke 4:31–37): Early in His ministry, while teaching in a synagogue in Capernaum, Jesus is confronted by a man possessed by an unclean spirit. The demon recognizes Jesus as the "Holy One of God." Jesus commands the spirit to be silent and come out of the man, which it does, leaving onlookers amazed.

- The Gerasene Demoniac (Mark 5:1–20; Matthew 8:28–34; Luke 8:26–39): One of the most dramatic exorcisms, this account features a man (or, in Matthew's account, two men) possessed by a legion of demons. The dark spirits plead with Jesus not to send them into the abyss but to allow them to enter a herd of pigs nearby. Jesus grants their request, and the possessed pigs rush down a steep hill into a lake and drown.

- Daughter of a Canaanite Woman (Matthew 15:21–28; Mark 7:24–30): A Canaanite (or Syrophoenician, in Mark's account) woman pleads with Jesus to heal her daughter, who is tormented by a demon. Initially, Jesus responds negatively to the woman, but after witnessing her faith, He commends her and heals her daughter.

- Boy with an Evil Spirit (Mark 9:14–29; Matthew 17:14–20; Luke 9:37–43): After the Transfiguration, Jesus descends a mountain to find His disciples unsuccessfully trying to exorcise a demon from a boy. The boy's father explains that the demon often throws his son into fire and water. After a brief conversation about faith, Jesus rebukes the demon, and the boy is healed. Later, the disciples ask Jesus privately why they couldn't drive out the demon, and Jesus speaks about the necessity of prayer (and, in some accounts, fasting).

- Woman Crippled by a Spirit (Luke 13:10–17): Jesus encounters a woman in a synagogue who has been crippled for eighteen years due to an evil spirit. Jesus calls her over, rebukes the demon, and immediately she straightens up. This healing on the Sabbath leads to a confrontation with the synagogue leader.

- Mute Man Possessed by a Demon (Matthew 9:32–34; Luke 11:14–23): After Jesus casts out a demon from a man who couldn't speak, the man begins to talk. Some of the onlookers accuse Jesus of driving out demons by the power of Beelzebul (another name for Satan), leading Jesus to deliver a teaching on the kingdom of God and the absurdity of the claim that Satan would drive out his own.

SAMAEL

Samael is a demon who appears in Talmudic, Midrashic, and Gnostic texts. His name translates to "the venom of God," and he is often depicted as a fallen angel or the ruler of the demonic hierarchy. The lore surrounding Samael is varied and complex, with many conflicting interpretations of his character and significance.

In Jewish mythology, Samael is often described as the "angel of death" responsible for carrying out God's judgment on mortals. He is sometimes identified as the angel who wrestled with Jacob, the husband of Lilith after she left the Garden of Eden, or a chief of evil angels. He is also associated with the serpent who tempted Adam and Eve to eat from the Tree of Knowledge. According to some interpretations, because Samael was jealous of Adam and Eve's relationship with God, he sought to disrupt that closeness by leading them astray. In one story, he is the planter and gardener of the Tree of Knowledge of Good and Evil, and in others, he is portrayed as a loyal servant of God who is simply carrying out his orders to test the first humans.

In some Christian folklore, Samael is said to have seduced Eve and fathered Cain, the first murderer in the Bible, casting him as a symbol of evil and corruption, a figure to be feared and reviled. While his role has been discussed in Christian demonological texts over the centuries, he holds no place in Christian theology and does not appear in either the Old or New Testament.

Samael is frequently identified with the demiurge in Gnostic belief systems. The demiurge is an ignorant, lesser deity who creates the material world and believes himself to be the one true God, unaware of the higher spiritual realities above him. In this context, Samael often is associated with blindness and ignorance. Texts like *Pistis Sophia*, possibly a third- or fourth-century Gnostic text about Jesus, post-Transfiguration, depict Samael as the ruler of the material world, and are associated with archons, which are lesser rulers or powers of the material realm, sometimes called the Kingdom of Darkness.

SATAN

Satan, also known as the devil, diablos, slander, Accuser, the Serpent, the Dragon, the Wicked One, the Father of All Lies, Old Scratch, and a host of other names, is the prince of all demons. Some traditions believe that Satan was the Angel of the Angels, the commander of the Seraphim, the leader of the Virtues, until his fall from Heaven. In the Bible, Satan's presence is ubiquitous and multifaceted.

In Genesis 3, the serpent tempts Eve to eat the fruit from the Tree of the Knowledge of Good and Evil, leading to the ouster of Adam and Eve from the Garden of Eden. While the serpent is never explicitly identified as Satan in this narrative, it is described as a crafty creature created by God. The association of the serpent with Satan comes from later Christian interpretations and is particularly evident in the writings of early Church Fathers and texts like the book of Revelation. In her influential work *The Origin of Satan*, scholar Elaine Pagels notes that the transformation of the serpent's identity to become synonymous with Satan represents broader shifts in religious thought.

Satan as a concept appears in Numbers 22, manifesting as an angelic figure to block Balaam's path, signaling opposition and divine intervention.

In the book of Job, Satan is often referred to as "the Adversary," the Hebrew term used is *ha-satan*, which translates to "the accuser." Here, Satan challenges God regarding Job's faithfulness, positing that Job's piety is merely a byproduct of his blessings and prosperity. Satan insinuates that if Job's blessings were stripped away, he would renounce God. Accepting the challenge, God permits Satan to test Job, first by taking away his wealth and family and then by afflicting him with painful sores, with the sole condition being that Job's life be spared. Throughout these trials, Job expresses deep anguish and confusion, and questions the reasons for his suffering, but he does not denounce God.

In the Gospels, Satan emerges as the chief tempter, seeking to divert Jesus from His divine mission during His time in the wilderness. Taking advantage of Jesus's vulnerable state as he fasted for forty days, Satan tempts Jesus to transform stones into bread, questions Jesus's divine identity, and challenges Jesus's reliance on God. He then manipulates Scripture, urging Jesus to jump from Jerusalem's pinnacle, hinting that angels would shield Him. Finally, to derail Jesus from his sacrificial path, Satan offers the splendor of all earthly kingdoms in exchange for Jesus's worship. Throughout these encounters, Satan's role is to challenge, deceive, and divert, but Jesus counters each temptation with steadfast faith and a solid knowledge of Scripture. This narrative underscores Satan's persistent efforts to undermine God's plan, even as it highlights Jesus's unwavering resistance to these seductions.

The book of Revelation amplifies Satan's antagonistic nature. He is depicted as humankind's primary adversary, relentlessly endeavoring to thwart God's divine plan and torment believers. This portrayal is rich and multifaceted, painting him as a symbol of consummate evil and rebellion against the Divine. One of the most vivid descriptions of Satan is Revelation 12, where he is personified as the "great red dragon" with seven heads and ten horns. In this passage he attempts to consume the child birthed by a "woman clothed in the sun," a symbol often linked to Jesus and his mother, Mary. Satan's efforts, however, are in vain.

Thwarted, Satan then turns his wrath toward those unfaltering in their faith and in their commitment to Christ. Satan appears as chief protagonist in the book of Revelation. A dramatic scene unfolds as a celestial war erupts: Michael and his angelic hosts engage in fierce combat against the Dragon. Defeated, Satan and his fallen angels are cast down to Earth, prompting a stark warning: "Woe to the earth and the sea, for the devil has descended upon you in rage, knowing his time is limited" (Revelation 12:12). Further intensifying the narrative, Revelation 13 recounts how Satan empowers two beasts—one emerging from the sea (Leviathan) and another from the earth (Behemoth). Typically interpreted as representations of political or religious entities, these monsters violently oppose God's followers, and make it their mission to disseminate heretical teachings. Their demand to be worshipped mirrors Satan's incessant ambition to divert adoration and honor from God to himself. As the narrative progresses to Revelation 20, Satan is momentarily restrained; specifically, he is bound for a millennium. Yet, this respite is brief. Upon release, he musters nations for a conclusive assault against the holy city and its denizens. This act epitomizes the enduring, rebellious spirit of Satan.

PLATE X

Satan

Every tale has its denouement, however. Satan's machinations in Revelation culminate in his irrevocable defeat, where he, alongside the beast and false prophet, is consigned to the lake of fire, enduring eternal torment. This trajectory reinforces his roles throughout Revelation: the accuser, the deceiver, and the relentless persecutor. These Scriptures, in combination with others such as Isaiah 14:12–15 and Luke 10:18, collectively paint the narrative of a celestial being who, consumed by pride, falls from grace.

In Christian doctrine, Satan's roles and significance are manifold. Principally, he is seen as the seducer of souls, enticing humanity into the realms of sin and thereby severing their bond with the Divine. Symbolically, he epitomizes malevolence, representing the perpetual spiritual warfare between benevolence and evil within human existence. However, it's important to note that Christianity reiterates Satan's subservience to God. He is not a divine counterpart but a creature, albeit powerful, who once basked in God's favor but was subsequently condemned for his rebellion.

Satan's influence extends beyond theology, permeating cultural and artistic realms. Literary masterpieces like Dante Alighieri's *Divine Comedy* offers a harrowing characterization of Satan. John Milton's *Paradise Lost* provides a more empathetic portrayal, portraying Satan as a tragic, albeit defiant, hero who loved God with a passionate love until the creation of humans led to the Angel's jealousy, pride, and hate. Modern media, particularly in films like *The Exorcist* and *The Omen*, emphasize his terrifying unholy persona, which often parallel societal anxieties regarding malevolence and the unknown. Additionally, his image, often depicted with horns, red skin, and a trident, can be traced back to medieval and Renaissance art as symbolic of his role as a gruesome deceiver.

In essence, whether through religious Scriptures, classic literature, or evocative art, Satan's indelible mark on Christianity and the broader culture is a testament to the enduring influence and the complex interplay of good and evil in human consciousness.

THE WATCHERS

The Watchers, as depicted in the book of Enoch, are enigmatic celestial beings originally stationed in Heaven. They are associated with fallen angels. Seduced by the allure of Earth, two hundred of them, led by Semyaza, descended to Earth to the peak of Mount Hermon. Though their initial intent might have been to guide humanity, their purpose quickly went awry. Captivated by the beauty of women, they took them as concubines, producing the Nephilim, a race of giants who wreaked havoc, consuming vast resources, and spreading terror.

Beyond their transgressions with human women, the Watchers also introduced forbidden knowledge to humanity. As tradition holds, Azazel, one of their leaders, taught humans the art of warfare and the crafting of weapons, while others revealed secrets of magic, divination, and other esoteric arts. This infusion of forbidden knowledge further corrupted the world.

With the resulting chaos and upheaval, many people cried out to Heaven, capturing the attention of Archangels Michael, Raphael, and Gabriel. Tasked with restoring order, Raphael bound Azazel in darkness, Gabriel incited the Nephilim to destroy one another, and Michael confined Semyaza and his minions. Unfortunately, the actions of the Watchers and the subsequent decline in human behavior culminated in a divine judgment. The Earth, overwhelmed with wickedness, was cleansed by a Great Flood, sparing only Noah and those with him. (See Nephilim.)

ZIZ

In Jewish tradition, Ziz is a demon that takes the form of a giant, mythical bird. Ziz is mentioned in tandem with other legendary creatures like the Behemoth (a primordial land beast) and the Leviathan (a sea monster), all believed to have come into existence on the fifth day of creation. These creatures appear in various Jewish texts, often to symbolize the vastness and the mystery of God's creation. Ziz is sometimes described as having mighty wings that could block out the sun, and it oversees the domain of the sky, just as Behemoth and Leviathan represent the domains of the land and the sea, respectively. (See Behemoth, Leviathan.)

APPENDICES

TIMELINE TO SAINTHOOD

The road to sainthood in the Catholic Church is a rigorous and demanding journey, often spanning decades or even centuries. It's a path punctuated by meticulous examination, fervent prayer, and the need for undeniable evidence of divine intervention. The canonization process, in which an individual is formally recognized as a saint, is a testament to the Church's commitment to venerating those who have genuinely exemplified Christ's teachings and left an indelible mark on the Christian community.

The following are the steps involved:

1. WAITING PERIOD: Historically, there used to be a waiting period of fifty years after the death of a candidate before the process could begin. However, this has changed, and by the twentieth and twenty-first centuries, the waiting period was reduced to five years, though even this wait can be waived by the pope. For example, Pope John Paul II, who changed the waiting period, started the process for Mother Teresa just two years after her death.

2. SERVANT OF GOD: The process officially starts at the diocesan level. A local bishop investigates a candidate's life and writings to determine if he or she lived a holy and virtuous life. After this initial investigation, the individual can be titled a "Servant of God."

3. VENERABLE: The Vatican's Congregation for the Causes of Saints then examines the evidence of the candidate's holiness, sanctity, and miracles. If the candidate is deemed to have lived a life of "heroic virtue," the pope proclaims him or her "Venerable."

4. BEATIFICATION: For beatification, a miracle must be attributed to the Venerable, signifying that he or she is in Heaven and can intercede with God on our behalf. The miracle is usually a medically unexplainable healing. Martyrs (those who died for their faith) can be beatified without a miracle. Once beatified, the individual is given the title "Blessed."

5. CANONIZATION: For canonization, another miracle is required, attributed to the intercession of the Blessed after his or her beatification. Once this second miracle is confirmed, the individual can be formally recognized as a saint. However, as for beatification, martyrs can be canonized without a second miracle.

6. PAPAL APPROVAL: The pope has the final say in the process of beatification and canonization. Once the pope approves the canonization, a special Mass is celebrated in which the pope formally declares the person a saint.

7. FEAST DAY: Saints are usually given a feast day, celebrated annually, and they can be venerated (honored) by the Universal Church.

It's worth noting that the process is exhaustive, involving the collection of volumes of evidence, testimonies, and documentation about the person's life, teachings, and potential miracles. Furthermore, a postulator is appointed to oversee the cause, and an *advocatus diaboli*, a devil's advocate, formally known as a Promoter of the Faith, is tasked with critically evaluating the case to ensure it meets the highest standards of scrutiny.

TIMELINE OF ROMAN EMPERORS

The history of the Roman Empire is vast and complex, and continues to be the subject of research and debate to this very day. Spanning continents and centuries, the empire's legacy and intricacies have left an indelible mark on the world at large. From the inception of Rome to the fourth century, the empire was often unfriendly to Christians. Many emperors, driven by various motives, persecuted Christians for their beliefs and their refusal to embrace the state-sanctioned religions. This tension between the Roman Empire and a burgeoning faith would shape the course of Western history in profound and radical ways.

The following is a list of the primary emperors who lived from first century BC to fourth century AD.

AUGUSTUS (27 BC–AD 14)
First Roman emperor and founder of the Julio-Claudian dynasty. Ended the Roman Republic and initiated the Pax Romana.

TIBERIUS (AD 14–37)
Augustus's stepson and successor. His reign saw increasing autocracy and the notorious events surrounding Sejanus.

CALIGULA (AD 37–41)
Known for erratic behavior, possible madness, and extravagant spending.

CLAUDIUS (AD 41–54)
Proved to be an able administrator and began the conquest of Britain.

NERO (AD 54–68)
Persecuted Christians, blaming them for the Great Fire of Rome. Known for tyranny and extravagance.

VESPASIAN (AD 69–79)
Founder of the Flavian dynasty. Restored stability after a year of civil war and began the construction of the Colosseum.

TITUS (AD 79–81)
Saw the eruption of Mount Vesuvius and the completion of the Colosseum.

DOMITIAN (AD 81–96)
Known for autocratic rule, extensive building projects, and believed to have persecuted Christians and Jews.

TRAJAN (AD 98–117)
Empire reached its greatest territorial extent. Clarified policy on Christians, leading to sporadic persecutions.

HADRIAN (AD 117–138)
Traveled extensively, consolidated borders, and was a patron of Greek culture.

MARCUS AURELIUS (AD 161–180)
Philosopher-emperor with Stoic writings. Faced plagues and wars and saw sporadic persecutions of Christians.

COMMODUS (AD 180–192)
His erratic rule is often seen as marking the decline of the empire's golden age.

SEPTIMIUS SEVERUS (AD 193–211)
Strengthened the military and introduced reforms. Issued edicts leading to Christian persecutions.

DECIUS (AD 249–251)
Issued an empire-wide edict demanding sacrifice to the emperor, effectively targeting Christians.

VALERIAN (AD 253–260)
Initially tolerant of Christians; later edicts led to persecutions.

DIOCLETIAN (AD 284–305)
Responsible for the "Great Persecution," the last and most severe persecution of Christians.

CONSTANTINE THE GREAT (AD 306–337)
Unified the empire, founded Constantinople, converted to Christianity, and issued the Edict of Milan granting religious tolerance.

THEODOSIUS I (AD 379–395)
Last emperor to rule over both the East and West. Made Christianity the state religion and banned pagan rituals.

TIMELINE OF THE CATHOLIC FAITH

Here's a timeline of Christianity from the perspective of the Catholic Church. Note that this is a broad overview and not exhaustive.

1ST CENTURY
C. 4-6: Birth of Jesus Christ in Bethlehem.
C. 30: Crucifixion and resurrection of Jesus Christ.
33-34: Pentecost—descent of the Holy Spirit upon the Apostles.

C. 34-67: Apostle Peter becomes the first bishop of Rome; the Catholic Church sees him as the first pope.
60-99: Writings of the New Testament, including the Gospels, letters, and the Revelation.

2ND CENTURY

The Church distinguishes itself from Gnosticism and other early heresies.

150: St. Justin Martyr writes his Apologies, defending Christianity to the Roman Empire.

3RD CENTURY

The Church suffers from various persecutions by Roman emperors.

251: Cyprian becomes bishop of Carthage and writes on the unity of the Church.

4TH CENTURY

313: The Edict of Milan by Constantine the Great legalizes Christianity.

325: First Council of Nicaea—condemned Arianism and produced the Nicene Creed.

380: Christianity becomes the official religion of the Roman Empire under Emperor Theodosius I.

5TH CENTURY

410: Fall of Rome to the Visigoths.

431: Council of Ephesus—declared Mary as Theotokos (God-bearer or Mother of God).

451: Council of Chalcedon—affirmed Christ's divine and human natures.

6TH CENTURY

590-604: Pope Gregory the Great enhances the papacy's authority and role.

7TH CENTURY

632: The rise of Islam and its expansion into previously Christian territories.

8TH CENTURY

800: Charlemagne is crowned Holy Roman Emperor by Pope Leo III, reinforcing the bond between the Church and European rulers.

9TH CENTURY

869-870: Fourth Council of Constantinople—last ecumenical council the East and West participated in before the Great Schism.

10TH CENTURY

962: Formation of the Holy Roman Empire—the coronation of Otto I as Holy Roman Emperor in 962 marked the formal establishment of the Holy Roman Empire, which aimed to revive the glory of the ancient Roman Empire and played a central role in European politics and Christian history for centuries.

11TH CENTURY

1054: The Great Schism—formal split between the Roman Catholic Church and Eastern Orthodox Churches.

12TH–13TH CENTURIES

Crusades to reclaim the Holy Land.

1215: Fourth Lateran Council—clarified teachings and approved transubstantiation.

14TH–15TH CENTURIES

1309-1377: Avignon papacy—popes reside in Avignon, France, instead of Rome.

1417: End of the Western Schism with the election of Pope Martin V.

16TH CENTURY

1517: Martin Luther's 95 Theses—beginning of the rotestant Reformation.

1545-1563: Council of Trent—Counter-Reformation, clarified Church teachings in response to Protestantism.

LATE 16TH CENTURY ONWARD: Expansion of Jesuit missions—the Jesuits expanded Catholic influence in parts of Asia, Africa, and the Americas.

17TH–18TH CENTURIES

1633: The trial of Galileo—Galileo was tried and found "vehemently suspect of heresy" for supporting the heliocentric view, leading to house arrest.

MID-17TH CENTURY: Jansenism Controversy: a heretical movement within the Catholic Church, emphasizing original sin and predestination.

19TH CENTURY

1870: First Vatican Council—defined papal infallibility.

20TH CENTURY

1962-1965: Second Vatican Council—modernized the Church's practices and teachings.

1978: Pope John Paul II becomes the first non-Italian pope in 455 years and has a significant influence on the Church and the world.

21ST CENTURY

2013: Pope Benedict XVI resigns, the first pope to do so in 600 years. Pope Francis is elected, becoming the first Jesuit pope and the first from the Americas.

ICONOGRAPHY

Catholic iconography is rich and diverse, with many symbols used over the centuries to convey religious teachings, concepts, and stories.

Here's a short list of some prominent symbols and their meanings:

ALPHA (A) AND OMEGA (Ω): The first and last letters of the Greek alphabet represent Jesus as the beginning and end of all things, based on a description in the book of Revelation.

ANCHOR: Symbolizes hope and steadfastness in the faith.

ARROWS: Often seen with St. Sebastian, they represent martyrdom.

BEEHIVE: Symbolizes industry, diligence, and orderliness, but also the Church, with the bees representing Christians working together in community.

BOOK: Often held by saints; represents the Holy Scriptures or the teachings of that particular saint.

CENSER OR THURIBLE: Represents prayers rising to Heaven, based on the Biblical imagery of incense as prayers.

CHI-RHO (✗): Made up of the first two letters (X and P) of the Greek word for "Christ." It's a symbol for Jesus Christ.

CROSS/CRUCIFIX: Represents the sacrifice of Jesus Christ on the Cross for the salvation of humanity. The crucifix specifically depicts Jesus on the cross and is different from a plain cross, which is often found in Protestant churches.

CROWN: Represents victory, martyrdom, and the Kingdom of Heaven. Saints, especially martyrs, are often depicted with crowns.

DOVE: Represents the Holy Spirit and is often shown descending from the heavens, especially in depictions of Pentecost.

FISH: An ancient Christian symbol known as Ichthys. It represents Christ and originates in the early days of Christianity when it was used as a secret sign among believers.

FLEUR-DE-LIS: Traditionally used to represent the Holy Trinity, but also associated with the Virgin Mary and purity.

GRAPES AND WHEAT: Represent the Eucharist, with the grapes symbolizing the wine (blood of Christ) and the wheat the bread (body of Christ).

HIS (IHΣ): A monogram representing the first three letters of "Jesus" in Greek. It's a symbol for Jesus Christ.

ICXC: An ancient Greek Christogram, an abbreviation for "Jesus Christ."

IMMACULATE HEART: Depiction of the heart of the Virgin Mary, representing her pure love and sorrow. It's often surrounded by roses or thorns and pierced by a sword.

INRI: An abbreviation of the Latin phrase *Iesus Nazarenus, Rex Iudaeorum* meaning "Jesus of Nazareth, King of the Jews."

KEYS OF ST. PETER: Symbolizes the authority given by Jesus to Peter and, by extension, to the papacy.

LADDER: Often seen in depictions of the crucifixion, it recalls the tools used during the descent from the cross.

LAMB: Represents Jesus as the "Lamb of God" who takes away the sins of the world.

LILY: Associated with the Virgin Mary; represents purity and virtue. It is also linked with St. Joseph.

LOAVES AND FISHES: Recall the miracle of the multiplication of the loaves and fishes, representing the miracles and abundance of Christ.

MANTLE OR CLOAK: Associated with protection, especially in depictions of Mary, where she is shown spreading her mantle over the faithful.

MONSTRANCE: A vessel used to display the Eucharistic host. It represents the real presence of Jesus in the Eucharist.

OLIVE BRANCH: Symbolizes peace and reconciliation. The dove returning to Noah's Ark with an olive branch indicated the end of the Flood and God's reconciliation with humanity.

PALM BRANCH: Represents martyrdom and victory over death, as martyrs are often depicted holding palm leaves. It also recalls the entry of Jesus into Jerusalem (Palm Sunday) when he was greeted with waving palm branches.

PELICAN: Believed in medieval Europe to feed its young with its blood, the pelican symbolizes the sacrifice of Christ.

PHOENIX: A mythical bird that rises from its ashes, it symbolizes the resurrection.

SACRED HEART: Depicts Jesus's heart, often surrounded by thorns and topped with a flame, symbolizing his divine love and compassion, as well as his sacrifice.

SHELL: Particularly associated with St. James and pilgrimage (especially to Santiago de Compostela in Spain). It's also used in depictions of baptism, as water from a shell is traditionally poured over the person being baptized.

SHEPHERD'S CROOK (PASTORAL STAFF): Symbolizes the role of bishops and higher prelates as shepherds of the Lord's flock.

SHIP: Symbolizes the Church, with the idea of the Church guiding its followers through the "stormy seas" of life.

SWORD: Can symbolize martyrdom when depicted with a saint (like St. Paul). It can also represent the Word of God, which is described in the Bible as "sharper than any two-edged sword."

This list only scratches the surface of the vast iconography within Catholicism. Each symbol is imbued with deep meaning and history, often with layers of interpretation that have developed over the centuries.

FOUR EVANGELISTS

The four evangelists are the authors of the four Gospels in the New Testament of the Bible. Each of these evangelists is represented by a distinct symbol, often derived from the prophetic vision in the book of Ezekiel (1:1–14) and the book of Revelation (4:6–8). Here they are, along with their associated symbols:

1. MATTHEW: His symbol is a man or angel. This image represents the humanity of Christ and relates to Matthew's account, which begins with the genealogy of Jesus and emphasizes Jesus's human lineage. The Gospel of Matthew portrays Jesus as the promised Messiah who fulfills Old Testament prophecies, hence linking the human ancestry of Jesus to the Davidic lineage.

2. MARK: His symbol is a lion, often winged. This symbol represents royal majesty and resurrection. The Gospel of

Mark starts with John the Baptist's voice "crying out in the wilderness," and the lion is often associated with the desert. Moreover, the Gospel's focus on the power and authority of Jesus can be likened to the strength and majesty of a lion.

3. LUKE: His symbol is an ox or calf, often depicted with wings. The ox is a symbol of sacrifice, service, and strength. This image aligns with Luke's portrayal of Jesus as the compassionate healer and savior of all people, emphasizing His sacrificial love and service to humanity.

4. JOHN: His symbol is an eagle. The eagle represents the infinite sky and the divine nature of Christ. The Gospel of John is unique in its theological depth and focus on the divinity of Jesus Christ, starting with the prologue: "In the beginning was the Word, and the Word was with God, and the Word was God."

These symbols have often been used throughout Christian art and history to represent each evangelist. They are depicted in stained glass windows, paintings, and other artworks in churches and religious texts.

TWELVE APOSTLES

The twelve apostles were the original disciples of Jesus Christ, chosen by him to spread his teachings. They are central figures in Christianity:

1. SIMON PETER (OR PETER): He is often considered the leader of the apostles and was instrumental in the early growth of the Church. Jesus often referred to him as the "rock" on which He would build His church.

2. ANDREW: Peter's brother; he was the first disciple called by Jesus.

3. JAMES THE GREATER: The son of Zebedee and the elder brother of John. He is often called "the Greater" to distinguish him from the other James.

4. JOHN: James's younger brother is known as the Beloved Disciple and is traditionally believed to be the author of the Gospel of John, as well as three New Testament epistles and the book of Revelation.

5. PHILIP: Hailing from Bethsaida in Galilee, he evangelized and engaged in theological discussions with Jesus.

6. BARTHOLOMEW (OR NATHANAEL): He is sometimes identified with Nathanael, who appears in the Gospel of John.

7. MATTHEW (OR LEVI): He was a tax collector before being called by Jesus. Tradition holds that he is the author of the Gospel of Matthew.

8. THOMAS: Often referred to as Doubting Thomas because he initially doubted Jesus's resurrection until he saw Jesus's wounds.

9. JAMES THE LESSER: Often identified with James, the son of Alphaeus, he's called "the Lesser" or "the Younger" to differentiate him from James the Greater.

10. THADDEUS (OR LEBBAEUS OR JUDAS, SON OF JAMES): The names and identifications of this apostle vary between the Gospels and church traditions.

11. SIMON THE ZEALOT: Referred to as "the Zealot" to distinguish him from Simon Peter.

12. JUDAS ISCARIOT: He betrayed Jesus to the religious authorities, leading to Jesus's crucifixion. After his betrayal, Judas felt remorse and ended his own life.

After Judas Iscariot betrayed Jesus and subsequently died, the remaining eleven apostles felt the need to replace him to maintain the number twelve, which had symbolic significance. The replacement process is described in the book of Acts, chapter 1.

They proposed two men as potential replacements: Joseph, called Barsabbas (also known as Justus), and Matthias. They prayed for guidance and then cast lots, an ancient method of seeking divine guidance. The lot fell to Matthias, and he was added to the eleven apostles, thus becoming the twelfth apostle in place of Judas Iscariot.

DOCTORS OF THE CHURCH

The title "Doctor of the Church" is a special designation the Catholic Church gives to certain saints, recognizing them for their outstanding contributions to theology or doctrine. Each of these saints has made significant contributions to doctrine and teaching, and their works are often studied by theologians, seminarians, and the faithful for deeper understanding of the faith. It's worth noting that the recognition of someone as a Doctor of the Church does not imply infallibility in everything they wrote; rather, it signifies that their writings are particularly beneficial for understanding and living the Catholic faith.

Albert the Great
Alphonsus Liguori
Ambrose
Anselm
Anthony of Padua
Athanasius

Augustine
Basil the Great
Bede the Venerable
Bernard of Clairvaux
Bonaventure
Catherine of Siena

Cyril of Alexandria
Cyril of Jerusalem
Ephrem the Syrian
Francis de Sales
Gregory of Narek
Gregory of Nazianzus
Gregory the Great
Hilary of Poitiers
Hildegard of Bingen
Isidore of Seville
Jerome
John Chrysostom

John of Ávila
John of Damascus
John of the Cross
Lawrence of Brindisi
Leo the Great
Peter Canisius
Peter Chrysologus
Peter Damian
Robert Bellarmine
Teresa of Ávila
Thérèse of Lisieux
Thomas Aquinas

THE APOSTOLIC FATHERS

The Apostolic Fathers are a group of early Christian writers who lived and wrote primarily in the late first and early second centuries. They are so named because they were traditionally believed to have had direct personal contact with the apostles or to have lived during the Apostolic Age (the years after Jesus's death and resurrection). The writings of the Apostolic Fathers are not considered canonical (that is, they aren't part of the New Testament), but they have been highly revered throughout Christian history. They provide a bridge between the New Testament and the later writings of the Church Fathers like Sts. Augustine, Jerome, and Gregory the Great, and they offer critical insights into the development of early Christian thought, theology, and practice.

Here are some of the most notable Apostolic Fathers:

Clement of Rome (St. Clement I)
Ignatius of Antioch
Polycarp of Smyrna
Hermas

Papias of Hierapolis
Barnabas
The Author of the Didache
Clement II

THE FOURTEEN HOLY HELPERS

In Catholic tradition, the Fourteen Holy Helpers are a group of saints venerated together in parts of medieval Europe, especially in Germany, for their intercessory power, particularly during times of hardship. Their veneration likely became more widespread due to the need for heavenly assistance during the Black Death in the fourteenth century.

Each of these saints was invoked for specific ailments or protections.

Agathius (Acacius)
Barbara
Blaise (Blase, Blasius)
Catherine of Alexandria
Christopher (Christophorus)
Cyriacus
Denis (Dionysius)

Erasmus (Elmo)
Eustace (Eustachius, Eustathius)
George (Georgius)
Giles (Aegidius)
Margaret of Antioch
Pantaleon (Panteleimon)
Vitus (Guy)

MYSTICAL EXPERIENCES

Many mystics in the Catholic tradition have reported extraordinary experiences and miracles. The Catholic Church approaches these phenomena with caution and discernment. They're seen as signs of God's active presence, but not as necessary indicators of holiness or as essential for spiritual growth.

Here are definitions of some of the more notable ones:

AURORA OF SANCTITY (OR HALO): A radiant light signifying holiness.

BILOCATION: Being in two places at the same time.

ECSTASIES: States of deep contemplation and absorption in God.

ENDURANCE OF EXTREME HARDSHIPS: Facing physical challenges as a testament to faith.

EUCHARISTIC MIRACLES: Visible transformations of the Eucharist, often into flesh and blood.

GIFT OF HEALING: Ability to heal through prayer and touch.

GIFT OF MIRACULOUS KNOWLEDGE: Receiving knowledge beyond natural means.

GIFT OF PROPHECY: Foreseeing future events or understanding God's will.

GIFT OF TEARS: Overwhelming sense of God's presence or personal sin, leading to weeping.

GIFT OF TONGUES: Speaking in previously unknown languages.

***INCENDIUM AMORIS* (INFLAMING OF LOVE):** Intense spiritual longing for God.

INEDIA (OR FASTING MIRACLES): Surviving without food or drink, often excepting the Eucharist.

LEVITATION: Being lifted off the ground, especially during prayer.

LOCUTIONS: Supernatural communications, audible or internal.

MIRACULOUS HEALINGS: Curing of illnesses and ailments through divine intervention.

MIRACULOUS IMAGES: Sacred images appearing on objects or in natural phenomena.

MIRACULOUS PROTECTION: Divine protection in dangerous situations.

MYSTICAL MARRIAGE: Spiritual union between the soul and Christ.

OSMOGENESIA: Fragrant aroma from the body of a particularly holy deceased person. Otherwise known as the odor of sanctity.

READING OF HEARTS: Discerning inner thoughts, feelings, or sins of individuals.

STIGMATA: Bodily marks or pains corresponding to the crucifixion wounds of Jesus.

TRANSVERBERATION: A piercing or flaming arrow of love from God felt intensely in the heart.

VISIONS AND APPARITIONS: Supernatural appearances of saintly, demonic, or heavenly figures.

MYSTICS

The Catholic Church has a rich mystical tradition, with numerous saints and theologians who have explored and described the depths of spiritual experience. Some of the most notable Catholic mystics are:

Alexandrina of Balazar
Angela of Foligno
Anne Catherine Emmerich
Bernard of Clairvaux
Bridget of Sweden
Catherine of Siena
Venerable Conchita
Dina Bélanger
Elizabeth of the Trinity
Faustina Kowalska
Francis of Assisi
Gemma Galgani
Henry Suso
Hildegard of Bingen
Ignatius of Loyola

John Eudes
John of the Cross
Julian of Eucharist
Julian of Norwich
Lutgarde
Margaret Mary Alacoque
Maria Bolognesi
Venerable Marie of the Incarnation
Mary Magdalene de' Pazzi
Meister Eckhart
Pio of Pietrelcina
Teresa of Ávila
Thérèse of Lisieux
Veronica Giuliani

THE EDICT OF MILAN

The Edict of Milan refers to a significant historical document issued in 313 by the Roman emperors Constantine the Great and Licinius. It marked a pivotal moment in the Roman Empire's history and profoundly impacted the religious landscape of the time.

The Edict of Milan granted religious tolerance and freedom to Christians within the Roman Empire, effectively ending the persecution of Christians that had been occurring for several decades. The edict is particularly associated with Emperor Constantine, who is known for his role in the conversion of the Roman Empire to Christianity.

The proclamation was a response to the religious conflicts and persecutions that had characterized the empire for years, particularly against Christians. It granted Christians and other religious groups the right to openly practice their faith without fear of persecution, and it also restored confiscated properties and privileges to Christian communities.

By legalizing Christianity and granting it official recognition, the Edict of Milan contributed to accepting and spreading the religion throughout the Roman Empire. This shift in policy laid the groundwork for the eventual establishment of Christianity as the state religion of the Roman Empire under Emperor Theodosius I in 380.

HERESIES

The Catholic Church has faced various heretical movements and teachings throughout its history. In Christian theological context, a heresy refers to a belief or a collection of beliefs that are seriously at odds with established doctrine. Here are some of the major heresies that the Catholic Church has addressed:

ALBIGENSIANISM OR CATHARISM (12TH-13TH CENTURIES): Based in southern France, Albigensians believed in a dualistic view of good and evil deities and rejected many Catholic doctrines and practices. The Albigensian Crusade and the Inquisition were significant responses to this heresy.

ARIANISM (4TH CENTURY): Proposed by Arius, this heresy asserted that Jesus Christ was created by God the Father and therefore is not co-eternal with the Father. The First Council of Nicaea in 325 condemned Arianism and reaffirmed the full divinity of Jesus Christ.

DOCETISM (EARLY CENTURIES): Derived from the Greek *dokein* (to seem), Docetism claimed that Jesus did not have an actual physical body and only appeared to be human. Various Church Fathers refuted this heresy.

DONATISM (4TH-5TH CENTURIES): Donatists believed that the sacraments' efficacy depended on the minister's ethical character. They also maintained a rigorous stance on lapsed Christians during persecutions, saying they couldn't be easily readmitted to the Church.

GNOSTICISM (2ND CENTURY ONWARD): An ancient religious idea that posited a dualism between the material and spiritual worlds. Gnostics believed in secret knowledge for salvation and often viewed the material world as evil.

ICONOCLASM (8TH-9TH CENTURIES): This refers to the opposition to the veneration of icons and images in the Church. The Second Council of Nicaea in 787 affirmed the veneration (but not the worship) of icons.

MANICHAEISM (3RD CENTURY): A religious movement from Persia inspired by the dualism of Zoroastrianism and other Eastern philosophies that stressed the belief in two divine natures: one good, the other evil. St. Augustine was drawn to Manichaeism as a young man, and the Church continued to challenge this belief system well into the Middle Ages.

MODERNISM (19TH-20TH CENTURIES): A broad movement that sought to reconcile traditional Christian beliefs with modern science and philosophy. Pope Pius X condemned the more radical aspects of Modernism in the early twentieth century, including relativism and a rejection of dogma.

MONOPHYSITISM (5TH-6TH CENTURIES): Opposite of Nestorianism, Monophysitism held that Jesus had only one nature, which was either purely divine or a synthesis of divine and human. The Council of Chalcedon in 451 refuted this and established the doctrine that Christ has two distinct natures, divine and human, in one person.

NESTORIANISM (5TH CENTURY): This heresy, associated with Nestorius, argued that Jesus had two separate personhoods, one divine and one human, instead of one unified person. The Council of Ephesus in 431 refuted this.

PELAGIANISM (5TH CENTURY): Initiated by Pelagius, this heresy denied original sin and asserted that humans could achieve salvation through their own efforts without divine grace. It was condemned at multiple synods and councils.

COUNCILS

FIRST COUNCIL OF NICAEA (325): This council was convened to address the Arian controversy. It decisively condemned Arianism, which denied the divinity of Christ. The council produced the first part of the Nicene Creed to articulate the faith in Christ's true divinity.

FIRST COUNCIL OF CONSTANTINOPLE (381): Building on the work at Nicaea, this council further refuted Arianism and Macedonianism, the latter of which denied the divinity of the Holy Spirit. The Nicene-Constantinopolitan Creed, commonly recited today and known simply as the Nicene Creed, resulted from this council.

COUNCIL OF EPHESUS (431): The council tackled the Nestorian heresy, which argued that Jesus had two separate personhoods. The council asserted Mary's title as Theotokos, or God-bearer, and emphasized Christ's unity as one person with two natures, human and divine.

COUNCIL OF CHALCEDON (451): Against the Monophysite contention that Jesus had only one nature, this council defined the hypostatic union: Jesus is one person in two natures, fully divine and fully human, without confusion or separation.

SECOND COUNCIL OF CONSTANTINOPLE (553): This council confronted various interpretations of Christology that diverged from Chalcedonian understanding. It reaffirmed the decisions of previous councils and further condemned certain writings that veered toward Nestorianism.

THIRD COUNCIL OF CONSTANTINOPLE (680-681): The debate on Christ's nature continued, this time focusing on his wills. The council condemned Monothelitism, which claimed Christ had only one will, affirming instead that he had both a divine will and a human will.

SECOND COUNCIL OF NICAEA (787): Iconoclasm, or the opposition to religious images, was the key issue here. While the council confirmed the appropriate veneration of icons, it differentiated between the respect given to icons and the worship due only to God.

FOURTH COUNCIL OF CONSTANTINOPLE (869-870): Occurring amid political intrigue and ecclesiastical tensions, this council dealt with issues stemming from the Photian schism and further clarified the papacy's role in relation to other patriarchates.

FIRST LATERAN COUNCIL (1123): In the backdrop of the Investiture Controversy between the Church and secular rulers, this council asserted the Church's independence in making clerical appointments. It also began addressing disciplinary reforms in the Church.

SECOND LATERAN COUNCIL (1139): Following a schism, this council confirmed Pope Innocent II's papacy and tackled disciplinary issues, including condemning simony (buying or selling ecclesiastical positions) and clerical marriage.

THIRD LATERAN COUNCIL (1179): The council established the two-thirds majority rule for papal elections, ensuring more decisive outcomes. It also condemned heresies of the time and further addressed issues like simony and clerical discipline.

FOURTH LATERAN COUNCIL (1215): One of the most significant medieval councils, this gathering defined the doctrine of transubstantiation, which explains Christ's presence in the Eucharist and mandated annual confession and communion for the faithful.

FIRST COUNCIL OF LYON (1245):
Primarily political, this council reaffirmed the excommunicated Emperor Frederick II for his perceived offenses against the Church. Additionally, it called for support for the Holy Land against Muslim forces.

SECOND COUNCIL OF LYON (1274):
Amid ongoing tension between the East and West, this council attempted a short-lived reunion with the Eastern Orthodox Church. It also affirmed the primacy of the papacy and introduced new liturgical customs.

COUNCIL OF VIENNE (1311-1312):
The primary agenda was the suppression of the Knights Templar following allegations of heresy and misconduct. Additionally, it addressed issues concerning the Beguines and Beghards, lay religious movements of the time.

COUNCIL OF CONSTANCE (1414-1418): Amid the Western Schism with multiple claimants to the papacy, this council sought to resolve the crisis. It eventually ended the schism, electing Pope Martin V, and also, controversially, condemned Jan Hus, who was subsequently executed.

COUNCIL OF BASEL, FERRARA, AND FLORENCE (1431-1445): Moving locations multiple times, this council grappled with the challenge of conciliarism, which prioritized councils over popes. It also saw another short-lived reunion with the Eastern Orthodox Church.

FIFTH LATERAN COUNCIL (1512-1517): The last council before the Protestant Reformation discussed reforms but achieved limited results. The significant theological and ecclesiastical changes of the Reformation soon overshadowed its declarations.

COUNCIL OF TRENT (1545-1563):
In response to the Protestant Reformation, this council was pivotal in shaping Catholic Counter-Reformation efforts. It clarified and reaffirmed fundamental Catholic doctrines, addressed abuses, and set the direction for Catholicism for centuries.

FIRST VATICAN COUNCIL (1869-1870): This council is best known for defining papal infallibility, asserting that the pope, under certain conditions, could proclaim doctrines free from error. It also discussed the nature of the Church and its relation to modern thought.

SECOND VATICAN COUNCIL (1962-1965): Convened by Pope John XXIII, this landmark council sought to address the Catholic Church's relationship with the modern world. It introduced significant liturgical reforms, promoted ecumenism, and engaged with contemporary challenges like social justice and the Church's relationship with non-Christian religions.

CALENDAR OF SAINTS AND FEAST DAYS

JANUARY 1
- St. Zygmunt Gorazdowski
- Circumcision of Our Lord
- Octave Day of the Nativity
- Solemnity of the Blessed Virgin Mary, Mother of God

JANUARY 2
- St. Basil the Great
- St. Gregory Nazianzen

JANUARY 3
- St. Anterus
- St. Genevieve
- Most Holy Name of Jesus

JANUARY 4
- St. Elizabeth Ann Seton

JANUARY 5
- St. Genoveva
- St. John N. Neumann

JANUARY 6
- Sts. Caspar, Balthasar, and Melchior
- St. Raymond of Penyafort
- Epiphany of Our Lord

JANUARY 7
- St. Angela of Foligno
- St. Lucian of Antioch
- St. Raymond of Peñafort

JANUARY 8
- St. Apollinaris the Apologist
- St. Severinus of Noricum

JANUARY 9
- St. Adrian of Canterbury
- St. Julian the Hospitalarian and his wife, St. Basilissa

JANUARY 10
- St. John Camillus the Good
- St. Nicanor
- St. William of Bourges

JANUARY 11
- St. Hyginus
- St. Paulinus
- St. Theodosius the Cenobiarch

JANUARY 12
- St. Arcadius
- St. Benedict Biscop
- St. Marguerite Bourgeoys

JANUARY 13
- St. Hilary of Poitiers
- St. Veronica of Milan
- Commemoration of the Baptism of Our Lord

JANUARY 14
- St. Felix of Nola
- St. Sava

JANUARY 15
- St. Ita of Killeedy
- St. Paul the Hermit

JANUARY 16
- St. Fursey

JANUARY 17
- St. Antony the Abbot

JANUARY 18
- St. Margaret of Hungary
- St. Prisca
- St. Volusian
- Feast of the Chair of St. Peter at Rome

JANUARY 19
- St. Canute IV
- St. Wulfstan

JANUARY 20
- St. Fabian
- St. Sebastian

JANUARY 21
- St. Agnes
- St. Meinrad

JANUARY 22
- St. Anastasius XIV

JANUARY 23
- St. Emerentiana
- St. Marianne Cope
- St. Vincent

JANUARY 24
- St. Francis de Sales

JANUARY 25
- St. Ananias of Damascus
- Conversion of St. Paul

JANUARY 26
- St. Paula
- Sts. Timothy and Titus

JANUARY 27
- St. Angela Merici

JANUARY 28
- St. Peter Nolasco
- St. Thomas Aquinas

JANUARY 29
- St. Blath

JANUARY 30
- St. Bathildes
- St. Martina of Rome

JANUARY 31
- St. John Bosco

FEBRUARY 1
- St. Brigid of Ireland

FEBRUARY 2
- Feast of the Presentation of Our Lord and Purification of the Blessed Virgin Mary (Candlemas Day)

FEBRUARY 3
- St. Anne-Marie Rivier
- St. Ansgar
- St. Blaise
- St. Marie of St. Ignatius
- St. Simeon

FEBRUARY 4
- St. Andrew Corsini

FEBRUARY 5
- St. Agatha

FEBRUARY 6
- St. Dorothy
- St. Francis of Nagasaki
- St. Paul Miki

FEBRUARY 7
- St. Richard of Lucca

FEBRUARY 8
- St. Josephine Bakhita

FEBRUARY 9
- St. Apollonia
- St. Nicephorus

FEBRUARY 10
- St. Scholastica of Nursia

FEBRUARY 11
- St. Pascal I
- Our Lady of Lourdes

FEBRUARY 12
- St. Anthony of Saxony

FEBRUARY 13
- St. Apollos
- St. Catherine dei Ricci

FEBRUARY 14
- Sts. Cyril and Methodius
- St. Valentine

FEBRUARY 15
- St. Claude de la Colombière
- Sts. Faustinus and Jovita

FEBRUARY 16
- St. Juliana of Nicomedia
- St. Onesimus

FEBRUARY 17
- St. Donatus

FEBRUARY 18
- St. Flavian of Constantinople

FEBRUARY 19
- St. Barbatus

FEBRUARY 20
- St. Amata
- St. Eucherius
- Sts. Francisco Marto and Jacinta Marto

FEBRUARY 21
- St. Peter Damian

FEBRUARY 22
- Chair of St. Peter at Antioch

FEBRUARY 23
- St. Polycarp

FEBRUARY 24
- St. Adela

FEBRUARY 25
- St. Tarasius
- St. Walburga

FEBRUARY 26
- St. Alexander

FEBRUARY 27
- St. Gabriel of Our Lady of Sorrows
- St. Leander of Seville

FEBRUARY 28
- St. Romanus
- St. Hilary

MARCH 1
- St. Albinus
- St. David

MARCH 2
- Blessed Charles the Good

MARCH 3
- St. Cunegundes
- St. Katharine Drexel

MARCH 4
- St. Casimir
- St. Lucius I

MARCH 5
- St. John Joseph of the Cross

MARCH 6
- St. Colette
- St. Fridolin

MARCH 7
- Sts. Felicitas and Perpetua

MARCH 8
- St. John of God

MARCH 9
- St. Catherine of Bologna
- St. Frances of Rome
- St. Gregory of Nyssa

MARCH 10
- St. Victor

MARCH 11
- St. Eulogius of Cordoba

MARCH 12
- St. Theophanes the Chronicler

MARCH 13
- St. Euphrasia of Constantinople
- St. Roderic

MARCH 14
- St. Matilda

MARCH 15
- St. Longinus
- St. Louise de Marillac

MARCH 16
- St. Julian of Antioch

MARCH 17
- St. Joseph of Arimathea
- St. Patrick

MARCH 18
- St. Cyril of Jerusalem

MARCH 19
- St. Joseph

MARCH 20
- St. Photina
- St. Wulfran

MARCH 21
- St. Edna

MARCH 22
· St. Nicholas Owen

MARCH 23
· St. Felix
· St. Turibius of Mogrovejo

MARCH 24
· St. Catherine of Vadstena
· St. Oscar Arnulfo
  Romero y Galdámez
· St. Simon of Trent

MARCH 25
· St. Dismas
· Annunciation of
  the Lord

MARCH 26
· St. Castulus
· St. Ludger

MARCH 27
· St. Augusta
· St. John of Egypt
· St. Rupert of Salzburg

MARCH 28
· St. Alexander

MARCH 29
· St. Eustace of Luxeuil
· St. Joseph of Arimathea

MARCH 30
· St. John Climacus
· St. Quirinus of Neuss

MARCH 31
· St. Balbina of Rome
· St. Benjamin

APRIL 1
· St. Hugh of Grenoble

APRIL 2
· St. Francis Paola

APRIL 3
· St. Irene of Thessalonica
· St. Richard of Chichester

APRIL 4
· St. Benedict the Moor
· St. Gaetano Catanoso
· St. Irene of Rome
· St. Isidore of Seville

APRIL 5
· St. Vincent Ferrer

APRIL 6
· St. Celestine I

APRIL 7
· St. John Baptist de
  La Salle

APRIL 8
· St. Julie Billiart

APRIL 9
· St. Gaucherius

APRIL 10
· St. Fulbert of Chartres

APRIL 11
· St. Gemma Galgani
· St. Stanislaus of Kraków

APRIL 12
· St. Julius
· St. Sabbas the Goth

APRIL 13
· St. Hermenegild
· St. Martin I

APRIL 14
· St. Lambert of Lyon
· St. Lydwine of Schiedam
· Sts. Tiburtius, Valerian,
  and Maximus

APRIL 15
· St. Paternus

APRIL 16
· St. Bernadette Soubirous
· St. Drogo

APRIL 17
· St. Anicetus
· St. Stephen Harding

APRIL 18
· St. Apollonius
  the Apologist

APRIL 19
· St. Alphege
· St. Expeditus
· St. Leo IX

APRIL 20
- St. Agnes
  of Montepulciano

APRIL 21
- St. Anselm
- St. Conrad

APRIL 22
- Sts. Epipodius
  and Alexander

APRIL 23
- St. Adalbert
- St. George

APRIL 24
- St. Mary Cleophas

APRIL 25
- St. Mark the Evangelist

APRIL 26
- St. Alda
- St. Cletus

APRIL 27
- St. Zita

APRIL 28
- St. Gianna Beretta Molla
- St. Louis de Montfort
- St. Peter Chanel

APRIL 29
- St. Catherine of Siena
- St. Hugh the Great
- St. Peter of Verona

APRIL 30
- St. Pius V
- St. Quirinus

MAY 1
- St. Joseph the Worker
- St. Peregrine Laziosi

MAY 2
- St. Athanasius the Great

MAY 3
- St. Alexander
- St. Juvenal of Narni
- Sts. Philip and James
  the Lesser

MAY 4
- St. Florian

MAY 5
- St. Jutta

MAY 6
- St. Dominic Savio
- St. Evodius
- Blessed Edward Jones
  and Anthony Middleton

MAY 7
- St. Domitian of Huy
- St. Rosa Venerini

MAY 8
- St. Desideratus
- St. Magdaline of Canossa

MAY 9
- St. Pachomius

MAY 10
- St. Damian
- Sts. Gordian
  and Epimachus
- St. John of Ávila
- St. Solange

MAY 11
- St. Francis di Girolama

MAY 12
- Sts. Nereus and Achilleus

MAY 13
- Our Lady of Fatima

MAY 14
- St. Boniface of Tarsus
- St. Matthias

MAY 15
- St. Dymphna
- St. Gerebernus
- St. Isidore the Farmer

MAY 16
- St. Brendan
  the Navigator
- St. John Nepomucen
- St. Simon Stock
- St. Ubaldus

MAY 17
- St. Paschal Baylon

MAY 18
- St. Eric IX of Sweden
- St. John I
- St. Venantius

MAY 19
- St. Celestine V
- St. Dunstan
- St. Ivo
- St. Pudentiana

MAY 20
- St. Bernardino of Siena

MAY 21
- St. Christopher
  Magallanes
- St. Constantine
  the Great
- Cristero Martyrs

MAY 22
- St. Rita of Cascia

MAY 23
- St. John Baptist de Rossi
- St. Julia of Corsica

MAY 24
- Sts. Donatian and
  Rogatian (brothers)
- St. Joanna

MAY 25
- St. Bede the Venerable
- St. Gregory VII
- St. Mary Magdalene
  de' Pazzi
- St. Urban I

MAY 26
- St. Augustine
  of Canterbury
- St. Eleutherius
- St. Philip Neri

MAY 27
- St. Augustine
  of Canterbury

MAY 28
- St. Bernard of Montjoux

MAY 29
- St. Maximinus of Trier

MAY 30
- St. Ferdinand III
- St. Joan of Arc

MAY 31
- St. Camilla Battista
  da Varano
- The Visitation of the
  Virgin Mary

JUNE 1
- St. Justin

JUNE 2
- St. Erasmus
- Sts. Marcellinus
  and Peter

JUNE 3
- St. Charles Lwanga
  and companions
- St. Clothilde
- St. John XXIII

JUNE 4
- St. Francis Caracciolo

JUNE 5
- St. Boniface of Mainz

JUNE 6
- St. Norbert

JUNE 7
- St. Robert
  of Newminster

JUNE 8
- Sts. Medard and Gildard

JUNE 9
- St. Columba
- Sts. Primus and Felician

JUNE 10
- St. Landericus

JUNE 11
- St. Barnabas

JUNE 12
- St. Gaspar Bertoni
- Blessed Jolenta of Poland

JUNE 13
- St. Anthony of Padua

JUNE 14
- St. Elgar

JUNE 15
- Sts. Vitus, Crescentia,
  and Modestus

JUNE 16
- St. John Francis Regis

JUNE 17
- St. Botolph
- St. Gregory Barbarigo
- St. Harvey (Hervé)

JUNE 18
- Venerable Matt Talbot

JUNE 19
- Sts. Gervase and
  Protase (brothers)
- St. Juliana Falconieri
- St. Romuald

JUNE 20
- St. Silverius

JUNE 21
- St. Aloysius Gonzaga
- St. Terence

JUNE 22
- St. John Fisher
- St. Paulinus of Nola
- St. Thomas More

JUNE 23
- St. Etheldreda (Audrey)

JUNE 24
- St. John the Baptist
- María Guadalupe
  García Zavala

JUNE 25
- St. Prosper of Aquitaine
- St. William of Vercelli

JUNE 26
- St. Anthelm
- St. Josemaria Escriva
- Sts. John and Paul
- St. Pelagius

JUNE 27
- St. Cyril of Alexandria
- Our Lady of
  Perpetual Help

JUNE 28
- St. Irenaeus

JUNE 29
- St. Paul
- St. Peter

JUNE 30
- First Martyrs of the Holy
  Roman Church

JULY 1
- St. Junípero Serra

JULY 2
- St. Bernardino Realino
- Sts. Processus
  and Martinian

JULY 3
- St. Thomas the Apostle

JULY 4
- St. Elizabeth of Portugal
- St. Theodore of Cyrene

JULY 5
- St. Anthony
  Mary Zaccaria

JULY 6
- St. Goar
- St. Maria Goretti

JULY 7
- St. Astius

JULY 8
- St. Grimbald
- St. Kilian
- Sts. Priscilla and Aquilla

JULY 9
- Sts. Augustine Zhao
  Rong and companions
- St. Veronica Giuliani

JULY 10
- Sts. Rufina and
  Secunda (sisters)

JULY 11
- St. Benedict of Nursia
- St. Pius I

JULY 12
- St. John Gualbert
- Sts. Louis and
  Zélie Martin
- Sts. Nabor and Felix
- St. Veronica

JULY 13
• St. Henry II

JULY 14
• St. Kateri Tekakwitha

JULY 15
• St. Bonaventure

JULY 16
• Our Lady of
  Mount Carmel

JULY 17
• St. Alexis

JULY 18
• St. Camillus de Lellis
• St. Frederick

JULY 19
• St. Arsenius the Great
• St. Epaphras

JULY 20
• St. Margaret of Antioch

JULY 21
• St. Lawrence of Brindisi
• St. Praxedes

JULY 22
• St. Mary Magdalene

JULY 23
• St. Apollinaris
  of Ravenna
• St. Bridget of Sweden
• St. Liborius

JULY 24
• St. Kinga of Poland
• St. Sharbel Makhluf

JULY 25
• St. Christopher
• St. James the Greater

JULY 26
• Sts. Joachim and Anne

JULY 27
• Sts. Nathalia, Aurelius,
  Liliosa, Felix, and George
• St. Pantaleon

JULY 28
• St. Alphonsa
• Sts. Nazarius and Celsus
• St. Victor I

JULY 29
• St. Martha
• St. Olaf

JULY 30
• Sts. Abdon and Sennen
• St. Peter Chrysologus

JULY 31
• St. Ignatius of Loyola
• St. Neot

AUGUST 1
• St. Alphonsus Liguori
• Sts. Faith, Hope,
  and Charity
• St. Peter in Chains

AUGUST 2
• St. Peter Julian Eymard

AUGUST 3
• St. Lydia Purpuraria
• St. Nicodemus

AUGUST 4
• St. John Vianney

AUGUST 5
• St. Emygdius

AUGUST 6
• Transfiguration of
  Our Lord

AUGUST 7
• St. Cajetan

AUGUST 8
• St. Cyriacus
• St. Dominic
• St. Mary of the
  Cross MacKillop

AUGUST 9
• St. Edith Stein (St. Teresa
  Benedicta of the Cross)

AUGUST 10
• St. Lawrence of Rome

AUGUST 11
• St. Clare of Assisi
• St. Philomena
• Sts. Tiburtius
  and Susanna

AUGUST 12
- St. Euplius
- St. Jane Frances de Chantal

AUGUST 13
- St. Hippolytus
- St. Radegund

AUGUST 14
- St. Maximilian Mary Kolbe

AUGUST 15
- St. Tarcisius
- Assumption of the Blessed Virgin Mary

AUGUST 16
- St. Roch
- St. Stephen of Hungary

AUGUST 17
- St. Jeanne Delanoue

AUGUST 18
- St. Agapitus
- St. Helena

AUGUST 19
- St. John Eudes

AUGUST 20
- St. Bernard of Clairvaux

AUGUST 21
- St. Pius X

AUGUST 22
- Queenship of the Blessed Virgin Mary

AUGUST 23
- St. Philip Benizi
- St. Rose of Lima

AUGUST 24
- St. Bartholomew

AUGUST 25
- St. Genesius of Rome
- St. Joseph Calasanz
- St. Louis IX
- St. Patricia

AUGUST 26
- St. Zephyrinus
- Our Lady of Czestochowa

AUGUST 27
- St. Caesarius of Arles
- St. Monica

AUGUST 28
- St. Augustine of Hippo
- St. Hermes
- St. Mose the Black

AUGUST 29
- Martyrdom of St. John the Baptist

AUGUST 30
- Sts. Felix and Adauctus
- St. Jeanne Jugan

AUGUST 31
- St. Aristides
- St. Raymond Nonnatus

SEPTEMBER 1
- St. Anna the Prophetess
- St. Giles
- St. Simeon Stylites the Elder

SEPTEMBER 2
- St. Agricola
- St. Ingrid

SEPTEMBER 3
- St. Gregory the Great

SEPTEMBER 4
- St. Marinus
- St. Rosalia

SEPTEMBER 5
- St. Bertin
- St. Lawrence Justinian
- St. Teresa of Calcutta

SEPTEMBER 6
- St. Eleutherius

SEPTEMBER 7
- St. Anastasius the Fuller
- St. Cloud
- St. Regina

SEPTEMBER 8
- St. Adrian
- St. Corbinian

SEPTEMBER 9
• St. Peter Claver

SEPTEMBER 10
• St. Peter Martinez

SEPTEMBER 11
• St. Adelphus
• St. Paphnutius
• Sts. Protus and Hyacinth

SEPTEMBER 12
• Most Holy Name
  of Mary
• St. Ailbe of Emly

SEPTEMBER 13
• St. John Chrysostom

SEPTEMBER 14
• St. Maternus
• St. Notburga
• Exaltation of the Holy
  Cross of Our Lord
  Jesus Christ

SEPTEMBER 15
• St. Nicomedes
• Our Lady of Sorrows

SEPTEMBER 16
• St. Cornelius
• St. Cyprian
• Sts. Euphemia, Lucy,
  and Geminianus

SEPTEMBER 17
• St. Robert Bellarmine
• St. Hildegard of Bingen
• Feast of the Stigmata of
  St. Francis of Assisi

SEPTEMBER 18
• St. Joseph of Cupertino

SEPTEMBER 19
• St. Januarius

SEPTEMBER 20
• Sts. Andrew Kim Taegon,
  Paul Chŏng Hasang,
  and companions
• Sts. Eustachius
  and companions

SEPTEMBER 21
• St. Matthew
  the Evangelist

SEPTEMBER 22
• Sts. Maurice
  and companions
• St. Thomas of Villanova

SEPTEMBER 23
• St. Constantius
  the Sacristan
• St. Linus
• St. Pio of Pietrelcina
  (Padre Pio)
• St. Thecla
• St. Zechariah

SEPTEMBER 24
• St. Gerard Sagredo

SEPTEMBER 25
• St. Cleophas

SEPTEMBER 26
• Sts. Cosmas and Damian
• St. Paul VI

SEPTEMBER 27
• St. Vincent de Paul

SEPTEMBER 28
• Sts. Lawrence Ruiz
  and companions
• St. Wenceslaus
• Blessed John of Dukla

SEPTEMBER 29
• Sts. Michael, Gabriel,
  and Raphael

SEPTEMBER 30
• St. Jerome

OCTOBER 1
• St. Remigius
• St. Thérèse of Lisieux

OCTOBER 2
• Holy Guardian Angels

OCTOBER 3
• St. Gerard of Brogne

OCTOBER 4
• St. Francis of Assisi

OCTOBER 5
- St. Faustina Kowalska
- St. Flora of Beaulieu
- St. Galla
- Blessed Raymond of Capua

OCTOBER 6
- St. Bruno
- St. Mary Frances of the Five Wounds (Anna Maria Gallo)
- Blessed Marie Rose Durocher

OCTOBER 7
- Our Lady of the Rosary

OCTOBER 8
- St. Pelagia

OCTOBER 9
- St. Denis
- St. John Henry Newman
- St. John Leonardi
- St. Louis Bertrand

OCTOBER 10
- St. Francis Borgia

OCTOBER 11
- St. Firminus
- St. John XXIII

OCTOBER 12
- St. Wilfrid

OCTOBER 13
- St. Gerald of Aurillac

OCTOBER 14
- St. Angadrisma of Beauvais
- St. Callistus I
- St. Cosmas

OCTOBER 15
- St. Teresa of Ávila

OCTOBER 16
- St. Gerard Majella
- St. Marguerite Bay
- St. Marie Marguerite d'Youville

OCTOBER 17
- St. Ignatius of Antioch
- St. John the Dwarf
- St. Margaret Mary Alacoque

OCTOBER 18
- St. Luke the Evangelist

OCTOBER 19
- St. Bruno of Querfurt
- St. Noël Chabanel
- Canadian/North American Martyrs

OCTOBER 20
- St. Irene of Tomar
- St. Paul of the Cross
- Blessed Adeline

OCTOBER 21
- St. Cilinia
- St. Hilarion
- St. Ursula

OCTOBER 22
- St. John Paul II
- St. Mary Salome

OCTOBER 23
- St. John of Capistrano

OCTOBER 24
- St. Anthony Mary Claret

OCTOBER 25
- Sts. Chrysanthus and Daria
- Sts. Crispin and Crispinian
- St. Tabitha

OCTOBER 26
- St. Demetrius
- St. Evaristus

OCTOBER 27
- St. Frumentius

OCTOBER 28
- Sts. Simon and Jude

OCTOBER 29
- St. Narcissus

OCTOBER 31
- St. Alphonsus Rodriguez
- St. Quintin

NOVEMBER 1
- All Saints' Day

NOVEMBER 2
- All Souls' Day

NOVEMBER 3
• St. Malachy
• St. Martin de Porres

NOVEMBER 4
• St. Charles Borromeo
• Sts. Vitalis and Agricola

NOVEMBER 5
• St. Bertille
• Sts. Zachary
  and Elizabeth

NOVEMBER 6
• St. Leonard of Noblac

NOVEMBER 7
• St. Engelbert
• St. Willibrord

NOVEMBER 8
• Four Crowned Martyrs:
  Severus, Severian, Car-
  pophorus, and Victorinus

NOVEMBER 9
• St. Theodore Tyro

NOVEMBER 10
• St. Andrew Avellino
• St. Leo the Great
• Sts. Tryphon, Respicius,
  and Nympha

NOVEMBER 11
• St. Martin of Tours
• St. Mennas

NOVEMBER 12
• St. Josaphat

NOVEMBER 13
• St. Didacus of Alcalá
• St. Frances
  Xavier Cabrini
• St. Stanislaus Kostka

NOVEMBER 14
• St. Lawrence O'Toole

NOVEMBER 15
• St. Albert the Great
• St. Leopold

NOVEMBER 16
• St. Agnes of Assisi
• St. Gertrude the Great

NOVEMBER 17
• St. Gregory
  Thaumaturgus
• St. Roque Gonzalez

NOVEMBER 18
• St. Rose-
  Philippine Duchesne

NOVEMBER 19
• St. Mechtild

NOVEMBER 20
• St. Bernward
• St. Felix of Valois

NOVEMBER 21
• Presentation of the
  Blessed Virgin Mary

NOVEMBER 22
• St. Cecilia

NOVEMBER 23
• St. Clement I
• St. Columban
• St. Felicity of Rome

NOVEMBER 24
• Sts. Andrew Dung-Lac
  and companions
• St. Chrysogonus

NOVEMBER 25
• St. Catherine
  of Alexandria

NOVEMBER 26
• St. John Berchmans
• St. Leonard of
  Port Maurice

NOVEMBER 27
• St. Maximus of Reiz
• Our Lady of the
  Miraculous Medal

NOVEMBER 28
• St. Catherine Labouré

NOVEMBER 29
• St. Saturninus

NOVEMBER 30
• St. Andrew
• St. Maura

DECEMBER 1
- St. Edmund Campion
- St. Eligius

DECEMBER 2
- St. Bibiana

DECEMBER 3
- St. Frances Xavier

DECEMBER 4
- St. Barbara
- St. John of Damascus

DECEMBER 5
- St. Gerald
- St. Sabas

DECEMBER 6
- St. Nicholas

DECEMBER 7
- St. Ambrose

DECEMBER 8
- Feast of the Immaculate Conception of the Blessed Virgin Mary

DECEMBER 9
- St. Juan Diego
- St. Leocadia

DECEMBER 10
- St. Eulalia
- St. Gregory III

DECEMBER 11
- St. Damasus I

DECEMBER 12
- St. Finnian
- Our Lady of Guadalupe

DECEMBER 13
- St. Lucy

DECEMBER 14
- St. John of the Cross
- St. Lucy of Syracuse
- St. Venantius Fortunatus

DECEMBER 15
- St. Maria di Rosa

DECEMBER 16
- St. Adelaide

DECEMBER 17
- St. Olympias

DECEMBER 18
- St. Gatian

DECEMBER 19
- Blessed Urban V

DECEMBER 20
- St. Dominic of Silos

DECEMBER 21
- St. Peter Canisius

DECEMBER 22
- Sts. Chaeremon and Ischyrion

DECEMBER 23
- St. Servulus

DECEMBER 24
- Sts. Adam and Eve
- Vigil of Christmas

DECEMBER 25
- St. Anastasia of Sirmium
- Nativity of Christ

DECEMBER 26
- St. Stephen
- St. Zosimas

DECEMBER 27
- St. John the Evangelist
- St. Fabiola

DECEMBER 28
- Holy Innocents

DECEMBER 29
- St. Thomas Becket of Canterbury

DECEMBER 30
- St. Sabinus

DECEMBER 31
- St. Sylvester I

GLOSSARY

ABSOLUTION: The declaration of forgiveness for sins by a priest in the sacrament of reconciliation.

ACOLYTE: A person who assists a priest or deacon during a religious service or procession.

ANGEL: A messenger from God.

APOSTLE: One of the twelve original disciples of Jesus Christ.

APOSTOLATE: The religious work or mission of an apostle or a religious group.

APOSTOLIC SUCCESSION: The uninterrupted passing of authority from the apostles through successive popes and bishops.

ARCHANGEL: A high-ranking angel; Michael and Gabriel are the most commonly recognized Archangels in Catholic tradition.

ASCENSION: The ascent of Christ into Heaven on the fortieth day after the resurrection.

ASH WEDNESDAY: The first day of Lent when believers are blessed and marked by the imposition of ashes.

ASSUMPTION: The taking up of the Virgin Mary into Heaven when her earthly life was finished.

BAPTISM: The sacrament in which a person is initiated into the Christian community.

BEATIFICATION: The second step in the canonization process when a person is given the title "Blessed."

BENEDICTION: A short service for invoking God's blessing.

BISHOP: A senior member of the clergy who usually oversees a diocese.

CANON: A title bestowed by a bishop upon a priest who assists the bishop with special duties involving liturgy, pastoral care, and/or teaching.

CANONIZATION: The official declaration by the pope that a deceased person is a saint.

CATECHISM: A summary of the principles of the Catholic Church.

CATECHUMEN: An individual preparing to receive the sacrament of Baptism.

CHALICE: A large cup or goblet used during communion or the Eucharist.

CHARISM: A special grace or gift given by God for the good of the Church.

CHRISM: A consecrated oil used in various sacraments.

COMMUNION OF SAINTS: The spiritual union of all living and deceased members of the Church.

CONFIRMATION: A sacrament in which a baptized person is anointed with chrism and receives the Holy Spirit.

CONSECRATION: The dedication of something or someone for a divine purpose.

CONVENT: A community of priests, religious brothers, religious sisters, monks, or nuns.

COVENANT: A formal alliance or agreement made by God with a religious community or humanity in general.

DEACON: Ministers ordained for tasks of service in the Church.

DEITY: The state of being a god; divinity.

DEMON: A fallen angel; a malevolent spiritual entity.

DEVIL: A synonym for Satan; the chief evil spirit.

DIOCESE: A district under the pastoral guidance of a bishop.

DISCIPLE: A follower of Jesus, but not one of the twelve apostles.

ENCYCLICAL: A letter written by the pope, distributed to the Church globally to express Church teaching.

EUCHARIST: The Christian ceremony commemorating the Last Supper, in which bread and wine are consumed.

EVANGELIST: An individual aiming to persuade others to embrace the Christian faith.

EVENSONG: An evening prayer or liturgy.

EX CATHEDRA: A Latin phrase that means "from the chair" and refers to infallible teachings issued by the pope on faith or morals.

EXCOMMUNICATION: The formal act of barring someone from engaging in the sacraments and services ceremonies of the Christian Church.

EXORCISM: The act or practice of expelling evil spirits.

FAITH: Complete trust or confidence in God.

FRIAR: A member of a religious community committed to vows of poverty, chastity, and obedience.

GOSPEL: The teachings of Jesus, and the term used for the first four books of the New Testament.

GUARDIAN ANGEL: A personal angel assigned to protect and guide a particular person.

HAGIOGRAPHY: A biography of a saint, often mixing history with legend.

HEAVEN: Union with God, the angels, and the righteous after death.

HELL: The place of eternal punishment for the sinful after death.

HERESY: A belief that does not agree with official Church doctrine.

HOLY ORDERS: The sacrament by which a man is ordained as a bishop, priest, or deacon.

ICON: A devotional painting, especially one of Christ or a saint.

IMMACULATE CONCEPTION: The belief that the Virgin Mary was conceived without original sin.

INCARNATION: The doctrine that Jesus was conceived in the womb of Mary by the Holy Spirit and that Jesus is both true God and true man.

INCENSE: A substance that is burned for the smell it produces; it is used in religious rituals.

INDULGENCE: A forgiveness of the earthly consequences of wrongdoing.

INFALLIBILITY: The doctrine that the pope is incapable of making errors when proclaiming *ex cathedra* on subjects of faith and morality.

INTERCESSION: The action of intervening on behalf of another, especially by prayer.

LAITY: Laypeople, as distinct from the clergy.

LAUDS: A service of morning prayer in the Divine Office of the Western Christian Church.

LECTERN: A stand on which the Bible rests and from which lessons are read in a church service.

LECTOR: A person who reads aloud certain of the scriptural passages used in a church service.

LIMBO: A place or state of oblivion for souls of righteous individuals who died before the resurrection of Jesus.

LITURGY: The public worship and ritual practices of the Church, particularly the celebration of the Eucharist (Mass) and other sacraments.

MAGISTERIUM: The Church's authority or office to establish its own authentic teachings.

MARTYR: A person who is killed because of their religious beliefs.

MASS: The central act of worship in the Catholic Church.

MIRACLE: An extraordinary event that is believed to be caused by the intervention of God.

MONASTERY: A place that houses a community of monks living under religious vows.

MONSTRANCE: A vessel used to display the consecrated Eucharistic host.

MORTAL SIN: A grave sin that causes a person to lose sanctifying grace.

NOVENA: A nine-day devotion of special prayers and actions.

NUN: A member of a religious community of women.

OBLATE: A person who is dedicated to God or to God's service.

ORIGINAL SIN: The inherent condition passed down to all humans due to Adam and Eve's act of defiance in the Garden of Eden. It is a state of separation from God and a tendency toward sin that is passed down through generations.

PAPACY: The office or authority of the pope.

PARISH: A small administrative district typically having its own church and a priest or pastor.

PASCHAL MYSTERY: The central mystery of Christ's life, death, and resurrection, which encompasses the events of His passion, crucifixion, burial, and triumphant rising from the dead. It is the core belief that, through these events, Christ's sacrifice and victory over sin and death offer redemption and eternal life to humanity.

PASTORAL LETTER: A written communication from a bishop or group of bishops to offer guidance, teachings, and encouragement on matters of faith, morals, and pastoral concerns. It aims to provide spiritual direction and practical advice to the faithful based on Church tradition and teachings.

PENANCE: Repentance of sins and the associated rite.

PREACHER: A person who proclaims the Gospel, especially a cleric.

PRELATE: An individual who holds a high-ranking position of authority within the Church hierarchy. This term generally includes bishops and archbishops but can also extend to certain ecclesiastical officials who have been granted specific privileges and responsibilities by the pope.

PRESBYTERY: The part of a church reserved for the clergy.

PRIEST: An ordained minister within the Catholic Church who has received the sacrament of Holy Orders, and is thereby empowered to offer the Eucharist, administer other sacraments, preach the Gospel, provide spiritual guidance, and act as a mediator between God and the faithful community.

PURGATORY: A temporary state after death in which souls who have died in a state of grace undergo purification to cleanse any remaining imperfections before entering the fullness of God's presence in Heaven. It is seen as a place of spiritual healing and preparation for those not yet fully perfected, but ultimately destined for eternal union with God.

RECTOR: A clergyman who has charge of a parish.

RELIC: An object, typically a part of the body or belongings of a saint or a significant individual from the past, that holds spiritual significance and is venerated as a link to the person's holiness and God's grace.

ROMAN MARTYROLOGY: An official listing of Roman rites and listing of saints and martyrs.

ROSARY: A form of prayer used especially in the Catholic Church, in which repetitions of the Lord's Prayer are followed by ten repetitions of the Hail Mary and a single saying of "Glory Be to the Father."

SACRAMENT: A sacred and visible sign established by Christ, entrusted to the Church, through which God's grace is conveyed to believers, fostering spiritual growth and a deeper connection with God.

SACRAMENTAL: A sacred object, sign, or devotion that elevates a person's prayer life, such as a rosary, medal, making the sign of the cross, or performing novenas.

SACRISTY: A chamber within a church where a priest readies himself for a service, and where liturgical garments and other items employed in worship are stored.

SANCTUARY: A sacred or holy place in the church.

SATAN: A fallen angel; the adversary of God and the instigator of evil.

SIN: The violation of God's moral law, resulting in a separation from God's grace and a disruption of one's relationship with Him.

TABERNACLE: The place where the Eucharist is kept in a church.

THEOTOKOS: A title of Mary, mother of Jesus, used especially in Eastern Christianity. It means "God-bearer" or "Mother of God."

TRANSUBSTANTIATION: The Catholic doctrine that during the Eucharist at Mass, bread and wine of the Eucharist become the actual body and blood of Christ.

TRINITY: The Christian doctrine that God exists as three persons in one substance: Father, Son, and Holy Spirit.

VATICAN: The spiritual and administrative center of the Roman Catholic Church, in Vatican City.

VENERATION: Great respect or reverence inspired by a saint or something sacred.

VESPERS: An evening prayer service in the Western Christian tradition.

VICAR: A representative or deputy, especially an ecclesiastical one.

VIRGIN BIRTH: The belief that Mary conceived Jesus by the power of the Holy Spirit and was a virgin at the time of Jesus's birth. Catholics believe Mary maintained her virginity throughout her life.

VIRTUE: Moral excellence; goodness; righteousness.

VOCATION: A call from God to live a certain way of life, often used to describe a call to ordained or lay ministry.

VOTIVE OFFERING: A gift of gratitude to a deity, typically used in the context of Christian saints and the Virgin Mary.

WORSHIP: The feeling or expression of deep respect and reverence toward God.

YAHWEH: The name of the God of Israel, revealed to Moses.

ACKNOWLEDGMENTS

The creation of this book coincided with a time of significant loss. First, my mother-in-law, who had suffered a heart attack right before the start of COVID-19 and contracted a non-contagious infectious disease in her lungs, died after a very long illness. Three months later, my mother fell at work and broke her pelvis. A CT scan revealed advanced lung and brain cancer. She opted against treatment, and as I write these acknowledgments, my mom is in hospice, inching moment by moment toward Heaven. Both women were the bedrock of our family, and their loss has sent shockwaves through me and those I love most dearly. We are feeling the after-affects every day. Both women were people of great faith and sacrifice, people who celebrated and suffered life in their own distinct ways. Had they lived during the Middle Ages, they might be venerated as saints today. In my heart and soul, they are Sacred Ones, and this book is dedicated to them.

After embarking on a project of this magnitude, it quickly became apparent how little I knew about anything, especially the lives of the saints and their heavenly companions and hellish adversaries. One of the challenging aspects of this topic was the multiplicity of information, meaning the differing details from one book or article to another. I relied heavily on the scholarship of Matthew and Margaret Bunson, whose *Encyclopedia of Saints* was a great source of concise and vital information. Rosemary Guiley's *Encyclopedia of Saints* and her *Encyclopedia of Angels* provided great insight into the mystical experiences of many of these holy men and women. Ann Ball's *Modern Saints* and Joan Carroll Cruz's *Mysteries, Marvels, and Miracles* were also invaluable resources. I extend my most heartfelt thanks to these scholars and the many authors who have written on the saints over the years.

In creating this book, I endeavored with utmost diligence to ensure the accuracy of information. Extensive research and cross-referencing were employed to avoid errors. However, since accounts vary from book to book and generation to generation, the lives of the saints can be a tricky subject, which means that discrepancies or oversights may have occurred inadvertently. I am committed to rectifying any such issues in subsequent editions, and I welcome constructive feedback from readers. Additionally, as I mentioned in the introduction, this book was never intended to be an academic tome but rather an easy-to-read introduction to the topics at hand, an amalgam of more than three thousand years of religious history; hence the absence of footnotes or citations. Should there be any instance where proper acknowledgment is lacking, I wish to state unequivocally that the omission is unintentional and will be corrected in future editions of this work.

I want to thank my friend Monsignor Stephen J. Rossetti, Chief Exorcist of Washington, D.C., for reviewing the material on angels and demons and for providing nuances that better explained the history and background of these enigmatic figures.

ACKNOWLEDGMENTS

Special thanks to Maura Poston for her friendship and assistance throughout the years and throughout this project.

Thank you to Joellyn Cicciarelli, Santiago Cortes, Anthony DeStefano, Kimberly Snyder and Dr. Deepak Chopra for their support and encouragement. Special thanks to illustrator Katie Ponder for her beautiful renderings and unique approach to these inhabitants of Heaven and Hell. And thank you to Katie Benezra for her elegant design and her incredible attention to detail. The two of them created a book to remember.

Thanks to the intrepid team at Hachette and Black Dog & Leventhal for their support, including Melanie Gold, Betsy Hulsebosch, Becky Maines, Kara Thornton, and Seta Zink. A particular word of thanks to my editor, Becky Koh, who gracefully honed this manuscript, patiently talked me off the ledge several times, and helped me cross the finish line on time. I am most grateful to you, Becky, for not taking no for an answer when I first declined this project ("How many saints?? How much time to get it done??").

Last but certainly not least, I want to thank my beautiful and brilliant wife, Grace, and my inspiring sons, Edward and Charles. Your unwavering support and specific contributions—like Grace's late-night pep talks and the boys' invaluable patience during my countless hours of research—have been my project's unsung melody. Your graciousness and resilience allowed me to pursue this endeavor, and for that, I am profoundly thankful. The joy of closing my books and turning off my computer screen is only surpassed by the delight of finding you there at the finish line.

BIBLIOGRAPHY

Anderson, Carl. 2009. *Our Lady of Guadalupe: Mother of the Civilization of Love.* New York: Image Books.

Augustine. 1961. *Confessions.* New York: Penguin Classics.

Ball, Ann. 1991. *Modern Saints: Their Lives and Faces.* Rockford, IL: TAN Books.

Bunson, Matthew (Ed.). 2003. *Our Sunday Visitor's Encyclopedia of Saints, Second Edition.* Huntington, IN: Our Sunday Visitor.

Butler, Alban. 1991. *Lives of the Saints.* San Francisco: Harper San Francisco.

Catholic Encyclopedia. Accessed October 2022–September 2023. https://www.newadvent.org/.

Catholic Online. Accessed October 2022–September 2023. https://www.catholic.org/.

Connolly, S. 2020, May 7. "Calling upon St. Michael the Archangel on Mount Gargano." *Catholic World Report.* Accessed January 2024. https://www.catholicworldreport.com/2020/05/07/calling-upon-st-michael-the-archangel-on-mount-gargano/.

Cruz, Joan Carroll. 1997. *Mysteries, Marvels, and Miracles: In the Lives of the Saints.* Rockford, IL: TAN Books.

Danielou, Jean. 2009. *The Angels and Their Mission.* Manchester, NH: Sophia Institute Press.

Encyclopedia Britannica. Accessed October 2022–January 2024. https://www.britannica.com.

Graham, Albert E. 2013. *Compendium of the Miraculous.* Gastonia, NC: TAN Books.

Guiley, Rosemary Ellen. 2001. *The Encyclopedia of Angels.* New York: Facts on File.

Guiley, Rosemary Ellen. 2004. *The Encyclopedia of Saints.* New York: Facts on File.

Guiley, Rosemary Ellen. 2009. *The Encyclopedia of Demons and Demonology.* New York: Facts on File.

Hahn, Scott. 2014. *Angels and Saints: A Biblical Guide to Friendship with God's Holy Ones.* New York: Image.

The Holy See. Accessed October 2022–September 2023. http://www.vatican.va/.

Kreeft, Peter. 2009. *Angels and Demons: What Do We Really Know about Them?.* San Francisco: Ignatius Press.

The Loyola Treasury of Saints. 2003. Chicago: Loyola Press.

Mack, Carol K., and Dinah Mack. 1998. *A Field Guide to Demons, Fairies, Fallen Angels, and Other Subversive Spirits.* New York: Owl Books.

Patella, Michael, 2012. *Angels and Demon: A Christian Primer of the Spiritual World.* Collegeville, MN: Liturgical Press.

INDEX

Page numbers of illustrations appear in italics.

SAINTS